GCSE Accounti

GCSE
Accounting

D. E. Turner
P. H. Turner

© D. E. Turner and P. H. Turner 1991

All rights reserved. No reproduction, copy or transmission
of this publication may be made without written permission.

No paragraph of this publication may be reproduced, copied
or transmitted save with written permission or in accordance
with the provisions of the Copyright, Designs and Patents Act
1988 or under the terms of any licence permitting limited copying
issued by the Copyright Licensing Agent, 33–4 Alfred Place,
London WC1E 7DP.

Any person who does any unauthorised act in relation to
this publication may be liable to criminal prosecution and
civil claims for damages.

First published 1991

Published by
MACMILLAN EDUCATION LTD
Houndmills, Basingstoke, Hampshire RG21 2XS
and London
Companies and representatives
throughout the world

Printed in Hong Kong

British Library Cataloguing in Publication Data
Turner, D. E. (Daphne E.)
GCSE accounting.
1. Accounting
I. Title II. Turner, P. H.
657

ISBN 0–333–52979–0

Contents

(Asterisked (*) units or sections cover the more difficult concepts, which may be omitted from an initial or basic course.)

About this Book *xi*
Acknowledgements *xi*

Part One
A BIRD'S EYE VIEW

Unit 1
Accountancy: What it is all about 3
- 1A. The first questions *3*
- 1B. Structure of the accounting system *4*
- 1C. Accounting conventions *5*
- 1D. Help from machines *6*

Part Two
SUMMARISING THE NET WORTH

Unit 2
Balance sheets: what they try to show 11
- 2A. Personal worth *11*
- 2B. Clubs and commercial firms: what they are worth *13*

Unit 3
Keeping track of the changes: 1 19
- 3A. The changing pattern *19*
- 3B. Types of records *20*
- 3C. Bank accounts *22*
- 3D. Cash and security *23*

Unit 4
Keeping track of the changes: 2 28
- 4A. The fuller picture *28*
- 4B. The trial balance *32*
- 4C. The accounting cycle *34*

Unit 5
Reading meaning into balance sheets 39
- 5A. Balance sheet subgroups *39*
- * 5B. Interpretation *41*
- * 5C. Understanding the ratios *43*
- * 5D. The ratios and change *44*

Part Two
Multiple-choice test 49

Contents

Part Three
CALCULATING THE PROFIT

Unit 6
Earning a living: 1. The profit and loss account 55
- 6A. What is profit? 55
- 6B. Tracking the profit 56
- 6C. The nature of ledger accounts 59

Unit 7
Earning a living: 2. The accounts of traders 65
- 7A. The idea of gross profit 65
- 7B. Accounting for 'goods' 65
- 7C. Some more conventions 73
- 7D. The accounting cycle 74

Unit 8
Complications in traders' accounts 77
- 8A. Returns and allowances 77
- 8B. Transportation costs 80
- 8C. Discounts 81
- 8D. Wages and salaries 85

Unit 9
A closer look at trading: the use of day books 87
- 9A. The need for day books 87
- 9B. Day books of commercial concerns 88
- 9C. The journal 90
- 9D. Cycle of operations—updated 92

Part Three
Multiple-choice test 97

Part Four
MORE ABOUT PROFIT

Unit 10
Calculating profit: some complications 103
- 10A. Accrued charges 103
- 10B. Pre-payments 106
- 10C. Accruals and pre-payments, and examination questions 107
- 10D. The 'matching' convention 107

Unit 11
Calculating profit: further complications 111
- 11A. Bad debts 111
- 11B. Bringing home the bacon 114

*****Unit 12**
Stock and its complications 118
- 12A. Valuation of closing stock 118
- 12B. Delayed stock-taking calculations 121

*****Unit 13**
Understanding profit 125
- 13A. Profit and capital 125
- 13B. Profit and turnover 128
- 13C. Rate of stock turnover 129

13D. Turnover of debtors and creditors *130*
13E. Use of the ratios *131*
13F. The problem of inflation *131*

Part Four
Multiple-choice test *135*

Part Five
BEING REALISTIC

Unit 14
Accounting for wear and tear *141*

14A. The nature of depreciation *141*
14B. Accounting methods *141*
14C. Calculating the depreciation *143*
* 14D. Sale of a depreciated asset *144*
14E. Examination questions *145*

Unit 15
Providing for bad debts *150*

15A. Potential bad debts *150*
15B. Bad-debts provision and the trial balance *152*

* Unit 16
A further look at business transactions: capital and revenue transactions *158*

16A. Types of transactions *158*
16B. Capital gains and losses *161*
16C. Materiality *162*

Unit 17
A look back at ledger posting *166*

17A. Ledger posting: the background *166*
17B. The posting of transactions *167*

Part Five
Multiple-choice test *175*

Part Six
SOME ROUTINE APPLICATIONS

Unit 18
Looking after the pounds: another look at cash *179*

18A. Specialised cash books *179*
* 18B. Cash flows *184*
18C. Looking after the pence: petty-cash accounting *185*

Unit 19
Reconciling the bank balance *190*

19A. Bank statements *190*
19B. Further complications *193*

* Unit 20
Paying the wages *198*

20A. The wages system *198*
20B. Ledger postings *201*
20C. Wage payment procedures *201*

Contents

* Unit 21
Paying tax *205*

21A. Tax and the business organisation *205*
21B. VAT: the general idea *206*
21C. Book-keeping procedures *207*
21D. Complications *208*

Part Six
Multiple-choice test *213*

Part Seven
ACCOUNTS OF PARTICULAR
ORGANISATIONS

* Unit 22
Accounting for clubs and societies *219*

22A. Receipts and payments accounts *219*
22B. Income and expenditure accounts *221*
22C. Other final accounts of clubs and societies *223*

* Unit 23
Accounting for partnerships *230*

23A. General considerations *230*
23B. Accounting procedures *231*
23C. Goodwill in partnership accounts *234*

Unit 24
Accounting for companies: 1. The background *239*

24A. General considerations *239*
24B. When not to form a company *241*

* Unit 25
Accounting for companies: 2. Accounting procedures *244*

25A. Ledger procedures *244*
25B. Company final accounts *247*

* Unit 26
The accounts of manufacturers *256*

26A. The problem *256*
26B. Form and content of manufacturers' accounts *257*
26C. Alternative structure *260*

Part Seven
Multiple-choice test *265*

Part Eight
CHECKING UP, SUMMING UP AND
SELLING UP

Unit 27
Getting the books right: 1. The correction of errors *271*

27A. Errors and their effect *271*
27B. The correction of errors *272*
* 27C. Correction through a suspense account *273*
* 27D. Errors and examination questions *274*
27E. Other uses of suspense accounts *276*

viii

* Unit 28
Getting the books right: 2. Control accounts *279*
  28A. General principles *279*
  28B. Complications *283*

* Unit 29
Incomplete records: putting the pieces together *288*
  29A. Statements of affairs *288*
  29B. Preparation of conventional final accounts *289*
  29C. Conversion to double entry *292*

* Unit 30
Selling up the business *296*
  30A. Winding up *296*
  30B. Sale of an existing firm *297*

Part Eight
Multiple-choice test *303*

General revision: multiple-choice test *307*

Appendix A. Coping with percentages *311*
Appendix B. Using graphs and charts *316*
Appendix C. Balancing accounts—the rules *319*

Index *321*

About this book

This book gives a wide introduction to modern accounting, and emphasises the logic and reason behind the procedures involved. We have designed the book to be used in a number of different ways. It may be used as an intensive one-year course, or as a 'straight-through' two-year course—an appropriate aim for the end of the first year would be unit 17. Alternatively, it is possible to choose some of the units to form a basic and balanced course, with the possibility of suitable students proceeding later to a course comprising the more difficult units (those marked with an asterisk in the *Contents*).

The book attempts to involve the student as the course proceeds, and to develop a questioning and intelligent approach to the issues involved. Students are recommended to keep a record of the activity work suggested in each unit, together with their answers to other practical assignments.

Acknowledgements

The authors wish to thank Mrs Judith Johnson and Miss Helen Turner for their considerable help in preparing this book.

PART ONE

A Bird's Eye View

UNIT 1 ACCOUNTANCY
WHAT IT IS ALL ABOUT

Before you read this unit, try activity 1.1.

Activity 1.1

Suppose that you are 'in the market' for a second-hand car. You see one advertised in a local newspaper and you arrange to see it.

As you walk up the road towards it, what questions will you have in mind?

1A. The First Questions

In studying a new subject, the first question must be:

What is it all about?

In accounting, you can understand the answer to that question best by putting yourself in the position of someone who suddenly has to take charge of a small business. The firm has an accountant. What types of information about the firm would you expect the accountant to be able to give you?

Try listing them.

The information you would expect the accountant to give you would probably not be very different from that which you would expect from the previous owner of the car you are thinking of buying in activity 1.1.

In the case of the car, as you walk up the road to the house of the seller, you would be concerned, first, with what the car is going to look like as it stands there at the roadside—what might be called the *stationary* picture. How many miles are 'on the clock'? Is the paintwork in reasonable condition? What about body rust? What is the upholstery like? Is the exhaust about to fall off?

But, as a separate issue, you will want to know how well the car runs over a given distance—the *running* picture. Does it give a comfortable ride? How many miles does it do to the gallon? Does it use much oil?

Also, what of the longer-term future? Will the car 'get you places'—to college or work, for instance, or away for the week-end. Will it be able to take you on a holiday with friends in the summer?

Finally, you will expect the present owner to come up with reliable, detailed records to support his or her claims about the vehicle.

If you become the owner of a firm, the questions are much the same. You will expect the accountant to give you both a 'stationary' picture of the firm's current financial position, and a 'running' picture of how well—or badly—it is doing. You will expect the accountant to be able to advise you how well the firm could do in the future. Finally, you would expect to be shown detailed records to support these claims.

Display 1 sets out the information you would expect from your accountant. It is important to remember this list, because it is the key to what the accounting system is all about.

A bird's eye view

> *Display 1:* **Information Provided by an Accounting System**
>
> 1 The current financial state of the firm—put simply, whether it is in a strong financial position or whether the creditors are already 'knocking at the door'.
>
> 2 How well the firm is running—i.e. whether it is running at a profit or at a loss.
>
> 3 Where the firm should go in the future—should it expand or contract, develop new products, look for new customers, ...
>
> 4 Detailed records supporting all of the above.

These requirements are common to all organisations whether they are small social clubs, mini-enterprises, companies, local authorities, or huge multi-national conglomerates. But the nature of any particular organisation may well mean that certain objectives differ in importance. The main requirement of a small social club, for instance, may be simply that of recording money spent—and its accounting system will be designed to meet that simple need. A large commercial concern, on the other hand, will be much more concerned with profit trends and planning for the future. So its accounting system will be much more complex.

1B. Structure of the Accounting System

Because the accounting *requirements* of all organisations are similar, the *structure* of their accounts is also very similar. The structure breaks down into several different parts, and each part satisfies a different need.

The foundations of any accounting system consist of the **original documents** such as invoices, credit notes and receipts—in fact, any business document which shows that something has 'happened' between two people or firms. Examples include payments of expenses, and the purchase or sale of goods—whether they are paid for at the time or not. These 'happenings' are known as *transactions*. If a transaction happens for which there is no original document, an entry has to be made in a special book known as a **journal** to prevent it from being forgotten.

Where there is a lot of one type of original document (imagine the number of invoices that a large mail-order firm issues each day), they are grouped together and summarised in **day books**. The information is then fed through to the main book of account, the **ledger**. Here, the full effects of all the transactions are recorded.

So, the original documents, day books and ledger provide the detailed information from which we can obtain the answers to the main questions.

To obtain those answers, the information in the ledger is fed periodically—usually once a year—through to the *final* accounts. The names of these will vary with the exact nature of the organisation concerned. In the case of a trading organisation, the final accounts consist, *firstly*, of a **trading and profit and loss account**. This summarises the profit for the period, showing how well the organisation has been running over a period of time. *Secondly*, there is the **balance sheet**, which attempts to show the financial position of the organisation—the 'stationary' picture—at a particular date.

In the case of a club concerned solely with social activities or a 'non-profit-making' concern such as a charity, the trading and profit and loss account is usually replaced by an **income and expenditure account**, and the balance sheet is *sometimes*, although not always, called a **statement of assets and liabilities**. But these are changes in name only, designed to reflect the type of organisation concerned, and there is little difference in the content.

But no single part of an accounting system states what the firm should do and where it should go in the future, and what its financial policy should be. To be able to answer this question, you must have a full appreciation of the whole accounting system and be able to interpret all the information within the framework of other relevant knowledge—such as important aspects of law and of current social, political and moral issues.

Figure 1.1 summarises this structure. It will help you to understand accounting if you keep it in mind throughout your study, not only the structure itself but also which of the requirements each part of the accounting structure is designed to meet. Notice how the information 'flows through' the system from the original documents to the final balance sheet.

Figure 1.1
The structure of the accounting system, and flow of information.

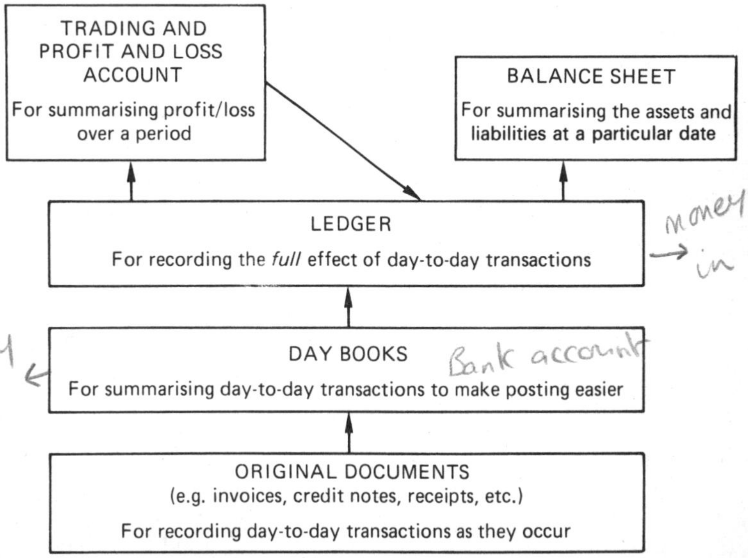

```
                    TRADING AND
                  PROFIT AND LOSS                BALANCE SHEET
                      ACCOUNT                For summarising the assets and
                For summarising profit/loss   liabilities at a particular date
                      over a period

                              LEDGER
                 For recording the full effect of day-to-day transactions

                             DAY BOOKS
                 For summarising day-to-day transactions to make posting easier

                         ORIGINAL DOCUMENTS
                    (e.g. invoices, credit notes, receipts, etc.)
                  For recording day-to-day transactions as they occur
```

1C. Accounting Conventions

Most subjects start off with certain basic assumptions. Although, with some, their truth can be proved, many are regarded either as simply 'self-evident' or as purely practical 'reasonable working assumptions'. One example from mathematics, for instance, is that the shortest distance between any two points is a straight line—though even that only applies to flat surfaces and would not be true if, for example, you were trying to fly round the world.

Accountancy also has its rules and 'reasonable working assumptions'. They are known as **conventions**. One basic rule is that the accounts should only record things that have a money value—money is the measuring rod of accountancy (though this does not prevent social and other issues being taken into account in the *interpretation* of accounts and in the making of financial decisions). Another rule is that the same procedures should be followed consistently from year to year. One of the 'reasonable assumptions' is that, in normal circumstances, we can assume that the organisation concerned will be continuing its operations in the future. These conventions will be described as you meet them in the book. Be prepared to make a note of each as it is dealt with, and watch out for more examples of their uses as you study. They often come up in examinations.

1D. Help from Machines

Most organisations these days use some form of mechanical or electronic aid in their accounting. These aids range from pocket calculators to full-scale computers. When properly used, they can save accountants many hours of boring routine work and enable them to devote their time to the sort of work that machines cannot do—work requiring understanding, interpretation and intelligence. The value of machines lies in the following:

(i) *Number crunching*. Machines cope speedily and efficiently with the routine processing of vast quantities of numerical information.
(ii) *Simplifying and speeding up calculations*. The pocket calculator has brought about a revolution in this respect, just as microcomputers, minicomputers and main-frame computers have done with more complex calculations. Their use, however, must not make the accountant blind to the need to understand the nature and purpose of the calculations being performed, and to the importance of correctly interpreting the resulting answers.
(iii) *Action indicating*. Computers in particular can be programmed to indicate what courses of action should be taken or to suggest decisions that should be made in particular situations. But again you must remember that computers are nothing more than machines, and can only work on the basis of programs put into them by humans. Any 'advice' that a computer gives is purely a mechanical reaction determined by those programs.

Most examining bodies allow the use of pocket calculators, though it is always wise to check in good time before an exam. They are used extensively in accounting work, particularly for calculating percentages. A good knowledge of percentage calculations is essential in accounting, and if you need to revise your knowledge of the basic processes, look at appendix A at the end of the book.

Computers, for their part, deal with an enormous amount of routine accounting work. They have made it even more important that accountants know what the data being produced are all about, and understand their importance and implications. Above all, any machine can only do what is asked of it.

Unless you know the questions to ask, the machines will never give you the answers.

Check Your Understanding

1 What are the four main questions that an accounting system is designed to answer?

2 What are the names of the main 'parts' of an accounting system?

3 Which question is each part of an accounting system designed to answer?

4 What is the proper name for the working assumptions or 'rules of convenience' accepted by accountants?

5 List the main functions of computers in accounting.

6 What are the limitations of machines?

Practical Assignments

1 Discuss the ways in which the accounting system of a club might be different from that of a large commercial organisation.

2 Identify and describe as many documents as you can which provide the 'raw information' for an accounting system.

3 A friend has written to you asking you what this accountancy business is all about. Write out your reply.

4 A firm is considering closing its factory in a congested and depressed part of Newcastle, and building a new one in Kent near a terminal for the new channel tunnel.

What (a) financial considerations and (b) non-financial considerations do you think the management of the firm should bear in mind when making the decision?

PART TWO
Summarising the Net Worth

UNIT 2 BALANCE SHEETS WHAT THEY TRY TO SHOW

Before you read this unit, try activity 2.1.

Activity 2.1

(i) How would you set about summarising what someone is really worth (not just in terms of how much money he or she has)?

(ii) How would you compare that person's worth with that of others?

(iii) Set out a statement showing the 'real worth' of a typical club or society.

The last unit suggested that, if you wished to buy a car, you would want to know something about its condition as it stood at the roadside—i.e. its 'stationary' or static picture at a particular point in time. This static picture would be one of the two main things you would take into account in deciding whether or not the car was worth the asking price.

This unit looks at the 'static' picture—not of a car but, first, of private individuals, and then of businesses and other organisations. It will look at balance sheets—note where their position is on the 'map' of the accounting system in figure 1.1, and bear in mind their purpose as listed on page 4.

2A. Personal Worth

1. Money measurement

In order to compare one thing with another, we need to be able to *measure*. And in order to measure, we must have some sort of measuring unit.

A person's worth may be measured by using many different types of measuring unit. The hours of community work that he or she does may be one. The goals he scored last season may be another. Another way would be to add up the value of their possessions. One of the best measuring units for doing this is money—or, to be more precise, the *money value* of the possessions concerned.

In the world of finance and accounting—the world this book is all about—the **worth** of firms is calculated by adding up the net value of their possessions in terms of money. This does not mean that accountants are *mercenary*—that is, concerned solely with money, and with the idea of making more and more of it just for its own sake. Accountants simply use money as a basic measuring unit. It is their way of comparing one thing with another.

This does not mean that something that is worth more (in terms of money) is a 'better' thing—or more worth while—than some other item. But it does mean that, in formal accountancy, we do not include

11

Summarising the net worth

items that cannot be measured in terms of money units. This brings us to one of the basic working rules—or **conventions** as they are properly called—of accounting.

> ***Accounting Convention No. 1***
> **The Money Measurement Convention**
>
> Accountants only deal with things that have a money value and so can be measured in money units.

Just because accountants limit themselves to money values, this does not mean that they can ignore the broader social and human implications of the problems they have to deal with. It may make *financial* sense to close a factory down, but they should also consider the unemployment problems that it might cause. Also, a firm may find it possible to manufacture and sell a new product at a very large profit—but what if it involves a serious health risk? In recent years, increasing importance has been attached to these broader issues when making accounting decisions.

2. Summarising personal worth

In activity 2.1 above, you probably listed the cash in your pocket and any savings you have at home or in the bank. Did you include anything else? And what did you include in the estimate for the club or society?

You were right to include cash and savings. But you should also have included every other possession—items such as radios, clothes, furniture, cycles and cars—on which a money value could be placed. Any debts owed to you should also have been added and, to be fair about it, any debts owed by you to others should have been deducted (taken away).

An informal summary of an individual person's financial position at a particular time is usually known as a **statement of affairs**, as opposed to the term 'balance sheet', which is used for the more formal statement that forms part of a proper accounting system. Example 2.1 is typical.

Example 2.1

Draw up a statement of affairs for Joe Black, which relates to his position on 30 June last. You can assume that his house has a current market value of £50 000, against which a mortgage of £30 000 is owed. His furniture is worth £10 000 and other personal property £9000. He has savings of £700 and cash in his possession of £50. He owes £120 on his credit card.

Note: The value of the house itself, and the mortgage on it, are considered as two quite separate items, just as any personal items bought by credit card are listed quite separately from the debt due to the credit card company.

SOLUTION

Joe Black: Statement of affairs as at 30 June 19--

Value of:	£
House	50 000
Furniture	10 000
Personal property	9 000
Savings	700
Cash	50
	69 750

Debts due in respect of:	
Mortgage	30 000
Credit card	120
	30 120
Net worth	39 630

Balance sheets

Now try activity 2.2.

Activity 2.2

Harry wants to know whether he can raise £300 within a week in order to join a skiing trip to Austria. He has £52.50 in cash and £175.40 in the bank. He has a motor cycle, which originally cost £300, but Harry thinks he would now find it difficult to get more than about £40 for it on the open market. He has some hi-fi equipment, which he bought from a friend for £50 a few weeks ago. His younger brother Alf owes him £10. Harry himself owes the local youth club his annual subscription of £15 and he owes £50 on his credit card.

(i) *Draw up a summary of Harry's financial worth today. Consider carefully the value that should be placed on items. Do you think he will be able to find the money for his trip?*

(ii) *What else could he do about his problem and what effect would this have upon the summary?*

2B. Clubs and Commercial Firms: What They Are Worth

1. Balance sheet summaries: vertical presentations

Although it is often helpful for individuals, like Harry in activity 2.2, to know their proper financial worth at a particular time, it is essential for any club, society or commercial firm to know the same thing if they are to be efficiently run.

Precise terms are used in connection with all of these statements, and you should remember the meaning of the terms. They will be used time and again throughout your study of accountancy.

The possessions owned by an individual person, club, society or commercial firm are known as **assets**; the debts owed to others are known as **liabilities**. The difference between the two—the real or *net* worth—is known as the **capital** in commercial concerns, and as the **accumulated fund** where clubs, societies and non-profit-making organisations (such as charities) are concerned. The term *accumulated fund* is used, as it is thought that the word *capital* sounds too commercial for non-trading organisations. Whatever term is used, the meaning is the same: namely, it is the true worth (i.e. *net* worth) of the person or organisation after all liabilities have been deducted from assets.

Activity 2.3

Look back to your summary of Harry's position in activity 2.2, and state the total amount of his

(i) assets,
(ii) liabilities, and
(iii) capital (i.e. *net worth*).

Where the summary refers to organisations such as clubs, societies and commercial firms, the term **balance sheet** is usually used instead of statement of affairs.

There are various ways in which balance sheets can be set out. Anyone responsible for drawing one up should bear in mind the people to whom it is to be sent, and then prepare it in a form which those people will understand. This is part of the essential art of communication. In the past, accountants have not always been very successful at communicating. They have often prepared their accounts and summaries in ways that they understood, but that have had little meaning to others.

Nobody is doing their job properly unless they pass information on to others in a way in which it can be understood.

Summarising the net worth

One of the simplest ways of presenting such information is in the form used in example 2.1, with all the assets grouped together in one subtotal, and all the liabilities in another. Then one subtotal is taken away (deducted) from the other to give the final net worth (i.e. the *capital* or *accumulated fund* as the case may be). It is important that you give the summary a clear and proper heading, together with the date to which the information refers.

Example 2.2

At the end of its season on 30 September last, the Pendennis Sports Club owned a house worth £10 000. It also owned furniture worth £1000 and equipment of £2000. The club was owed £110 by members to whom it had sold old equipment. It had a balance in its bank account of £326 and had cash-in-hand of £55.

The club owed £1000 to the Sports Council in respect of a loan, repayable in five years' time. It also owed £240 to Imogen Ltd in respect of the supply on credit of sports equipment.

You are required to draw up the club's balance sheet at 30 September last.

Note: The accumulated fund would have been termed 'capital' had the organisation concerned been a commercial concern.

SOLUTION

Pendennis Sports Club: Balance sheet as at 30 September 19--

Assets		£
Premises	10 000	
Furniture	1 000	
Equipment	2 000	
Debtors	110	
Cash: at bank	326	
in hand	55	13 491
Liabilities		
Loan (from Sports Council)	1 000	
Trade creditor (Imogen Ltd)	240	1 240
Accumulated fund (i.e. net worth)		12 251

You should notice the following points from the example:

(i) The title of the summary clearly states what it is, i.e. a balance sheet, to whom it refers, i.e. the Pendennis Sports Club, and the date concerned, i.e. 30 September 19--.

(ii) The *single* underline indicates where the subtotal is 'extended' to the main column, and the *double* underline (the 'full stop' of book-keeping) shows the end of the summary.

(iii) The assets are listed in order of **liquidity**—that is, in order of how easy they are to turn into ready cash. Note that the most liquid comes at the end of the group.

(iv) The liabilities are listed in the order in which they will become due for payment, with the one that will fall due for payment earliest at the end of the group.

The same format is often followed for a commercial concern (except that the term *capital* replaces the term *accumulated fund* to indicate the net worth of the firm).

Balance sheets

> **Activity 2.4**
>
> Sandra Jones runs a retail shop. At 31 December last, her shop premises were estimated to be worth £20 000, and the fittings and furniture £3500. She also owned a small delivery van worth, at that date, about £2000. She valued the stock in her shop at £12 500; she had £5040 owing to her by debtors and had cash-in-hand of £175.
>
> Her brother had loaned her £8000 with which to start the business. She owed £3528 to her suppliers and had a bank overdraft of £2500.
> *Draw up a balance sheet summarising her financial position at 31 December last.*

2. Balance sheets: 'T account' form of presentation

The way in which the data were set out in example 2.2 (and in activity 2.4) is known as the *vertical* presentation or format of balance sheets (in other words, reading from top to bottom). Another way in which the same information may be presented is in the *'T' account* format. This title comes from the fact that the presentation is based upon a 'T', the downward stroke of the 'T' dividing the page into two halves. The assets are listed on one side of the 'T', and the capital and the liabilities on the other.

Look at the statements in example 2.2 and activity 2.3. What, in effect, they say is that

Assets − Liabilities = Capital (or accumulated fund in the case of a club or non-profit organisation)

From this, it follows that it would be equally true to say that

Assets = Capital + Liabilities

Presented in this form, the balance sheet for Sandra Jones (activity 2.4), becomes:

Sandra Jones: Balance sheet as at 31 December 19--

Assets	£		£
Premises	20 000	Capital	29 187
Fixtures and fittings	3 500	*Liabilities*	
Van	2 000	Loan	8 000
Stock	12 500	Trade creditors	3 528
Debtors	5 040	Bank overdraft	2 500
Cash	175		
	43 215		43 215

Note: It is important to note that the total of the two columns must be on the same level, even if it means leaving a space on one side or the other.

> **Activity 2.5**
>
> Take the information for the Pendennis Sports Club given in example 2.2 and present it in a balance sheet following the 'T' account format.

Summarising the net worth

Until recently, it was customary in the UK to present the T form balance sheet with the above columns reversed—that is, in the form of

$$\text{Capital} + \text{Liabilities} = \text{Assets}$$

and you may still see this format. But larger companies—those known as public limited companies—*must* now present their balance sheets either in the vertical format or in the form shown on page 15. It is recommended that smaller companies do so also, though it is not compulsory. There are a number of reasons why it is better practice to follow one or the other of the formats recommended for companies, and these formats will be followed in this book. The balance sheet of a large company is, of course, a much more complicated document than the simple presentations shown above.

The vertical format has the advantage—at least with simple balance sheets—of being easier to understand, particularly by those with no accounting knowledge. We shall see later, however, that a number of accounting advantages spring from the 'T' format with its two columns of figures that 'balance', i.e. come to the same total.

3. Other methods of presentation

If balance sheet information is to be circulated for general information, various forms of graph may be used to make it more interesting and intelligible to those with no accounting knowledge. Some of the more common methods that may be used are described in appendix B at the end of the book.

Activity 2.6

The chairman of the Pendennis Sports Club approaches you and says that, for the purposes of his annual report for the season ended 30 September last, he would like to include diagrams showing the financial position of the club. He is anxious, he says, to get away from 'all these figures'.

What would you produce for him?

---

4. Business versus private interests

When drawing up balance sheets for businesses, it is essential to distinguish between the assets and liabilities which refer to the business, and those which are the private concern of the owner outside of the business. So no reference is made in the balance sheet to the owner's private house (not used for business purposes), personal possessions and any debts that might be due other than in connection with the business. This is known in accounting as the 'business entity' convention.

Accounting Convention No. 2
The Business Entity Convention

In accounting, a distinction is always drawn between the affairs of the business and the private affairs of the owner. The business accounts only deal with the affairs of the business as such and do not include the other personal possessions and liabilities of the owner.

Balance sheets

Check Your Understanding

1 What 'measuring unit' is used in accountancy?
2 Is the accountant only interested in 'the money side of things' when it comes to business matters?
3 What is the meaning of the word *mercenary*? Do you think it fair to say that accountants are mercenary individuals?
4 What is an *accounting convention*? Describe, in your own words, the two mentioned in this unit.
5 What is the difference between an asset and a liability?
6 What are the capital plus the ~~assets~~ liabilities of an organisation each equal to?
7 In a club or a society, the 'capital' is usually known by another name. What is it?
8 In a commercial organisation, what equals the total of the capital and the liabilities added together?
9 What is the name given to the summary of an organisation's assets, liabilities and capital?
10 What is meant by 'order of liquidity'?
11 In what order are liabilities usually listed?
12 What should be the guiding principle in deciding the form of presentation of any accounting statement?
13 This unit suggested three major forms of presentation of balance sheet information. Describe each briefly. Which two of the forms accord with the requirements for public limited companies?
14 In what ways, other than the three major formats, can you present balance sheet information?

Practical Assignments

1 a. What is a balance sheet?
 b. For what purpose is it prepared?
 c. What are the three main groups of information shown in a balance sheet?
 d. What is the basic 'accounting equation' upon which the balance sheet is based? What are the three ways in which it can be expressed?
 e. Describe the three main ways in which accountants set out formal balance sheets.
 f. Why should a balance sheet always have a full and proper title? What items of information should be included in this title?
 g. Why do clubs and societies often prefer to use the term *accumulated fund* rather than *capital*?
 h. Classify the following items into assets or liabilities:

 (i) motor vehicles; (ii) cash;
 (iii) loan to a friend; (iv) machinery;
 (v) stock of goods; (vi) loan from the bank;
 (vii) debts owed by other firms; (viii) premises;
 (ix) office furniture; (x) debts owed to suppliers of goods.

2 Joan Smith commenced business at the beginning of the week with cash-in-hand of £1200, cash-at-bank £6000, trading stock £7200 and with premises that she had purchased for £9600.
 a. What was her capital on the day she commenced business?
 b. Draw up Joan Smith's balance sheet as at commencement of business.
 c. Illustrate the position by means of a pie chart.

3 The following information refers to the Zingo Hi-Fi Club on the first day of the present month.
 Assets: equipment £6000; subscriptions owed to the club £50; balance at the bank £150.
 Liabilities: Owing to CD Supplies Ltd £80.
 The following are needed:

 a. a calculation of the 'accumulated fund';
 b. a balance sheet in 'T' account form;
 c. a bar chart illustration of the balance sheet information;
 d. suggestions of other ways in which the information might be illustrated.

4 Draw up what you consider might be a typical balance sheet of a school or college mini-enterprise. Present the information in an alternative way which you think might make the situation clearer to someone with no accounting knowledge.

5 The following information refers to the Kenwell Repair Service at 31 July last:

	£
Cash	1800
Debts due to Kenwell	900
Debts owed by Kenwell	1020
Stock of spare parts	3800
Tools	4300
Bank overdraft	3000
Equipment	6700

 a. What is the amount of Kenwell's capital?
 b. Prepare Kenwell's balance sheet, setting it out in each of the three formats described in this unit. How else could it be presented?

17

6 Joe is a friend of yours. Recently, Joe's Uncle Sam, who owned a fish and chip shop, died. The uncle had always been very concerned about Joe's employment problems and so, shortly before his death, he left instructions that Joe could have the fish and chip shop as a gift provided he took it 'lock, stock and barrel'. Joe asks your advice concerning the sort of things he should enquire into before accepting the gift.

Outline the advice you would give him.

7 The following balance sheet was prepared at the end of June by a club treasurer, who has since resigned. You have been asked to correct it. (You may assume that the figures are correct.)

Balance sheet of the Victoria Club up to June last

	£		£
Cash	2 100	Bar stocks	4 200
Debts due to club	3 000	Accumulated fund	11 900
Loan from bank	1 400		
Debts due by the club	2 800		
Sports equipment	6 800		
	16 100		16 100

8 Sarah hopes to start business as a market trader. She realises that she will need a certain amount of capital and is anxious to know exactly what she is worth. She has asked you to help her and she supplies you with the following information:

(i) The total amount she has available in 'actual cash' is £160.
(ii) She is a keen member of the local hockey club and intends to continue playing. She owes the annual membership subscription of £15 and this will have to be paid within a few days.
(iii) She has £450 in a high-interest savings account with a building society. She has to give four weeks' notice if she wishes to withdraw the money.
(iv) She also has £150 in her current account at the bank.
(v) She owns surplus furniture which she intends to sell in order to raise funds for her business. She paid £750 for it a few years ago, but feels she would be lucky to get £100 for it today.
(vi) She is purchasing a motor-cycle under a hire purchase agreement. The cash price was £3200 and the hire purchase price was £5000. She paid a deposit of £200, and has paid sixteen monthly instalments, also of £200. She has another eight to pay.
(vii) She owes £5 to her newsagent for newspapers and magazines.
(viii) Her friend Bill owes her £50, which he borrowed a week ago in order to buy some fishing tackle. Bill has promised to repay the debt at the end of the month.
(ix) She has a car which she bought new two years ago for £7000.

Required:
a. A summary in suitable form of Sarah's present financial position. (Note: Think carefully about the value you put on the possessions.)
b. A calculation of the 'ready cash' she could raise within the week.
c. A calculation of the amount of cash she could hope to raise by the end of next month (use only the information given above: ignore any income Sarah might receive in the future).

Sarah later changes her plans and decides that, instead of becoming a market trader, she and Bill (to whom she lent money for the fishing tackle) will put their resources together and form the Trojan Window Cleaning Co. Bill has cash of £30 available and ladders and other equipment that will be of use in the firm of a value of £80. He also has a car and trailer suitable for use within the firm: the car cost £4000 and is a year old. He has no debts other than the one due to Sarah for the fishing tackle. Unfortunately, the tackle was stolen while he was asleep on the river bank and was not insured.

Required:
a. A calculation of the total capital of the new firm.
b. A statement summarising the financial position of the firm.

UNIT 3 KEEPING TRACK OF THE CHANGES: 1

Before you read this unit, try activity 3.1.

Activity 3.1

Is the cash you have 'in-hand' today correct? Check back over the last week or so and see if you can agree the amount with what you have received and with what you have paid out.

How accurate is your memory?

3A. The Changing Pattern

A balance sheet summarises an organisation's assets, liabilities and capital in order to show its financial position at a particular date—but *only* at that particular date. As the days go by, money will be spent, assets will be bought and stock will be sold. This means that the position will change. In order to keep track of the financial position of a firm, a day-to-day record has to be kept of these changes. This is kept in the **ledger**, one function of which is to provide up-to-date information for the balance sheet as and when required.

As for your own personal 'cash-in-hand', you may be quite happy to keep track of the changes in your head. Your main concern will probably be how much you actually have 'in-hand', and you may not be too concerned with where that cash has come from—or where the cash you had last week has gone to. You will know only too well that some of what you had last week 'has gone' and is no longer there to be spent.

Most of us occasionally become worried when there is a little less money in our pockets than we think there should be. Convinced that some has been lost or stolen, we do a quick mental check.

What goes on in our minds when we do this?

We usually think back to what we know we had at some point in the past. This, in accounting terms, is our **opening balance**. We then try to remember what we have had 'come in' and what was 'spent'. The first we add to the opening balance, the second we take away (deduct). The final figure—the **closing balance**—is what should be in our pockets now.

As far as pocket money is concerned, most of us are happy to rely solely on occasional mental checks. It is only when we get particularly worried about where the money is going, or might go if we are not careful, that—for a time at least—we might keep some form of written record. A record becomes even more important if our money is being kept elsewhere—in a bank, for example. Banks can make mistakes, and it happens rather more often than most people think. If we are responsible for the money of others—as the treasurer of a club or an accountant with a firm—it is *essential* that a proper written record be maintained.

Summarising the net worth

3B. Types of Records

Activity 3.2

The treasurer of Green Street Youth Club retains a cash balance from which to make small payments, as well as a deposit account with a building society. The following records the transactions for March last:

March		£
1	Balance of cash-in-hand	42.50
2	Subscriptions received in cash	120.26
3	Paid part-time cleaner's wages	15.00
5	Cash received from sale of refreshments	34.93
6	Subscriptions received in cash	35.60
8	Deposited in building society	120.00
10	Receipts from sale of refreshments	45.13
15	Paid part-time cleaner's wages	15.00
20	Paid for supply of table-tennis balls	10.50
21	Entrance fees paid by non-members	7.60
23	Deposited in building society	80.00
30	Paid to supplier of refreshments	35.10

You are now asked to calculate the amount of cash-in-hand at 31 March

(Keep a note of how you worked it out.)

---

1. Single-column cash book

There are a number of ways of recording cash transactions. The most obvious way is in a *single-column cash book*. Receipts are simply added to, and payments deducted from, the balance in hand. The cash book for Green Street Youth Club (activity 3.2) in single-column form is shown in example 3.1.

Example 3.1

March		£ p
1	Balance	42.50
2	Subscriptions received	120.26
		162.76
3	Cleaner's wages	15.00
		147.76
5	Sale of refreshments	34.93
6	Subscriptions received	35.60
		218.29
8	Deposit in building society	120.00
	c/f	98.29

		b/f	98.29
10	Refreshments		45.13
			143.42
15	Cleaner's wages		15.00
			128.42
20	Purchase of table-tennis balls		10.50
			117.92
21	Non-members' entrance charges		7.60
			125.52
23	Deposit in building society		80.00
			45.52
30	Supplier of refreshments		35.10
			10.42

What do you think are the main disadvantages of this type of record?

Keeping track of the changes: 1

2. Running balance form

The main problem with the single-column cash book method is that the additions can easily become muddled with the deductions. It becomes very cumbersome when there are several deductions together. Also, since every item takes an additional line, and further lines are needed again for the balances, it tends to take up a lot of space. A clearer way of doing the same job is to keep the additions (known in accounting terms as the **debit** items) in a separate column from the deductions (known in accounting as the **credit** items), and to have a third column for the balance. This means that the balance after each item can be seen and, for that reason, this form of account is known as the **running balance** type. In running balance form, the youth club's account would appear as in example 3.2.

Example 3.2

March		Debit £	Credit £	Balance £
1	Balance			42.50
2	Subscriptions received	120.26		162.76
3	Cleaner's wages		15.00	147.76
5	Sale of refreshments	34.93		182.69
6	Subscriptions received	35.60		218.29
8	Building society deposit		120.00	98.29
10	Sale of refreshments	45.13		143.42
15	Cleaner's wages		15.00	128.42
20	Purchase of table-tennis balls		10.50	117.92
21	Non-members' admission charges	7.60		125.52
23	Building society deposit		80.00	45.52
30	Costs of refreshments		35.10	10.42

This form of account has the clear advantage that the balance after each transaction is clearly displayed. The problem is the tedium—if machines are not available—of doing all the additions and subtractions, and of entering the balance, each time an entry is made. Also—and perhaps surprisingly—it is very easy for mistakes to be made. Once one is made, it affects all subsequent balances.

3. Conventional 'T' form accounts

Another way of keeping the record is by a 'T' account. Where accounting is done 'manually'—that is, without the aid of machines—this is the most common form of account.

As with the 'T' style balance sheet (see page 15), the page is divided into two halves. The left-hand side lists the *debit* entries, and the right-hand side the *credit* entries. In dealing with a cash account, this means that when money is paid into the account, it is entered on the debit (i.e. left-hand) side, and when it is paid out, it is entered on the credit (i.e. right-hand) side. Also, any opening balance of cash would appear on the debit side. On each side of the account, there are columns for the date, for the 'particulars' and for the cash figure. There is also, sometimes, a 'folio' column immediately preceding the cash column, which, as we shall see later, can be used for cross-referencing purposes.

The youth club's cash account in 'T' form is shown in example 3.3.

Summarising the net worth

Example 3.3

March		£	March			£
1	Balance	42.50	3	Wages		15.00
2	Subscriptions received	120.26	8	Building society		120.00
5	Sale of refreshments	34.93	15	Wages		15.00
6	Subscriptions received	35.60	20	Table-tennis balls		10.50
10	Refreshments sales	45.13	23	Building society		80.00
21	Non-member entrance	7.60	30	Refreshments, costs		35.10
			31	Balance	c/d	10.42
		286.02				286.02
April						
1	Balance b/d	10.42				

The final cash balance is the amount by which the debit (i.e. the 'heavier') side is greater than the credit (i.e. the 'lighter' side). In this example, we have a debit balance of £10.42, since this is the amount by which the debit side is greater than the credit side. The figure is, however, first entered on the credit side and the two columns added (coming to the same total 'proves' that we've got the right figure for the balance) and then it is 'carried down' (note the abbreviation c/d) to the debit side—simply and solely because it really is a debit balance. It is entered on the debit side with the abbreviation b/d, meaning 'brought down'. The closing balance of the one period becomes the opening balance for the next period and is usually dated for the following day for this reason. (The detailed rules for balancing 'T' accounts are described in appendix C at the end of the book.)

3C. Bank Accounts

When money is placed in a bank, both the person or firm depositing the money, and the bank itself, will keep records. Each will record the transactions *from their own point of view*.

When Mrs X pays money into the bank, for example, her cash-in-hand is reduced (i.e. a credit entry in cash account) and the bank becomes *her debtor*. Therefore, in her books the bank account will show a debit balance.

From the bank's point of view, however, Mrs X becomes *their creditor*, and this is what the bank's records will show. Consequently, if Mrs X has 'money in the bank' and she receives a statement (which is a copy of her account in the bank's books), she will be shown as having a *credit* balance, which will match the debit balance recorded against the bank in her own books.

One complication can arise with bank accounts which cannot arise with cash accounts. It is possible, with the bank's approval, to draw more money out of the bank account than has been paid in. This is known as an **overdraft** and will be shown by a credit balance in the customer's own books, and as a debit balance in the bank's books. The account for cash-in-hand can never have a credit balance, since it is physically impossible to pay out more actual cash than there is in the cash box.

Keeping track of the changes: 1

Activity 3.3

On 1 June last, the Albion Athletics Club opened an account with the Midland Bank and paid in £100 as the opening balance. The following transactions then took place:

June		£
5	Paid affiliation fees by cheque	75
10	Received subscriptions from members and paid them into bank	160
15	Purchased equipment by cheque	200
20	Received more subscriptions and paid them into the bank	80
25	Paid out cheque for hire of gymnasium	75

Prepare the following:

(i) *The bank account as it would appear in the books of the club in 'T' form, showing the balance carried down at the end of the month.*
(ii) *The account in 'running balance' form. What problems arise with the running balance form in this particular case?*
(iii) *If statements had been received from the bank listing all transactions up to (a) 19 June and (b) 30 June, what would the balances on the statements have been (state whether debit or credit)?*

When money is paid into a bank, a *paying-in slip* is completed, a copy of which is retained by the customer. This is an important document, as it is from this 'original document' that the bank account is entered up. It should be retained as evidence that the money was, in fact, paid in. The auditor will want to check it later.

Payments from bank accounts are usually made by 'drawing' (i.e. writing out) cheques. Payments can also be made by *standing orders*—this is a system by means of which a customer directs the bank to make payments of a stated amount either on the dates that he orders, or regularly, such as on the first of every month or at a certain date each year. It is obviously a convenient way of paying regular amounts such as subscriptions or rent. Payments can also be made by *direct debit*. Under this system, the customer authorises the bank to pay from his or her account whatever amount a particular person or organisation demands. This can be a convenient way of paying regular charges—such as that for electricity—which are likely to vary. One problem, however, is that the person's or firm's own bank records cannot be made up until the statement is received from the bank, as it is not usually known until then how much has been demanded by the creditor.

An overdraft should not be confused with a **bank loan**. An overdraft amounts to taking out from a bank account more money than there is in it, and interest is charged by the bank on the amount overdrawn from day to day. A **bank loan** is a formal agreement by the bank to lend a customer a specified amount and—usually—for an agreed period. The amount of the loan is paid into the customer's bank account to draw on as he or she wishes. The customer pays interest on the full loan, whether he or she draws the money out or not. The loan, and the money in the bank account, must be considered as two separate items, and each appears as separate items in balance sheets. A bank overdraft is a short-term (current) liability, and a bank loan is normally a long-term liability (except for the year in which it falls due for repayment).

3D. Cash and Security

Of all assets, cash is the one which is most likely to be lost, stolen or subject to fraud. Even where quite small amounts are concerned—amounts far less than a pound—some people will always be tempted

Summarising the net worth

to 'help themselves', usually with the firm intention of 'putting it back' at some future date. Unfortunately, such intentions are seldom realised. Also, what starts off in a very small way can very easily become a habit, and before the individual realises it, he or she is so much in debt that there is no hope of paying it back. And that can lead to even bigger problems, such as illegal attempts to alter the books in order to cover up the theft.

Those people responsible for keeping the cash accounts must ensure first that the cash receipts and payments system is designed to reduce to a minimum the risk of fraud or theft—by themselves as well as by others. Secondly, it must be obvious to all that such a system exists. In other words, in accounting:

It is not only important to be honest, but it is equally important that it should be clear to everyone that you (and indeed everyone else) are being honest.

Several simple rules exist which help to improve the security of cash accounting systems. These are shown in display 2. The rules should be strictly followed, no matter how big or small the organisation is, and no matter whether it is a major cash fund of a multinational, or a more modest cash holding of a club, or collection, or raffle.

Display 2: Keeping the Cash Safe—The Essential Ten Points

1 Numbered receipts should be given, if possible, when cash is received. The receipt number can be entered in the folio column in the ledger.

2 If it is not possible to give receipts (e.g. in a busy 'shop' situation), then there should be some other control, such as a proper cash till with a 'tally' roll, or a second person present. The amount of cash taken should be counted and the amount certified by those concerned. One of the reasons why shops price goods at (say) £4.99 instead of £5 is because the 1p change required forces the assistant to 'ring up' the sale.

3 Receipts should always be obtained, if possible, for any cash payments made and these should be filed in the order in which the items are entered in the cash account. If a formal receipt cannot be obtained, then a 'voucher' should be prepared. A voucher is a simple note recording the payment, and signed or initialled by the person receiving or authorising the payment.

4 All payments should, if possible, be authorised by someone other than the person actually handling the cash or the person receiving it.

5 Cash should always be kept in a safe place and kept under lock and key.

6 If large sums are involved, the money should be transferred to a bank account as quickly as possible.

7 An independent person should have the authority and responsibility of checking the cash-in-hand against the cash records, and have the right to do this without notice or warning.

8 Cheque books should always be kept in a safe place and—in the case of a club or firm—should have to be signed by at least two people. Only 'crossed' cheques should be used—this means that they can only be 'cashed' by being paid into a bank account. For additional security, cheques should be marked 'not negotiable'. This simply means that, should one be stolen, no one (not even someone who takes it innocently) obtains any right to it. It does *not* prevent the cheque being transferred.

9 If *you* are to be responsible for any cash-count checks, ensure that *all* cash funds are produced to you at the *same* time and that you are not called away during the cash count. If possible, have the total of the check certified by an independent person.

10 If you are unable to be present for any necessary checks of goods or cash, ensure that the check is carried out by at least two responsible persons, both of whom should sign an appropriate certificate.

Now try activity 3.4.

Activity 3.4

Assume that a club of which you are a member is considering setting up a coffee bar to be run by volunteers.

(i) Discuss, with a group of others, the major problems that would exist concerning security of the cash and stock.

(ii) Prepare a set of rules to ensure that cash or goods do not go astray.

(iii) Compare your list of rules with those produced by other groups. Are any of the suggested rules impracticable—try to think about the practical problems in running bars in this sort of situation?

(iv) Describe the form and style of any certificates you would want signed by others in respect of checks it might be difficult for you to carry out personally.

(v) Prepare a 'final' list of rules incorporating the best suggestions from all of the groups.

Check Your Understanding

1 What do the terms *opening balance* and *closing balance* refer to in the case of a cash account?

2 What are the advantages of keeping a proper cash record?

3 What are the disadvantages of the single cash column type of cash account?

4 What problems could a large commercial firm run into if it did not keep a proper record of cash?

5 What are the advantages and the disadvantages of the running balance form of cash account?

6 Rule up a 'T' balance form of cash account, and head the columns.

7 What is the difference between a balance marked 'c/d' and a balance marked 'b/d'?

8 Can a cash account (note: *not* a bank account) have a credit balance? What is the reason for your answer?

9 What is the reason for entering the balance on the lighter of the two sides of a 'T' form account, and then carrying the figure down to the heavier side?

10 Why should the totals of the two columns of a 'T' form account both appear on the same line—even though it may mean leaving a gap between the last entry and the total on one side of the account?

11 What are the main ways in which the cash account of a major business firm would differ from that of a private person?

12 Why is *special* care needed to prevent fraud where cash-in-hand is concerned?

13 List the major steps that can be taken to increase security where cash-in-hand is concerned.

14 What are the differences between a bank overdraft and a bank loan?

15 Describe (a) standing orders and (b) direct debits. In what circumstances might each be used?

Practical Assignments

1 Complete the following paragraph, choosing one of the options listed in the brackets following each blank.

A cash account commences with the _____ (opening balance/closing balance) of cash-in-hand. Entries are made on the ____ (debit/credit) side in respect of cash received, and on the ____ (debit/credit) side in respect of cash payments. The amount of cash-in-hand at the end of the period is known as the _____ (opening/closing) balance, and is carried forward to the next accounting period. It is _____ (possible/impossible) to have a

Summarising the net worth

credit balance to a cash account. This is because one cannot pay more actual cash out than there is in the account.

2 Among the items in Simon Noakes' cash account are the following:

A. On the *debit* side:

			£
April 13	Cash sales		24
27	Interest received from investments		78

B. On the *credit* side:

			£
April 29	Rent		120
30	Balance	c/d	460

What does each of these entries mean?

3 Joe Smith is a window cleaner. The following is a list of his cash transactions for the week ending 28th June 19—.

			£
June 23	Cash balance brought forward from the previous week		42.20
23	Cash receipts from cleaning windows		18.50
23	Payment for insurance		30.00
24	Cash receipts from cleaning windows		25.00
24	Purchase of new bucket		5.00
24	New ladder bought from DIY shop		15.00
25	Money received for window cleaning		10.00
25	Cost of repairing trailer		10.50
26	Window cleaning receipts		22.30
26	Purchase of window cleaning materials		12.00
27	Payments by customers for window cleaning		15.00
28	Receipts from customers for window cleaning		18.00
28	Wages of part-time assistant		40.00

Write up Joe's cash account for the week, showing clearly the balance to be carried forward to the next week. Is this balance more, or less, than the balance he started the week with? What is the amount of the difference?

4 From the following, prepare the cash account of the Fitzwilliam Cricket Club for the month of June 19—. Balance the account at the end of the month, and show the balance carried forward to 1 July.

			£
June 1	Balance of cash brought forward from May		40.35
3	Collection at home match		30.65
3	Receipts from players for teas and refreshments		20.00
5	Cost of teas supplied on June 3		22.40
6	Purchase of new bats and pads		75.00
10	Collection at home match		45.20
10	Receipts from players for teas		18.30
12	Cost of teas supplied on June 10		25.00
17	Hire cost of bus for an away match		30.00
17	Receipts from players and supporters for transport		31.00
20	Purchase of new score book		3.50
20	Purchase of new accounts book		2.40
24	Collection at home match		15.00
24	Receipts from players for teas supplied		20.00
29	Cost of teas supplied on June 24		24.00

5 Complete the following table summarising the cash position of Ajax Ltd for the period 1 January–30 June last:

Month	Opening balance (£000)	Receipts (£000)	Payments (£000)	Closing balance (£000)
January	250	360	120	490
February	490	280	...	650
March	650	142	530	...
April	262	360	428	...
May	...	200	123	...
June	...	...	640	483

6 Enter the following in the cash account of Amanda Hawke, who commenced business at the beginning of January, and balance at 31 January.

			£
Jan 1	Sold goods for cash		175.00
2	Paid to G. Watson for goods received		30.50
4	Paid J. Jackson		22.75
6	Cash sales		386.44
7	Paid for goods		150.00
8	Purchased stationery for office use		25.00
10	Paid into the bank		300.00
12	Sold goods for cash		250.87
15	Paid rent for warehouse		150.00
19	Purchased stamps		36.50
25	Cash sales		420.00
31	Paid wages		350.00

7 Enter up the cash account of Farflung Enterprises Ltd for the quarter ending 31 March last. The account should be balanced at the end of each month and the balance carried down.

			£
Jan 1	Balance of cash-in-hand		246.22
5	Cash sales		1 985.25
5	Paid wages		1 200.00
12	Paid rent		750.00
13	Cash sales to date		2 500.00
15	Paid wages		946.78
18	Paid for advertising		1 500.00
Feb 5	Cash sales		2 500.00
15	Paid wages		1 350.46
16	Paid rent		1 200.00
20	Cash sales		876.55

	28	Paid the balance of cash-in-hand into the bank with the exception of £1 000 which was carried forward to March	
Mar	5	Paid for advertising	1 000.00
	8	Paid postage and related expenses	546.22
	12	Paid wages	1 350.67
	15	Cash sales to date	4 684.56
	30	Paid wages	1 482.36

8 One of your uncles has recently decided to take a lease on a small corner shop, which will sell newspapers, stationery, confectionery and tobacco. This means that almost all of his trade will be 'cash over the counter'. As he has other commitments, he will have to leave the shop for long periods in the charge of two assistants, who have yet to be recruited. Your uncle has heard that you are studying accountancy, and he has written to you to ask your advice on what he should do to reduce the risk of cash losses. Write your reply to him.

9 At the start of term last September, a number of students obtained permission to form a small company in order to produce a college Christmas magazine. The college principal was rather dismayed at the end of term to find that no proper accounts had been kept, but fortunately the pupils had made a careful note of all items concerning cash receipts and payments in a notebook. From this information, you are asked to write up the cash account of the magazine for submission to the principal, who is, of course, responsible to the college governors for making certain that no money has gone astray. The items in the note book read as follows:

15 Sep	Sold 100 shares in the company at 25p each to college students and staff.
9 Oct	Received £20 from local retailers for advertising space in the magazine.
15 Oct	Purchased printing paper from W. H. Smith £20.
16 Oct	Paid to the college for telephone calls £3.
23 Oct	Gave £2 to the editor as refund of bus fares incurred by him in obtaining adverts.
Nov 5	More telephone calls £5.
23 Nov	Received bill from college, £7, for more phone calls, which was paid.
25 Oct	Issued 80 more shares at 25p each.
20 Nov	Received from advertisers £60.
27 Nov	Another 80 shares issued and paid for.
Dec 4	Paid £28 for a printing block containing the college crest and the title of the magazine. Paid travelling costs to the editor (£3, I think).
Dec 10	Sold 300 copies of the magazine. They are priced 15p each. Also paid £15 to the college for the hire of a room as the office of the magazine.
15th	Paid to the college £30 as the printing cost of the magazine. Last day of term. Sold 200 more magazines.

Required:
a. Write up and balance the cash account.
b. What check could you carry out immediately to see if all cash items had been included in your account?
c. The principal is not very happy about the way the records have been kept. What suggestions can you make for an improved system for the next magazine, which might make him feel a little happier?

UNIT 4 KEEPING TRACK OF THE CHANGES: 2

Before you read this unit, try activity 4.1.

Activity 4.1

Richard Jones started business buying and selling second-hand cars on 1 May and paid £30 000 into the firm's bank account from his private resources as capital.

Draw up his balance sheet as at 1 May.

			£
May			
1	Capital		30 000
3	Loan (from relative)		20 000

The next day, he obtained a ten-year loan from a relative, and arranged with the bank to have an overdraft. He spent the month of May 'setting up' the business, purchasing cars at auctions and arranging his premises. At 31 May, the firm's bank account kept by Richard appeared as follows:

Bank account

May		£
5	Premises	10 000
7	Cars	4 500
9	Fixtures and fittings	1 000
13	Cars	6 200
15	Office equipment	1 000
18	Cars	3 000
21	Fixtures and fittings	2 000
22	Office equipment	2 500
23	Cars	10 500
25	Display equipment	500
26	Cars	12 000

What information is it possible to obtain from the account?

4A. The Fuller Picture

1. Cash transactions

The debit side of Richard's bank account shows the sums of money that he paid into the bank. The credit side lists the various payments.

But can the account tell us anything else?

It is obviously possible to find the state of Richard's bank balance at the end of the month by finding the difference between the two sides. It is in fact a credit balance of £3200, indicating an overdraft. Remember that when Richard receives a statement from the bank, the entries will be reversed, as the bank will be looking at it from *their* point of view. The account can, of course, be balanced (see page 22), and the balance carried forward to the next month. It is also possible to see exactly where the income came from. Also, by selecting and adding together the appropriate items on the credit side, it is possible to find out how much was spent on (i) premises, (ii) purchase of cars,

(iii) fixtures and fittings, (iv) office equipment and (v) display equipment.

In this case, it is not difficult to obtain the answers by a quick glance at the account. But it would be much more difficult if the account had consisted, not just of 13 entries on one page, but perhaps of 110 items on each of 51, 63 or even many more pages.

Would Richard Jones want to know such figures?

Yes, he would. First, it is obviously important for him to know just what his cash balance is from time to time. Secondly, the figures would be needed from time to time to draw up balance sheets and other summaries. Thirdly, it is equally important—if not *more* important—to know where the cash received over a period has come from, and on what it has been spent.

Each of the entries in Richard's bank account refers to what in accounting is known as a **transaction**. A *transaction* is an event that affects the *financial* position of the person or firm concerned. Examples include all receipts of cash, and any form of payment. A transaction need not necessarily involve money. For instance, as we shall see later, the purchase of goods on credit (i.e. goods that are bought but not paid for at the time) is a transaction, since it affects the financial position of the firm.

Each of the transactions in Richard's account could be looked at in another way. As regards the payments *into* the account, one could ask the question: Where did they come from? In his case, one came from his own resources, and one by way of a loan. As regards the payments *out of* the account, we can list the various items on which the money was spent. This brings us to a fundamental rule in accounting—namely that:

Each and every transaction affects two items with which we are concerned.

Each time cash is received, it is important to know exactly where it has come from. In addition, it is equally important to know, each time money is paid out, exactly what it is spent on. Only in this way can we build up a full picture of what is going on.

This brings us to the idea of **double-entry** book-keeping. The rule is, simply, that, for each transaction, entries are made in *two* separate accounts, not just one. This means that:

(i) If cash is received, it is recorded not only on the *debit* side of cash account, but also on the *credit* side of an account that states where the cash has come from.
(ii) If cash is paid out, an entry is made not only on the *credit* side of cash account, but also on the *debit* side of an account that states what it was spent on.

If this procedure is carefully followed, then a complete picture is built up of what has happened. In order to answer the questions asked in activity 4.1, we have only to turn to the appropriate account or accounts. The position is even clearer if the accounts are totalled and balanced, and the balances carried down. (The detailed rules for balancing accounts are described in appendix C at the end of the book.)

Entering up the accounts in this way is known as **posting**. The accounts are all kept together in a **ledger**, which may consist of a bound book, a loose-leaf file or a computer print-out. The ledger of Richard Jones (activity 4.1), when posted and balanced, would consist of the cash account set out at the start of this unit, and of the following accounts.

Summarising the net worth

For each item entered in Richard's cash account, find and tick the appropriate 'double entry' in the other accounts.

Capital account

				£
	May 1	Bank		30 000

Loan account

				£
	May 5	Bank		20 000

Premises account

			£
May 5	Bank		10 000

Motor cars account

			£					£
May 7	Bank		4 500	May 31	Balance	c/d		36 200
13	Bank		6 200					
18	Bank		3 000					
23	Bank		10 500					
26	Bank		12 000					
			36 200					36 200
Jun 1	Balance	b/d	36 200					

Fixtures and fittings account

			£				£
May 9	Bank		1 000	May 31	Balance		3 000
21	Bank		2 000				
			3 000				3 000
Jun 1	Balance	b/d	3 000				

Office equipment account

			£					£
May 15	Bank		1 000	May 31	Balance	c/d		3 500
22	Bank		2 500					
			3 500					3 500
Jun 1	Balance	b/d	3 500					

Display equipment account

			£
May 25	Bank		500

2. Credit transactions

So far, only the posting of transactions that involve either the actual receipt of money or the actual payment of it have been considered. These are not the only types of transactions that concern the accountant. He is interested in *any* transaction that affects the financial position, whether or not it involves the payment of money at the time.

An example is the purchase of, say, equipment *on credit*. This means that, although the goods have been legally purchased and the legal ownership transferred, they were not paid for at the time. Consequently, the firm is the owner of the equipment but, for the time being, the firm has a **creditor**—i.e. someone to whom the firm owes money. Payment will, of course, be made eventually, but that must be considered as a separate transaction.

Keeping track of the changes: 2

Example 4.1

Check through the double-entry postings for each of the following transactions in the accounts listed:

March		Debit	Credit
4	Purchased equipment by cheque £200	Equipment	Bank
10	Purchased equipment £75 on credit from Allsports Ltd	Equipment	Allsports Ltd
20	Paid cheque £75 to Allsports Ltd	Allsports Ltd	Bank

```
                  Equipment account
March  4  Bank              200
      10  Allsports Ltd      75

                 Bank account (extract)
                              March  4  Equipment      200
                                    20  Allsports Ltd   75

                      Allsports Ltd
March 20  Bank       75     March 10  Equipment       75
```

Notes:
(i) Each posting truly reflects the change in the firm's position. If a balance sheet is prepared before payment is made, Allsports Ltd will appear as a creditor—i.e. a current liability. There are usually a number of creditors, and they are added together as one figure in the balance sheet. It is important that, in the ledger itself, individual creditors each have a separate account so that the firm knows how much is owed to each creditor.

(ii) After the payment to Allsports Ltd has been made, there is a 'nil' balance on its account—which means that nothing is owed to or by either firm. This, of course, is the true position.

(iii) If payment is made immediately for purchases, we are not interested—from an accounting point of view—in who the supplier was. The name of the supplier is only of importance in credit transactions. In a posting exercise, therefore, if the name of the supplier is given, it may be assumed that the transaction is a credit one.

(iv) It is usual to omit the word 'account' in the title of personal accounts such as that of Allsports Ltd.

Similar considerations apply to sales on credit. The purchaser becomes a debtor until he pays the amount owing.

Example 4.2

Richard Jones (activity 4.1) found that he did not need all the premises that he had bought for £10 000 and could sell part of them to Diana Fletcher on 13 June for £4000. Diana paid part of the amount (£2500) on 30 June, the balance being carried forward for payment at a later date.

June		Debit	Credit
13	Sale of premises (£4000) to D. Fletcher	D. Fletcher	Premises
30	Receipt of cheque (£2500) from D. Fletcher	Bank	D. Fletcher

```
                          Premises account
May 5   Bank              10 000    June 13  D. Fletcher             4 000
                                    June 30  Balance          c/d    6 000
                          ──────                                    ──────
                          10 000                                    10 000
Jul 1   Balance     b/d    6 000

                            D. Fletcher
Jun 13  Premises           4 000    Jun 30   Bank                    2 500
                                         30  Balance          c/d    1 500
                          ──────                                    ──────
                           4 000                                     4 000
Jul 1   Balance     b/d    1 500
```

Summarising the net worth

It is useful to remember the following simple rule:

Debit the account that 'receives'.
Credit the account that 'gives'.

With more complicated transactions later, this rule has to be modified, but it is helpful at this stage.

Similar items can often be posted to the same account, depending upon how much detail is necessary in the accounts. For example, the purchase of cricket balls and stumps by a cricket club can often both be posted to equipment account.

Activity 4.2

Draw up the balance sheet of Richard Jones as at 31 May. Take the information from the balance of his ledger accounts shown in the unit.

4B. The Trial Balance

1. General principles

Accounting records are useless unless they are accurate. And if we are handling large sums of *other* people's money—often thousands of pounds—then it is doubly important that the records are correct. Not only must they be correct, but the accountant must be able to *show* that they are correct.

One advantage of the double-entry system is that, if a mistake is made, the final balance *may* not balance—only 'may' because there are some errors that do not show up in this way, such as the complete omission of a transaction. At least it is possible to say that, if a final balance sheet does not balance, then it is certain that a mistake has been made.

It is particularly useful to know that the accounts are (probably) correct immediately after the ledger posting has been completed. But, if there is a great deal of posting to be done over a period of time, it is often worth while to do a check periodically—say, once a month or once a week, or even once a day, depending on the need for 'on-going' accuracy. Some organisations can 'carry' a mistake in their accounts for a short while. But, in general, the sooner it is known that a mistake has occurred, the easier it is to find and correct it.

One of the most common ways of checking for errors in accounting is by means of a **trial balance**. A trial balance is simply a list of the balances in each of the accounts in the ledger at a particular time. These are set out in two columns—one for debit balances and one for credit balances. *If* the ledger posting has been correct, then the totals of the two columns will be the same.

A trial balance drawn up from the balances in Richard Jones' ledger (shown earlier in this unit) at the end of his first month as a second-hand car dealer would therefore appear thus:

[handwritten margin note: Trial balance stepping stone to final account]

Richard Jones: Trial balance at 31 May 19--

	Debit £	Credit £
Bank		3 200
Capital		30 000
Loan		20 000
Premises	10 000	
Motor cars	36 200	
Fixtures and fittings	3 000	
Office equipment	3 500	
Display equipment	500	
	53 200	53 200

If the two sides of an account 'balance' (i.e. come down to the same total so that there is no balance to carry down), it is not entered in the trial balance.

It is usual to prepare a trial balance at the end of an accounting period after all the ledger posting has been completed. This serves as a check on the accuracy of the posting. But also it is a useful working list of balances needed when preparing the balance sheet and the other summaries to be discussed later. A trial balance may be drawn up at *any* stage during the ledger posting process. As such, it acts as a check on the posting up to that point in time.

2. Why a trial balance may not balance

There are several reasons why a trial balance may not balance. These are summarised in display 3, together with the steps that should be taken to remedy the position.

3. Immediate correction of errors

Sometimes, errors are not found in accounts until quite a long time after they have been made, and correction of the original figure will mean correction of a very large number of figures—balances at the bottom of each page, for example—which occur after the error. In such instances, special rules apply, and these will be considered in unit 27. However, a mistake is often noticed almost immediately and a correction can be made 'on the spot'. This will happen where a wrong figure has been entered and it is noticed almost immediately.

Where it is necessary to alter a figure of this nature, the rules in display 3 should be strictly followed.

Finally, the following three points must be emphasised in connection with trial balances:

(i) Care must be taken to distinguish a trial balance from a balance sheet. Although the names are similar, they are two quite different documents.

(ii) The trial balance is *not* part of the double-entry system, and the accounts are in no way transferred to it. It is purely an independent and external check.

(iii) Only some errors are shown up by the trial balance; others do not affect it. This means only that if the trial balance 'balances', the accounts *may* be right. However, if the trial balance does *not* balance, it means that there definitely are errors.

Summarising the net worth

Display 3: Trial Balances—Which Don't

THE REASONS

1. A balance may have been entered in the wrong column of the trial balance.

2. One or more ledger accounts have been accidentally omitted from the trial balance.

3. Only one entry may have been made in the ledger for a transaction (for example, only the debit—not the credit—entry, or vice versa).

4. Both entries in the ledger may have been made on the same side (e.g. two debit, or two credit, entries instead of one of each).

5. Wrong figures may have been entered in one or more accounts.

6. Figures may have been 'reversed' (e.g. 2769 may have been entered as 2679). This is a very easy error to make, particularly when carrying balances forward.

7. The balance themselves may have been wrongly calculated or transferred.

8. The trial balance itself may have been incorrectly added.

HOW TO FIND THE ERROR

1. Check the addition of the trial balance.

2. Look for 'obvious' errors (e.g. capital or sales listed on the debit side or machinery on the credit side). 'Nonsense' figures for an account may also give a clue.

3. Check that all ledger balances have been included which should have been included.

4. Find out the difference in the trial balance totals and check whether there is a transaction for:
(a) the same amount, which would indicate that one entry of a transaction had not been made; or
(b) *half* the amount, indicating that both entries had been made on the same side of the ledger.

5. Check whether the difference in the trial balance is divisible by 9. If it is, then it could indicate that numbers had been reversed. Whenever this is done, the difference that results will be divisible by 9.

6. Check the accuracy of each ledger balance.

7. Check that the ledger 'balanced' at the start of the accounting period.

8. Check the whole posting, transaction by transaction. Neat pencil ticks should be used to show that a figure has been checked.

THE RULES FOR CORRECTING A WRONG FIGURE

1. Do *not* alter a figure until you are certain you have got the correct one. Nothing looks worse than the same figure altered several times.

2. When you are satisfied that you know the correct figure, strike the wrong figure through once (*and once only*) and insert the correct figure above it.

3. Always ensure that the wrong figure can be read for what it was. In no circumstances must anything appear as if it has been 'covered up' in any way at all.

4. For the same reason, do not use liquid paper (Snopake, Tippex, etc.).

Activity 4.3

One example of an error that will not show up in a trial balance is the complete omission of a transaction from the books.

Can you think of any others? Also, describe an error that will show up in a trial balance.

(*Keep your answer safely, as you will need to refer back to it when you read unit 27.*)

4C. The Accounting Cycle

The example of the accounts of Richard Jones (above) illustrates the basic **accounting cycle**. The cycle starts with the balance sheet at the beginning of the period (the 'opening' balance sheet). This leads on to the ledger and the posting of the transactions recording the effect of the changes, and ends with the balance sheet at the end of the period (the 'closing' balance sheet).

The closing balance sheet of one period is the opening balance sheet of the next period, and the closing balances of the ledger accounts of the first period are carried down in order to become the opening balances of the next. They are 'on-going' from one accounting period to the next. Note that the ledger accounts are *not* transferred to the balance sheet: the balance sheet merely *summarises* what, from time to time, happens to be in the ledger. The trial balance is included in the cycle of operations, but it must be remembered that it is an optional procedure. Though it is usually prepared at the completion of the posting, it can in fact be taken out at any point.

We can show the cycle of operations as a diagram, like that in figure 4.1.

Figure 4.1
The accounting cycle.

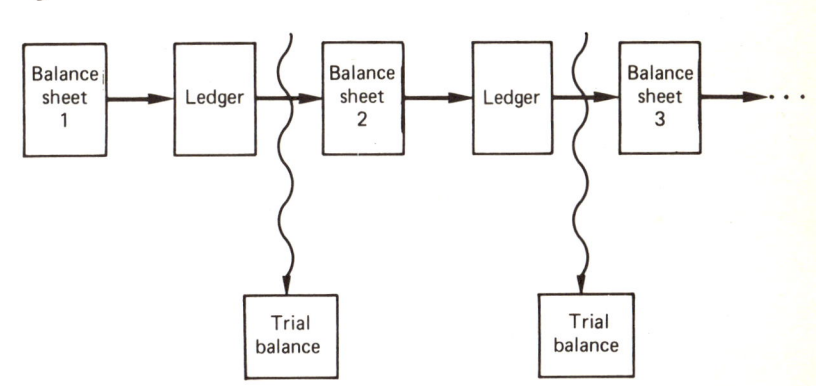

Check Your Understanding

1. What do we mean by the word *transaction* in accounting?

2. What is meant by the term *double-entry* book-keeping?

3. What does the term *posting* mean?

4. Why is it necessary to make two entries for every transaction?

5. What ledger entries should be made for the following:
    (i) Purchase of equipment from A. Filey.
    (ii) Loan of cash to D. Watson.
    (iii) Payment of a cheque into a building society account.
    (iv) Payment of cash into the bank.
    (v) Repayment of loan by cheque by D. Watson.
    (vi) Withdrawal of cash from the bank.
    (vii) Payment of cheque to A. Filey.
    (viii) Transit van purchased by cheque.

6. What does the term *balancing* mean in connection with accounts?

7. When balancing accounts, what should be done with:
    (i) an account with only one entry in it?
    (ii) an account with the same figure entered on each side of the account?

8. List the rules for balancing a ledger account in which there are a number of entries on each side of the account.

9. What is the difference between a balance 'carried down' and a balance 'brought down'?

10. What is the difference between a balance 'brought down' and a balance 'brought forward'?

11. What is meant by the term *credit transaction*?

12. Why is it not necessary, from an accounting point of view, to know the name of the supplier when goods are purchased for cash?

13. Define the term *creditor*.

14. What name does a firm give to a person to whom it sells goods on credit and who has not yet paid for them?

15. Where do (a) creditors and (b) debtors appear in a balance sheet?

16. What is meant by the term *accounting cycle*?

17. What is the main purpose of a trial balance?

18. What other function does a trial balance have?

Summarising the net worth

19 What, if anything, can be said about the ledger if the trial balance agrees?

20 What can be said about the ledger if the trial balance does not agree?

21 Give as many examples as possible of mistakes that will now show up in the trial balance.

22 What are (a) the similarities and (b) the differences between a trial balance and a balance sheet.

23 Why should we take out a trial balance as often as is convenient?

Practical Assignments

1 Fill in the blanks in the following sentences:
   a. The left-hand side of a 'T' form ledger account is known as the _Debit_ side, and the right-hand side as the _Credit_ side.
   b. If a fork-lift truck is bought and paid for immediately by cheque, a debit entry would be made in the _Vehicles_ account and a credit entry in the _bank_ account.
   c. If furniture is purchased on credit from Homesales Ltd, a debit entry would be made in the _Furniture_ account and a credit entry in the _HSL_ account.
   d. When payment is made, by cheque, to Homesales Ltd in respect of the furniture purchased on credit, the entries will be a debit entry in the _HSL_ account and a credit entry in the _Bank_ account.
   e. If surplus equipment is sold to D. Foukes, a club member, on credit, the entries in the club's books would be a debit entry in the _D Foukes_ account and a credit entry in the _equipment_ account.

2 Describe in your own words the transactions that would have given rise to each of the following postings in the ledger:
   a. A debit entry in the bank account and a credit entry in the cash account.
   b. A debit entry in the motor vehicles account and a credit entry in the Europa Car Co. account.
   c. A credit entry in the bank account and a debit entry in the Europa Car Co. account.
   d. A debit entry in bank account and a credit entry in the loans account.
   e. A credit entry in the bank account and a debit entry in the account of Business Loans Ltd.

3 Complete the following statements:
   a. A debit balance in an account for J. Smith indicates _he owes us money_
   b. A credit balance in an account for Office Supplies Ltd indicates _we owe_
   c. A debit balance in equipment account indicates _Fixed Asset_
   d. A credit balance in bank account indicates _overdrawn_
   e. A debit balance in cash account indicates _cash in hand_

4 Enter in the appropriate columns the accounts that should be debited and credited in respect of each of the following transactions. The organisation concerned is a social club.
   a. Purchase of premises from the Local Authority.
   b. Purchase of equipment by cheque.
   c. Cheque paid to Local Authority in respect of purchase of premises.
   d. Cash drawn from bank.
   e. Equipment purchased from D. Sorell Ltd.
   f. Sale of surplus equipment for cash.
   g. Cash paid into the bank.
   h. Surplus equipment sold to Ken Jackson.
   i. Purchased office equipment by cash.
   j. Purchase of furniture from Modern Furnishings Ltd.
   k. Paid Modern Furnishings Ltd by cheque.
   l. Ken Jackson pays by cheque for the equipment he bought.

5 Tom Edwards commenced business as a travel agent on 1 January last. His assets, at that date, were: cash-in-hand £10 000; cash-at-bank £16 000; office equipment £6 000; lease on premises £20 000. His liabilities at the same date were: loan owing to Mercantile Finance Ltd £10 000, repayable in two years' time; owing to Office Supplies Ltd in respect of purchase of the office equipment £4 000.

   Draw up his opening balance sheet, open his ledger and then post the following transactions. Then extract a trial balance and draw up a balance sheet as at the close of business on 12 January.

		£
Jan 2	Bought an electronic typewriter by cheque	800
3	Purchased filing cabinets from Office Supplies Ltd	260
5	Withdrew cash from bank for office use	500
9	Bought car, for the firm's use, from Ace Motors Ltd	8 500
10	Sent cheque to Mercantile Finance Ltd to reduce outstanding loan	2 500

		£
11	Paid cheque to Ace Motors Ltd on account	6 000
11	Tom Edwards paid additional cash into the firm by way of additional capital from his private resources	3 000
12	Paid wages in cash	250
12	Paid into the bank	10 000

6 Tom Cobley started business on 20 April last as a furniture repairer and restorer with £10 000 cash, which he deposited in a bank account in the firm's name. Between then and the end of the month, he entered into the following transactions:

April 22	Bought furniture from Furnisales Ltd, £50 000
24	Borrowed from Trade Loans Ltd, £6 000, and deposited same amount with the bank
25	Bought various items of equipment, £2 500, and paid by cheque
27	Withdrew £500 from bank for use as office cash
29	Paid Furnisales Ltd by cheque the sum of £8 000

Open Cobley's ledger at 20 April, and post the transactions to the relevant accounts. Extract a trial balance and draw up his balance sheet as at 30 April last.

7 a. What is a trial balance?
b. Give *three* examples of errors that will show up in a trial balance.
c. Give *two* examples of errors that will not show up in a trial balance.
d. State why the following trial balance *must* be incorrect:

	£	£
Capital	8 000	
Cash-at-bank	10 000	
Debtors		30 000
Plant and machinery	20 000	
Cash-in-hand	15 000	
Trade creditors	4 000	
Long-term loan		3 000
Stock	6 000	
	48 000	48 000

8 Sheila McDonald opened the McDonald Secretarial Bureau on 1 August last with a capital of £20 000, which she paid into the bank account of the new firm. During August, the following transactions took place:

		£
Aug 2	Drew cash from bank for office use	250
5	Received a loan from her parents	5 000
10	Purchased lease of an office, by cheque	15 000
15	Bought office equipment from Ajax Ltd	850
20	Purchased office equipment by cash	100
25	Purchased by cheque furniture for office	1 500
28	Drew cash from bank	100
29	Returned faulty equipment to Ajax Ltd and was allowed the full cost	200

Draw up a trial balance, balance the ledger at 31 August, and then post the following transactions, which refer to September:

		£
Sep 8	Paid Ajax Ltd by cheque	650
10	Purchased office equipment from Menser Ltd	500
15	Purchased filing cabinet and paid in cash	75
20	Sheila paid additional capital into the firm's bank account	2 000
21	Purchased car for use on firm's business and paid by cheque	8 000

Post the transactions, extract the trial balance as at 30 September, and then draw up Sheila's balance sheet as at that date.

9 Tony Ashcroft commenced business as a travel agent on 1 January last. His assets, at that date, were cash-in-hand £500, cash-at-bank £16 000, office equipment £6 000, lease on premises £40 000. His liabilities at the same date consisted of a loan from his brother for £10 000, and owing to Office Supplies Ltd £4 000.

Draw up a balance sheet as at 1 January, open his ledger, and post the following transactions:

		£
Jan 2	Bought an electronic typewriter by cheque	800
3	Purchased filing cabinets from Office Supplies Ltd	400
5	Withdrew from bank for office cash	250
9	Sent cheque to brother in reduction of loan	2 000
9	Bought car from Ace Motors Ltd	8 000
10	Sent cheque to Ace Motors Ltd	5 000
11	Tony Ashcroft paid a cheque for £1 000 into the firm's bank account, from his private resources, as additional capital	
12	Cash paid into the bank	150

Extract a trial balance; then draw up a balance sheet as at the close of business on 12 January.

10 Elizabeth recently commenced business and has drawn up the following statement of the firm's assets and liabilities, but fears she may have gone wrong somewhere. She asks you to redraft it for her. (You may assume that the items are listed at correct valuations.)

	£	£
Premises	40 000	
Mortgage	30 000	
Stock	19 600	
add Creditors	6 200	
	25 800	
less Debtors	2 400	23 400

Summarising the net worth

Cash loan	5 000	
add cash-in-hand	3 000	
	8 000	
less bank overdraft	4 500	4 500
Fixtures and fittings		2 000
		99 900
less Capital paid in at start		21 300
Net worth of the business		78 600

After redrafting the statement, add a short note explaining to Elizabeth any significant differences between your draft and hers.

11 Alan Rhodes, an engineer, was recently made redundant and decided to set up his own small engineering firm to be known as Rhodes Fabrications. He set the firm up at the start of the first full week of last month, and spent the Monday in detailed discussions with his bank manager. As a result, he opened a current account in the name of the firm and paid into it his redundancy money of £20 000 as his initial capital. In addition, his brother John agreed to advance him £30 000 as a long-term loan and this Alan also paid into his bank account.

a. On the Tuesday, John arranged a five-year lease of workshop premises at a cost of £15 000. He obtained a loan for the full amount from the Enterprise Finance Co. and agreed to commence repayments in three years' time.
b. On Wednesday, he drew a cheque for £1200 to provide the firm with some cash-in-hand. He also purchased some machinery by cheque for £10 000.
c. On Thursday, he bought further machinery for £15 000 on credit from Ajax Engineering Ltd, and agreed to pay as soon as possible.
d. Also on Thursday, he bought a second-hand pick-up utility van for £5500 from Roadsales plc. He paid a deposit by cheque of £1500, and agreed to pay the balance in three months' time.
e. On Friday, he purchased a range of loose tools for £600 cash.
f. On the Friday afternoon, he reviewed his financial position and paid £300 of the cash-in-hand back into the bank. He also took the bank manager's advice to transfer £20 000 from the firm's current account to a deposit account.

You are asked to do the following:

(i) Prepare the opening balance sheet for Rhodes.
(ii) Open his ledger and post the transactions.
(iii) At the end of the period: balance the accounts; draw up a trial balance; and draw up the closing balance sheet.

Discussion points
Alan took a lease on his workshop premises. Instead, he could either have rented them, or bought the freehold. What are the differences between these, what are their respective advantages and disadvantages, and how would the accounts have been affected by each?

Why do you think Alan was wise to have a long talk with his bank manager before starting his business? Bearing in mind that the manager is not an engineer, what sort of help and advice do you think he was in a position to give?

Towards the end of the week, when Alan realised he had surplus cash-in-hand, he paid some back into the bank. Bearing in mind that he would probably need it at some future point in time, was this wise? What are the dangers in keeping large amounts of cash-in-hand in a firm?

What are the main differences between a bank current account and a bank deposit account?

What do you think were the reasons that the bank manager had in mind in advising Alan to transfer some of the current account balance into a deposit account? Is there anything else he might consider doing with the money?

Alan purchased a vehicle from Roadsales plc. What is the meaning and significance of the abbreviation 'plc'?

UNIT 5 READING MEANING INTO BALANCE SHEETS

Before you read this unit, try activity 5.1.

Activity 5.1

The following information refers to the business of Alan Andy, a taxi-cab operator, at 1 June last. At that date, he owned the freehold of a garage valued at £36 000, of which he owed £24 000 to a building society on a 15-year mortgage. He owned three cars currently valued at £10 000 each and various items of office equipment of a total value of £3600. At his garage, he had in stock £600 worth of petrol; he still owed £240 on this. His balance at the bank was £2400 and his cash-in-hand was £400.

Prepare Alan's balance sheet as at 1 June last. Add a comment saying (with reasons) whether you think he was in a satisfactory financial position and whether the business appears to be well managed.

5A. Balance Sheet Subgroups

1. Fixed and current assets

A balance sheet is much more than just two columns of figures which—by chance or good fortune—happen to come to the same total. It is even something more than just a bland statement of the assets, liabilities and capital of a business at a certain date. To someone who knows how to 'read' a balance sheet, it gives much insight into the position, strength and viability of the business concerned.

In order to make the task of 'interpretation' (i.e. that of understanding the real meaning of a balance sheet) easier, it is helpful to arrange the assets into two main subgroups. These are:

(i) fixed assets, and
(ii) current assets.

Fixed assets are those which an organisation keeps in its permanent possession. Examples include land, buildings, machinery, fixtures and fittings, office equipment and motor vehicles.

Current assets are those which are continually being 'turned over' in the course of the firm's normal operations. In the case of a retail trader, the current assets would include trading stock, debtors, cash-at-bank and cash-in-hand. The current assets are sometimes termed the *circulating assets* because of the movement between them—stock is sold to debtors, who pay cash, which is used for paying creditors, from whom more stock is purchased. The circulating assets are sometimes known as circulating 'capital'—i.e. the amount of capital invested in the circulating assets. This movement is shown diagrammatically in figure 5.1.

Summarising the net worth

Figure 5.1
The movement of assets.

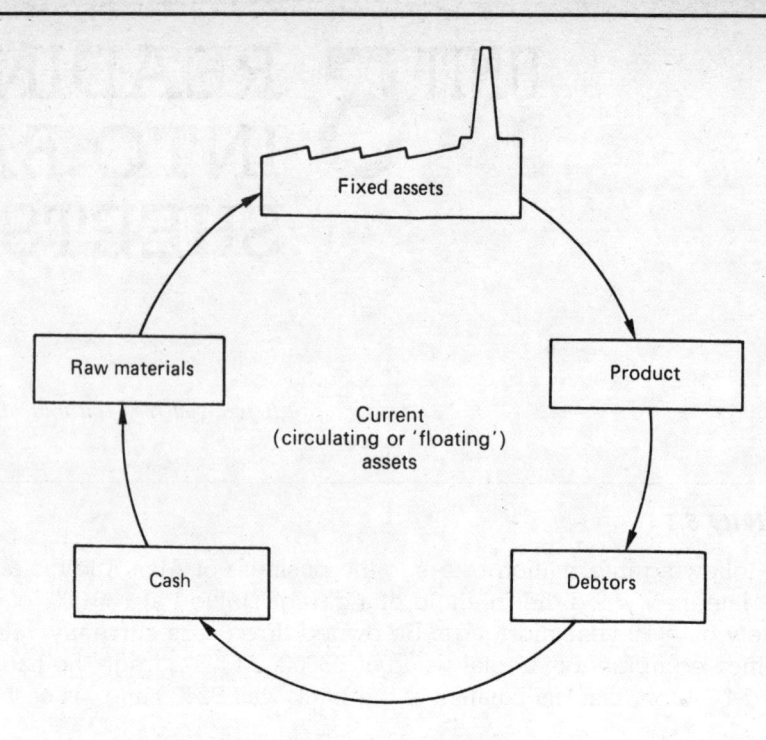

[Diagram: circular flow showing Fixed assets → Product → Debtors → Cash → Raw materials → back to Fixed assets. Labelled "Current (circulating or 'floating') assets".]

2. Long-term and current liabilities

We have already seen that liabilities should be listed in their date order for repayment. Again, they can be divided into two main subgroups:

  (i) long-term liabilities, and
  (ii) current liabilities.

Long-term liabilities are those which will not become due for repayment within the next 12 months. A common example is long-term loans; these may be from individuals, banks or other financial institutions.

Current liabilities are those which will become due for repayment within the next 12 months. The main example consists of trade creditors—i.e. people or firms who have supplied trading goods or services to the organisation on credit. Another example is a bank overdraft. All long-term liabilities will become current liabilities once they are within 12 months of having to be repaid. Also, although loans may be long-term, any interest due on them is a current liability.

You should now be able to rewrite Alan's balance sheet (activity 5.1), showing the total of each of the subgroups. It should appear as follows:

Alan Andy: Balance sheet as at 1 June 19--

	£	£		£
Fixed assets			Capital	48 760
Garage	36 000			
Cars	30 000		*Long-term liabilities*	
Office equipment	3 600	69 600	Mortgage	24 000
			Current liability	
Current assets			Creditors	240
Petrol stock	600			
Bank	2 400			
Cash	400	3 400		
		73 000		73 000

Activity 5.2

Rewrite Alan's balance sheet in the vertical format (see page 4), again showing clearly the subtotals.

5B. Interpretation

1. Long-term solvency

An examination of Alan Andy's balance sheet above shows clearly that, on 1 June last, he had assets worth a total of £73 000, but the total of his liabilities—both short-term and long-term—came only to £24 240. There is therefore no doubt that, if he had to do so, he could pay all of his debts in full. He is therefore **solvent**.

Activity 5.3

The following information refers to the business of Brenda Black, who, at 1 June last, owned premises valued at £100 000, stock of £20 000 and cash of £17 500. Against these assets she owed £70 000 on a mortgage, £30 000 on a long-term loan and £40 000 to her trade creditors.

Draw up Brenda's balance sheet and compare it with Alan's. What significant difference do you notice?

You should have found that Brenda's total liabilities are more than her total assets. Instead of having 'capital', which can be listed on the same side as the liabilities, she has a *deficit*, which has to be inserted on the liabilities side in order to make the balance sheet balance.

Brenda is **insolvent**—that is, if her creditors demanded payment, she could not pay them. Care must be taken here to avoid the use of the word *bankruptcy*. This word can only be used after a certain legal process has been followed, and a 'decree in bankruptcy' issued. Bankruptcy proceedings cannot be taken against companies; if these become insolvent, the legal process is one of 'winding up' the company concerned.

2. Current ratio

Although it is important that an organisation should have more total assets than total liabilities, it is even more important that it should be able to meet all the debts that are likely to arise *in the near future*. This is because of the simple fact that, if it cannot survive in the short term, it is not even going to get the chance to survive in the long term.

One way of checking whether a firm is likely to survive in the short term is to look at the relationship between its *current* assets and its *current* liabilities, because the current liabilities will have to be met out of the money coming in from the turn-round of the current assets. What we are looking at here is what is known as the **short-term solvency**.

If the current assets exceed (are more than) the current liabilities, the amount of the surplus is known as the **working capital** of the firm. If there is a deficit, i.e. the current liabilities exceed the current assets, the firm is said to be **overtrading**.

Summarising the net worth

Activity 5.4

At 1 June last, Christopher Cotton owned land and buildings valued at £240 000 and machinery valued at £180 000. He held trading stock valued at £40 000, debtors of £20 000 and cash-at-bank of £6000. He owed £90 000 to trade creditors.

Draw up Christopher's balance sheet at 1 June last, and compare his position with Alan and Brenda above. What significant difference do you notice?

Your balance sheet for Christopher should show that he is clearly solvent—in the long term. That is, his total assets are comfortably more than his total liabilities. However, it is a different story if his *current* assets are compared with his *current* liabilities—and it is from the current assets that the current liabilities will have to be met. Even if all of his stock is sold for cash, only £66 000 would become available to meet immediate debts of £90 000. Should the creditors start to want their money (and if they get wind of the situation, they are likely to), the only way to pay them would be to sell up at least some of the fixed assets—and that usually means selling up the firm.

A common measure of the short-term solvency position is the **current ratio**. This is a way of expressing the current assets as a percentage of current liabilities. It is found by taking

$$\frac{100 \times \text{Current assets}}{\text{Current liabilities}}$$

Thus the current ratio of Christopher Cotton is

$$\frac{100 \times 66\,000}{90\,000} = 73.3\%$$

This means that his current assets are less than three-quarters of his current liabilities. This compares with a current ratio for Alan Andy of

$$\frac{100 \times 3400}{240} = 1416.7\%$$

In other words, Alan's current assets are some 14 times his current liabilities.

Activity 5.5

Calculate the current ratio of Brenda Black. How does it compare with those of Alan Andy and Christopher Cotton? What can you say about the situations facing the three firms?

3. Quick ratio

One shortcoming of the current ratio is that it assumes that trading stocks are selling—and they may *not* be! So it is important to calculate the **quick ratio**. This is such an important ratio that it is sometimes called the *acid test*. It is similar to the current ratio, but stock is excluded. It is therefore found by taking

$$\frac{100 \times (\text{Current assets} - \text{Stock})}{\text{Current liabilities}}$$

The quick ratio for Christopher Cotton is, therefore,

$$\frac{100 \times 26\,000}{90\,000} = 28.9\%$$

> **Activity 5.6**
>
> Compare Christopher's quick ratio with those of Alan and Brenda.
>
> *What do you think the quick ratio of a small trading firm should stand at, and why?*

4. Cash ratio

A further ratio of importance is the **cash ratio**. This measures the ratio between cash—both at the bank and in-hand—and the current liabilities. Thus, in Christopher's case we have a cash ratio of

$$\frac{100 \times 6000}{90\,000} = 6.7\%$$

Compare this with both Alan's and Brenda's. Which firm do you think has the best ratio?

> **Activity 5.7**
>
> Draw up a table listing the three firms that have figured in this unit—those owned by Alan, Brenda and Christopher—and show their current, quick and cash ratios. Bearing in mind also their long-term solvency positions, write a short note stating which firm you consider to be in the best financial position, and why. What further information would you like about the firms?

5C. Understanding the Ratios

It is not sufficient just to know what the ratios are. It is vital to understand what they mean.

1. Long-term solvency

It is obviously desirable that a firm should be long-term solvent—that is, its total assets should exceed its total liabilities. It is difficult to say what, precisely, the surplus should be, but it is generally thought that the capital (i.e. the amount the owner has invested in the firm) should at least equal that of the total creditors. Consequently, the liabilities should be no more than half the total assets (remember, liabilities + capital = assets). This means that the total assets should be at least double the liabilities (i.e. a minimum ratio of 200%).

2. Current ratio

It is also considered that the current assets should be quite a bit larger than the current liabilities—again a ratio between 150% and 200% would normally be looked for. A higher figure than that could show that the firm was not using its assets effectively; a much lower figure would show that the firm might be approaching an 'overtrading' position—and that could be dangerous. However, what ratio is desirable is determined mainly by the nature of the trade or industry in which the firm is engaged. Although a 'norm' of between 150% and 200% has been suggested, it will be found that most supermarkets are way below that—often as low as 50%. In other words, their current assets are only half their current liabilities. This would seem to be a grossly overtrading situation, but it has to be remembered that such businesses buy their stock on extended credit, but sell very quickly for cash—and that every day of every week they have large amounts of cash coming in. This enables them to meet their immediate debts, as they become due, with a very much lower current ratio than firms that sell extensively on credit and have to wait a long time for their money.

3. Quick ratio

If a firm has a quick ratio of 110%—that is, its 'quick' assets are 10% more than its current liabilities—it is certainly in a very 'safe' position, since the cash it can expect within the near future will more than meet the demands of the creditors. Most firms, however, find that in practice they do not have to have a cash ratio nearly as high as this, and most seem to manage very well on quick ratios between 80% and 90%.

4. Cash ratio

Any well-managed firm will know how much (or, perhaps, how little) actual cash in-hand and at the bank will be needed to meet immediate debts. The amount is not nearly as high as most people would think—and the reason for that is the 'circulating' nature of current assets (see figure 5.1 earlier in this unit). Few debts will *have* to be paid 'tomorrow', and more money will be coming in by the day after. Therefore, provided there is very careful planning of the *cash flow* (that is, of money in and out), it is possible to manage with a running cash balance far below the level of the current liabilities. Again, it will depend very much on the type of trade, on how quickly stock is selling, on how soon creditors will have to be paid and on how long debtors are taking to pay up. Most firms find that cash ratios of 15–25% are satisfactory. Some manage on ratios as low as 4–5%. However, a firm must take great care not to allow the ratio to fall below whatever minimum is desirable in the particular trading conditions it is faced with.

Too high a cash ratio means that cash is simply lying idle within the firm.

Activity 5.8

Using what you have learnt about ratios in the last section above, look again at your table of ratios for Alan, Brenda and Christopher and check your opinion of the financial position regarding the three firms.

5D. The Ratios and Change

We have seen that the affairs of a firm do not usually remain constant for long. Changes occur in the balance sheet items as a result of transactions.

Each transaction, we have seen, always affects two items in the balance sheet. This means that, when a transaction takes place, the relationship between the items will change, and this will be shown up by a change in at least some of the ratios.

Consider the following balance sheet of J. R. Ross at 30 June last:

	£000	£000		£000
Fixed assets			Capital	80
Machinery		60		
			Current liabilities	
Current assets			Creditors	10
Stock	15			
Debtors	8			
Bank	5			
Cash	2	30		
		90		90

J. R. Ross are clearly solvent, with assets considerably in excess of their liabilities. Their working capital amounts to £20 000, and their liquidity ratios are

$$\text{Current ratio} = 100 \times (30 \div 10)\% = 300\%$$

$$\text{Quick ratio} = 100 \times (15 \div 10)\% = 150\%$$

$$\text{Cash ratio} = 100 \times (7 \div 10)\% = 70\%$$

Now assume that on 1 July, J. R. Ross obtain a long-term loan from Mercantile Credit Ltd for £20 000.

What difference will this make to their position?

The new balance sheet becomes:

	£000	£000		£000
Fixed assets			Capital	80
Machinery		60		
			Long-term liabilities	
			Loan	20
Current assets				
Stock	15		*Current liabilities*	
Debtors	8		Creditors	10
Bank	25			
Cash	2	50		
		110		110

Their long-term solvency remains as before. Their working capital, however, has increased to £40 000; their current ratio is now 500%, quick ratio 350% and cash ratio 270%.

Activity 5.9

Say whether J. R. Ross's current, quick and cash ratios will be increased, decreased, or remain unaffected, by each of the following transactions:

(i) Purchased premises by cheque, £18 000.
(ii) Purchased additional stock on credit for £5000.
(iii) Debtors pay cheques, £6000.
(iv) Creditors paid by cheque, £6000.
(v) J. R. Ross pay additional capital into the bank, £4000, from private resources.
(vi) Sold machinery to Apex Ltd, £2000.

Draw up a revised balance sheet for J. R. Ross after all the above transactions have taken place. Calculate their revised working capital and new current, quick and cash ratios.

Check Your Understanding

1 Name the two subgroups of assets that appear in a balance sheet.
2 What is the principal difference between them?
3 Give three examples of assets to be found in each group.
4 In what order are assets listed in each group?
5 Name two subgroups of liabilities found in a balance sheet.
6 What distinguishes one group from the other?
7 Give one example from each group.
8 What determines the order in which liabilities are listed?
9 What is the meaning of solvency? What is the difference between long-term and short-term solvency.
10 What is the difference between bankruptcy and insolvency.

Summarising the net worth

11 What are the names of the three main ratios used in connection with the interpretation of balance sheets? How is each calculated?

12 Define 'overtrading'.

13 Is it necessarily undesirable that a firm should be in an overtrading position? Mention three factors that should be taken into account in assessing the position.

14 What is the lowest ratio of total assets to total liabilities that would normally be acceptable.

15 What are the generally accepted norms for the balance sheet ratios?

16 By what other name is the quick ratio sometimes known?

17 If a loan is obtained, repayable in five years' time, what effect—if any—would it have on the current ratio?

18 If a firm draws cash from the bank, what effect—if any—would it have on its cash ratio?

19 A firm has a cash ratio of 10%. It then pays some of its creditors in cash. Would its cash ratio be increased, decreased or remain constant?

20 A firm has a current ratio of 150%. It pays some of its creditors in cash. Would the current ratio be increased, decreased or remain constant?

Practical Assignments

1 Marcus Derwent rents a garage and filling station. His assets and liabilities, as at today's date, comprise a loan from a finance company repayable in 10 years' time of £30 000, trade creditors of £25 000, cash-in-hand £2000, cash-at-bank £16 800, stocks of petrol valued at £30 000, debtors standing at £4000, equipment £40 000.

From this information, prepare a balance sheet and state:

a. the total of the fixed assets;
b. the total of the current assets;
c. whether the firm is solvent or insolvent;
d. whether or not the firm is overtrading;
e. the value, if any, of the working capital;
f. (i) the current, quick and cash ratios;
    (ii) whether you consider, with reasons, whether the ratios are satisfactory.

2 Explain whether it is possible for a firm to be insolvent without being bankrupt, and whether it can be bankrupt without being insolvent.

3 Discuss whether it is better for a firm to be (i) solvent but overtrading, or (ii) insolvent but with adequate working capital. What further information would be helpful to you in deciding?

In what circumstances do you consider that a firm can survive even though it is heavily overtrading?

4 The following information refers to the position of Harry Peterson as at 31 December last:

	£
Plant and machinery	50 000
Trade creditors	15 000
Stock	25 800
Balance of cash-in-hand and cash-at-bank	17 400
Trade debtors	22 000
Motor vehicles	25 000
Loan (repayable in 10 years' time)	20 000

During the period 1–5 January, the following transactions took place:

(i) a new machine was purchased on short-term credit for £10 000;
(ii) the sum of £4800 was paid to the trade creditors;
(iii) additional stock was purchased for £2000 and paid for by cheque;
(iv) a further £5000 was borrowed on a long-term basis;
(v) trade creditors were paid a total of £3000.

Required:

a. A definition of working capital.
b. A calculation of the working capital on the initial balances provided as at 31 December last.
c. A statement of the effects, if any, of each of the items (i)–(v) above on the firm's working capital.
d. A statement as at 5 January showing the revised working capital, giving full details.

5 'A balance sheet is a statement that reports the financial position of a business.'

Discuss this statement and explain why there are two separate sides to, or two separate sets of figures in, a balance sheet. What is the inter-relationship between these two sets of figures?

6 Your firm is considering purchasing the Optima Trading Corporation. The following information is available concerning its position over the last four years:

	1989 (£000)	1988 (£000)	1987 (£000)	1986 (£000)
Cash holdings	1	4	3	2
Bank balances	3	36	12	20
Equipment	75	69	65	65
Loan	80	—	—	—
Creditors	61	40	56	64

Factory premises	414	300	300	300
Debtors	36	31	35	37
Bank overdraft	25	–	–	–
Stocks	55	59	52	40

Your manager asks you to draw up for consideration by management a tabular statement showing such additional information from these figures as you think important, and to add a brief interpretation of them. In particular, he asks you to state, with reasons, whether you consider it was wise for Optima to have invested in additional fixed assets during 1989.

7 a. The following information related to the position of the Superbongo Toy Co. as at the last day of last month: stocks £90 000; mortgage against premises £60 000; trade creditors £216 000; cash holdings £29 400; equipment £360 000; land and buildings £540 000; debtors £45 000.

You are required to draw up a balance sheet of the company at the date in question and comment as fully as you can on its financial position. What other information, both financial and non-financial, would you like to know if you had to advise a firm of merchant bankers whether or not to grant Superbongo a substantial loan?

   b. Since the end of last month, Superbongo has engaged in the following transactions. Analyse carefully the effect of each on the affairs of the firm and on its financial position. Assume that the transactions occurred one after the other.

   (i) Additional capital of £30 000 was paid into the firm's bank account by the proprietor.
   (ii) A loan of £150 000 was obtained from Mercantile General, the firm's merchant bankers. Repayment is to consist of five annual instalments of £30 000, the first of which is due in a week's time.
   (iii) £45 000 worth of the stock was sold at its cost price in order to make warehouse space available for a new product.
   (iv) Surplus factory buildings, which are no longer required, were sold at their book value of £54 000. There was an immediate cash settlement by the purchaser.
   (v) Cash payments amounting to £27 600 were received from debtors.
   (vi) Additional equipment was purchased for £24 000 cash.
   (vii) Cash payments to creditors in the period amounted to £150 000.

8 James Usher has recently had the following balance sheet submitted to him by his newly appointed accounts supervisor:

Balance sheet as at 30 June 19--

1988			1989	
£000	£000		£000	£000
		Fixed assets		
20		Land and buildings	22	
12		Machinery	12	
	32			34
		Current assets		
9		Stock	6	
8		Debtors	8	
4		Cash	1	
21			15	
		Less		
		Current liabilities		
6		Creditors	2	
	15	Working capital		13
	47	Net assets		47

James asks your advice, as he is worried by the document. His queries are the following ones:

a. Is this a valid balance sheet? All the others I have seen have consisted of two sides coming to the same total. Why is this one different? Does my new man know what he is doing?
b. I have worked very hard this last year in order to reduce the amount owing to creditors, and to increase the amount of working capital I have in the firm—yet I see the working capital has decreased. I cannot understand this. Can you explain?
c. What is the point of putting in figures for last year? I thought the balance sheet was meant to be for this year.
d. How can my capital have remained the same although the working capital has dropped?
e. Why has the figure for 'land and buildings' come to be increased? I haven't bought any during the year.

Write out the letter you would send him in reply.

PART TWO Multiple-choice test

In Questions 1–39, state which option best answers the question.

1. Which of the following is in order of liquidity?
   a. premises, equipment, stock, debtors, cash
   b. premises, equipment, debtors, stock, cash
   c. premises, debtors, equipment, stock, cash
   d. premises, stock, equipment, debtors, cash

2. Which of the following is a direct responsibility of the accountant's department?
   a. recording the issue and receipt of stocks
   b. maintaining records of debtors and creditors
   c. ensuring proper personnel records are maintained
   d. ensuring output is according to budget.

3. What a firm legally owns is known as
   a. possessions
   b. assets
   c. property
   d. belongings

4. Money owed to other organisations is known in accounting as
   a. assets
   b. liabilities
   c. losses
   d. expenses

5. The working capital of an organisation measures the extent to which the current assets are
   a. more than the current liabilities
   b. less than the total liabilities
   c. more than the total liabilities
   d. less than the current liabilities

6. Which is the correct statement?
   a. assets plus capital equals liabilities
   b. liabilities plus capital equals assets
   c. assets plus liabilities equals capital
   d. assets minus liabilities equals capital

7. Which of the following is most likely to be a long-term liability?
   a. trade debt due to a supplier
   b. debt secured by a mortgage
   c. debt in respect of purchase of fixed assets
   d. debts arising from the purchase of trading stock

8. The balance sheet of an organisation summarises the
   a. financial position over a given period
   b. profit at a certain date
   c. financial position as at a certain date
   d. profits for a given period

9. The rule that a firm's affairs should be regarded completely separately from those of the proprietor(s) is known as the convention of
   a. objectivity
   b. consistency
   c. entity
   d. separation

10. Using accounting information to plan future activities is known as
    a. management accounting
    b. creative accounting
    c. policy accounting
    d. progressive accounting

11. Circulating capital consists of assets that
    a. remain as permanent fixtures in the firm
    b. can be transferred from one firm or process to another
    c. can be used time and time again
    d. are continually being used and replaced

12. Debts owed for trading goods bought on credit are
    a. current liabilities
    b. current assets
    c. long-term liabilities
    d. fixed assets

13. A debt owed as a result of purchasing premises on a 10-year mortgage plan is a
    a. fixed asset
    b. current liability
    c. long-term liability
    d. current asset

14. Premises that have been acquired by a loan repayable in 10 years' time are a
    a. long-term liability
    b. fixed asset
    c. current liability
    d. current asset

15. Which of the following is a long-term liability?
    a. bank overdraft
    b. debt in respect of purchase of trading goods
    c. loan repayable in 24 months
    d. debt in respect of purchase of machinery

16. Which of the following is part of the circulating capital of a railway company?
    a. rolling stock
    b. office equipment
    c. debtors
    d. premises

17. A firm commenced business with premises valued at £61 000, stock £40 000, creditors £10 000, debtors £8000 and cash £5000. It had also taken a bank loan of £12 000. Its opening capital was therefore
    a. £92 000
    b. £96 000
    c. £104 000
    d. £116 000

18. Current assets are normally expected to be
    a. more than current liabilities
    b. equal to total liabilities

49

Summarising the net worth

c. less than current liabilities
d. more than total liabilities

19. If a firm buys premises for £15 000 by cheque, the ledger entries would be
    Debit   Credit
    a. premises account   cash account
    b. bank account   premises account
    c. premises account   bank account
    d. cash account   premises account

20. In accounting, a transaction
    a. may concern two separate accounts
    b. will always affect two separate accounts
    c. will never affect two separate accounts
    d. may affect the same account twice

21. The account of Smith in the books of Johnson shows a debit balance of £634. This means that
    a. Smith owes Johnson £634
    b. Johnson owes Smith £634
    c. Smith is the creditor of Johnson for £634
    d. Johnson is the debtor of Smith for £634

22. Which of the following accounts would normally have a debit balance in the ledger?
    a. accounts of persons owing money to the firm
    b. capital account of the proprietor
    c. accounts of persons owed money by the firm
    d. accounts of those who have lent money to the firm

23. Which is the correct statement?
    a. liabilities minus capital equals assets
    b. assets minus capital equals liabilities
    c. assets plus liabilities equals capital
    d. assets plus capital equals liabilities

24. The main purpose of the trial balance is to
    a. provide a working list of balances for the balance sheet
    b. check the arithmetical accuracy of the ledger
    c. ensure that every transaction has been posted
    d. pinpoint the exact location of errors

25. John Harris pays £5000 into his firm's bank account as additional capital. The ledger entries are
    Debit   Credit
    a. bank account   capital account
    b. capital account   John Harris
    c. John Harris   capital account
    d. capital account   bank account

26. The ledger entries in respect of the purchase of a new motor vehicle from Island Traders Ltd are
    Debit   Credit
    a. bank account   motor vehicle account
    b. Island Traders Ltd motor vehicle account
    c. motor vehicle account Island Traders Ltd
    d. motor vehicle account bank account

27. In posting a transaction to the ledger, the number of accounts usually concerned is
    a. one
    b. two
    c. three
    d. four

28. If there is a debit balance of £500 in cash account it means that
    a. £500 has been paid out
    b. there is £500 in hand
    c. £500 has been received
    d. the account is overdrawn by £500

29. A 'running balance' ledger account is one in which the balance is
    a. shown after each posting
    b. maintained at an agreed level
    c. carried forward from one accounting period to the next
    d. always changing

30. A debit balance in capital account indicates that the firm is
    a. overtrading
    b. not overtrading
    c. insolvent
    d. not insolvent

31. Cash-in-hand and cash-at-bank is usually
    a. less than current liabilities
    b. roughly equal to current liabilities
    c. a little more than current liabilities
    d. considerably more than current liabilities

32. A trial balance
    a. always proves the accuracy of the books
    b. sometimes proves the accuracy of the books
    c. seldom proves the accuracy of the books
    d. never proves the accuracy of the books

33. Most firms prepare a balance sheet
    a. daily
    b. weekly
    c. monthly
    d. yearly

34. The 'acid test' is another name for the
    a. cash ratio
    b. short-term solvency ratio
    c. quick ratio
    d. working capital

35. A firm is 'overtrading' if its
    a. total assets are less than the total liabilities
    b. current liabilities exceed current assets
    c. total assets exceed total liabilities
    d. current assets exceed current liabilities

Questions 36–39 are based on the following balance sheet:

	£		£
Premises	35 000	Capital	60 000
Equipment	15 000	Loan	10 000
Stock	15 000	Creditors	5 000
Debtors	8 000		
Cash	2 000		
	75 000		75 000

36. The firm is
    a. solvent
    b. insolvent
    c. overtrading
    d. bankrupt

37. The quick ratio of the firm is
    a. 13.3%
    b. 33.3%
    c. 166.6%
    d. 200.0%

38 The working capital of the firm is
  a. £10 000
  b. £20 000 ✓
  c. £35 000
  d. £50 000

39 The cash ratio of the firm is
  a. 2.6%
  b. 8.0%
  c. 13.3%
  d. 40.0% ✓

40 Complete the table by inserting the missing items.

	Capital (£000)	Long-term liabilities (£000)	Current liabilities (£000)	Fixed assets (£000)	Current assets (£000)
a.	?	421	768	5219	3126
b.	26	?	15	38	26
c.	490	300	nil	?	540
d.	6200	nil	300	3281	?

PART THREE
Calculating the Profit

UNIT 6 EARNING A LIVING: 1 THE PROFIT AND LOSS ACCOUNT

Before you read this unit, try activity 6.1.

Activity 6.1

On 1 January 1981, John Haynes started business as a self-employed joiner with machinery worth £5000, tools worth £3000 and cash of £1500. Against this, he owed his sister £2000 on an interest-free long-term loan, repayable as and when convenient.

During the following year, John earned a total of £31 000 cash but paid out £11 500 for materials, £1000 for electricity, £500 for the occasional hire of a van, £2000 rent and rates for his workshop, and £5000 to part-time assistants. He also paid off the loan. His assets other than cash, and the loan, remained as they were at the beginning of the year.

Draw up his balance sheets (a) at the start of business and (b) at the end of his first year. What are the main differences that you notice in the two documents?

6A. What is Profit?

The transactions we have been concerned with so far have all had a common characteristic—they have not involved a 'profit' element. They were simply concerned with 'transfers' between the assets and liabilities.

No organisation—no matter whether it is a multinational corporation, a college mini-enterprise or a social and leisure club—will be content with just simply shuffling its assets and its liabilities around for very long. It will have been set up for a purpose—to make profit or to provide a service—and its owners or members will want it to get on and do just that.

This brings us, then, to another group of transactions—those concerned with making profit.

The accounts of a small commercial firm—such as John Haynes' joinery business in activity 6.1—show how it all works out in practice.

The purpose of such a firm is (putting it simply) to 'make money'; that is, to end up with more money—or other assets—than it started with. In other words, the purpose is to increase its capital.

Capital can change for reasons other than trading. The owner may put more money into the firm, or may take some out of it. But, at the moment, we are only going to consider changes *as a result of the normal business of the firm or organisation*.

Remember the definition of capital, namely: assets − liabilities. What the above paragraph is saying is that, if a firm has done well in a trading period, its capital (i.e. assets − liabilities) will be greater at the end of the trading period than at the beginning.

This increase in capital during a trading period as a result of trading activities is known as the **net profit** and amounts to the increase in the net value of *all* of the assets, not just of the cash.

Calculating the profit

6B. Tracking the Profit

If you drew up the two balance sheets for John Haynes correctly (activity 6.1), and calculated the correct cash balance at the end of the period, you should have found that his capital increased from £7500 to £18 500; in other words, he made a profit of £11 000.

One way of measuring the profit over a period is to calculate the increase in capital as shown by two balance sheets. It is sometimes done in this way when no other information is available. But calculating profit only by comparison of balance sheets has a major limitation.

Can you guess what it is?

Here is a clue. What if you were asked '*How* did the profit arise?'? Could you answer if the only information you had was that provided by the two balance sheets?

The answer can be obtained by calculating profit in a completely independent way from the balance sheet. The method employed is to summarise what *caused* the changes. This amounts to adding the *sources* from which income has flowed, and deducting the various payments made or debts incurred.

In the case of John's joinery business, the arithmetical calculation of profit looks like this:

John Haynes: Calculation of net profit for year to 31 December 1981

	£	£
Income earned		31 000
Expenses incurred:		
Materials	11 500	
Electricity	1 000	
Hire of van	500	
Rent and rates	2 000	
Wages	5 000	
		20 000
		11 000

If you look at the calculation closely, you will see that the items are the ledger 'double entries' in the cash account. This means that, if the double entries are fully completed in the normal book-keeping way, the information for the independent calculation of profit is immediately available.

These ledger accounts for items of income and expenditure can be brought together by transferring them to a 'summary' account known as a **profit and loss account** (usually abbreviated to P&L). The P&L for John Haynes is shown as part of example 6.1 below.

The ledger procedures leading up to the profit and loss account can be seen by posting the transactions of John Haynes—following full double-entry principles—to the ledger. Since any receipts of cash must be debited to cash account, an account in respect of the 'source' must be credited. Similarly, since any payments must be credited to cash account, an account for the particular expense concerned must be debited.

These new accounts build up a picture of how the change in cash took place—in other words, they provide the information needed for the P&L to which the balances in them will be *transferred* at the end of the year.

Earning a living: 1

Example 6.1

In the following set of accounts for John Haynes, check carefully each of the following:

(i) The posting of the opening balances in the ledger at 1 January.
(ii) The full double entry for each of the transactions during the month. These will be:

Transaction	Debit entry	Credit entry
Cash earned from joinery	Cash account	Income earned account *sales account*
Payments for:		
materials	Materials used account *purchases a/c*	Cash account
rent	Rent account	Cash account
electricity	Electricity account	Cash account
van hire	Van hire account	Cash account
wages	Wages account	Cash account

(iii) The transfers of the balances of the accounts for materials used, electricity, rent and rates, and wages to the P&L. (Note: Since the balances are transferred, there are no balances to carry down; this is, of course, different from the situation with real and personal accounts (the ones summarised in the balance sheet).)
(iv) The entry for net profit in the P&L is matched by a credit entry in capital account, thus increasing its balance.
(v) The carrying down of the remaining ledger accounts to the next accounting period. These are the balances that are summarised in the balance sheet as at 31 August.

Capital account

Dec 31	Balance	c/d	18 500	Jan 1	Balance		7 500
				Dec 31	Profit		11 000
			18 500				18 500
				Jan 1	Balance	b/d	18 500

Loan account

Dec 31	Cash		2 000	Jan 1	Balance		2 000

Cash account

Jan 1	Balance		1 500	Dec 31	Sundry payments:		
Dec 31	Sundry receipts		31 000		Materials		11 500
					Electricity		1 000
					Van hire		500
					Rent		2 000
					Wages		5 000
					Loan		2 000
					Balance	c/d	10 500
			32 500				32 500
Jan 1	Balance	b/d	10 500				

Income earned account

Dec 31	P&L		31 000	Dec 31	Cash		31 000

Materials used account

Dec 31	Cash		15 000	Dec 31	P&L		15 000

57

Calculating the profit

Electricity account
Dec 31	Cash	1 000	Dec 31	P & L	1 000

Van hire account
Dec 31	Cash	500	Dec 31	P & L	500

Rent account
Dec 31	Cash	2 000	Dec 31	P & L	2 000

Wages account
Dec 31	Cash	5 000	Dec 31	P & L	5 000

Profit and loss account for the year to 31 December 1981
Materials	11 500	Income earned	31 000
Electricity	1 000		
Van hire	500		
Rent and rates	2 000		
Wages	5 000		
Net profit, to capital a/c	11 000		
	31 000		31 000

Balance sheet as at 31 December 1981
Fixed assets			*Capital*			
Machinery	5 000		as at 1 Jan		7 500	
Tools	3 000	8 000	Profit		11 000	18 500
Current assets						
Cash		10 500				
		18 500				18 500

Although a P & L account has certain similarities with a balance sheet, there are also some significant differences.
Can you spot what they are? (Display 4 may help you identify them.)

Display 4: The Major Characteristics of Profit and Loss Accounts

1 The P & L is only drawn up at the *end* of an accounting period. In this respect, it is similar to the balance sheet.

2 The P & L is a *summary* covering a period. Note how this is reflected in the title of the account. In this respect, it is different from a balance sheet, which is a picture of the firm *at* a certain date only.

3 The information for the P & L is obtained by *transferring* the items from the respective ledger accounts. This means that the profit and loss account, unlike the balance sheet, is an integral part of the ledger and must follow all the rules of the ledger.

4 Since the balance (i.e. net profit) of the P & L represents the net increase in the capital, this figure can be transferred from the profit and loss to the capital account, thus completing the full double entry and enabling capital account to show a full and up-to-date picture of the firm.

6C. The Nature of Ledger Accounts

> *Activity 6.2*
>
> Compare very carefully the profit and loss account and the balance sheet above of John Haynes. What difference or differences do you see in the nature of the items that appear:
>
> (i) on the debit side of the profit and loss account and the assets side of the balance sheet?
> (ii) on the credit side of the profit and loss account and the liabilities side of the balance sheet?

The nature of the accounts that appear in a balance sheet is very different from those in a profit and loss account. If you know the difference it helps greatly in understanding what a set of accounts is really 'all about'. Let us compare the two types of statement carefully:

(i) *Assets in the balance sheet and debit balances in the P & L.* Each of the items on the assets side of a typical balance sheet is either a real or a personal account, and represents something that actually exists. But the items that appear on the debit side of P&L accounts refer to things such as rent paid, the cost of electricity consumed, telephone expenses, rates, advertising expenditure, and the cost of materials and supplies which have been used up. In other words, the accounts *describe* something on which money has been spent, but they do not refer to things that continue to exist—there is not a 'box' of rent, or of insurance, or of telephone calls, which can be taken away, split up and sold to several different people. Because they are *descriptions* and cannot exist on their own, these accounts are known as **nominal accounts**.

(ii) *Liabilities in the balance sheet and credit items in the P & L.* Similar considerations apply 'on the other side of the page'. The items on the liabilities side—usually creditors—really do exist. But the items on the credit side of a P&L show the sources of income over a period; they do not refer to debts at a certain date.

The differences in meaning are summarised in display 5. They are important because, if we see a list of ledger balances, we should recognise in each case whether it is a real, personal or nominal account—and this means that we should be able to interpret the meaning of its balance.

Display 5: Interpretation of Ledger Balances

Type of account	Type of balance	Meaning
Real and personal accounts	Debit	Something that is *owned* by the organisation concerned as at a certain date
	Credit	An amount *owed* by the organisation concerned as at a certain date
Nominal accounts	Debit	An expense incurred during an accounting period
	Credit	Income that has been earned during an accounting period

Calculating the profit

For example, let us consider a debit balance of £5000 in a club's equipment account. If we think of the type of transaction (or series of transactions) that could have caused that balance (e.g. bought equipment from Supersports Ltd), then we would expect that there was equipment, of that approximate value, actually within the club at the date of the balance sheet (remember that the balance sheet is a picture of a firm *as at* a certain date only).

But if we see a debit balance of £500 on the wages account and we think of the type of transaction or transactions that would have caused that balance (e.g. paid wages in cash, £500), we know that a total of £500 has been spent on wages during the period concerned (remember that a profit and loss account covers a period). In other words, it is an expense incurred during a period, and not something that is owned at a particular date.

Activity 6.3

The ledger balances below are from the books of the Cloud Nine Youth Club. In respect of each:

(i) state whether the account concerned is a real, personal or nominal account;
(ii) describe a transaction that could have caused the balance indicated;
(iii) state whether the account would be *transferred* at the end of the accounting period to the profit and loss account, or whether the balance would be *carried down* to the next period but be included in the balance sheet summary.

	£
Debit balances:	
Hire of hall account	200
Sports equipment account	750
Insurance account	60
Advertising account	35
Cash-in-hand account	26
Travelling expenses account	120
Crockery account	80
Equipment account	500
Hire of coach account	250

	£
Debit balances (cont.):	
Raffle prizes account	54
Stationery account	36
Cash-at-bank account	320
Credit balances:	
Bank loan account	120
Subscriptions account	540
Raffle tickets account	89
Hire of equipment account	136

Check Your Understanding

1 What do you think is the main objective of a commercial firm?

2 Is the main objective of a club or a society the same as that of a commercial organisation? If not, what is it?

3 How can you calculate profit for a period simply by reference to the opening and closing balance sheets?

4 Define 'profit'.

5 Why are the balances of accounts that appear in the profit and loss account actually *transferred* to it at the end of the period, thus closing the ledger account concerned, while the balances of accounts that appear in the balance sheet are not transferred to it, but have their balances carried down to the start of the next accounting period?

6 Net profit appears as a debit entry in the profit and loss account. Where is the corresponding double entry made?

7 Profit may be calculated either by comparison of the opening and closing balance sheets for the period, or by drawing up a profit and loss account for the period concerned. What does a profit and loss account show that a balance sheet does not show?

Earning a living: 1

8 Describe the main characteristics of a profit and loss account.

9 How would a loss appear in a profit and loss account?

10 Why would it be wise to take the advice of others before setting up your own business? What sort of advice do you think it would be useful to have, and from whom could it be obtained?

11 What are the three main types of ledger account called?

12 Why is it important to be able to distinguish between them?

13 What do the following indicate:
   (i) A debit balance in a real account?
   (ii) A credit balance in a real account?
   (iii) A debit balance in a nominal account?
   (iv) A credit balance in a nominal account?

14 What type of balance, and what type of account, would indicate:
   (i) An asset owned by an organisation?
   (ii) An expense incurred during an accounting period?
   (iii) Income earned during an accounting period?
   (iv) A liability?

15 Describe a transaction that would give rise to a credit balance in a nominal account.

Practical Assignments

1 Fill in the blanks in the following sentences:
   a. There are two types of transactions. Some are concerned with making _____; some are not.
   b. Profit is equal to the net increase in _____ during a period as a result of normal business.
   c. The credit side of the profit and loss account shows _____ and the debit side shows the _____.
   d. Accounts which are transferred to the profit and loss account are known as _____ accounts.
   e. Entries in respect of payments by cheque for electricity consumed are _____ (debit) and _____ (credit).

2 Describe in your own words the transactions that would have given rise to each of the following postings in the ledger:
   a. A debit entry in the stationery account and a credit entry in the cash account.
   b. A debit entry in the motor vehicles account and a credit entry in the Europa Car Co. account.
   c. A credit entry in the bank account and a debit entry in the Europa Car Co. account.
   d. A debit entry in cash account and a credit entry in subscriptions account.
   e. A credit entry in bank account and a debit entry in subscriptions account.

3 Complete the following statements:
   a. A debit balance in an account for J. Smith indicates _____.
   b. A credit balance in an account for Office Supplies Ltd indicates _____.
   c. A debit balance in rent account indicates _____.
   d. A credit balance in bank account indicates _____.
   e. A debit balance in cash account indicates _____.

4 On 1 March a club started with a bank balance of £8756. During the month of March, the following transactions took place:

		£
Mar 2	Paid for stationery	45
3	Refunded postage expenses to the club secretary	23
4	Purchased equipment	560
6	Paid for room hire	50
7	Paid cleaning expenses	30
9	Paid wages	90
10	Received subscriptions	120
11	Paid stationery expenses	60
12	Paid wages	85
12	Paid for purchase of Vim and polish	8
13	Postage expenses refunded to secretary	36
15	Purchased envelopes and typing paper	14
18	Paid for room hire	50
20	Paid wages	90
27	Paid cleaning expenses	45
29	Purchase of equipment	260
30	Paid for window cleaning	20

(All payments were made by cheque, and all receipts paid directly into the bank.)
   Required:
   a. The bank account for the month, completing the double entry to the other accounts concerned. Balance all accounts at 31 March.
   b. Using information obtained from the accounts, a statement showing under suitable headings the totals of (i) receipts and (ii) payments, for the month.

61

Calculating the profit

5 At the beginning of February, a firm had a balance of £250.25 cash-in-hand and £1150 cash-at-bank. During the month, the following transactions took place:

			£
Feb	3	Purchased tools from Acme Ltd	520.00
		(Remember, if the name of the firm is given, you should assume it is a credit transaction)	
	5	Paid cash for stationery	15.75
	6	Sold surplus tools to Bloom & Co.	135.50
	7	Paid wages by cheque	360.85
	10	Paid general expenses, cash	15.20
	11	Paid Acme Ltd by cheque	300.00
	12	Paid advertising costs by cheque	54.00
	14	Paid wages by cheque	104.20
	16	Withdrew cash from the bank	50.00
	17	Bloom & Co. sent a cheque for the full amount owed	
	18	Purchased stationery by cheque	200.50
	21	Paid wages by cheque	95.60
	23	Overcharge for advertising refunded by cheque	9.00
	28	Paid wages by cheque	89.10

Tasks:
a. Post the transactions to all the relevant accounts and balance them as at 28 February, showing the amounts to be carried forward to March.
b. State how much is owing, at 28 February, by Acme Ltd and by Bloom & Co.
c. Calculate the *differences* in the cash and bank balances at the beginning and the end of the month.

6 Draw up the profit and loss account of the City Cab Co. for the month ending 30 June last from the following information:

	£
Income from hire of taxi cabs	22 924
Expenses paid:	
petrol	14 400
oil	600
rents	400
telephone	120
secretarial expenses	200
wages and salaries	2 460
other sundry expenses	160

7 Freddie Flower commenced business as an independent electrical repairs specialist on 1 October 19— with equipment worth £20 000 and cash of £1000. The following summarises his work for the month:

		£
(i)	Cash received for repairs undertaken	1500
(ii)	General expenses paid in cash	400
(iii)	Rent of workshop, paid in cash	100
(iv)	Work undertaken, but not paid for	150
(v)	Cost of advertising, paid in cash	300
(vi)	Insurance for the month, paid in cash	160

Required
a. A balance sheet as at 1 October.
b. The ledger accounts for the month.
c. A profit and loss account for the month ended 31 October.
d. A balance sheet as at 31 October.

8 Tom Harris commenced work as a jobbing gardener on 1 January 19— with cash £200, tools and equipment £100 and a debt owing to Gardening Supplies Ltd (in respect of some of his equipment) of £30. Draw up his balance sheet as at 1 January, open his ledger, then post the following transactions:

			£
Jan	5	Cash earned from working	120
	10	Bought a spade for cash	20
	15	Bought a tool shed from Gardening Supplies Ltd	300
	20	Paid Gardening Supplies Ltd, cash	100
Feb	2	Received cash for working	75
	6	Paid cash for advertising	15
	10	Paid travelling expenses, cash	10
	15	Bought additional equipment from Gardening Supplies Ltd	35
	20	Received cash for working on various sites	50
	25	Undertook gardening for the vicar, Rev. Jones, for an agreed figure of £40, to be paid later	
	26	Purchased fertiliser for cash, £10, to replace that used on the vicar's garden	

Balance each of the ledger accounts and extract a trial balance at this point; then continue by posting the following transactions:

			£
Mar	6	Cash earned from lopping trees at the parish hall	40
	6	Purchased for cash a first-aid kit in order to treat saw-cut of hand sustained when lopping trees at the parish hall	15
	10	Bought for cash new saw to replace one broken when lopping trees at the parish hall	10
	11	Paid advertising expenses, cash	22
	15	Cash received for weeding the doctor's garden	10

20 Purchased additional tools from
Gardening Supplies Ltd   30
22 Received cash from the vicar, £25,
in partial payment of what he owes
28 Paid cash to Gardening Supplies Ltd   150

Further tasks:
a. Extract a trial balance *without* balancing the accounts; then undertake the following:
b. State whether Harris could, or could not, pay the amount still owing to Gardening Supplies Ltd.
c. List the factors that you think Harris should bear in mind when deciding whether to pay Gardening Supplies Ltd in full, or not.
d. Prepare Harris' profit and loss account for the quarter ending 31 March 19--, transferring the balances of the accounts concerned.
e. Prepare Harris' balance sheet as at 31 March 19--.

9 a. What is the purpose of a profit and loss account?
   b. In what way do the items that appear in a profit and loss account differ, in nature, from those in a balance sheet?
   c. A. Driver commenced a private car-hire firm on 1 June 19-1 with premises worth £30 000, vehicles worth £20 000, equipment worth £5000 and cash-at-bank of £1500. He had a creditor, Mortec Ltd, for £1200.
   Calculate Driver's capital at this stage. Open the ledger and post with the appropriate entries. Then post the following items, which summarise his transactions for the year ended 31 May 19-2:

		£
(i)	Cash receipts for the year, paid into bank	23 000
(ii)	Purchase of equipment from Mortec Ltd	2 000
(iii)	Purchase by cheque of petrol for the year's operations	8 000
(iv)	Advertising costs paid by cheque	250
(v)	Paid telephone bills by cheque	300
(vi)	Purchase of second-hand vehicle from New Garage Co.	4 000
(vii)	Repairs and maintenance of vehicles, paid by cheque	1 500

Required:
d. A trial balance extracted after completion of the posting.
e. A profit and loss account for the year ended 31 May 19-2.
f. A balance sheet as at 31 May 19-2.

10 Rosemary Fisher is in business as an interior decorator. On 1 January 19-1, she had premises worth £15 000, a van worth £4000, equipment amounting to £300, and a bank balance of £50. She owed £1000 to Vehicle Supplies Ltd and £100 to Office Equipment Ltd.
The following summarises her transactions for the year then following. All cash receipts were paid into the bank, and all payments made by cheques.

		£
(i)	Value of work undertaken and invoiced out to sundry debtors	13 600
(ii)	Cash receipts from debtors	12 400
(iii)	Proceeds of sale of van	4 000
(iv)	Cost of purchasing second-hand pick-up	7 500
(v)	Payments for advertising	1 000
(vi)	Cost of road-fund licence for pick-up	100
(vii)	Payments for casual labour	4 000
(viii)	Payments for materials used (wallpaper, paint, etc.)	8 000
(ix)	Payment to Vehicle Supplies Ltd	750
(x)	Payment to Office Equipment Ltd	100

You are required to:
a. open and post the ledger in the normal way; then draw up the profit and loss account for the year ended 31 December 19--, and the balance sheet as at that date;
b. prepare a statement describing Fisher's financial position, as disclosed by the balance sheet, at 31 December 19--.

11 Anita Brock commenced business on 1 January 19-1 as a hairdresser with a capital in cash of £250, which she had borrowed from her Aunt Susie. During the month, the following transactions took place:

Jan		£
2	Purchased equipment for cash	100
6	Cash receipts from hairdressing	50
8	Opened a bank account and paid in cash	80
13	Cash receipts from hairdressing	100
14	Paid rent in cash	50
16	Cash loan received from her brother, James	500
17	Cash paid into the bank	400
20	Purchased equipment by cheque	300
22	Paid electricity by cheque	60
25	Cash receipts from hairdressing	100
30	Withdrew cash from bank	120

Open Anita's ledger and post the above transactions. Extract a trial balance and then draw up a profit and loss account for the month ended 31 January last, and a balance sheet as at that date.

12 J. Soap commenced business as a freelance painter and decorator on 1 March last with equipment valued at £2000 and cash £500. During the month he earned £600 cash and paid out, also in cash, £200 for materials (all used) and £10 for general office expenses.
Required:
a. Soap's opening and closing balance sheets, and his profit and loss account for the month.
b. A statement of the difference that would have resulted from buying additional equipment on credit from B&Q Ltd for £100.

Calculating the profit

13 Albert provides financial services and advice. He commenced on 1 January last with premises £20 000, cash-at-bank £2000, and cash-in-hand £300. The following transactions then took place:

January		£
5	Charged clients for advice	500
9	Clients paid by cheque	100
10	Albert withdrew £100 from bank for office purposes	
20	Albert paid office rent by cheque	50
25	General expenses paid in cash	30
30	Received £50 for rent of spare room leased to another firm in cash	
31	Paid lighting and heating by cheque	60

Required:
a. Albert's balance sheets as at the beginning and the end of the month.
b. A calculation of the difference in Albert's cash and bank balances at the end of the month compared with the beginning.
c. A calculation of the increase in capital over the month.

Open Albert's ledger on the basis of his opening balance sheet, post his transactions, and draw up his profit and loss account for the month, transferring the accounts concerned. Carry down the balances on the remaining accounts.

Required:
d. A calculation of the variation in Albert's cash holdings, and the amount of his profit or loss.
e. A reasoned statement explaining whether or not it would be possible for Albert's cash to increase at the same time as making a loss.
f. An explanation of whether it would be possible for Albert's cash to decrease while at the same time running at a profit.
g. A statement explaining the difference *in the principles involved* in the posting of transactions to, and the meaning of the balances resulting in,
   (i) the cash and the clients accounts on the one hand, and
   (ii) the lighting and heating, rent, and general expenses accounts on the other?
h. An explanation of the significance of (i) a debit balance and (ii) a credit balance in the accounts that appear in the (1) balance sheet and (2) profit and loss account?

UNIT 7 EARNING A LIVING: 2 THE ACCOUNTS OF TRADERS

Before you read this unit, try activity 7.1.

Activity 7.1

Sheila White is a market trader who regularly takes a stall at three markets each week. Last week, she started with a stock of clothes that had cost her £340 and she purchased a further £210 worth. She sold part of the stock for £530. At the end of the week, she had stock left over that had cost her £325.

Set out a neat calculation of her basic profit or loss on the purchase and sale of the goods.

Out of her basic profit, Sheila had to pay £45 for hire of stalls, £40 for hire of a van, and £30 general expenses.

Calculate her final profit or loss for the week.

7A. The Idea of Gross Profit

The last unit showed how the profit and loss account is used to summarise the income and expenses for the accounting period in order to give the *net profit*—which is equal to the net increase in assets for the period.

This normal profit and loss account can be set out differently to suit the needs and special problems of various types of organisations. Trading firms are an example. Their main function is buying goods and then re-selling them at a higher price. It is important to traders to know the basic profit made on just the buying and selling of the goods (ignoring other costs) as well as the overall net profit on the whole business operation. This basic profit is known as the **gross profit**.

The gross profit is calculated in the **trading account**. The trading account is a specialised subsection of the main profit and loss account.

After the gross profit has been calculated in the trading account, it is transferred to the profit and loss account, where the general expenses are deducted in order to arrive at the net profit.

7B. Accounting for 'Goods'

Certain problems crop up when we have to bring both buying and re-selling of the same goods into the accounts. The problems are best overcome by having *three* separate accounts. These are:

(i) purchases account,
(ii) sales account, and
(iii) stock account.

Each of the accounts deals with a particular type of transaction. Its use has to be limited to that type of transaction, and we must not be misled by the words that might be used.

1. Purchases

The **purchases account** is used to record the purchase of goods, during any particular trading period, which we intend to re-sell. If we take the transaction:

Bought goods for £40 cash

the entries would be:

Debit Purchases account
Credit Cash account. — money out

If the goods are bought 'on credit', for example:

Purchased stock from J. Armstrong Ltd, £500

the entries would be:

Debit Purchases account
Credit J. Armstrong Ltd.

Note the entry would still be in purchases account, although the word 'stock' is used.

In the ledger, the entries for both transactions would appear like this:

Purchases account
Cash   40.00
J. Armstrong Ltd   500.00

Cash (extract)
                Purchases   40.00

J. Armstrong Ltd
                Purchases   500.00

It is important to note the following with regard to purchases account:

(i) Purchases account is *only* used for goods bought with the intention of re-selling them at a profit. It is *not* concerned with the purchase of fixed assets. In such cases, the asset account itself must be debited, not purchases account.
(ii) Purchases account is only used for goods actually purchased within the trading period concerned. We shall see in a moment what happens when goods are left over at the end of a period.
(iii) Purchases account is used for such transactions, no matter what the form of words, e.g. even if the words 'bought stock' are used.

2. Sales

The problem is that goods are not normally re-sold for the same price at which they were bought. It would be very confusing if we were to use the same account for goods at two different values—at cost price when they are purchased, and at selling price when some of them are sold. So a separate account—the **sales account**—is used to record all sales of trading goods during the accounting period concerned. Therefore, for the transaction:

Sold goods for cash, £20

Debit cash
credit sales

the entries would be

Debit Cash account
Credit Sales account.

For credit transactions such as:

Sold goods to G. Forrester, £5000

the entries would be:

Debit G. Forrester
Credit Sales account.

In the ledger, the entries would appear like this:

Sales account
Cash	20.00
G. Forrester	5000.00

Cash account (extract)
Sales 20.00

G. Forrester
Sales 500.000

As with purchases account, it is important to note that the sales account is only used for trading goods sold within the normal course of business. It is *not* used for the sale of fixed assets. We shall discuss how we sell fixed assets later in the book.

Note that purchases account only has *debit* entries and sales account only has *credit* entries. Also note that entries in purchases account refer to goods at their *cost* price; those in sales account refer to goods (often the same goods) at their *selling* price.

How this works out in practice is shown in example 7.1 below. Note that the example involves no opening or closing stocks.

Example 7.1

(i) Joe decided to set up a stall on Saturdays as a market trader. He started on 1 May 1990 with a capital in cash of £500.
(ii) During the month, he purchased goods for re-sale for £300 cash.
(iii) The goods were sold for £700 cash. There was no stock of goods left at the end of the month.
(iv) He paid £80 rent in cash for his market stall.

Check through each of the above transactions in the solution that follows. In order to aid checking, dates have been replaced by the numbers such as (i) and (ii) used in the question.

Capital account

May 31	Balance	c/d	850.00	May 1(i)	Cash			500.00
				31	Net profit			350.00
			850.00					850.00
				June 1	Balance	b/d		850.00

Cash account

May 1	Capital		500.00	(ii)	Purchases			300.00
(iii)	Sales		700.00	(iv)	Rent			50.00
				May 31	Balance	c/d		850.00
			1200.00					1200.00

Calculating the profit

June	1	Balance	b/d	850.00					

Purchases account

(ii)	Cash	300.00	May	31	Trading account	300.00

Sales account

May	31	Trading account	700.00	(iii)	Cash	700.00

Rent account

(iv)	Cash	50.00	May	31	P & L	50.00

Trading and profit & loss account for month ended 31 May 1990

Purchases		300.00	Sales		700.00
Gross profit	c/d	400.00			
		700.00			700.00
Rent		50.00	Gross profit	b/d	400.00
Net profit		350.00			
		400.00			400.00

Balance sheet as at 31 May 1990

Cash	850.00	Capital at 1 May	500.00
		Profit	350.00
	850.00		850.00

In the above example note:

(i) how the net profit does, in fact, represent the net increase in assets—i.e. the increase in capital—during the period, and

(ii) how the trading account and the profit and loss account are combined into one statement.

3. Stock

Now look at activity 7.2 and see if you can work out for yourself what the answers must be.

Activity 7.2

In month 1, Alison purchased goods for £500 and sold half of them for £300. During month 2, she sold the other half for £400.

Calculate her profit for each month, and state which was her 'better' trading month.

This activity shows how important it is, at the end of month 1, to 'carry forward' the cost of the unsold stock, and to charge it against the income earned in month 2. Otherwise, we get some nonsense results.

We now come to the third of the accounts mentioned above, the **stock account**. The purpose of the stock account is to bring into account any goods unsold at the end of the accounting period, known in accounting as the *closing stock*. The closing stock for one period is, of course, the *opening stock* for the next.

At the end of the accounting period, the stock left on hand is valued—usually at its original cost price—and this is then *deducted* from the cost of the purchases in the trading account. Hopefully this is what you did anyway in activity 7.1 at the start of this unit—so you see in accounting we are only doing the obvious and sensible thing! A deduction has the same arithmetical effect as a credit entry, so what we effectively do is to make a credit entry in the trading account.

The entry in the trading account (i.e. a deduction on the debit side with the same effect as a normal credit entry) is matched by a debit entry in a new account, namely *stock account*. Thus the double entry is correct.

It is allowable to show closing stock as an entry on the credit side of trading account, and some firms do follow this practice. The advantage of showing closing stock as a deduction on the debit side is that it produces a very useful figure, namely the *cost of the goods sold*. We shall see the importance of this figure later in the book.

Example 7.2

(i) William Holt started business on 1 August with £600 cash.
(ii) He purchased goods for £800 from Wilco Ltd (on credit).
(iii) Some of the goods were sold for £950 cash.
(iv) He paid £60 in cash as rent for his stall and £30 in cash as general expenses.
(v) At the end of the month, he found he had goods left over that had cost him £300, and these goods he expects to sell in September.

Capital account

Aug	31	Balance	c/d	960.00	Aug	1	Cash		600.00
					Aug	31	Net profit		360.00
				960.00					960.00
					Sept	1	Balance	b/d	960.00

Cash account

Aug	1	Capital		600.00	(iv)		Rent		60.00
	(iii)	Sales		950.00	(iv)		General expenses		30.00
					Aug	31	Balance	c/d	1460.00
				1550.00					1550.00
Aug	31	Balance	b/d	1460.00					

Purchases account

(ii)	Wilco Ltd	800.00	Aug	31	Trading a/c		800.00

Sales account

Aug	31	Trading a/c	950.00	(iii)	Cash		950.00

Wilco Ltd

		(ii)	Purchases	800.00

Rent account

(iv)	Cash	60.00	Aug	31	Trading a/c	60.00

General expenses

(iv)	Cash	30.00	Aug	31	Trading a/c	30.00

Stock account

Aug	31	Trading a/c	300.00	

Calculating the profit

Trading and profit and loss account, month ended 31 August

Purchases		800.00	Sales		950.00
Less stock, 31 Aug		300.00			
Cost of goods sold		500.00			
Gross profit	c/d	450.00			
		950.00			950.00
Rent		60.00	Gross profit	b/d	450.00
General expenses		30.00			
Net profit		360.00			
		450.00			450.00

Balance sheet as at 31 August

Current assets			*Capital* at 1 May	600.00
Stock	300.00		Net profit	360.00
Cash	1460.00			960.00
			Current liabilities	
	1760.00		Wilco Ltd	800.00
				1760.00

Note that the credit transaction is included in the profit calculation, and that at the end of the trading period, stock account is an 'open account' with a current balance in it. So it must appear as a current asset in any balance sheet drawn up at that date.

This is not the end of the story. If a trader *finishes* one trading period with goods still in hand (the *closing stock*), it follows that he *commences* the next period with the same goods, still in hand and still represented by the figure in stock account. This same figure, then, becomes the *opening stock* for the new period.

At the end of the second period, both the opening stock *and* the purchases during the period must be transferred to the trading account, and added together. There will then be a new closing stock, and this must be deducted as before, with a corresponding entry back in stock account in the ledger. Check the procedure through entry by entry in the following example.

Example 7.3

William Holt (see example 7.2 above), who ended August with stock in hand of £300, carried on trading in September. During the month he:

(i) purchased additional stock for £200 cash and for £950 credit from Wilco Ltd;
(ii) sold goods, all for cash, for £1775;
(iii) paid (in cash) rent for his stall of £75 and general expenses of £40; and
(iv) had a closing stock of £350.

Capital account

Sept 30	Balance	c/d	1520.00	Sept 1	Balance	b/f	960.00
				Sept 30	Net profit		560.00
			1520.00				1520.00
				Oct 1	Balance	b/f	1520.00

Cash account

Sept	1	Balance	b/f	1 460.00	(ii)	Purchases		200.00
	(ii)	Cash		1 775.00	(iii)	Rent		75.00
					(iv)	General expenses		40.00
					Sept 30	Balance	c/d	2 920.00
				3 235.00				3 235.00
Oct	1	Balance	b/d	2 920.00				

Stock account

Aug	31	Trading a/c	b/f	300.00	Sept 30	Trading a/c	300.00
Oct	1	Trading a/c		350.00			

Wilco Ltd

Sept	30	Balance	c/d	1 750.00	Sept	1	Balance	b/f	800.00
						(i)	Cash		950.00
				1 750.00					1 750.00
					Oct	1	Balance	b/d	1 750.00

Purchases account

	(i)	Cash		200.00	Sept	30	Trading a/c	1 150.00
	(i)	Wilco Ltd		950.00				
				1 150.00				1 150.00

Sales account

Sept	30	Trading a/c	1 775.00	(ii)	Cash	1 775.00

Rent account

Sept	30	Cash	75.00	Sept	30	P & L	75.00

General expenses account

Sept	30	Cash	40.00	Sept	30	P & L	40.00

Trading and profit and loss account for month ended 30 Sept

Stock at 1 Sept		300.00	Sales		1 775.00
Purchases		1 150.00			
		1 450.00			
Less Stock at 31 Sept		350.00			
		1 100.00			
Gross profit	c/d	675.00			
		1 775.00			1 775.00
Rent a/c		75.00	Gross profit	b/d	675.00
General expenses		40.00			
Net profit		560.00			
		675.00			675.00

Balance sheet as at 30 Sept

Current assets			Capital at 1 Sept	960.00
Stock		350.00	Profit	560.00
Cash		2 920.00		1 520.00
			Current liability	
		3 270.00	Wilco Ltd	1 750.00
				3 270.00

4. Closing stock, and examination questions

The figure for closing stock, in the real situation, is usually obtained by checking the stock on hand (a process known as **stock-taking**) at the end of the accounting period. The figure is not brought into account

Calculating the profit

until the trading account is drawn up, so does *not* appear in the trial balance extracted immediately after the posting of the transactions. This means that any stock figure appearing in the trial balance will normally be that for *opening* stock, and not that for *closing* stock.

Examination questions often consist of a trial balance, from which you are asked to draw up the final accounts (trading and profit and loss account, and the balance sheet). The routine posting of the ledger is not asked for. The figure for closing stock is given as a statement after the end of the trial balance, i.e. it will *not* form part of the trial balance itself. Example 7.4 below is a simplified example.

Example 7.4

The following trial balance was extracted from the ledger of Anne Smith, a retailer, at 31 December 1981. From the information given, prepare a trading and profit and loss account for the year to 31 December 1981, and a balance sheet as at that date.

	£	£
Capital		24 000
Premises	30 000	
Equipment	21 000	
Creditors		10 200
Debtors	15 500	
Purchases	200 500	
Sales		284 500
Stock	5 800	
General expenses	26 200	
Salaries and wages	35 600	
Cash-at-bank	4 100	
Loan (repayable in 5 years)		20 000
	338 700	338 700

Stock at 31 December (i.e. closing stock) was valued at £4200.

Trading and profit & loss account, year to 31 December 1981

Stock, at 01/01/81	5 800		Sales		284 500
Purchases	200 500				
	206 300				
Less Stock at 31/12/81	4 200				
Cost of goods sold		202 100			
Gross profit	c/d	82 400			
		284 500			284 500
General expenses		26 200	Gross profit	b/d	82 400
Salaries & wages		35 600			
Net profit		20 600			
		82 400			82 400

Balance sheet as at 31 December 1981

Fixed assets			Capital, at 01/01/81	24 000	
Premises	30 000		Profit	20 600	
Equipment	21 000				44 600
		51 000	Long-term liabilities		
Current assets			Loan		20 000
Stock	4 200		Current liability		
Debtors	15 500		Wilco Ltd		10 200
Cash	4 100				
	23 800				
	74 800				74 800

A word of warning. Although trial balances in examination questions are *usually* those drawn up immediately after the end of the posting and before the preparation of the trading account (as in the example above), trial balances are sometimes given *after* the trading account has been drawn up. This means that the closing stock will already have been written back to the ledger, and will appear in the trial balance itself. Also, in the trial balance, there will be a figure for the gross profit (i.e. the balance of the trading account). From this information, you will be expected to draw up only the profit and loss account, and the balance sheet.

A trial balance may also be given after the profit and loss account has been prepared, in which case it will contain both the closing stock figure and the net profit. From this information, you will be asked to draw up only the balance sheet.

In an examination, make sure that you know and understand at what stage a given trial balance has been extracted, and exactly what you are being asked to do with it.

7C. Some More Conventions

Two examples of conventions in accounting—the 'working rules and assumptions' of the subject—were given on pages 12 and 16.

If you do not remember what they were, look them up now.

We can now identify three more.

Accounting Convention No. 3
The Continuity Convention

Unless there are reasons for believing otherwise, it is always assumed that the firm will continue to operate in the future.

Example The cost of the closing stock is carried forward and charged against the income in the period during which it is expected to be sold.

Accounting Convention No. 4
The Consistency Convention

Accountants should always adhere to the *same* rules, definitions, procedures or principles unless there is a very good reason for departing from them.

Example Profit should always be calculated for the same period (usually 12 months) if results of one period are to be compared with those of another.

Calculating the profit

> **Accounting Convention No. 5**
> **The Prudence Convention**
>
> Profit should not be anticipated—i.e. it should not be brought into account until it has been earned. Possible losses should be allowed for as soon as possible.
>
> *Example* Closing stock should be carried forward to the next period at its cost price, *not* at its anticipated selling price.

7D. The Accounting Cycle

At the end of unit 4, an initial diagram of the accounting cycle was shown. It is now possible to draw a more detailed one, and this is shown in figure 7.1.

Balance sheet 1 → Ledger → Trading account 1 → Profit and loss account 1 → Balance sheet 2 → Ledger → Trading account 2 → Profit and loss account 2 → Balance sheet 3 → ...

(Ledger → Trial balance)

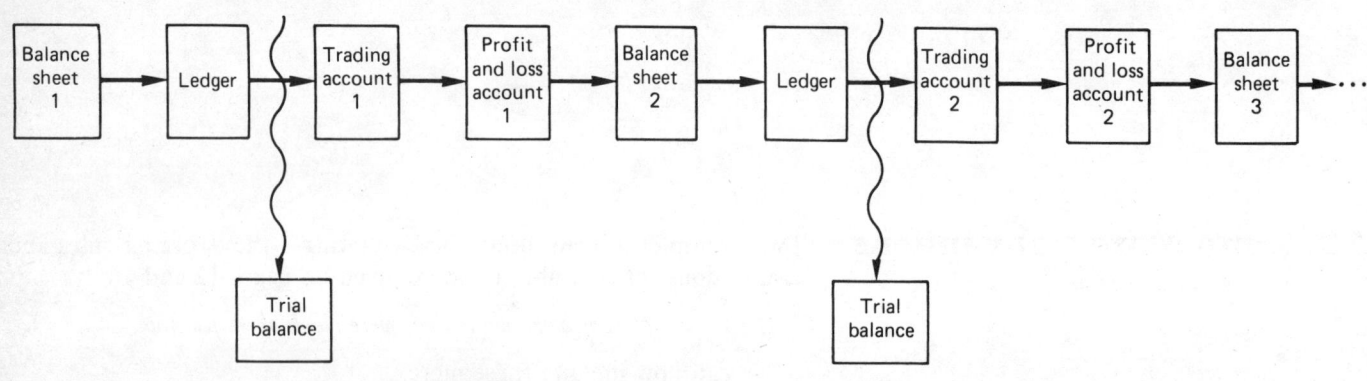

Figure 7.1
The accounting cycle in more detail.

Activity 7.3

1. Can you think of any more examples of the accounting conventions that have already been described? Keep a note of them, and add to them as your study proceeds. It is a common examination topic.
2. The published profit and loss accounts of many commercial organisations state whether, for any particular year, the accounts are based on a 52- or a 53-week year. With which accounting convention is this concerned, and why is it important that it should be stated? How does there come to be a 53-week year in any case?
3. What would be:
   (i) the danger, and
   (ii) the effect upon profit for both the current year and the following year

   of ignoring the convention and carrying stock forward to the following year at its probable selling price?

Check Your Understanding

1. What is the purpose of the trading account?
2. The record for goods intended for re-sale is divided into three separate accounts. What are they?
3. What type or types of transactions are entered in the purchases account?
4. Entries for what are recorded in the stock account?

5 What are the ledger entries for:
   (i) cash sales;
   (ii) credit sales?

6 Why does an error in the valuation of 'closing stock' show up in the profits of the *next* period as well as in the profits of the current period?

7 What is the advantage of showing closing stock as a deduction on the debit side of the trading account, instead of as a normal credit entry?

8 Although a trial balance may be drawn up at any point in the cycle of accounting operations, when is the most common time? What *two* functions does it serve if drawn up at this time?

9 What does the *consistency* convention state?

10 What would be the effect of carrying forward closing stock at its likely selling price instead of its cost price? Which convention would you be ignoring if you did so?

Practical Assignments

1 Supertrader Stores commenced business on 1 January 1989 with stock of £20 000. During the year, purchases of £360 000 were made and sales of £504 000. At 31 December 1989, the stock remaining was valued at £180 000.
   Prepare the firm's trading account for the year to 31 December 1989.

2 a. What is the purpose of trading and profit and loss account?
   b. List the ways in which the trading section differs from the profit and loss section.
   c. From the following information, which has been extracted from the books of Traders Ltd, prepare the trading and profit and loss account for the year to 30 September 1989.

	£
Sales	1 270 721
Stock at 1 October 1988	180 346
Purchases	784 248
Stock at 30 September 1989	214 628
Wages and salaries	150 000
Advertising	5 600
Insurance	8 000
Miscellaneous expenses	2 540

   d. Write up the firm's stock account as it would appear in the ledger.

3 The following balances have been extracted from the trial balances of Penrose & Co. at 30 September 1989:

	£	£
Stock at 1 October 1988	250 000	
General expenses	85 200	
Sales		1 126 400
Purchases	1 300 500	

The stock at 30 September 1989 was valued at £300 000.

   a. Prepare the trading and profit and loss account for the year.
   b. What would have been the effect upon the accounts had closing stock been valued at: (i) £500 000, (ii) £750 000, (iii) £250 000.

4 From the following trial balance, draw up the trading and profit and loss account for the year to 31 December 1989, and the balance sheet as at that date.

Capital		172 000
Stock at 1 January 1989	40 000	
Purchases	160 000	
Sales		134 000
Advertising	12 000	
Insurance	3 000	
Rent	4 000	
Bank	15 000	
Sundry debtors	44 000	
Sundry creditors		32 000
Premises	60 000	
	338 000	338 000

Stock at 31 December was valued at £130 000.

5 The following balances appeared in the ledger of Betty Brady on 31 December 1989: premises £30 000; equipment £10 000; stock £16 000; debtors £2400; bank £3400; mortgage £16 000; trade creditors £6000.
   Draw up her balance sheet at this date, open her ledger and then post the following, which refer to the month of January 1990:

	£
Cash sales for the month	2 400
Credit sales for the month	10 800
Cash purchases for the month	1 800
Credit purchases for the month	8 400
Cash received from debtors	9 800
Cash payments to creditors	7 600
Cash paid for	
electricity	600
advertising	500
new equipment	1 600
sundry expenses	300
Stock on hand at 31 January	16 200

Calculating the profit

All cash received is immediately banked and all payments are made by cheque.

Prepare a trading and profit and loss account for the month ended 31 January 1990, and a balance sheet as at that date.

Comment on her financial position.

6. a. A retailer purchases goods for £200 000 and sells them at a mark-up (profit as a percentage of cost price) of 40%. What was the selling price of the goods?
   b. Another retailer sold goods for £160 000. This gave him a profit margin (profit as a percentage of selling price) of 20%. What was the cost price of the goods?
   c. A wholesaler bought goods for £940 000 from a manufacturer, and sold them to retailers for £1 410 000. How much was his profit? What percentage was the profit of (i) cost price and (ii) selling price?
   d. If goods were sold for £150 000 subject to a mark-up of 25%, what was their cost price?
   e. Goods were purchased for £320 000 and were sold with a profit margin of 20%. What was the selling price?

(Note: If you have any difficulty in making the above calculations, then reference should be made to appendix A. It is very important that the basic procedures should be understood, since this type of calculation frequently arises in accounting work.)

7. a. Complete the following trading and profit and loss account. The trader concerned has a mark-up on cost of 40%.

	£		£
Opening stock		Sales	
Purchases	90 000		
less Closing stock	30 000		
Cost of goods sold			
Gross profit c/d			
	140 000		
Advertising	4 000	Gross profit b/d	
Salaries	25 000		
Rent and rates	3 000		
Net profit			

b. What was his profit margin?

8. Stuart Bradley commenced business on 1 November last with the following assets: debtor (A. N. Smith) £5000; equipment £12 000; stock £30 000; vehicles £8000; premises £25 000; cash-at-bank £3000; cash-in-hand £250. In addition, he owed B. Brown £10 000 in respect of a long-term loan and W. White £3000 in respect of an ordinary trade debt.

Draw up his balance sheet as at 1 November and open his ledger. Then post the following transactions:

		£
Nov 2	Purchased goods by cheque	2 000
4	Sold goods for cash	10 000
5	Paid cash into the bank	8 000
7	Purchased goods from W. White	68 000
9	Sold goods for cash	15 000
10	Returned goods to W. White	1 000
11	Paid advertising by cheque	1 500
13	Paid cheque to B. Brown in part settlement of loan	4 000
14	Purchased additional premises by cheque	2 000
15	Cash sales	20 000
17	Paid cash into the bank	25 000
18	Paid advertising by cash	500
20	Paid electricity by cheque	300
22	Sold goods to X. Checker	67 000
25	Goods returned by X. Checker	2 000
27	Paid cheque to W. White	500
28	Drew cash from bank	10 000
29	Paid salaries by credit transfer	10 000
30	Paid rent by cheque	500

a. Draw up Bradley's trading and profit and loss account for the month, and his balance sheet as at 30 November, bearing in mind that the value of stock at the close of business on 30 November was £20 000.
b. After seeing the final accounts, Bradley asked the following questions. What would you say in answer to each?

   (i) How can I have made a profit when I see that my stocks, cash and bank balances are less than they were when I started. Surely I must have made a loss?
   (ii) I can see the distinction between the balance sheet and the other two accounts, but I don't understand the difference between a trading and a profit and loss account. What is the difference between the two and what point is there in separating them?

UNIT 8 COMPLICATIONS IN TRADERS' ACCOUNTS

Before you read this unit, try activity 8.1.

Activity 8.1
Assume that you are the manager of a general store. You order a range of goods from a catalogue at their 'catalogue price'. The bills that you finally pay for the goods you order may well be different from their catalogue prices.

List all the reasons that you can think of why this might be so.

The last unit showed that gross profit is the difference between sales and their cost, and that this cost is obtained by adding purchases to opening stock and deducting closing stock. There are a number of items that may have to be considered in order to obtain the true cost of goods sold.

8A. Returns and Allowances

1. General nature
The first complicating factor concerns the problems that crop up when goods have to be returned.

There are a number of reasons why goods may have to be sent back to the supplier. They may have been damaged in transit, or they may be faulty. The goods sent to a customer may not be exactly what he or she ordered, or they may be the wrong type or colour. The wrong quantity may have been sent. It may simply be that the customer has had a change of mind, and asks the supplier to take them back 'out of the goodness of his heart'.

Whatever the reason, there will be occasions with all organisations when goods have to be returned to suppliers, and when goods have to be accepted back from customers.

Activity 8.2
Imagine you are the manager of a retail store. Describe what action you would take in each of the following situations and the factors you would bear in mind in making your decision. In particular, say whether the reason behind the action that you suggest is legal, moral or commercial.

(i) You have received a consignment of tinned beans from a wholesaler you have dealt with for a number of years. You actually ordered 100 dozen tins, but have actually received—and been charged for—110 dozen.

(ii) You ordered 100 pints of fresh milk, and have been sent 500 pints.

(iii) Customer 'A', who recently purchased a packet of tea bags from you, complains that they taste 'musty'.

(iv) Customer 'B', who recently bought two dozen tins of sardines in tomato sauce, says that she has 'gone off fish' and wants you to take them back.

(v) Customer 'C' recently purchased from you 100 tins of an unusual type of cat food, which you had to obtain by special order. He now tells you that Tiddles doesn't really like that food after all, and will you take back the remaining 95 tins.

77

Calculating the profit

When a firm has goods returned to it *from* customers, the goods are known as **returns-in**. When a firm finds that it has to return goods *to* its suppliers, they are called **returns-out**.

When goods are sold on credit, a document is issued, which is known as an **invoice**. We shall be looking more closely at invoices, and indeed other documents connected with trading, in unit 10. But for the moment it is enough to know that an invoice is the document that tells the customer the price to be paid.

If all or part of a batch of goods has to be returned, appropriate allowance will have to be made. This may amount to an immediate cash refund or—as is much more common in business—it may take the form of an 'allowance', which authorises the customer to deduct an appropriate sum from his or her next payment.

It would lead to considerable confusion, and risk of error, if any attempt was made to alter the original invoice. So the normal practice is for the supplier to whom the goods are being returned to issue an additional document, known as a **credit note**. This is sent to the customer who has returned the goods, and states the amount that the customer can deduct from the next payment. Credit notes are usually printed in red to distinguish them from invoices.

2. Accounting for returns

The ledger entries for returns-in are:

Debit Returns-in account.
Credit Personal account of the debtor from whom the goods have been returned.

The ledger entries for returns-out are:

Debit Personal account of the creditor to whom the goods are being returned.
Credit Returns-out account.

At the end of the trading period, the sales account, purchases account and the two returns accounts are transferred to the trading account. The returns-in account, which has a *debit* balance, is shown as a *deduction* from the sales, and the returns-out account, which has a *credit* balance, is shown as a deduction from purchases. In this way, the real value of those items—i.e. 'net sales' and 'net purchases'—are shown. This is shown in the following example.

Example 8.1

A firm's purchases and sales for March were as follows:

March 5 Sold goods to J. Machin, £200
March 6 Sold goods to A. N. Other, £10 000
March 10 Purchased goods from H. George, £600
March 12 Purchased goods from Suppliers Ltd, £3000
March 20 J. Machin returns faulty goods, £80
March 21 Returned goods to H. George, £100

Show the relevant accounts and transfers to the trading account at 31 March.

			Sales account				
Mar 31	Trading account		10 200	Mar 5	J. Machin		200
				6	A. N. Other		10 000
			10 200				10 200

			Purchases account				
Mar 10	H. George		600	Mar 31	Trading account		3 600
12	Suppliers Ltd		3 000				
			3 600				3 600

			Returns-in account				
Mar 20	J. Machin		80	Mar 31	Trading account		80

			Returns-out account				
Mar 31	Trading account		100	Mar 21	H. George		100

			J. Machin				
Mar 5	Sales		200	Mar 20	Returns-in		80
				Mar 31	Balance	c/d	120
			200				200
Apr 1	Balance	b/d	120				

			A. N. Other				
Mar 6	Sales		10 000				

			H. George				
Mar 21	Returns-out		100	Mar 10	Purchases		600
Mar 31	Balance	c/d	500				
			600				600
				Apr 1		b/d	500

			Suppliers Ltd				
				Mar 12	Purchases		3 000

		Trading account (extract)			
Purchases	3 600		Sales	10 200	
Less returns-out	100		Less returns-in	80	
	3 500			10 120	

Another way of doing this is to enter the returns directly in the sales and purchases accounts, so that only the net figure is transferred to the trading account. Although simpler, there is a particular disadvantage to this method, which will be demonstrated later in this unit.

Can you think what it is?

Activity 8.3

Post the following transactions to the ledger by directly debiting sales account (in the case of returns-in) and by directly crediting purchases account (in the case of returns-out), and draw up the trading account.

	£
Stock at 1 October	26 000
Purchases from sundry creditors during October	12 600
Sales to sundry debtors during October	23 600

Calculating the profit

Purchases returns (i.e. returns-out to sundry creditors	4 600
Sales returns (i.e. returns-in from sundry debtors)	11 600
Stock at 31 October	24 000

Do you think, from the trading account you have just prepared, that the firm has made a reasonable profit for the month?

Note: For the purpose of this exercise, it is enough to make the entries to a 'sundry debtors' account and to a 'sundry creditors' account ('sundry' meaning 'several' or 'various'). In practice, detailed individual records would, of course, have to be kept.

Post the transactions again from the beginning, this time opening a 'returns-in' account and a 'returns-out' account. Prepare a trading account, showing the returns as deductions from sales account and purchases account, respectively.

Answer the following questions by looking at the second trading account:
 (i) *Are you still satisfied that the firm has made a reasonable profit?*
 (ii) *Does anything significant stand out that was not immediately apparent in the first trading account?*
 (iii) *What are the problems involved in the situation now shown up by the trading account?*
 (iv) *What further enquiries should the manager of the firm now make, and what action might he or she possibly have to take?*

3. Allowances

Suppliers often grant retailers special allowances, which are deducted from the normal catalogue price. There are a number of reasons for doing this: one may be to allow suppliers to clear old stock to make way for new lines; another may be to enable suppliers to offer the goods to customers at very competitive prices.

The book-keeping is very similar to that for returns. The firm receiving the allowance would *debit* the supplier (thus reducing the amount owed) and *credit* allowances account. The firm giving the allowance would *debit* allowances and *credit* the customer. The totals of the allowances account would be deducted from purchases (in the case of the retailer receiving the allowance) or from sales (in the case of the supplier giving the allowance).

8B. Transportation Costs

Catalogue prices sometimes include the costs of delivery to the customer; sometimes they do not. If the transport and delivery costs have not been included in the catalogue price, they have to be paid for by someone—either by the purchaser as an addition to the catalogue price of the goods, or by the seller as an additional cost.

In accounting, a rather old-fashioned term is often used to describe these costs—it is *carriage*. Thus, as regards transport costs on purchases, a firm may find itself paying **carriage-in**, while on sales it may find itself liable for the **carriage-out**.

Both carriage-in and carriage-out are expenses—in both cases the respective account (either carriage-in account or carriage-out account) has to be debited, while cash account is credited. It is extremely important to maintain *separate* accounts for carriage-in and carriage-out, and not to combine them. This is because of a rather fine distinction that is always drawn in accounting, which we shall now look at.

Carriage-in is always thought of as an essential part of the cost of purchases, and is therefore added to purchases in the trading account. Also, it is a figure that tends to vary with the amount of purchases being made, and also with turnover.

Carriage-out, on the other hand, is thought of as an independent expense, not directly connected with the selling price of goods. It is therefore taken to the profit and loss account at the end of the accounting period, *not* to the trading account.

You may well think this distinction is splitting hairs a little, but it is a firm rule of procedure in accounting, and must always be followed—particularly in examination work.

Example 8.2

From the following balances, which have been extracted from the trial balance of George Fox at 31 December last, show the trading and profit and loss account for the year to that date.

	£	£
Stock at 1 January	40 500	
Purchases	29 100	
Sales		50 700
Returns-in	400	
Returns-out		100
Carriage-in	1 200	
Carriage-out	3 500	
Other expenses	10 000	

The estimated value of stock-on-hand at 31 December was £52 000.

G. Fox: Trading and profit and loss account for year ended 31 December 19--

		£	£			£	£
Stock at 1 Jan			40 500	Sales		50 700	
Purchases		29 100		Less returns-in		400	50 300
Add carriage-in		1 200					
		30 300					
Less returns-out		100					
			30 200				
			70 700				
Less stock 31 Dec			52 000				
Cost of goods sold			18 700				
Gross profit	c/d		31 600				
			50 300				50 300
Carriage-out			3 500	Gross profit	b/d		31 600
Other expenses			10 000				
Net profit			18 100				
			31 600				31 600

8C. Discounts

A further reason why customers may not find themselves paying the actual catalogue price for an order of goods is that they may be entitled to a discount. There are two main types of discount: one is *trade discount* and the other is *cash discount*.

1. Trade discount

Trade discount is usually allowed by wholesalers to retailers. It is used when goods are invoiced to the retailer at what is expected to be their full retail selling price, i.e. the price that the retailer will charge his customers. In other words, it amounts to the profit margin that the retailer can expect to make on the goods. The important thing about trade discount is that it is *always* allowed, and has no connection with the speedy payment of the debt. It is usual for different rates of trade discount to be allowed to different customers depending upon the quantities of goods they order, the length of time they have been trading with the wholesaler, the competition they are having to face in order to sell the product, and their general 'credit worthiness'. Occasionally, a very large trade discount is allowed to enable retailers to sell goods very cheaply; this often happens when a manufacturer or wholesaler wishes to 'clear' an old product from their shelves in order to make space for a 'new line'.

When trade discounts are allowed, the retailer never owes to the wholesaler the full amount of the invoice. The maximum amount he owes is the invoice figure *after* the trade discount has been deducted. So this is the only figure that is of interest to the accountant, and the only one that goes into the books.

2. Cash discount

Cash discount is an amount that may be deducted if payment is made within a certain period of time. It is usually described as a percentage—that is, a percentage calculated on the amount *after* the trade discount has been deducted.

Example 8.3

A retailer purchases goods from a wholesaler for £2000, less trade discount of 40%, and subject to a cash discount of 5%, one month—this means that if the amount is paid within one month, 5% discount (i.e. cash discount) may be deducted.

Show the amount that the retailer will pay, if he or she settles within one month.

	£
Gross amount of invoice	2 000
Trade discount (40% of £2000)	800
Amount net of trade discount	1 200
Cash discount (5% of £1200)	60
Net amount payable	1 140

Note: The original debt was £1200, not £2000. No more than £1200 will be payable no matter when payment is made. The cash discount, on the other hand, may only be deducted if the account is paid within the stated period of time (in this case, one month).

---

3. Book-keeping procedures for discount

No entries are made in the accounting books for trade discount. This is because the net amount of the invoice *after* its deduction is the only figure entered in the books. The accountant, therefore, ignores it completely.

A cash discount does have to go through the books because, at the time the invoice is sent, it is not known whether the discount will be claimed or not. Cash discount may be either **discount-allowed** (to a debtor) or **discount-received** (from a creditor).

When a debtor pays his or her account and is allowed discount, the entries are:

(i) *Debit*   Cash (or bank) account.
Credit   Personal account of the debtor concerned, with the amount of the actual cash received.
(ii) *Debit*   Discount-allowed account.
Credit   Personal account of the debtor concerned, with the amount of the discount.

Similar entries are made when payment is made to a creditor and discount is received:

(i) *Debit*   Personal account of the creditor.
Credit   Cash (or bank) account, with the amount of the actual cash payment.
(ii) *Debit*   Personal account of the creditor.
Credit   Discount-received account, with the amount of the discount.

Example 8.4

(i) A firm sells good to Barbara Black for £8000, less 25% trade discount, and 10% cash discount, one month. Barbara pays within one month, and is therefore allowed the cash discount.

Note: The amount owed by Barbara, in the first instance, is £6000 (i.e. £8000 less the 25% trade discount of £2000), and so £6000 is the amount that is entered in the ledger. The cash discount is 10% of the £6000 (i.e. £600). The actual payment therefore is £5400.

(ii) Goods are purchased from William White for £9000. He is paid by cheque for £8600 in settlement (i.e. the balance must be regarded as discount).

Sales account

		B. Black	6 000

Barbara Black

Sales	6 000	Cash	5 400
		Discount-allowed	600
	6 000		6 000

Purchases account

W. White	9 000		

William White

Cash	8 600	Sales	9 000
Discount-received	400		
	9 000		9 000

It should be noted that the *discount-allowed* account always has a *debit* balance. At the end of the accounting period, it is transferred to the debit side of the profit and loss account as an expense of trading during the period.

The *discount-received* account always has a *credit* balance. At the end of the period, it is transferred to the credit side of the profit and loss account, thus increasing the profit.

Care must be taken in the use of the words *discount-allowed* and *discount-received*. These are the recognised accounting terms and they should be used only within their strict accounting meaning, i.e. *discount-allowed* for discount allowed *by* a firm to its debtors, and *discount-received* by a firm *from* its creditors. Examiners often deliberately word questions misleadingly. It helps to remember that a

Calculating the profit

transaction is always looked at from the point of view of the person whose accounts are being kept. Thus

Paid ABC £2000 and received £100 cash discount

has exactly the same meaning as

Paid ABC £2000 and was allowed £100 cash discount

In both cases, it is discount-received from the point of view of the person paying the money, and must be treated as such.
Similarly,

Received cheque from XYZ for £500 and allowed them discount of £10

has exactly the same meaning as

XYZ paid cheque for £500 and received discount of £10

In both cases, it is a matter of discount-allowed by the person receiving the money and is so entered in his or her books.

Activity 8.4

Listed below are samples of the different ways in which transactions involving discount can be worked. Complete the table, indicating which accounts are to be debited, and which credited, in each case.

Note: It is again emphasised how important it is to decide whether, within the accounting meaning of the terms, it is discount-allowed or discount-received that is involved.

Transaction	Account or accounts to be debited and amount (£)	Account or accounts to be credited and amount (£)

1. Paid A £200 by cheque and received discount £10
2. Received cash £30 from B and allowed him discount £1.50
3. C settled the amount she owed, £500, by cheque less 10% discount
4. Paid D a cheque £600 in settlement of a debt of £620
5. E paid a cheque £140 and received discount £5
6. Received cheque from F £200, on account
7. G owes £500. He pays £490 in settlement by cheque
8. Paid H cheque £100 and was allowed discount of £5
9. Paid J a cheque £400 on account
10. K is paid a cheque in respect of goods ordered at a catalogue price of £800 subject to 25% trade discount and 5% cash discount
11. A cheque is received from L for £504, which is in settlement of her debt less 10% cash discount
12. We offer goods at a catalogue price of £60 subject to a cash discount of 10% one month, 5% three months, and a trade discount of 40%. Customer M orders the goods and pays within the one-month period

Complications in traders' accounts

8D. Wages and Salaries

Wages are sometimes recorded separately from salaries. To the accountant, **wages** are payments which tend to vary with the amount of work being done, such as where payment is 'by the hour'. **Salaries** are 'fixed' payments such as managerial salaries which do not vary with output.

At this stage, wages and salaries should both be taken to the profit and loss account. We shall see later (in Unit 26) that the rule is modified where manufacturing firms are considered.

Check Your Understanding

1. Give four reasons why goods may be returned to a supplier.

2. When goods are returned to a supplier, what are the entries on the debit and credit sides in the *supplier's* books?

3. When goods are returned to a supplier, what are the entries on the debit and credit sides in the *customer's* books?

4. Give two reasons why a special allowance may be given to a customer.

5. In accounting, what do the terms *carriage-in* and *carriage-out* refer to?

6. In the trial balance, on what sides do the following accounts appear:
   (i) returns-in account,
   (ii) returns-out account,
   (iii) carriage-in account,
   (iv) carriage-out account,
   (v) discount-received account,
   (vi) discount-allowed account?

Complete the following sentences:

7. At the end of the accounting period, (i) the carriage-in account is transferred to the _____ account and is added to the cost of _____, and (ii) the carriage-out account is transferred to the _____ account and appears on the _____ side.

8. At the end of the accounting period, (i) the returns-in account is shown on the _____ side of the _____ account as a deduction from _____, and (ii) the returns-out account is shown on the _____ side of the _____ account as a deduction from _____.

9. (i) Trade discount is an allowance made by _____ to _____ and _____ (always/sometimes/never) appears in the ledger accounts.
   (ii) Cash discount is an allowance in respect of _____ and _____ (always/sometimes/never) appears in the ledger accounts.

10. At the end of the accounting period, (i) discount-allowed is transferred to the _____ account and appears on the _____ side and (ii) discount-received is transferred to the _____ account and appears on the _____ side.

Practical Assignments

1. A firm had an opening stock of £50 000 and during the year purchased goods for cash of £5000 and on credit from Alimo Ltd £80 000. Some of the goods that were substandard had to be returned and £3000 was allowed.
   Cash sales of the same firm amounted to £100 000, and sales on credit to Bax Ltd to £20 000. Of these, goods to the value of £2000 had to be returned. Stock at close was valued at £55 000.
   Required: the trading account of the firm for the period concerned.

2. a. What is the purpose of the trading account?
   b. What is the purpose of the profit and loss account?
   c. In what way or ways do the trading and profit and loss accounts differ from the balance sheet?
   d. State whether the following would normally have a debit or a credit balance in the trial balance:
      (i) purchases account
      (ii) discount-allowed account
      (iii) returns-in account
      (iv) returns-out account
      (v) carriage-in account
      (vi) carriage-out account
      (vii) discount-received account.

3. The following account appears in the books of Northern

85

Calculating the profit

Traders Ltd, a firm of wholesalers. State concisely what is meant by each entry in the account:

19-1

Ridgeway Retailing Ltd

			£			£
Jan 1	Balance	5 000		Feb 28	Bank	4 875
Aug 12	Sales	7 500			Discount	125
				Sep 5	Returns	300
				30	Bank	3 500
				Dec 31	Balance c/d	3 700
			12 500			12 500

19-2
Jan 1   3 700

4 The following table was prepared from the trading records of Mackenzie & Co. Show the ledger accounts as they would appear in the ledger *after* the balance sheet for the period had been completed:

Accounts	Opening balance Debit	Opening balance Credit	Purchases	Sales	Returns	Payments	Cash discount
	£	£	£	£	£	£	£
Adamson	6400	–	–	2000	400	7650	350
Batman	1600	–	–	500	–	2000	100
Etchley	–	5000	1300	–	300	5700	300
Foster	1000	–	–	600	–	1420	80
Hill	200	–	–	5000	50	3600	–
Munn	–	8000	500	–	100	8380	20
Pink	–	1200	–	–	80	1080	40
Turner	–	–	3000	–	150	–	–
Williams	1400	–	–	200	60	1320	80

5 From the following trial balance, draw up the trading and profit and loss account for the year to 31 December 19-1, and the balance sheet as at that date.

	£	£
Capital		86 000
Stock as at 1 January 19-1	20 000	
Purchases	80 000	
Sales		67 000
Discount allowed	200	
Advertising	6 000	
Returns-in	600	
Carriage-in	400	
Insurance	1 500	
Discount received		300
Rent	2 000	
Returns-out		1 200
Bank	7 500	
Carriage-out	300	
Sundry debtors	22 000	
Sundry creditors		16 000
Premises	30 000	
	170 500	170 500

Stock at close   £65 000

6 The following details refer to Horizon Ltd for the year ended 31 December last:

	£
Stock at 1 January	20 000
Purchases	70 000
Sales	130 000
Returns-in	5 000
Returns-out	3 000
Advertising	1 500
Insurance	3 000
Rent	2 500
Carriage-in	1 000
Carriage-out	2 000
Wages	20 000
Salaries	15 000
Discounts allowed	1 500
Discounts received	4 200

Stock at 31 December was found to be £35 000.

Prepare the trading and profit and loss account of Horizon Ltd for the period concerned.

7 a. What is the purpose of a trial balance?
b. What is the main limitation of a trial balance?
c. Eastern Traders decided to employ an unqualified and inexperienced book-keeper in order to save money. At 31 March 19-2, he produced the following trial balance.

	£	£
Capital rec'd from proprietor	192 800	
Debtors	36 000	
Stock at 1 April 19-1	200 000	
Premises	300 000	
Salaries paid by bank credit		152 500
Plant and machinery	180 000	
Returns from debtors		5 000
Returns to creditors	7 500	
Carriage-in	5 400	
Carriage-out		7 500
Goods rec'd from trade creditors	480 000	
Goods rec'd by customers		980 500
General expenses	60 000	
Creditors		250 000
Discount received	3 400	
Discount allowed		2 800
Stock at 31 March 19-2		86 800
Cash in hand and at bank	20 000	
	1 485 100	1 485 100

In view of the fact that the trial balance balanced, the proprietor of the company assumed that it was in order to proceed with the preparation of the final accounts. Was he justified in making this assumption?

You are required to redraft the trial balance; then prepare a trading and profit and loss account for the year, and a balance sheet as at 31 March 19-2. Add a comment on the firm's position at this date.

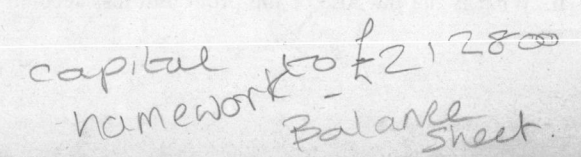

UNIT 9 A CLOSER LOOK AT TRADING THE USE OF DAY BOOKS

Before you read this unit, try activity 9.1.

Activity 9.1

A relative recently started a mail-order business, which has been much more successful than anticipated. The result is that he has recently suffered a nervous breakdown and you have been asked to sort out the office in his absence. You arrive to find large numbers of invoices, credit notes, even cheques, together with 'final demands' from suppliers, advertising circulars and a wide range of other documents, all piled on top of one another in a varied assortment of cardboard boxes. More documents arrive by every post.

What would you do to bring some sort of order into the chaos, and to ensure that essential information is fed through to the accounts?

9A. The Need for Day Books

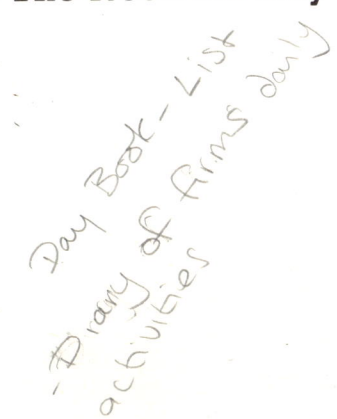

In the units up to now, we have seen that each business transaction should be backed by a specific document, examples of which are invoices and credit notes. These 'original documents' provide an immediate record of what has happened, and they provide the essential information for writing up the accounts. But there is one problem that they do not solve.

The problem is that of coping with the large number of transactions involved. For instance, even a medium-sized organisation may well issue (send out)—and receive—several hundred invoices a week. It is therefore necessary to 'streamline' the system, and to speed up the work involved.

This streamlining and speeding up is achieved by 'grouping' all similar transactions together, listing them, and then—where possible—posting only the totals to the ledger. For example, if an organisation sells goods on credit to 1000 customers during a particular period, it will issue 1000 invoices. Posted one by one to the sales account and to the respective debtor account, 2000 ledger entries would be needed. But if they are listed and a total figure for credit sales obtained, it will mean that only one entry need be made in sales account, although individual entries will still have to be made in the personal accounts. This will mean that only 1001 entries will have to be made instead of 2000. In other words, the ledger work is effectively halved without any loss of accuracy—in fact, the risk of mistakes can be much reduced.

This work of collecting and summarising is carried out in the **day books**—sometimes called the *journals*. Students of French will no doubt recognise the word *jour* which, of course, means 'day'. The

Calculating the profit

purpose of the day books is to record, group and summarise particular types of transactions daily as they occur.

There is usually a *separate* day book, with its own name, for each of the main types of transactions that an organisation deals with. The actual names of them, and their functions, will differ according to the type of organisation concerned, and the nature of its work.

Activity 9.2

You have been appointed treasurer of a sports club with a large membership. In addition to the income from subscriptions and from court fees, the club runs a shop for the sale—both for cash and on credit—of equipment to the members. The club also has a refreshment bar.

Consider the different types of transactions that take place from day to day. What original documents, if any, are likely to exist in respect of them and how could the data from them be grouped and fed into the accounting system? What safeguards could be developed to prevent any of the original documents going astray?

9B. Day Books of Commercial Concerns

Day books show the nature of the work of the organisation concerned. The main business of commercial concerns is buying and selling goods, very often on credit, and there are four important areas to consider:

(i) credit purchases;
(ii) credit sales;
(iii) returns-in;
(iv) returns-out.

1. Purchases day book

The purpose of the purchases day book (sometimes called the purchases *journal*) is to record the appropriate details of trading goods (i.e. goods intended for re-sale in the normal course of trade), which have been bought *on credit*. It does not record the purchase of goods for cash (which are entered directly into cash or bank account), nor is it concerned with the purchase of *capital* goods, such as fixed assets (which are entered in a special day book known as a journal, dealt with later in this unit). This is important to remember, as it is vital that only exactly similar transactions are grouped together in it.

The information needed for writing up the purchases day book is obtained from the relevant original document—i.e. the invoices received in respect of the purchase of trading goods. The information that the accountant will need from the document is:

(i) the name of the person or firm from which the goods have been purchased;
(ii) the date of the transaction;
(iii) the amount owing as a result of the transaction.

This is the basic information that is recorded in the purchases day book. Sometimes, details of the individual goods that have been purchased are listed, but this is unnecessary if the invoices are properly filed. In addition, the amount of any *trade* discount (see page 8) is sometimes recorded, but this is not normally necessary since it is recorded on the invoice, and is not entered in the accounts in any case. The important thing is that the actual amount owed *should* be listed.

From time to time, a *posting run* is carried out. This involves posting the total of the day book for the period of the posting run to the debit

A closer look at trading

of purchases account, and crediting the individual creditors' accounts with the relevant amounts.

In the past, day books used to be entered up by hand from the original invoices, and the entries to the ledger made as a separate operation. This was a long and tedious job and increased the risk of errors. In these days of mechanised or computerised accounts, it is possible to program a machine to compile the purchases day book (and to keep a running total to be posted to the purchases account), and to make entries in the personal ledger accounts, all in one operation.

Since ledger postings follow from the entries in the day book, it is important to be able to link the entry in the day book with the subsequent posting of the ledger. This is necessary both for audit reasons and for general checking purposes. If the day book is entered up by hand, a reference to the page number of the ledger entry can be made in the single column that usually appears to the left of the cash column—the **folio column**. An entry can also be made in the folio column of the ledger as a cross-reference to the day book. This provides what is known as the *audit trail*; it should be possible for an auditor to trace a transaction through the books from the original invoice to the final postings in the ledger. Alternatively, the creditor concerned may be identified by a code number. If ledger accounts are held on a loose-leaf or card system and are filed alphabetically, it may not be necessary to cross-reference in this way.

The mechanics of a simple purchases day book and the subsequent ledger posting are illustrated in example 9.1.

Example 9.1

PURCHASES DAY BOOK

			£
May	5	Andrews Ltd	150 000
May	7	Black & Co.	360 000
May	9	Candy & Rice	580 000
May	10	Featherstone Inc.	20 000
May	11	Wessex Stone	680 000
			1 790 000

LEDGER

Purchases account

May 11   Sundries   1 790 000

Andrews Ltd

May 5   Purchases   150 000

Black & Co

May 7   Purchases   360 000

Candy & Rice

May 9   Purchases   580 000

Featherstone Inc.

May 10   Purchases   20 000

Wessex Stone

May 11   Purchases   680 000

2. Sales day book

The procedure for the sales day book is essentially the same as that for the purchases day book, except that the original documents on which the procedure is based are copies of invoices issued. The information from them is summarised in the sales day book. The total of sales for the period concerned is then credited to the sales account, and individual entries made in the personal accounts of the various debtors concerned. Again, the complete operation is ideal for mechanisation or computerisation: the machine prepares the invoices (at the same time as other documents such as the consignment note and address labels), records the entry in the debtor's account, and accumulates (adds up) the total for the day book and the sales account.

3. Returns day books

Exactly similar procedures are followed for both returns-in and returns-out. The originating documents for the returns-in are the copies of credit notes issued. These are summarised in the returns-in day book and posted from there to the debit of the returns-in account (in total), and to the credit of the individual personal accounts of the debtors concerned.

The original documents for the returns-out are the credit notes received. After listing them in the returns-out day book, the total for the posting run goes to the credit of returns-out account, and the individual debits go to the personal accounts of the creditors concerned.

4. Other day books

It must be emphasised that the sales, purchases and returns day books are restricted to recording *credit* transactions within the normal course of trade. They are *not* used to record cash purchases and sales, nor for transactions outside the course of normal everyday trade—such as the purchase and sale of fixed assets.

Cash sales and purchases, after some form of initial recording such as a cash-till roll or a payment voucher, are posted directly to the cash or bank account; these serve as day books as well as ledger accounts, as will be seen in unit 18. Other specialised records—performing in essence the function of day books—may be used in any situation where much detail has to be recorded, but only summarised totals need be entered in the ledger. Wages are a good example: the pay-roll of almost all organisations of any size is maintained in a separate, specially ruled, wages book and only the summarised totals posted to the ledger.

One further day book—the *journal*—is so important that it deserves a special section to itself.

9C. The Journal

Activity 9.3

You have been asked to check the accounts of a club to which you belong. You find that, early in the year, cash account was credited and John Jakes personal loan account was debited with £500. John Jakes is the club secretary.

You also note that, later in the year, the balance of Jakes' loan account was transferred to the general expenses account, and the loan account closed.

Are you happy to pass the accounts as being satisfactory?

A closer look at trading

1. General principles

In addition to specialised day books such as the sales, purchases and returns day books, there is the **journal**. At one time, all transactions were entered in this book before being posted to the ledger, and the other day books did not exist. But now the journal is reserved for occasional or unusual transactions, which do not fit conveniently into other day books, and are not sufficient in number to justify a day book of their own.

Because the transactions concerned do not fit into any general pattern, it is not possible to post 'totals'. Each transaction has to be dealt with separately, and both the debit and the credit entries listed. So there is no question of 'speeding up' the process of ledger posting, and the sole functions are simply those of:

(i) listing the ledger postings to be made; and
(ii) giving more information about the transaction concerned with a reference to any appropriate authorisation.

When checking the club accounts in activity 9.3 above, you may well have thought that there should have been some explanation and authorisation concerning the granting of the loan to the secretary in the first place, and of 'writing it off' to general expenses in the second.

The journal has two cash columns on the right-hand side. One column is for the debit entry, which is listed first; the other column is for the credit entry, entered on the line below. These entries are followed by the **narration**. This is a brief statement explaining what the transaction was all about, and—if appropriate—stating the authority for having entered it.

Example 9.2

Enter the following in the journal of the ABC Club:

March 15   Loan of £15 cash made to Joe Brown
       20   Purchase of new equipment, on credit, from Hi-Fi Sales Ltd, £250
       30   Surplus equipment sold to Jean White, £50

Notes:
(i) The credit entry is usually indented (moved across to the right) in order to avoid confusion with the debit entry.
(ii) It used to be the practice to enter 'Dr' at the end of the first line immediately before the figures and to precede the credit entry by the word 'To', but this practice has now largely died out.

SOLUTION

		£	£
Mar 15	Joe Brown loan account	15.00	
	Cash account		15.00
	Loan to J. Brown authorised by the committee on 12 March.		
Mar 20	Equipment account	250.00	
	HiFi Sales Ltd		250.00
	Purchase of equipment per order dated 17 February		
Mar 30	Jean White	50.00	
	Equipment account		50.00
	Sale of surplus equipment authorised by Club President		

From time to time, the entries in the journal are posted to the ledger, any necessary references being made in the folio columns in order to provide the audit trail. The actual posting is usually carried out by a junior member of the accounting team, but the journal itself should be written up by someone with a good knowledge of accounting principles. One of the common reasons for the transaction being in the journal is that it is 'out of the ordinary', and the ledger entries for it may be complicated.

2. Common uses of the journal
The following are among the entries that will be found in journals:

(i) the 'opening entries' of a new organisation;
(ii) purchase and sale of fixed assets;
(iii) writing off bad debts and recording bad debts recovered (to be dealt with in unit 15);
(iv) correction of errors (to be dealt with in unit 27);
(v) transfers to the trading and profit and loss account at end of the accounting period.

Illustrations of item (ii)—the purchase and sale of fixed assets—were shown in example 9.1 above. Examples of the others, as they might appear in the journal, are as follows:

Jan 1	Premises account	12 000	
	Equipment account	9 000	
	Stock account	11 000	
	Cash account	2 000	
	Bank loan account		8 000
	Capital account		26 000

Opening entries on commencement of business.

| Aug 6 | Bad debts account | 360 | |
| | John Soper | | 360 |

Notice of Soper's insolvency received 5 August.

| Sep 8 | William Batty | 27 | |
| | Sales account | | 27 |

Correction of error; sale of goods to Batty on Aug 14 posted as £69 instead of £96.

Dec 31	Profit and loss	41 820	
	Advertising account		3 000
	Salaries account		36 450
	General expenses account		2 370

Transfer of nominal accounts to profit and loss account at end of financial year.

9D. Cycle of Operations—Updated

At the ends of units 4 and 7 diagrams showing the cycle of accounting operations were given. They were correct in respect of the work done up to those units. A more complex pattern has emerged with the work covered since, and the diagram should be redrawn as shown in figure 9.1.

A closer look at trading

Figure 9.1
The accounting cycle—updated.

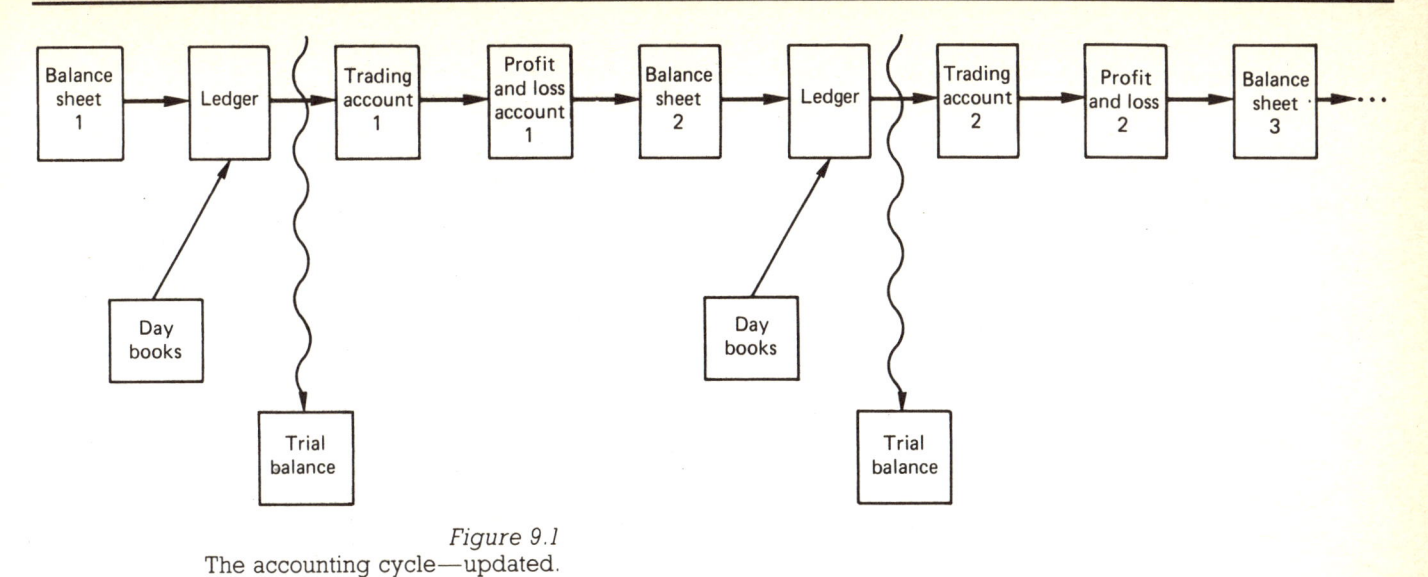

Activity 9.4

In which day book would the following transactions be entered:

(i) sales on credit to J. Smith;
(ii) cash purchases;
(iii) goods returned to J. Smith;
(iv) purchase of new premises;
(v) goods returned to a supplier.

With which ledger account is each concerned?

Check Your Understanding

1. What is meant by the term *original documents*?
2. Summarise the functions of the day books.
3. List the typical day books of a commercial concern. Describe the precise type of transactions to which each refers.
4. Copies of invoices that have been issued form the basis for entries in which day book? What entries are later made in the ledger?
5. Credit notes received are summarised in which day book? What entries are later made in the ledger?
6. What function or functions does the journal serve?
7. What is meant by the *narration* and what purpose does it serve?
8. Give an example of a typical journal entry.

Practical Assignments

1. a. From which original document will data concerning credit purchases be obtained?
   b. For what purpose are copies of invoices issued used in accounting?
   c. What are the original documents from which data concerning (i) returns-in and (ii) returns-out are obtained?
2. State in which book of account you would make the original entry for each of the following:

   a. purchase of goods on credit;
   b. purchase of new machinery on credit;
   c. credit sales;
   d. the return of goods previously sold to a customer;
   e. goods returned to a supplier;
   f. stocks destroyed by fire.

3. Explain how the following documents are used in the entry of data into the books of account in a conventional

93

Calculating the profit

double-entry book-keeping system:
a. copies of sales invoices;
b. an invoice received in respect of the purchase on credit of equipment to be used in the business;
c. credit notes received;
d. cheque book counterfoils;

4 Write up the journal in respect of the following transactions:
a. Machinery purchased from Tring & Co. £30 000.
b. Purchase of investments by cheque £6000.
c. Stock destroyed by fire £8000. Full liability is accepted by the Star Insurance Co. Ltd.
d. Additional capital paid into the firm's bank account by the proprietor, £10 000.
e. Loan of £5000 received from Enterprise Services Ltd and paid into the bank.

5 The Oregon Trading Co. issued the following invoices during the course of last week:

Day	Addressee	Amount (£)
Monday	Atcheson Ltd	540
	Batchelor & Co.	1240
	Watson & Truelove	980
Tuesday	H. Grantham	580
	Leeds Construction Ltd	6780
	Northern Lights Ltd	2460
Wednesday	Pompey Brick Co.	980
	Atcheson Ltd	620
	Watson & Truelove	400
Thursday	Fox and Coe	2567
	Apex Construction	666
	H. Grantham	3800
Friday	Atcheson Ltd	447
	Leeds Construction Ltd	3500

The company also issued the following credit notes:

Thursday	Atcheson Ltd	230
	Batchelor & Co.	120

Prepare the appropriate day books and post to the ledger.

6 Enter the following in the purchases day book and post to the ledger:

May 1 Purchased goods from Sing Ltd for £580 less 10% trade discount.
    5 Bought from Northern Traders Ltd, goods £5000.
    8 Bought from Electra Ltd, goods £4000 subject to 5% cash discount, one month.
   10 Purchased from Sing Ltd, goods £750 less 10% trade discount.
   15 Purchased from Johnson Ltd, goods £6000 subject to 20% trade discount and 5% cash discount, one month.

7 The following credit notes were received by Selina's Fashions:

May 5 From Centre Fashions Ltd
    10 metres material invoiced Apr 15 at £3 per metre
May 10 From Dressy Wholesalers Ltd
    5 dresses stained in transit invoiced on April 1 at £540 less 10% trade discount.
May 20 From Baldwin and Baldwin
    2 doz handbags not up to sample invoiced April 5 at £20 each less 20% trade discount $2\frac{1}{2}$% cash discount three months.

Write up the day book concerned, showing clearly the amounts to be posted to the ledger.

8 From the following details, enter up the purchases, sales, returns-in and returns-out day book of Cave and Cave, and post the relevant amounts to the ledger:

Feb 5 Credit purchases from Upton Ltd £300, O'Donnell & Co. £750 and French & Co. £600.
    8 Credit purchases from Oaklands Ltd £3000, J. and T. Kensington £2500 and Walton Industries £2750.
   10 Credit sales to B. Barker £1500, and I. Smith £4000.
   11 Credit sales to H. Horner £900 and G. Kirby £1250.
   13 Goods returned to Oakland Ltd £600 and to J. and T. Kensington £320.
   14 Goods returned to Horner £60 and Kirby £250.
   16 Goods purchased on credit Eros Ltd £2500 and from T. Oliver £1500.
   18 Goods returned to Eros Ltd £30 and to Oliver £100.
   19 Credit sales to Lanchester Sports £3500.
   24 Credit sales to Universal Trading Co. £4000.
   27 Goods returned by Lanchester Sports £5000.

9 Sheila works as a sole trader and on 1 Jan 19-1 had the following assets and liabilities: cash-at-bank £8000; stock £40 000; debtors—L. Kitchener £750, J. Fox £100; creditors—Suppliers Ltd £2000, Highlights Ltd £1500; premises £30 000; fittings and furnishings £8000.
Prepare her balance sheet at this point and open her ledger with the appropriate balances. Then enter the following transactions in the appropriate day book. At the end of the month, post the relevant amounts to the ledger.
(*Note*: Cash transactions should be posted directly to the bank account and not entered in a day book.)

		£
Jan 1	Drew from bank for office cash	500
3	Paid general expenses by cheque	100
5	Kitchener returned goods	20
8	Sales takings banked	2000
9	Paid Suppliers Ltd £2000 less 5% cash discount	
10	Purchased from Suppliers Ltd, goods £3000 subject to 10% trade discount	
11	Paid takings into bank	1500
12	Paid Highlights Ltd in settlement	1475

15	Received from Highlights Ltd, goods	2000
16	Sales takings to date, banked	3500
17	Returned damaged goods to Suppliers Ltd	300
18	Received goods from Highlights Ltd £400 subject to 10% trade discount	
19	Sold goods on credit to L. Kitchener	40
20	Sold goods to J. Fox on credit	500
21	Purchased office fittings and equipment on credit from Acme Shop Fitters Ltd	3000
25	J. Fox returned faulty goods	40
26	Returned the goods received from Highlights Ltd on January 16, not as ordered	
27	Purchased goods from P. and Q. Ltd	2000
28	Paid general expenses by cheque	500
31	Paid wages of assistant by cheque	320
	Closing stock	40 320

Extract a trial balance; then prepare a trading and profit and loss account for the month of January, and a balance sheet as at 31 January 19-1.

PART THREE
Multiple-choice test

Homework

In each of the following, state which option best answers the question.

1. A firm's rent account has a debit entry for £800. This represents an amount
   a. paid in respect of rent ✓
   b. received in respect of rent
   c. owed to the firm for rent
   d. owed by the firm for rent

2. The entries in a firm's ledger for stock sold to it by ABC Ltd would be

Debit	Credit
a. stock account	purchases account
b. ABC Ltd	stock account
c. ABC Ltd	sales account
d. purchases account	ABC Ltd ✓

3. Accounting operations follow a sequence of
   a. original documents, subsidiary books, ledger posting, final accounts ✓
   b. original documents, ledger posting, subsidiary documents, final accounts
   c. final accounts, subsidiary books, ledger posting, original documents
   d. subsidiary books, original documents, ledger posting, final accounts.

4. If a firm has made a trading profit, it means that the cash and bank balances
   a. will be greater than previously ✓
   b. will be less than previously
   c. are likely to be unaffected
   d. may either be greater or less than previously

5. Which of the following is likely to have a debit balance in the ledger?
   a. personal accounts of those to whom the firm owes money
   b. the proprietor's capital account
   c. personal accounts of those who owe money to the firm
   d. nominal accounts in respect of income received by the firm

6. Personal accounts appear in the
   a. trading account
   b. profit and loss account
   c. trading and profit and loss account ✓
   d. balance sheet

7. If at the end of a trading period a firm's cash and bank balances are low, it means the firm
   a. has purchased a lot of goods
   b. is making a loss
   c. is making a profit
   d. may be making either profits or losses ✓

8. The following information refers to the affairs of a trader:

	Position at Start of year £	End of year £
Stocks	150 000	140 000
Debtors	25 000	28 000
Creditors	85 000	62 000
Cash	122 000	151 000
Fixed assets	200 000	220 000
Loan	–	8 000

   The trader's profit or loss for the year was:
   a. £27 000 loss
   b. £57 000 profit
   c. £73 000 loss
   d. £27 000 profit

9. Debit balances in ledger accounts may refer to
   a. income or assets
   b. income or liabilities
   c. expenses or assets ⓒ
   d. expenses or liabilities

10. A payment by cheque in respect of advertising should be recorded in the ledger by

Debit	Credit
a. general expenses account	cash account
b. advertising account ✓	bank account
c. general expenses account	advertising account
d. advertising account	cash account

11. A trader purchases goods for £5000 and re-sells half of them for £6000. His gross profit is
    a. £1000
    b. £2500
    c. £3000
    d. £3500 ✓

12. Which of the following normally has a credit balance:
    a. bank account
    b. purchases account
    c. sales account
    d. stock account

13. The purchases day book is entered up from information obtained from
    a. invoices received ✓
    b. copies of invoices issued
    c. cash receipts issued
    d. delivery notes received

97

Calculating the profit

14 The double-entry system concerns
a. all accounting records
b. subsidiary books and the ledger
c. the ledger, trading and profit and loss account, and the balance sheet
d. the ledger, trading and profit and loss account only ✓

15 An item for £300 appears in the credit column of a trial balance in respect of rent. This means that £300 rent
a. has been paid ✓
b. has been received
c. is owing
d. has been overpaid

16 Information from copies of credit notes issued would be used in making up the
a. purchases day book
b. returns-in day book
c. sales day book
d. returns-out day book ✓

17 An invoice is received for £200 less 10% trade discount and 5% cash discount and is paid immediately. The amount debited to purchases account in respect of the transaction would be
a. £171
b. £180 ✓
c. £190
d. £200

18 Which of the following is not a book of original entry:
a. sales day book
b. ledger ✓
c. purchases day book
d. journal

19 A net loss is indicated by a
a. debit balance in the profit and loss account
b. credit balance in the trading account
c. credit balance in the profit and loss account ✓
d. debit balance in the trading account

20 Information for the returns-out day book is obtained from
a. debit notes received
b. debit notes issued ✓
c. credit notes received
d. credit notes issued

21 The 'continuity' convention assumes that a firm's affairs
a. are not likely to undergo fundamental change
b. do not relate to a particular accounting year
c. should be regarded as 'on-going' for the time being ✓
d. are not likely to be wound up

22 Trade discount received by a trader is entered in
a. discount-received account
b. discount-allowed account
c. trade discount account
d. none of the ledger accounts ✓

23 In adding up the sales account, an entry for £10 is mistakenly read as £100. The error will cause gross profit to be
a. overstated by £90 ✓
b. understated by £110
c. understated by £90
d. overstated by £110

24 The rule that profits should not be assumed until they have actually been made is known as the convention of
a. materiality
b. prudence ✓
c. continuity
d. consistency

25 Information for the sales day book is obtained from
a. invoices received
b. copies of invoices issued ✓
c. cash payments received
d. delivery notes issued

26 A firm is allowed both trade and cash discount. In the ledger accounts
a. both trade and cash discount are posted
b. the trade but not the cash discount is posted ✓
c. the cash but not the trade discount is posted
d. neither the cash nor the trade discount is posted

27 'Net sales' equals sales minus
a. returns-in ✓
b. carriage-out
c. carriage-in
d. returns-out

28 The total of the sales day book at the end of the accounting period is transferred to the
a. credit of the trading account
b. debit of the respective personal accounts
c. debit of stock account
d. credit of the sales account ✓

29 The purchase account is over-cast by £5000. This error will
a. increase gross and net profit
b. decrease gross and net profit ✓
c. affect neither gross nor net profit
d. affect gross profit only

30 A journal is used
a. to reduce the amount of posting in the ledger
b. in order to satisfy legal requirements
c. because it is an essential part of the double-entry system
d. so that detailed information concerning particular transactions is available ✓

31 The rule that the same accounting rules and procedures should always be followed is known as the convention of
a. consistency ✓
b. continuity
c. perpetuity
d. prudence

32 Discount allowed by a creditor is entered in a firm's
a. discount-allowed account
b. discount-received account ✓
c. trade discount account
d. trading account

33 The purpose of the subsidiary records is to
a. record transactions not recorded elsewhere
b. summarise particular types of common transactions
c. provide additional information to that recorded in the ledger
d. feed information into the final accounts

34 Gross profit is equal to
a. net sales less cost of goods sold ✓
b. net profit less indirect expenses
c. net profit less direct expenses
d. gross sales less direct expenses

35 The 'cost of goods sold' is calculated by adding
  a. opening and closing stock and deducting purchases
  b. purchases to opening stock and deducting closing stock
  c. opening stock and purchases, and deducting these from closing stock and sales
  d. sales and closing stock, and deducting opening stock and purchases

36 Nominal accounts refer to
  a. items of income and expenditure
  b. assets and liabilities
  c. accounts in the names of individuals
  d. capital accounts

37 Which of the following ledger accounts can never have a debit balance
  a. capital account
  b. rent account
  c. returns-out account
  d. bank account

38 If a retailer has a profit margin of 33.3%, his mark-up will be
  a. 25%
  b. 33.3%
  c. 50%
  d. 66.6%

39 If you wished to check the accuracy of a purchases day book, to which of the following would you refer:
  a. invoices received
  b. copies of invoices issued
  c. credit notes received
  d. copies of credit notes issued

40 A retailer bought £6000 worth of goods subject to 20% trade discount, 10% cash discount one week, 2½% cash discount one month, net thereafter. If he settles the bill 21 days later, he would pay
  a. £6000
  b. £4800
  c. £4680
  d. £4320

PART FOUR
More About Profit

UNIT 10 CALCULATING PROFIT SOME COMPLICATIONS

Before you read this unit, try activity 10.1.

Activity 10.1

Basil Smith is a hire-car operator. He started his business on May 1, and in his first month of business he earned £1430 cash. From this, he paid out £386 for petrol, £154 general running expenses and £100 for hire of garage. At the end of the month, he owed £55 for petrol.

In June, he earned £1510, from which he paid out £508 for petrol—this included the £55 owing from the previous month. He also paid £160 general running expenses and £100 for the hire of his garage. There were no debts owing at the end of the month.

(i) *What were the differences between his cash receipts and cash payments at the end of each month?*
(ii) *What do you consider was his profit for each month?*
(iii) *Which of the two months was the better one from a business point of view?*

10A. Accrued Charges

1. What profit really is

Basil Smith's experience is not an unusual one. Most businesses will have debts at the end of one trading period which will be carried forward and paid early in the next. The important question is: How does this situation affect profit?

In working through activity 10.1 you should have found that, in May, Basil Smith actually received £790 more from his business than he paid out. But in June the difference was only £742.

Does this mean that, in May, he made more profit than he made in June? If so, then what we are saying is that he made a bigger profit in May than in June, simply because he did not pay all of his bills!

'Making profit' is not the same as receiving cash. Turn back and revise the objectives of the accounting system, which we listed on page 4. We saw that the idea behind profit is to calculate how well the business is running. It cannot be said to be running more efficiently because the owner is not paying his or her bills!

Profit is the difference, *not* between cash receipts and payments, but between:

(i) the **income** that has actually been *earned* in a period (whether or not that income has been received), and
(ii) the **expenditure** that has been *incurred* in the period (whether or not those expenses have been paid).

The terms *income* and *expenditure* must always be used strictly within those definitions.

More about profit

2. Accrued charges and profit

Expenses that are owing at the end of a period are known as **accrued charges**, or simply as **accruals** for short. It is essential that they be added to actual payments if a proper view of profit is to be obtained.

This means that the correct calculation of profit for each of the two months for Basil Smith's hire-car operation (activity 10.1) becomes:

	May		June	
	£	£	£	£
Income earned		1430		1510
Expenditure incurred				
Petrol: paid	386		508	
add owing	55			
less paid for May			55	
	441		453	
General expenses	154		160	
Garage rent	100		100	
Total expenditure incurred		695		713
Profit		735		797

We see that although Basil's net cash receipts were higher in May than in June, his profit was in fact less.

3. Book-keeping for accrued charges

The book-keeping procedures for accruals are quite simple. Any payments actually made during the trading period are entered up in the usual way—i.e. *credit* to bank or cash, and *debit* to the expense account concerned. Any amount owing at the end of the period is added to that which has already been paid (enabling the full *expenditure incurred* to be written off to P&L) and is carried down to the credit on the account for the new period. This credit balance must appear in the balance sheet as a current liability—which is, of course, what it is.

Basil Smith's petrol account for May would appear as follows (dates have been assumed for the actual payments for petrol):

			£				£
May 9	Cash		120	May 31	P&L		441
16	Cash		139				
23	Cash		127				
31	Balance	c/d	55				
			441				441
				June 1	Balance	b/d	55

Note: It is customary to date the balance carried down as the first day of the new period.

If a balance sheet is prepared as at 31 May, the amount of the balance will appear as an accrual immediately after the trade creditors:

	£	£
Current liabilities		
Trade creditors (say)	5000	
Accruals	55	
		5055

When the amount is eventually paid, it will disappear from the account and will not affect the figures, either in the profit and loss or in the balance sheet, in the following period. Basil Smith's petrol account, continued into June, might therefore appear as:

			£					£
Jun	5	Cash	55	Jun	1	Balance	b/d	55
	12	Cash	127		30	P&L		453
	19	Cash	185					
	26	Cash	141					
			508					508

Notes
(i) The above account is a *continuation* of the one for May and not a separate one. The entry for the balance b/d for June 1 is, in fact, the credit balance that appeared at the end of the account in May.
(ii) The charge to P&L for June is less than the payments during June—this is because of the £55 charge to May.

Activity 10.2

A club's accounting year ends on 31 December. During the year to 31 December 1981, quarterly payments were made for electricity by cheque as follows:

£148 on April 28 for the period January–March 1981
£130 on August 15 for the period April–June 1981
£94 on October 5 for the period July–September 1981

At the end of the financial year, it was estimated that approximately £160 was owing for the period October–December 1981.

During the year to 31 December 1982, the payments were:

£156 on February 14 for the period October–December 1981
£178 on May 5 for the period January–March 1982
£160 on August 30 for the period April–June 1982
£130 on October 15 for the period July–September 1982

At the end of the second financial year, it was estimated that approximately £200 was owing for the period October–December 1982.

(i) *Write up the club's electricity account for the two years, showing clearly the amounts transferred to P&L at 31 December of each of the two years.*
(ii) *State what entry will be made in each of the two balance sheets.*
(iii) *Do you think it matters that the estimate for electricity owing at 31 December 1981 was slightly more than the amount of the bill that was paid on 14 February?*

A situation can arise in which there is an accrual at the end of the year for an item in which there is not an existing account. The entries are quite simple, namely:

Debit P&L account with the amount owing.
Credit Expense account concerned (this will mean opening a new one in the ledger).

The credit balance will, of course, appear in the balance sheet together with the other accruals.

More about profit

10B. Pre-payments

Activity 10.3

Tom Cobley runs a consultancy business and regularly receives £3600 each month in fees. His regular monthly expenses amount to £1250; in addition, on April 1, he paid his rates for the forthcoming year of £2400.

(i) *What was the difference between Cobley's cash receipts and payments for the month of April?*
(ii) *Did he make a profit or a loss in April, and how much was it?*
(iii) *How successful was he likely to be in May compared with April?*

1. Pre-payments and profit

If an allowance is to be made for expenses still owing at the end of a trading period, it is only reasonable that a similar allowance should also be made for expenses paid in advance.

Tom Cobley, in activity 10.3, is a typical example. Since he pays the whole of his rates for the year in April, his cash balance drops considerably as is shown by the following summary:

	£	£
Cash receipts in April		3600
Cash payments in April		
General expenses	1250	
Rates	2400	3650
Cash reduction		(50)

(In accountancy, brackets indicate minus or negative figures.)

But it would be wrong to argue that Cobley made a loss in April, and that his consultancy work for that month was less successful than that for the other months of the year—simply because he paid his full rates for the year in that month. To obtain a true and fair view of how his consultancy business operated during each month of the year, a fair proportion of the cost of rates should be allocated to each of the months that will benefit. A true picture of the *success*, or running efficiency, of his firm can only be obtained by charging against each month's income just that portion of the rates which refers to that month, and carrying forward any balance referring to future months. A correct view of Cobley's profit or loss for April is therefore shown by:

	£	£	£
Income earned in April			3600
Expenditure incurred			
General expenses		1250	
Paid for rates	2400		
Amount carried forward	2200		
		200	
			1450
Profit for the month			2150

2. Book-keeping for pre-payments

The book-keeping for pre-payments is simple and straightforward. The full amount paid must obviously be debited to the expense account concerned. The amount to be charged against profit and loss is then simply transferred to profit and loss at the end of the trading period concerned, and the balance is carried down. This balance will come down on the debit side and appear as an asset in the balance sheet. Cobley's rates account would therefore appear as:

			£				£
Apr 1	Cash		2400	Apr 30	P & L		200
					Balance	c/d	2200
			2400				2400
June 1	Balance	b/d	2200				

In the balance sheet, the amount of pre-payments at the date concerned is set out immediately after the normal trade debtors:

	£	£	£
Current assets			
Stock		90 000	
Debtors (say)	9 500		
Pre-payments	2 200	11 700	
Bank		15 000	
			116 700

Activity 10.4

A club commenced operations on 1 January 1971 with an accounting year to 31 December. At the end of March of its first year, the club acquired premises of its own and took out insurance to cover the building and its contents. The sum of £400 was paid on 1 April 1981 to cover the premiums (i.e. cost of the insurances) on both policies for one year as from that date. The policies were renewed on 1 April 1972 in the sum of £600, again for one year from that date. The increased sum was to cover additional fixtures and fittings acquired by the club.

Show the club's insurance account and the appropriate extracts from the balance sheets.

10C. Accruals and Pre-payments, and Examination Questions

Examination questions dealing with accruals and pre-payments sometimes require the writing-up of the expense account itself in a way similar to the examples and activities set out above. The question will require you to show the figure charged to P & L and the amount carried down to the next period—as either an asset or a liability.

A more common type of question takes the form of a trial balance with the expense items included, and with additional information being given regarding the accruals and pre-payments to be allowed for. The figures in the trial balance represent the actual payments made in respect of the expenses concerned. The question will require you to draw up the final accounts, making the appropriate adjustments to the expense figures in the trial balance. It will require you to 'visualise' the entries that would have been made in the ledger accounts had you been required to write these out. Have a go at one—if in difficulties, actually write out the ledger accounts concerned.

10D. The 'Matching' Convention

The idea of 'profit' as the difference between *income that has been earned* (whether or not received) and *expenditure that has been incurred* (again whether or not it has been paid) is crucial to a proper understanding of the accounting system, and to the correct calculation of profit or loss—which measures the efficiency with which organisations are operating. This brings us to a further accounting convention: it is known as the 'matching' or 'accruals' convention. The book-keeping for goods purchased and sold on credit, and that for accruals and pre-payments, are all examples of the convention in practice.

More about profit

> **Accounting Convention No. 6**
> **The Matching (or Accruals) Convention**
>
> The income earned in a trading period (whether received or not) should be matched against the expenditure incurred (whether paid or not) in order to obtain a true figure for profit.

Activity 10.5

The following trial balance was extracted from the books of Hensall Home Bakery at 31 December 1981:

	£	£
Capital		100 000
Loan		40 000
Cash	3 400	
Stock	45 200	
Sales		207 920
Purchases	143 900	
Advertising	800	
Rent	1 900	
Premises	94 000	
Wages	21 000	
Equipment	31 000	
General expenses	13 200	
Insurance	1 120	
Debtors and creditors	13 500	21 100
	369 020	369 020

Prepare the trading and profit and loss account for the year to 31 December 1981, and the balance sheet as at that date, taking into account:

(i) Stock at 31 December 1981 was valued at £50 500.
(ii) Interest at 10% per annum was owing on the loan for the full year.
(iii) Owing at 31 December in respect of:
   Wages   £500
   Advertising £300
(iv) Amounts paid in advance at 31 December
   Rent   £900
   Insurance £600

(*Answers*: gross profit £69 320; net profit £28 000)

Check Your Understanding

Complete the following:

1 The amount of *cash payments* and the total of *expenditure incurred* may differ because of ~~whether payment received/exp. paid (Time period)~~

2 *Income*, from an accounting point of view, refers to ~~amount earned in period~~

3 An accrual is ~~an Expense owing at end of period~~ and the ledger entries in respect of one is to debit ~~expense acc~~ and to credit ~~bank/cash~~.

4 A pre-payment is ~~expense paid in advance~~ and the ledger entries in respect of one is to debit ~~expense acc~~ and to credit ~~P+L~~.

5 Accounting for an accrual has the effect of ~~N affecting~~ (increasing/decreasing/not affecting) the amount actually paid on the expense item concerned. It also appears in the balance sheet as a ~~c/liability~~

6 Accounting for a pre-payment has the effect of ~~N/A~~ (increasing/decreasing/not affecting) the amount actually paid on the expense item concerned. It also appears as a ~~c/asset~~ in the balance sheet.

7 The principle of accounting for accruals and pre-payments is in accordance with the ~~Matching~~ convention.

Practical Assignments

1. a. Distinguish between an accrued charge and a pre-payment.
   b. Why is it important to allow for them when preparing a profit and loss account?

2. a. A firm rents an office block at a cost of £500 per month. During the year to 31 December 19-1, the firm paid £5500 for rent for the months January to November inclusive, but had not paid the rent (£500) for December, which remained owing. What figure will appear as regards rent in the:
   (i) bank account for the year to 31 December 19-1
   (ii) profit and loss account for the year ended 31 December 19-1
   (iii) balance sheet as at 31 December 19-1?
   b. What will each of these figures mean?

3. a. A firm started business on 1 January 1988 and on 1 April paid £400 in respect of insurance for one year in advance as from that date. Show the ledger account made up to the end of the financial year at 31 December 1988.
   b. The firm renewed the insurance policy on 1 April 1989 at the increased premium of £600. Show the same ledger account made up to 31 December 1989.
   c. On 1 April 1990, the insurance policy was again renewed, the premium being reduced to £500. Show the ledger account made up to 31 December 1990.
   d. What entries would appear in the balance sheet as at 31 December of each of the three years?

4. a. In the year to 31 March 19-1, a firm paid by cheque advertising costs of £24 000. A bill for £6000 in respect of further advertising was owing. Prepare the ledger account, showing clearly the amounts transferred to the profit and loss, and any balances carried down.
   b. During the year to 31 March 19-2, the same firm paid an additional £50 000 in advertising costs, and had bills owing at the end of the year of £8000. Continue its ledger account for the second year, again showing clearly the transfers to the profit and loss account at 31 March 19-2, and the balance (if any) carried down.
   c. During the year to 31 March 19-3, the firm paid bills for advertising amounting to £46 000. This included an amount of £10 000 paid in advance for a series of television advertisements, which are not to be screened until June 19-4. Continue the ledger account, and show the balances as at 31 March 19-3.
   d. State what entries would appear in the balance sheets as at 31 March of each of the three years.

5. The following is the trial balance of L. Piper at 31 December 1989:

	£	£
Capital		218 840
Stock at 1 Jan 1989	90 000	
Purchases	80 000	
Sales		160 000
Returns-in	2 800	
Returns-out		1 200
Carriage-in	360	
Carriage-out	1 280	
General expenses	40 200	
Wages	10 200	
Salaries	18 600	
Fixed assets	80 900	
Bank	60 200	
Creditors		4 500
	384 540	384 540

Stock at 31 December 1989 was valued at £84 000. The figure for general expenses includes an amount of £300 prepaid for the year 1990. Wages owing at year-end amounted to £1300.

Prepare Piper's trading and profit and loss account for the year ended 31 December 1989, and the balance sheet as at that date.

6. The following is the trial balance of Alison Rigg, who owns an advertising agency, at 31 December last.

	£	£
Capital		56 650
Income earned		53 060
Premises	40 000	
Cash	5 610	
Advertising	6 000	
Loan		10 000
Motor vehicles	25 000	
Rent	1 500	
Insurance	5 200	
Sundry debtors	6 400	
Salaries	23 260	
Sundry creditors		5 260
Equipment	12 000	
	124 970	124 970

Prepare the profit and loss account of the agency for the year to 31 December, and the balance sheet as at that date, taking into account:
a. advertising is to be written off over a three-year period;
b. £300 of the rent refers to the current year;
c. insurance is £1000 prepaid;
d. salaries accrued at the end of the year amount to £2500.

7. Andrew Sharp is in business as a general dealer. At 31 March 1990, he extracted the following trial balance from his books:

	£	£
Capital		83 548
Sales		142 880
Stock at 1 April 1989	52 400	

Purchases	57 700	
Returns-in	1 000	
Loan		3 000
Returns-out		2 500
Carriage-in	3 000	
Carriage-out	1 200	
Wages	10 000	
Motor vehicles	57 080	
Cash in hand and at bank	2 164	
Debtors and creditors	5 300	3 246
Office equipment	18 000	
Stationery and printing	1 500	
Rent	2 000	
Insurances	2 850	
Electricity	800	
Advertising	3 000	
Salaries	13 350	
Travelling expenses	2 250	
Postage	1 580	
	235 174	235 174

The following amounts were owing at 31 March: stationery £150; rent £500; electricity £150.

Of the insurance, £300 referred to the year beginning 1 April 1990 and it was agreed that £1000 of the advertising should also be charged against the following year.

Stock at the end of the year was valued at £64 080.

Prepare Sharp's trading and profit and loss account for the year ended 31 March 1989, and his balance sheet as at that date.

8 Terry Adams runs a business operation under the trade name Adams Car Insurance Services. At 30 September 1989, he extracted the following trial balance from his ledgers:

	£	£
Capital		36 000
Advertising	7 200	
Mortgage		5 000
Cash	4 000	
Debtors and creditors	5 000	6 000
Equipment	20 000	
Premises	40 000	
Commission earned on sales of insurance policies		59 400
Rates	6 000	
Electricity	3 400	
Office expenses	13 800	
Salaries	7 000	
	106 400	106 400

Draw up his profit and loss account for the year ended 30 September 1989, and his balance sheet as at that date, taking into account the following:
a. The amount for rates includes £1000 paid in respect of the year beginning 1 October 1989.

b. It was estimated that £500 was owing for electricity as at 30 September 1989.

9 Joanne Harrison is in business as a retailer. On 31 December last, the following trial balance was extracted from her books:

	£	£
Cash	260	
Bank	2 180	
Stock (as at 1 January previous)	24 500	
Interest on loan	800	
Returns in and out	2 180	3 300
Purchases and sales	147 820	177 400
General expenses	236	
Fixtures and fittings	10 000	
Premises	50 000	
Debtors and creditors	12 500	20 790
Carriage-in	580	
Capital		62 000
Rent received		1 000
Wages and salaries	30 488	
Loan		20 000
Carriage-out	540	
Advertising	1 290	
Insurance	1 116	
	284 490	284 490

You are required to draw up the trading and profit and loss account for the year ended 31 December, and the balance sheet as at that date, taking into account the following:
a. A further £250 was owing in respect of advertising.
b. £300 of the amount paid for insurance referred to the following year.
c. Stock on hand at 31 December was valued at £25 300.

10 During the first year of its operation, an organisation paid the following sums in respect of insurance:

Type of insurance	Date paid	£
Burglary	1 April 1988	360
Plate glass	1 May	240
Motor vehicle	1 July	480
Accident	1 Sep	240
Fidelity	1 January 1989	120

In each case, the premium was for one year's cover in advance. The firm's accounts are made up to 31 March each year. Each of the above insurances was renewed on the date it fell due, the premiums remaining the same in each case except for motor vehicle insurance, which qualified for a 10% no-claims bonus in 1989 and a 25% no-claims bonus in 1990. Write up the insurance account to 31 March 1990, showing clearly the amounts transferred to the profit and loss account each year, and the amounts carried forward.

UNIT 11 CALCULATING PROFIT FURTHER COMPLICATIONS

Before you read this unit, try activity 11.1.

Activity 11.1

Your firm is owed three debts—£5 by Richard Green, £90 by Graham Brown and £900 by Sarah Black. All three have been on your books for some while, and you think it is doubtful whether the persons concerned intend to pay.

State, with reasons, the actions that you would take—or that could perhaps be taken—in respect of each.

11A. Bad Debts

1. Nature and accounting procedure

All firms that sell goods on credit have to face the problems of bad and doubtful debts [*or Bad Debts*]. These are debts which it is considered are unlikely to be paid—this may be because of the length of time they have been owing, or because you have received definite information that the debtor is insolvent, or possibly because he or she has moved, and the new address is not known.

The accounting procedure is simple. As soon as it is realised that there is little chance of a debt being paid, it should be cleared from the books. This is done by transferring it to a 'collecting box'—a *bad-debts account*—and then, at the end of the accounting period, transferring the total of that account to the debit of profit and loss, thus reducing the profit for the period. Both the transfer of the debt to the bad-debts account, and the subsequent clearing of the bad-debts account to the profit and loss, will require journal entries. Look at the following example:

Example 11.1

At the end of an accounting period, the following debts are among those in a firm's ledger:

    T. Anderson £500; C. Cliff £300.

The account for Terry Anderson has been outstanding for a considerable period and it is now considered unlikely that it will ever be paid. It is known that Celia Cliff is insolvent and has gone out of business. Again, it is unlikely that the debt will be paid in the near future. So the journal entries are as follows:

	£	£
Bad-debts account	800	
T. Anderson		500
C. Cliff		300
Bad debts written off.		
Profit and loss account	800	
Bad-debts account		800
Bad debts for year transferred to P & L.		

111

More about profit

2. Bad debts recovered

Sometimes, payments are received from debtors which long ago had been written off as bad. When this happens, the entries are simple:

Debit Bank (or cash) account.
Credit Bad-debts recovered account.

The entry does not record from whom the money was received. This is because there is no account in the ledger for the debtor (it was written off as bad long ago) and so—from an accounting point of view—the name of the person is not important. This does not stop the full details being recorded in the journal or in some other document.

At the end of the accounting period, the balance of the bad-debts recovered account is transferred to the credit of the profit and loss account.

3. Dishonoured cheques

A further complication can arise where a cheque has been received from a debtor and posted in the ordinary way, and then the cheque is *dishonoured*—which means that the debtor's bank has refused to pay it. This may arise for a number of reasons—the cheque may have been incorrectly drawn (written out), be unsigned, be 'stale' (more than six months old), or (more seriously) there may not have been sufficient funds in the account to meet it. Whatever the reason, banks usually write simply *Refer to drawer* on it and leave the payee to take it up with the person who issued it (the drawer).

Where a cheque has been returned in this way, the original entries made when it was received must be *written back*—that is, entries made on the 'opposite' sides in the original accounts concerned. This has the effect of cancelling the original entries. Any discount allowed at the time must also be written back.

Having written back the entries, the firm would have to decide whether it would be wise to write the debt off as bad, or whether to retain it on the books in the hope of obtaining settlement.

Example 11.2

On 1 June, a customer, George Green, purchased goods for £20 000. A cheque is received on 29 June for £19 000, the balance being discount-allowed at 5%. On 5 July, the cheque is returned marked 'R.D.' (refer to drawer). It is decided to retain the customer on the books as a debtor pending the result of legal action. Show the relevant accounts:

G. Green

Jun 1	Sales	b/f	20 000		Jun 29	Bank		19 000
						Discount-allowed		1 000
			20 000					20 000
Jul 5	Bank		19 000					
	Discount-allowed		1 000					

Bank account (extract)

Jun 29	G. Green		19 000	Jul 5	G. Green		19 000

Discount-allowed account

Jun 29	G. Green	*1 000*	Jul 5	G. Green	*1 000*

Note: The entries necessary to write the dishonoured cheque back are in *italics*. Notice how they have the effect of cancelling the original entries.

4. Insolvency

Care must be taken to distinguish between *insolvency* and *bankruptcy*. A person or a firm is **insolvent** if there is not enough cash available to pay the debts in full. The term **bankruptcy** only refers to persons, not to companies, and must only be used after a legal process has been followed, and a decree in bankruptcy issued. The effect of this is that an official known as a 'receiver' is appointed to take over the affairs of the bankrupt person, and to pay the creditors as much as possible. Although a person cannot be made bankrupt unless he or she is also insolvent, it is possible to be insolvent without being bankrupt.

A limited company cannot be made bankrupt. All that the courts can do if it is insolvent is to order that it be 'wound up'.

If one of the debtors of a firm is declared bankrupt, it means that the person concerned does not have sufficient money to pay his or her debts in full. But there may be some funds available, and these will be divided among all the creditors according to the amount each is owed—in other words, the dividend (as it is called) will be at so many pence in the pound owed. This means that if a person is owed £200 and a dividend of 20p in the pound is paid, the person will receive £40. The creditor receiving the amount will then have to decide what to do with the balance—whether to keep it on the books for the time being in the hope of a further dividend, or to write it off as bad and, if a further dividend is received, to treat it as a bad debt recovered.

A similar procedure is followed if a company is insolvent and is wound up.

Example 11.3

On 1 December, a firm has W. Green and B. Brown on its books as debtors for £600 and £700 respectively.

Dec 4 B. Brown pays her debt by cheque £650, discount-allowed £50.

10 The bank returns B. Brown's cheque marked 'Refer to Drawer'.

12 Notice is received that W. Green is bankrupt. An initial dividend of 25p in the pound is paid; a cheque for this amount—i.e. £150—is enclosed with the notice. It is decided to write the remainder off as a bad debt.

Show the relevant accounts.

W. Green

		£			£
1 Dec	Balance	600	12 Dec	Bank	150
				Bad debts	450
		600			600

B. Brown

		£			£
1 Dec	Balance	700	4 Dec	Bank	650
				Disc. allowed	50
		700			700
10 Dec	Returned cheque				
	Bank	650			
	Disc. allowed	50			

More about profit

```
                        Bank account (extract)
4 Dec   Brown         650     10 Dec   Returned cheque         650
  12    Green         150

                  Discount-allowed account (extract)
4 Dec   Brown          50     10 Dec   Brown (returned cheque)  50

                      Bad-debts account (extract)
12 Dec  Green         450
```

11B. Bringing Home the Bacon

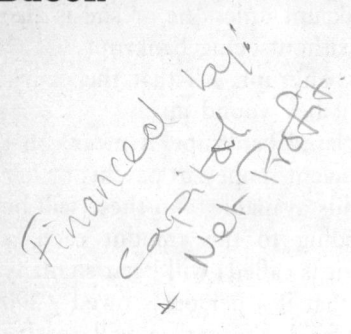

1. Drawings of cash

We have seen that, after the calculation of the net profit, the amount is added to the owner's capital—this is the correct procedure, but it is not the end of the story. Every business owner will need to take at least some of the profit out of the firm for his or her own use—it will, in fact, be personal income. In fact, in most firms, the owners withdraw cash for their own use regularly throughout the year—every week or every month.

The book-keeping for cash withdrawals of this nature is quite simple. At the time the money is taken, the entries are:

Debit Drawings account.
Credit Cash (or bank) account.

At the end of the year, the total of drawings account is transferred to the debit of capital account, so reducing the balance of that account. This means that an owner's capital account, at the end of the year, may appear as follows:

```
                        Capital account
                              £                                    £
19-1                                 19-1
Dec 31  Drawings        15 000       Jan  1   Balance        60 000
    31  Balance c/d     65 000       Dec 31   Net profit     20 000
                        80 000                               80 000
                                     19-2
                                     Jan  1   Balance b/d    65 000
```

In the balance sheet as at 31 December 19-1, the relevant figure for capital is the balance of the account—i.e. £65 000. It is customary—at least in examinations—to show how the figure has been made up. The entry would therefore appear as:

```
                £                                  £        £
Fixed assets:            Capital:
                         Balance at 1 Jan 19-1    60 000
                         Add Net profit           20 000
                                                  80 000
                         Less Drawings            15 000
                                                           65 000
```

2. Drawings of goods

It is not uncommon for business owners to take goods from the firm's stock for their own private use. This again amounts to 'drawings'. The entries will depend on whether the goods are being charged out at their cost price, or at their selling price. The entries are:

Debit Drawings account.
Credit Purchases account (if at *cost* price) or sales account (if at *selling* price).

If the drawings are recorded at cost price, this has the advantage that it keeps the goods concerned out of the normal trading of the firm, and the transaction therefore does not enter into the calculation of the gross profit.

3. Other benefits taken by the owner

The owner may receive other benefits from his or her firm. For example, the owner may use the firm's motor vehicles for private purposes, or the insurance of the owner's private premises may be covered by the general policy taken out by the firm. In each case, there should be a transfer of the appropriate amount from the expense account concerned to the drawings account.

Example 11.4

Show the ledger entries in respect of the following:

		£
Jan 1	Dickens & Co. paid insurance premium for the year (This premium included an amount of £100, which referred to the insurance of the owner's private house)	960
May 5	Paid motor-car running expenses (It is agreed that one-tenth of motor-car running expenses refer to the owner's use of the vehicle for private purposes)	1700

Insurance account

		£			£
1 Jan	Bank	960	31 Dec	Drawings	100
			31 Dec	P & L	860
		960			960

Motor expenses account

		£			£
5 May	Bank	1700	31 Dec	Drawings	170
			31 Dec	P & L	1530
		1700			1700

Drawings account (extract)

31 Dec	Insurance	100
31 Dec	Motor expenses	170

Activity 11.2

From the trial balance on page 116, draw up the trading and profit and loss account for the year to 31 March 19-2, and the balance sheet as at that date.

Note: The items in the trial balance have to be modified in respect of the adjustments listed. Remember the basic principles of double entry, and that each adjustment will require the modification of *two* terms in the trial balance.

More about profit

Trial balance at 31 March 19-2:	£	£
Capital		106 000
Stock at 1 April 19-1	50 000	
Purchases	75 000	
Sales		200 000
Drawings (cash)	10 000	
Bad debts	3 000	
Debtors and creditors	30 000	15 000
Bad debts recovered		2 500
Sundry expenses	86 000	
Sundry fixed assets	60 000	
Cash	9 500	
	323 500	323 500

Allowance should be made for the following:

(i) Stock at 31 March 19-2 was valued at £40 000.
(ii) No entries have been made in the accounts for two consignments (lots) of goods taken by the owner for his or her own use. One consignment consisted of raw materials to be charged at their cost price of £5000. The other consignment was of finished goods to be charged at their selling price of £3000.
(iii) It was decided to write off further debts amounting to £2000 as bad.

Check Your Understanding

1 Name and describe the convention that allows the practice of writing off debts as soon as it is clear that they are likely to be 'bad'.

2 State the ledger entries for:
   (i) a debt declared to be bad;
   (ii) a bad debt recovered.

3 What is meant by the *dishonour* of a cheque? List the ledger entries where a cheque is dishonoured which was accepted in payment of a debt and on which discount had been allowed.

4 Define precisely the difference between *insolvency* and *bankruptcy*.

5 What is the name of the procedure that should be followed if a company has more liabilities than it has assets?

6 What are the ledger entries if, for his own personal use, an owner:
   (i) withdraws cash from the firm;
   (ii) takes goods from the firm at cost price;
   (iii) takes goods from the firm at selling price?

Practical Assignments

1 Peters & Co. have an account on their books for Harry Smith with a debit balance for £540. The account has been outstanding for nearly two years and attempts to contact Smith have failed. It is decided to write the debt off as bad.
   a. State what is meant by a 'bad debt'.
   b. State the entries that will be made in order to write Smith's debt off.
   c. If the debt is written off as 'bad', does Smith cease to be liable for the amount?
   d. If, subsequently, the debt is paid, what entries will then be made in the ledger?

2 a. During the year ended 31 December last, the owner of a business withdrew a total of £15 600 cash from the firm for his personal use and also goods the cost price of which had been £850. Write up the drawings account as it would appear in the ledger *after* completion of the balance sheet as at 31 December last.
   b. What entries would have been made had the goods been charged to the owner at their selling price of £1120?

3 The ledger of Davis & Co. at 31 December last contained the following balances: capital £196 500; sundry fixed assets £212 840; debtors £2580; creditors £10 975; bank £1640; stock £30 600; purchases £56 340; sales £170 580; returns-in £680; returns-out £435; carriage-in £850; carriage-out £650; wages £25 430; salaries £16 650; sundry expenses £28 230.

No entries had been made for drawings by Davis for his own use of goods to the value (at cost) of £5000. He also decided to withdraw £2000 cash from the firm to finance a New Year party.

Stock at close amounted to £25 000.

Show the final accounts after allowing for the above.

Calculating profit

4 The following details refer to Horizon Leisure Services for the year ended 31 December last:

	£
Stock at 1 January	20 300
Purchases	69 750
Sales	180 050
Returns-in	4 850
Returns-out	3 000
Advertising	1 650
Insurance	3 200
Carriage-in	1 000
Carriage-out	2 000
Wages	20 250
Rent	2 300
Salaries	14 750
Proprietor's drawings	3 000
Debtors	7 300
Creditors	10 000
Capital	168 000
Cash	10 000
Sundry fixed assets	200 000
Bad debts	700

Stock at 31 December was valued at £35 000.

No allowance had been made for wages owing of £5000 and for a pre-payment of rent of £500. It was decided that further debts of £150 should be regarded as bad and written off. During the year, the proprietor had taken advantage of a holiday package offered by the firm at a sales price of £1000, and no entries had been made to record this in the books.

Show the trading and profit and loss account of the firm for the year to 31 December last, and the balance sheet as at that date.

5 The following information was extracted from the ledger and other records of Brian L. Zeebub at 31 December 19-1.

Trial balance at 31 December 19-1

	£	£
Capital at 1 January 19-1		257 420
Stock at 1 January 19-1	132 000	
Sundry debtors and creditors	36 000	120 200
Returns	720	640
Purchases and sales	126 280	366 380
Insurances	3 100	
Electricity	4 200	
Rents	3 000	860
Carriage inwards	320	
Wages	112 500	
Salaries	30 500	
Advertising	1 200	
Carriage outwards	580	
Drawings	8 000	
Mortgage		200 000
Premises	300 000	
Equipment	150 000	
Motor vehicles	20 000	
Cash: in-hand	2 300	
at-bank	14 800	
	945 500	945 500

Additional information at 31 December 19-1

	£
Stock at 31 December 19-1	125 200
Rent owing to B. L. Zeebub	400
Rent owing by B. L. Zeebub	150
Electricity owing	500
Insurance pre-paid	300

It is considered that £2500 owing by debtors should be regarded as bad.

The proprietor took for his own use goods that had cost £600. No entries had been made in respect of this.

B. L. Zeebub used one of his garages as a warehouse for some of his stock but this has never been recorded in the books of the firm. His accountant has advised him that this item, current value £5000, should be brought on to the books with effect from 1 January 19-1.

Answer the following questions:

a. In the trial balance, there are two entries on the same line for rent. What does each entry represent? Why have they not been combined into a net figure?

b. Why does the figure for stock at 31 December 19-1 not appear in the trial balance? Can the figure for closing stock ever appear in a trial balance?

c. What criteria can be used when deciding whether or not to write a debt off as bad?

d. Why is a distinction drawn between wages and salaries? On what basis are they differentiated?

e. What is meant by the term 'mortgage'. How does this item differ from other creditors?

f. Prepare the trading and profit and loss account of B. L. Zeebub for the year to 31 December 19-1, and his balance sheet as at that date.

UNIT 12 STOCK AND ITS COMPLICATIONS

Before you read this unit, try activity 12.1.

Activity 12.1

Brightgem Ltd manufacture jewellery mainly for the Christmas trade. Their purchases of 18-carat gold for manufacturing purposes during the financial year ended 31 December last were:

	Price (£/fine oz)	Purchases (fine oz)	Quantity used (fine oz)	Stock in hand (fine oz)	
Jan	175	300	100	200	(there was no opening stock)
Apr	215	400	250	350	
Jul	210	200	250	300	
Oct	225	100	160	240	

(i) *In how many different ways could Brightgem Ltd value its closing stock of 240 oz of gold?*
(ii) *Which way do you think would be the best, and why?*

12A. Valuation of Closing Stock

1. Valuation at cost

We saw in unit 7 that both the opening stock and the closing stock form an essential part of the calculation of the *cost of sales* in the trading account. If the figure for either of them is incorrect, then the calculation of gross profit will be affected. Try working out for yourself the effect upon gross profit if closing stock is either over-valued or under-valued.

The figure for closing stock is usually obtained by physical stock-taking. But this will only give a figure for the *quantity* of goods held in stock, and not its *value*. If a value is to be given to the stock, then further calculations are necessary.

The normal procedure is that stock should be valued at its cost price. To value it at its selling price would have the result of increasing profit—in other words, of assuming that a profit had been made which had not. This would be contrary to the prudence convention (see unit 7, page 74).

If the stock has been purchased at a constant price throughout the trading period, no great problems arise—it simply means multiplying the number of units that make up the closing stock by the purchase price. The situation becomes more difficult if stock has been purchased at different prices during the period. There are a number of different approaches to the problem; each has its advantages and its shortcomings.

(a) Ascertained, or 'unit', cost
Valuation of stock at cost presents no problems if it is known at exactly what price each unit was purchased. This is called the *ascertained cost* or *unit cost*. If, for instance, the records of Brightgem Ltd in activity 12.1 showed that the closing stock of 240 oz of gold was made up of 110 oz

purchased in April and 130 oz purchased in July, the valuation of the closing stock on this basis would be:

	£
110 oz at £215 per oz	23 650
130 oz at £210 per oz	27 300
240 oz	50 950

(b) FIFO (first in, first out)

It may be impossible—or at least too time-consuming—to match the various items in a large range of stock with the dates and prices at which individual batches had been purchased. So it is often assumed that stock is used in the order in which it is bought—i.e. that the stock that was 'first' into the stores is the 'first' to be issued or sold. This means that the closing stock is that which was bought most recently. On this basis, Brightgem's closing stock would be valued as:

	£
100 oz at £225 per oz	22 500
140 oz at £210 per oz	29 400
240 oz	51 900

FIFO has the advantage that it corresponds to the way in which most traders do, in fact, use their stocks. It is also simple to calculate. Its disadvantage is that it values the closing stock on the most recent prices—which very often tend to be the highest ones. This leads to a slightly higher profit figure than would otherwise be the case.

(c) LIFO (last in, first out)

LIFO assumes that the most recent stock to be purchased is that which is sold or issued first. If there have been several separate orders, and no stock is used until all orders have been received, then it means that any stock left over would be valued at the price of that first ordered. But it is more likely that, as stock comes in, some of it at least is used. In order to calculate the value of closing stock on a LIFO basis, it is necessary to compare the dates and quantities of stock received with the dates and quantities of stock issued, and to identify at which dates the closing stock was purchased. This means that you must maintain a 'running balance' of the purchase price of the units that make up the stock in hand.

If Brightgem Ltd used the gold as listed in the following table, then it is possible to show the running record. Note that if sales in any period exceed (are more than) the amount ordered in that period, the excess has to be deducted from the surplus stock purchased most recently before. This happens in the example below in both July and October, and the excess has to be deducted from the surplus of stock purchased in April.

	Price (£/fine oz)	Purchases (fine oz)	Quantity used (fine oz)	Stock in hand (fine oz)	LIFO cost of stock in hand
Jan	175	300	100	200	200 oz at £175/oz
Apr	215	400	250	350	200 oz at £175/oz
					150 oz at £215/oz
Jul	210	200	250	300	200 oz at £175/oz
					100 oz at £215/oz
Oct	225	100	160	240	200 oz at £175/oz
					40 oz at £215/oz

More about profit

On this basis, the valuation of the closing stock is:

	£
200 oz at £175	35 000
40 oz at £215	8 600
240 oz	43 600

In times of rising prices, LIFO has the advantage that it usually means that stocks are valued at a lower price than under FIFO. However, serious problems can arise if stock is *actually* rotated (used) on this basis—problems connected with obsolescence and deterioration of stock (e.g. stock getting out of date, out of use, going bad or off and getting damaged). Brightgem Ltd would not be likely to have this problem with gold, but a fruiterer would be in a different position! However, just because stock is *valued* on a LIFO basis, it does not mean that it has to be rotated or used on that basis.

(d) AVCO (average cost)

A fourth basis for valuation, sometimes used with commodities that vary a lot in cost, is their average cost of purchase. This means taking the *weighted average* of the purchases, and using this as the basis for the valuation of the closing stock. In the case of Brightgem Ltd, the calculation would be:

	Price (£/fine oz)	Purchases (fine oz)	Quantity used (fine oz)	Stock in hand (fine oz)	Total cost of purchases (£) (= price × purchases)
Jan	175	300	100	200	52 500
Apr	215	400	250	350	86 000
Jul	210	200	250	300	42 000
Oct	225	100	160	240	22 500
		1 000			203 000

$$\text{Average price per oz} = \frac{£203\,000}{1\,000} = £203$$

Valuation of the closing stock of 240 oz:

$$240 \times £203 = £48\,720$$

(e) What does it all add up to?

What conclusions can we draw from this? The value of Brightgem's closing stock varies, on the basis of the different methods above, from a low of £43 600 to a high of £51 900—a range that could make a difference of more than £8000 to the gross profit for the year. But does it matter if it is to be balanced out by the effect on the profit for the following year?

The answer is 'probably not', *provided* the same basis is employed each year. It would be bad accounting if the basis was varied each year in order to give the maximum (or minimum) profit for each year. Here we have a further example of the convention of consistency, also discussed in unit 7 (page 73).

2. Valuation other than at cost

There is one exception to the rule that stock should be valued at cost. This arises when the 'net realisable value' of the stock is *lower than*, not greater than, the cost price.

Stock and its complications

In the case of a normal retailer who buys goods and then re-sells them without processing (changing) them in any way, the net realisable value is in fact the selling price.

But a complication arises when work has to be performed on the stock before it can be sold. In such a case, we have to take a look at the *net realisable value*. The **net realisable value** (NRV) is the expected selling price less any expenses necessary to put the stock in a saleable condition.

The rule, therefore, is that:

Closing stock should be valued at the lower of cost or net realisable value.

Activity 12.2

Brightgem Ltd always value their closing stock on a FIFO basis and that valuation for the year ended 31 December last was £51 900. The costs of manufacturing the gold into saleable jewellery will amount to £10 500.

What figure should be included for closing stock in the trading account and the balance sheet if the anticipated selling price of the stock, when manufactured, will be (i) £75 000, (ii) £49 000?

12B. Delayed Stock-taking Calculations

It is often not possible to stock-take on the precise date for which the information is required. In such cases, stock-taking is performed as soon as is convenient afterwards and a calculation made bearing in mind the amount of the purchases and of the sales *at cost price* between the date of the stock-taking and the date for which the stock figure is required. The purchases have to be *deducted* because they would not have been in stock at the required date, and the sales have to be *added* because they would have been in stock.

In examination questions, sales are often quoted at their selling price with the percentage to be allowed as profit. Considerable care must be taken to check whether the profit is given as a percentage of selling price or of cost price, as this will greatly affect the calculation.

If you are not happy with 'cost-price/selling-price' calculations, work through 'Coping with Percentages' (appendix A on page 311).

Example 12.1

A supermarket's accounting year ended on 30 April, which happened to be a Tuesday. Stock-taking could not be carried out until the following week-end, when the following information was available (£m = million pounds):

	£m
Stock as valued on Sunday 5 May	212.4
Net purchases, 1–4 May	44.6
Net sales, 1–4 May	51.0
Mark-up on cost, 20%	

SOLUTION

(i) Reduction of sales to cost price:

$$\frac{£51m \times 100}{120} = £42.5m$$

(ii) Stock at 30 April:

	£m
Stock at 5 May	212.4
Add: Sales at cost, 1–4 May	42.5
	254.9
Less: Purchases, 1–4 May	44.6
Stock at 30 April	210.3

More about profit

A similar type of calculation arises when it is necessary to 'calculate forward'—i.e. to pick up the figure for a previous stock-take and to project it forward—this time *adding* purchases and *deducting* sales. This situation can arise when stock-taking is carried out *before* the end of the financial year, and it also arises when it is necessary to calculate the value of stock destroyed in a fire or flood, or which has been stolen. In such cases, it may be necessary to make an additional allowance for any stock salvaged or retrieved.

Example 12.2

On the night of 28 April, a firm had one of its warehouses destroyed by fire. The following information is available:

	£
Value of stock at 31 March previous	38 500
Purchases, 1–28 April	18 000
Sales, 1–28 April	27 000
Value of stock salvaged from the fire	5 000
Profit margin, 30% of selling price	

SOLUTION

(i) Calculation of sales at cost:
(note that on this occasion the profit is given as a percentage of selling price, not of cost price)

$$\frac{£27\,000 \times 70}{100} = £18\,900$$

(ii) Calculation of stock destroyed in fire:

	£
Stock at 31 March	38 500
Add: Purchases, 1–28 April	18 000
	56 500
Deduct: Sales at cost, 1–28 April	18 900
Stock at 28 April	37 600
Deduct: Stock salvaged	5 000
Value of stock destroyed in fire	32 600

Activity 12.3

The owner of Pluto Fashions carried out a stock-check at the end of the financial year. The check indicated that the stock had cost £80 000 and had an expected re-sale value of £100 000. The figures were handed to the firm's accountant, who produced a set of draft final accounts, based on normal accounting conventions, which showed a net profit of £29 000. Following a more detailed check, the following facts were discovered:

(i) A consignment of stock had been completely omitted. This was sold shortly after the end of the financial year for £2000, a mark-up of 25% on cost.

(ii) Various materials that had been damaged by water from a burst pipe had been included at their cost of £800. It is planned to sell the materials to staff for £300.

(iii) Supplies from Ajax Ltd had been included at their invoice price of £3500. Ajax always invoice goods subject to trade discount of 20% and cash discount of 10% if settlement is within one month.

(iv) A batch of goods that had been purchased some while ago for £1300 had been included. The cost of buying a similar batch now would be £1700.

(v) A consignment of materials had been included at its cost price of £750. Wages and other costs in processing the materials for re-sale are expected to amount to £320. When processed, the materials will be sold for £950.

Calculate a revised stock figure taking account, where necessary, of the effect of the above items; and an adjusted figure for profit taking account of the changed stock valuation.

Check Your Understanding

1. The valuation of stock at selling price and not at *possible* selling price is in accordance with which convention?
2. What is meant by FIFO?
3. What is meant by LIFO?
4. In a time of rising price levels, would FIFO or LIFO give the highest value for closing stock?
5. What is the effect of valuing stock at a higher figure:
   (i) in the current accounts;
   (ii) in the subsequent year's accounts?
6. What is the main advantage of FIFO over LIFO?
7. What is meant by NRV? Under what circumstances is it used as a basis for valuing stock?
8. How does the convention of consistency relate to closing stock?
9. Outline the main steps in the calculation of a value for closing stock when physical stock-taking has had to be delayed.
10. A large quantity of stock has been destroyed by fire. Some of the remainder was damaged by the water used to put out the fire, and by the heat generated by the fire. The last stock-take was two months ago. How would you set about calculating the value of stock remaining after the fire, and what additional information would you want?

Practical Assignments

1. What is meant by the
   a. FIFO,
   b. LIFO,
   c. AVCO
   methods of stock valuation? Give an example of each.

2. a. What is meant by the statement *stock should be valued at the lower of cost or net realisable value*?
   b. Raw materials were purchased by a firm for £280 000. They have been partly processed but will require further processing costing £10 000 to be carried out before they can be sold.
   At what price should the stock of raw materials be valued for balance sheet purposes if the anticipated selling price, when all processing has been completed, is likely to be £310 000?
   What would be the position if, as a result of a downturn in trade, the likely selling price was
   (i) £295 000, (ii) £283 000?

3. a. Explain, with an example, whether the FIFO or the LIFO basis of stock valuation will give the highest profit in a period of rapidly rising prices.
   b. If a firm overvalues its closing stock in one period, what effect will it have on the gross profit of
      (i) the period concerned;
      (ii) the subsequent period?

4. In January 1990, the Red Brick Construction Company was formed. Bricks were purchased during the first six months of the year as follows:

1 January	50 000 at £180 per thousand
1 February	70 000 at £200 per thousand
1 April	60 000 at £210 per thousand
1 June	30 000 at £220 per thousand

   The consumption of bricks during the months stated amounted to

January	30 000	April	20 000
February	25 000	May	40 000
March	40 000	June	20 000

   Calculate the value of the bricks in stock at 30 June 1990 on a LIFO, a FIFO and an AVCO basis.

5. The offices and warehouse of a trader were destroyed by fire on 10 April 1990. The stock was completely destroyed by the fire. Some of the accounting records were salvaged, and it proved possible to extract the following information:
   a. Stock at cost on 31 December 1989 was £145 600.
   b. Purchases between 1 January 1990 and the date of the fire had been £190 100. Of this, goods to the value of £3040 had not been delivered.
   c. Sales between 1 January 1990 and the date of the fire amounted to £280 060. Included within this figure were sales to customers of goods to the value of £10 560 which were in the warehouse pending delivery. These were destroyed in the fire.
   It is the practice of the firm to sell goods at a mark-up of $33\frac{1}{3}\%$ on cost.
   Calculate the cost of the goods destroyed in the fire.

6. The end of the financial year of Comely Cosmetics was on 30 April 1990—a Monday. Stock-taking could not take place until the week-end commencing Saturday 5 April, when it was found that the value of stock was £66 736. Between 1 April and 5 April, the following took place:

	£
Purchases of additional stock	5900
Recorded sales of stock	8640
Returns of sales from customers	480
Goods returned to suppliers	320

The firm has an average profit margin of 60% on cost. Calculate the value of stock as at the end of the firm's financial year.

7 The following information refers to the purchases and sales of a firm for the period 1 June to 30 September:

June	1	600 units purchased at £40 per unit
	15	100 units sold at £60 per unit
July	1	800 units purchased at £42 per unit
	15	600 units sold at £60 per unit
Aug	1	700 units purchased at £45 per unit
	15	550 units sold at £60 per unit
Sep	1	1200 units purchased at £48 per unit
	15	470 units sold at £60 per unit.

Compute the gross profit of the firm on both a LIFO and a FIFO basis.

8 The stock records of Jo-jo Ltd for the month of January 1990 were as follows:

January	3	Purchased 65 units at £200 each
	5	Sold 60 units at £260 each
	10	Purchased 98 units at £220 each
	16	Purchased 40 units at £225 each
	21	Sold 35 units at £275 each
	26	Purchased 50 units at £280
	30	Sold 86 units at £280 each

a. Draw up a draft trading account for Jo-jo Ltd, valuing the closing stock on a FIFO basis. Will any other method of stock valuation give a greater gross profit for the month?
b. Why is it important that the same method of stock valuation be employed for each accounting period?
c. The rule that the same basis of valuation should be used for successive accounting periods is an example of which accounting convention?

9 A firm's financial year ended on 30 September but stock-taking had to be delayed until 5 October. From the following information, calculate the value of stock at the year-end:
a. Value of stock at 5 October, £100 104.
b. Purchases, 1–5 October, £8850.
c. Sales, 1–5 October, £12 960.
d. A burglary took place on the night of 3 October when goods valued at a selling price of £6250 were stolen.

The firm's percentage of gross profit averages at 25% on cost. On checking the sales records after obtaining the figures stated, it was found that a sale for £582 had been mistakenly recorded as £528.

10 Fire badly damaged a stockroom of Belvoir Ltd on the night of 20 June. Stock had been valued on 1 January previously at £1 356 978. The records indicated that, since that time, purchases amounted to £25 700 and that returns-out amounted to £200. Net sales amounted to £163 680. Stock valued at £10 680 was salvaged from the fire. The Excelsior Insurance Co. have agreed to accept liability for the loss. Profit margin 20% on sales.
a. Calculate the amount of the claim against Excelsior Insurance.
b. State the entries that will be made in Belvoir Ltd's ledger pending the settlement of the claim.
c. If Excelsior Insurance accepted liability for only two-thirds of the loss, how would the balance be treated?

UNIT 13 UNDERSTANDING PROFIT

Before you read this unit, try activity 13.1.

Activity 13.1

(i) If you owned a small business and last year it made a profit of £30 000, would you feel it had done well or badly? What would be your reasons?

(ii) Would you say the same thing if the capital you had invested in the business had been (a) £100 000, (b) £600 000?

(iii) In which of the two situations *might* you have been better advised to have put your capital into a building society? Why? What 'non-financial' factors might you have thought about when making a decision?

13A. Profit and Capital

1. Return on capital invested

Unit 5 showed how it is possible to interpret a balance sheet—i.e. to read greater meaning into it than is immediately apparent from just the figures—by applying, to the figures, the various measures of liquidity.

If you do not remember them, revise them now: then attempt activity 13.2.

Example 13.1

THE ACCOUNTS OF WHITTAKER NOVELTIES

These accounts form the basis for the activities and examples in this unit.

Whittaker Novelties: trading and profit and loss account for year ended 31 December 1982

1981 £000	1981 £000		1982 £000	1982 £000	1981 £000		1982 £000
50		Opening stock	80		200	Sales (note 1)	270
180		Purchases	256				
230			336				
(80)		Closing stock	(120)				
	150	Cost of sales		216			
	50	Gross profit c/d		54			
	200			270	200		270
		General expenses			50	Gross profit b/d	54
	14	Administrative		15			
	8	Selling		9			
	3	Interest		3			
	25	Net profit		27			
	50			54	50		54

More about profit

Balance sheet as at 31 December 1982

	1981			1982		1981				1982	
	£000	£000		£000	£000	£000	£000			£000	£000
			Fixed assets					Capital			
	20		Premises	18			135	at 1 Jan		140	
	18		Equipment	13			25	Profit		27	
		38			31		(20)	Drawings		(22)	
							140				145
			Current assets					*Long-term liabilities*			
	80		Stock	120							
	50		Debtors	61			20	Loan			20
	10		Cash	5							
		140			186			*Current liabilities*			
							18	Creditors			52
		178			217		178				217

Note: All purchases were on credit. In 1981, cash sales amounted to £10 000 and in 1982 to £20 000, and these are included in the total sales listed in the trading account.

Activity 13.2

Example 13.1 shows the final accounts for Whittaker Novelties. Calculate the

(i) current ratio,
(ii) quick ratio,
(iii) cash ratio

for each of the two years for which information is given, and comment on any significant changes in the firm's position.

By applying certain measures—known as the measures of **profitability**—it is possible to read more meaning into profit (i.e. to 'interpret' profit) than is suggested by the figure itself. Activity 13.1 gives one clue as to how it is done—namely, by comparing it with the capital that the owner has put into the business. A profit of £30 000, in itself, sounds fine, and if only £100 000 had been invested at the start, then it would represent a 'return' of 30%—reasonable by any standards and certainly better than could be obtained by investing the money in, say, a building society.

But if £600 000 had been invested in order to produce the £30 000 profit, then another picture emerges—one in which the owner is obtaining only a 5% return on capital. Unless his or her trade is likely to improve, the owner might be well advised to look for another way of investing his or her money.

This first measure of profitability is known as the **return on capital invested**. The 'return' refers to the firm's net profit—before any deductions are made for drawings or for tax—and the 'capital invested' refers to the amount put into the firm by the owner. For the purpose of calculating the ratio—which is always expressed as a percentage—it is important to take the capital invested as at the beginning of the period (i.e. the capital that subsequently produced the profit), not the capital invested at the end of the year after the profit has been added to it. The formula is:

$$\text{Return on capital invested} = \frac{\text{Net profit before drawings or tax}}{\text{Owner's capital}}$$

Taking the accounts for Whittaker Novelties (example 13.1), the owner's return on capital invested for each of the two years is:

$$1981: \quad \frac{£25\,000 \times 100}{£135\,000} = 18.5\%$$

$$1982: \quad \frac{£27\,000 \times 100}{£140\,000} = 19.3\%$$

The ratios indicate that the *rate* of return, as well as the actual amount, has improved over the two years. The answers have, of course, been 'rounded'. Common sense should dictate whether rounding is necessary, and to how many places of decimals a calculation should be taken.

2. Return on capital employed

The return on capital invested indicates the worth of a business to the owner *as an investment*. It does not necessarily indicate how efficiently the firm is being run, since some of its assets may have been financed by 'borrowed' money, as shown by the liabilities listed in the balance sheet. So a second measure of profitability is a calculation of the **return on capital employed**. The 'capital employed' is made up of the owner's capital, plus the long-term liabilities. The calculation is based on these two items on the assumption that the main 'profit-producing assets' are financed either by capital or by loans.

But a complication arises with the definition of 'return'. Just as the year's profit had to be excluded when looking at capital invested, so also the year's interest payments on the loans must be excluded. So the formula for calculating the return on capital employed is:

$$\text{Return on capital employed} = \frac{\text{Net profit before drawings and interest payments}}{\text{Owner's capital plus long-term liabilities}}$$

In the case of Whittaker Novelties, this becomes:

$$1981: \quad \frac{£(25\,000 + 3000) \times 100}{£(135\,000 + 20\,000)} = 18.1\%$$

$$1982: \quad \frac{£(27\,000 + 3000) \times 100}{£(140\,000 + 20\,000)} = 18.8\%$$

The improved ratio in year 1982 shows that the firm's assets are being managed more efficiently than in year 1981.

3. Return on total assets

Some accountants prefer to look at the **return on total assets**. This measure indicates how well the assets *as a whole* have been managed, not just those financed by the capital and the long-term loans. Again, the figure for 'return' must be the net profit figure before drawings and before any interest payments. In the case of Whittaker Novelties:

$$1981: \quad \frac{£28\,000 \times 100}{£178\,000} = 15.7\%$$

$$1982: \quad \frac{£30\,000 \times 100}{£217\,000} = 13.8\%$$

The drop in the ratio is interesting. It indicates that significant changes must have taken place in the structure of the net current assets—changes which may (or may not) be for the good of the firm.

What changes can you spot in the current assets and liabilities, and what is your comment on them?

13B. Profit and Turnover

1. Profit on turnover (i.e. sales)

A firm's capital is not the only item that profit can be compared with. Directly connected with profit is the total sales or 'turnover'. Not surprisingly, any business owner will want to increase the percentage of sales that is received back as profit—and the owner will get very worried if the percentage starts to drop. For this and other reasons, a close watch is always kept on the **profit on turnover** ratio. Again, the net profit *before* the payment of interest and the deduction of drawings must be taken. In the case of Whittaker's Novelties the ratios for the two years are:

$$1981: \quad \frac{£28\,000 \times 100}{£200\,000} = 14.0\%$$

$$1982: \quad \frac{£30\,000 \times 100}{£270\,000} = 11.1\%$$

This shows a marked drop in the *percentage* return—but it should be interpreted with caution. Note that, although the percentage return is reduced, the amount in terms of actual money has increased. In a sense, the firm is having to work harder, pound for pound, for the profit than it did before—but the owner may be quite happy to do this!

2. Expenses on sales

Expenses fall into two distinct groups. First, there are the **direct expenses**, which tend to vary directly with output—and hopefully with sales. Secondly, there are the **indirect expenses**. These are the 'overheads', and variations in them are not reflected in sales, i.e. they do not depend on the amount of sales. In a retailing firm the only major direct cost is the cost of the goods sold, and this appears in the trading account. The overheads are those which appear in the profit and loss account.

The distinction is important because, if we have a constant price level, an increase in the amount spent on direct costs should result in a proportionate (corresponding) increase in output and sales, and this in turn to a *more than proportionate increase* in profit. But if there is an increase in the indirect expenses (not reflected in output or sales), there will be a *more than proportionate decrease* in profit.

Understanding profit

In order to keep track of changes in costs which might need investigation, many firms add a further column to the working drafts of the trading and profit and loss account in order to show the percentage of sales of each expense. Such accounts are known as percentage profit and loss accounts.

13C. Rate of Stock Turnover

The total sales of a firm—its turnover—are achieved by buying, selling and replacing the stock. In most firms, the normal stock-holding at any one time is much smaller than the amount of annual sales. This means that the stock has to be sold and replaced several times during the course of a trading period. The number of times that stock is sold and replaced during such a period is known as the **rate of turnover**. In order to find the rate of turnover, the annual sales have to be divided by the average stock-holding. But there is a complication. Stock is usually valued at **cost price**; the figure for sales is always at *selling price*. If the two are to be used in the same calculation, then sales must be converted to cost. The formula for calculating the rate of turnover of stock is, therefore:

$$\text{Rate of turnover} = \frac{\text{Sales at cost price}}{\text{Average stock}}$$

If a trading account has been prepared with the closing stock shown as a deduction on the debit side, the *cost of sales* (i.e. sales at cost price) is automatically shown. Otherwise, it has to be calculated from whatever information is available. As regards the calculation of *average stock*, the opening and closing stocks are available in the trading account. If no further information is available, then the average of these two figures has to be taken. But this may be misleading as both the opening and closing stocks refer to the same point in the trading year—a time when stocks may be well below or well above average. If more frequent stock-take figures are available (say quarterly or monthly), then a much more accurate figure can be calculated.

In the case of Whittaker Novelties, the cost of sales is immediately available in the trading account. The average stock is calculated by taking the average of the opening and closing stocks (the only figures available), i.e. for 1981 the average of £50 000 and £80 000, and for 1982 the average of £80 000 and £120 000. The calculation of the rate of turnover for each of the two years is, therefore:

$$1981: \quad \frac{£150\,000}{£65\,000} = 2.3 \text{ times}$$

$$1982: \quad \frac{£216\,000}{£100\,000} = 2.16 \text{ times}$$

Notice that this calculation is *not* expressed as a percentage. What it means is that the rate at which the normal stock-holding of Whittaker Novelties was 'turned over' dropped slightly over the two years.

Activity 13.3

Draw up a table showing the possible causes (at least two in each case) of:

(i) a rise in the rate of turnover;

More about profit

> (ii) a decrease in the rate of turnover;
> (iii) the rate of turnover remaining constant.
>
> Add a note, beside each cause, of the problem it might pose for the firm, or the action that should be taken.

13D. Turnover of Debtors and Creditors

1. Turnover of debtors

Any business that sells on credit must keep a careful check not only on the length of time individual debtors may take to pay their accounts, but also on how long the debtors in general are taking to 'pay up'. If this is allowed to creep up unnecessarily, the firm may well find itself with a cash-flow problem on its hands—that is, not enough cash actually coming in to meet immediate needs.

The average number of days that the debtors of a firm take to pay their debts is given by the formula:

$$\frac{\text{Average of trade debts} \times 365}{\text{Credit sales}}$$

Often, the only available figure for debtors will be the one appearing in the balance sheet, and so this has to be taken instead of the average. Whittaker Novelties' turnover of debtors for the two years was:

1981: $\dfrac{£50\,000 \times 365}{£190\,000} = 97$ days

1982: $\dfrac{£61\,000 \times 365}{£250\,000} = 90$ days

Do you consider Whittaker Novelties are having to wait too long for their debts to be paid?

(Note: The answers are, strictly, 96.05 and 89.06 days. This means that it is not until the 97th day (in 1981) and the 90th day (in 1982) that the debts (on average) were paid. This is an occasion when the rounding must be to the next figure above, not to the nearest whole figure, if the answer is to have any sense.)

2. Turnover of creditors

The same form of calculation can be made in order to establish how long a firm is taking, on average, to pay its creditors. The formula is:

$$\frac{\text{Average trade creditors} \times 365}{\text{Credit purchases}}$$

Again, the balance sheet figure may be the only one available for creditors. For Whittaker Novelties, therefore:

1981: $\dfrac{£18\,000 \times 365}{£180\,000} = 37$ days

1982: $\dfrac{£52\,000 \times 365}{£256\,000} = 75$ days

Again, the rounding *has* to be up, and not down. The increase in the length of time being taken to pay creditors should be noted. There may be good reasons for it, but significant amounts of discount may be being lost, together with the goodwill of creditors, who may not be happy at waiting for their money.

13E. Use of the Ratios

What use are all these ratios once they have been calculated?

In general, they can be of use in three different ways. The first is, simply, as individual figures in their own right. For instance, the owner of Whittaker Novelties may feel that he or she should be getting a higher return on turnover than just 4.8%.

The second use is by an analysis of trends over a period of time. For example, a return of 19.3% on capital invested may sound satisfactory, but if it is found that the percentage has fallen steadily over the past five years from, say, 27% and that the downward trend looks likely to continue, then the owner may have cause for concern.

A third use is that of **inter-firm comparison**—this means comparing the ratios of a particular firm with others of comparable size and nature. There are agencies that, for a fee, will supply a wide range of information by which owners or managers can compare the structure and performance of their firm with those of others. But considerable care and skill has to be exercised in using such information.

13F. The Problem of Inflation

Accountants have, in the past, stuck firmly to the principle of recording assets in the balance sheet, and expenses in the revenue accounts, at their 'historical' costs—i.e. at the costs *at the time* the assets were bought or the expenses were incurred. This has the advantage of being:

   (i) simple and straightforward;
  (ii) convenient, since it does not disrupt the double-entry system;
 (iii) highly objective (i.e. the costs are not subject to doubt or dispute).

The practice of doing this is known as the *historical cost* convention (sometimes known as the *objectivity* convention).

> ***Accounting Convention No. 7***
> ***The Objectivity Convention***
>
> Accounts should be prepared on the basis of the actual costs incurred, or the income actually received, at the time—not on a 'present-day', replacement, or other assumed cost level.

Accounts are almost always prepared on the basis of the historical cost convention. It means that the ratios discussed in this unit must be interpreted within that light. Their value is limited when costs, prices and money valuations of different periods are compared. This is particularly the case at the present time, because of the sort of inflation that the world has seen since the early 1970s. If the costs of raw materials bought a year ago are compared with the price of finished goods sold today (e.g. as in cost/turnover ratios), the value of the result is questionable.

More about profit

Unfortunately, it is easier to identify the problems than it is to find the solutions, and there is still much debate about what should be done. Because we still await answers to the very great difficulties involved, the practice continues—and is likely to continue for the near future—of preparing accounts on a purely historical cost basis.

Activity 13.4

Your grandmother, who has recently won a *Readers' Digest* prize draw, wishes to invest the money in a business, which she proposes to leave to you in her will. The choice is between the following two businesses; the details below refer to their most recent financial years. She asks your advice as to which is the better investment.

Draft out a report for her.

	Business A £000	Business B £000
Net capital employed	65	80
Sales	100	160
Purchases	70	150
Variable expenses	5	13
Opening stock	30	10
Fixed expenses	2	3
Closing stock	20	24

Check Your Understanding

1. What do the measures of (i) liquidity and (ii) profitability each attempt to show?
2. What are the main measures of profitability?
3. Define *turnover*.
4. What is meant by the expression *rate of turnover*, and how is it calculated?
5. Give *two* possible explanations for a rising rate of turnover.
6. Under what circumstances can it be misleading to calculate the rate of turnover from the figures for opening and closing stock only?
7. What are the formulae for the calculation of the average time taken:
    (i) by debtors for the payment of their debts;
    (ii) by a firm to pay its creditors?
8. What importance would you attach to the average times referred to in question 7 above?
9. What is meant by *inter-firm comparison*? What do you have to be particularly careful of when interpreting such comparisons?
10. What is (i) the main advantage and (ii) the main disadvantage of recording costs on the basis of historical cost alone?

Practical Assignments

1. a. (i) What are the basic measures of liquidity?
      (ii) What do they attempt to show?
   b. (i) What are the basic measures of profitability?
      (ii) What do they attempt to show?
2. a. Distinguish between:
      (i) the rate of turnover of stock,
      (ii) the turnover of debtors,
      (iii) the turnover of creditors.
   b. How is each measured?
   c. What is the significance of each?

Understanding profit

3 The following is the trading account of a wholesale organisation specialising in toys for the year ended 31 December last.

	£000			£000
Stock at 1 January	23	Sales	215	
Net purchases	85	Returns	20	195
	108			
Stock at 31 December	15			
	93			
Gross profit c/d	102			
	195			195
Miscellaneous expenses	46	Gross profit b/d		102
Net profit	56			
	102			102

a. What is the wholesaler's percentage return on turnover?
b. What is his percentage mark-up?
c. What is his percentage profit margin?
d. Calculate his rate of turnover.
e. Why might it be misleading to base the calculation of the rate of turnover solely on data extracted from the trading account?
f. Calculate a revised rate of turnover, given the following monthly stock-take figures:

	£000		£000		£000
January	23	May	76	September	162
February	34	June	97	October	151
March	41	July	114	November	134
April	54	August	153	December	15

g. Prepare a graph or bar chart to illustrate the monthly stock-holdings.
h. Give a possible reason for the pattern of stock-holdings shown by the above figures.
i. Name two other types of firms that may have regular 'peaks' in their stock-holding patterns. State, with reasons, at what time or times of the year the peaks might occur.
j. List as many problems as possible of this pattern of stock-holding.

4. a. Give two measures used to judge a firm's profitability.
   b. Give two measures used to judge a firm's liquidity.
   c. Compare the data for the two businesses below as regards their respective profitability and liquidity:

	Business A £000	Business B £000
Capital	1000	800
Net profit	100	200
Debtors	100	50
Stock	100	100
Creditors	200	400
Equipment	900	200
Bank	200	50
Premises	–	700
Motor vehicles		300

More about profit

5 The following information was extracted from the books of Bill Ltd and Ben Ltd at 31 December last:

	Bill Ltd £	Ben Ltd £		Bill Ltd £	Ben Ltd £
Opening stock	260 000	530 000	Sales	4 890 000	4 350 000
Purchases	?	?	Returns-in	90 000	25 000
	?	?			
Closing stock	?	470 000			
	?	?			
Gross profit	?	?			
			Gross profit	?	?
General expenses	?	615 000			
Net profit	600 000	?			

Additional information:

	Bill Ltd	Ben Ltd
Capital employed	£2 000 000	£2 000 000
Rate of turnover of stock	16	?
Mark-up on cost	50%	25%

You are required to:
a. Complete the trading and profit and loss accounts for both firms.
b. Calculate in respect of each business:
   (i) the ratio of gross profit on sales,
   (ii) the ratio of net profit on sales,
   (iii) the return on capital employed.
c. State, with reasons, which of the two firms had the more successful year.
d. Give two other ratios that may be used when judging the performance of firms.

6 The records of Victoria Black for the year to 31 March 1990 showed:

	£
Credit sales	670 000
Cash sales	9 680
Purchases returns	5 480
Stock at 1 April 1989	27 560
Stock at 31 March 1990	36 280
Gross profit for the year	160 136
Expenses	74 506
Proprietor's capital at 1 April 1989	428 150
Long-term loan from finance company	20 000
Average debtors throughout the year	82 602
Average creditors throughout the year	43 419

All purchases were on credit.
Calculate the following:
a. Cost of goods sold during the year.
b. Purchases for the year.
c. Turnover (net sales) for the year.
d. Rate of turnover for the year.
e. Net profit for the year.
f. Return on capital employed.
g. Return on capital invested.
h. Average collection period, in days, of debts.
i. Average period of credit, in weeks, taken by the firm.

7 A trading organisation was advised by a management consultant that, if further working capital is invested in the firm, sales could be increased more than proportionately. The firm acted upon the advice and the following figures refer to the year immediately *before* and the year immediately *after* the additional investment.

Before the additional investment (£000): capital employed 202; general expenses 39; net sales 188; cost of sales 103.

After the additional investment (£000): sales 550; capital employed 400; general expenses 118; cost of sales 344.

a. Prepare a table showing the effects of the additional investment, calculating such figures as you think may be relevant.
b. Comment on whether you think the advice of the consultant has proved correct and whether, on the basis of the information available, the expansion has been worth while.
c. What other information would be helpful before coming to a final decision on the long-term advisability of the expansion.

PART FOUR: Multiple-choice test

In each of the following, state which option best answers the question.

1. At the end of the accounting period, the balance of the discount received account is
   a. listed in the balance sheet as a current asset
   b. transferred to the credit of the profit and loss account
   c. carried forward to the next trading period
   d. entered on the debit side of the trading account

2. Sums of money received by a trading firm in respect of selling goods are referred to in accounting as:
   a. extraordinary income
   b. non-revenue income
   c. revenue income
   d. capital income

3. FIFO assumes that stock is resold:
   a. in the date order of purchase
   b. in the reverse of the date order of purchase
   c. without reference to the date order of purchase
   d. previous to the date order of purchase

4. Credit balances on ledger accounts may refer to
   a. expenses or liabilities
   b. income or liabilities
   c. assets or expenses
   d. assets or income

5. John Bull withdrew £100 from his firm's bank account for his own private purposes. The ledger entries are:

	Debit	Credit
a.	J. Bull	drawings account
b.	cash account	bank account
c.	drawings account	bank account
d.	J. Bull	capital account

6. A cheque received as a refund of an overpayment of rent is recorded by:

	Debit	Credit
a.	rent received account	bank account
b.	bank account	rent received account
c.	bank account	rent paid account
d.	rent paid account	bank account

7. If a proprietor withdraws cash from the firm for his or her own use, the effect upon the balance sheet will be to:

	Increase	Decrease
a.	drawings and cash accounts	—
b.	drawings account	cash account
c.	—	drawings and cash account
d.	cash account	drawings account

8. An item for rent appears on the assets side of a balance sheet. This means that rent:
   a. has been paid in advance
   b. is owing
   c. has been received during the accounting period
   d. has been paid in advance

9. An accrued charge is
   a. an expense for a period that has been incurred but has not been paid
   b. an amount that is deducted from the total paid for the period
   c. an expense that has been paid during a period but was not incurred during it
   d. an amount that should be held over and not taken into account until the following period

10. Income earned in period 1 but received in period 2 should be included in the profit calculation for
    a. period 1
    b. period 2
    c. neither period
    d. partly period 1 and partly period 2

11. A nominal account shows
    a. the cause of a change in balance sheet item
    b. the net change in an asset or a liability
    c. the cause of a change in cash account
    d. changes not recorded elsewhere

12. After the preparation of a profit and loss account, an insurance account showed a debit balance of £650. This meant that in respect of insurance, £650
    a. was owing
    b. had been paid
    c. was prepaid
    d. had been received

13. Discount received will appear on the
    a. debit side of the trading account
    b. credit side of the profit and loss account
    c. credit side of the trading account
    d. debit side of the profit and loss account

14. A prepayment will appear in the
    a. profit and loss account and the balance sheet
    b. profit and loss account but not the balance sheet
    c. balance sheet but not the profit and loss account
    d. ledger but neither the profit and loss account nor the balance sheet

15. Which of the following ledger accounts can never have a credit balance:
    a. capital account
    b. personal accounts of customers
    c. carriage-out
    d. bank account

135

More about profit

16 Cash received in respect of work undertaken last year should be regarded as income earned in
  a. this year
  b. neither year
  c. last year
  d. partly this year and partly last year

17 Drawings are equal to
  a. closing capital plus net profit less opening capital
  b. profit less closing capital plus opening capital
  c. opening capital less profit plus closing capital
  d. profit plus closing capital less opening capital

18 Relating income earned to the expenditure incurred in the same period is known as the
  a. matching convention
  b. entity convention
  c. money measurement convention
  d. consistency convention

19 If the price at which stock is purchased tends to fluctuate considerably, the valuation of closing stock is best carried out on a
  a. revaluation basis
  b. AVCO basis
  c. LIFO basis
  d. FIFO basis

20 The rent account of a firm has a credit balance for £600. This means that £600
  a. has been paid for rent
  b. has been received in respect of rent
  c. is owing by the firm for rent
  d. is owed to the firm for rent

21 The rule that the same accounting rules and principles should be applied in each successive trading period is known as the convention of
  a. consistency
  b. continuity
  c. perpetuity
  d. objectivity

22 If closing stock is undervalued, the rate of turnover will
  a. be increased
  b. remain constant
  c. be reduced
  d. be unaffected

23 If a firm has made a net profit, it means that it
  a. must have had a gross profit
  b. probably had a gross profit
  c. was unlikely to have had a gross profit
  d. could not have had a gross profit

24 The rate of turnover is
  a. total value of turnover
  b. sales divided by selling price of goods sold
  c. sales at cost divided by average stock held
  d. sales divided by cost of sales

25 The net profit of an organisation shows the
  a. gross increase of assets over liabilities
  b. net increase of liabilities over assets
  c. gross increase of liabilities over assets
  d. net increase of assets over liabilities arising from trading activities

26 If a firm's credit sales for the year amounted to £2m and the average amount owed by debtors was £500 000, the collection period for debts (to the nearest whole day) is
  a. 4 days
  b. 25 days
  c. 91 days
  d. 1460 days

27 The cost of goods sold is approximately equal to stock
  a. multiplied by the rate of turnover
  b. divided by purchases
  c. multiplied by sales
  d. divided by the rate of turnover

28 If closing stock is overvalued, the net profit will be
  a. overstated
  b. correct
  c. understated
  d. not affected

29 The acid test refers to the ratio between
  a. current assets less debtors and all liabilities
  b. current assets plus stock and current liabilities
  c. current assets and current liabilities
  d. current assets less stock and current liabilities

30 A firm's stock was completely destroyed by fire. Stock had previously been valued at £42 000, since when purchases of £58 000 had been made of which £2000 worth had been returned. The cost of the goods sold since the fire was £60 000. The value of stock destroyed was:
  a. £98 000
  b. £74 000
  c. £46 000
  d. £38 000

31 Which of the following is likely to have the highest rate of turnover:
  a. a grocer
  b. a furniture store
  c. a car-sales organisation
  d. a jeweller

32 A firm purchased 800 components in April at £2 each and a further quantity of 800 in June at £3 each. In May 300 of the components were resold, and in July a further 500 were resold. Using the LIFO method of stock valuation, the value of components in stock at 31 July was
  a. £1600
  b. £1900
  c. £2100
  d. £2400

33 The following information refers to the position of a trader at 31 December, the end of his financial year:

	£		£
Fixed assets	100 000	Long-term loans	10 000
Current liabilities	30 000	Current assets	20 000
Net trading profit for the year to 31 December			£20 000

His net profit to capital invested ratio was:
  a. 25%
  b. 20%
  c. 14%
  d. 12½%

34 A firm's working capital was £36 000. Debtors owed £10 000. They subsequently paid £9000 and received discount of £1000. The working capital then became
  a. £35 000
  b. £33 000
  c. £25 000
  d. £24 000

136

35 The opening stock of a firm was £100 000 and the closing stock was £140 000. The purchases for the year amounted to £400 000 and the sales to £600 000. The rate of turnover was
  a. 5 times
  b. 3 times
  c. 2.5 times
  d. 1.2 times

36 The ledger entries when a proprietor takes stock at cost for his or her personal use are:

Debit	Credit
a. drawings account	sales account
b. capital account	stock account
c. drawings account	purchases account
d. sales account	capital account

37 A firm started a trading year with 500 items of stock, which had cost £2 each. There were further purchases during the subsequent trading year of 400 units at £2.50 each, 300 units at £3 each and 100 units at £3.50 each. At the end of the year, 450 units were held in stock. If valued on a FIFO basis, the closing stock would be
  a. £900
  b. £1375
  c. £1575
  d. £1735

38 If a retailer's profit margin is 25% on sales, his mark-up on cost will be
  a. 20%
  b. 25%
  c. 33⅓%
  d. 50%

39 A profit and loss account shows a net profit of £140 500. Accruals for £300 and pre-payments for £900 have been overlooked. The correct net profit should be
  a. £139 300
  b. £139 700
  c. £141 100
  d. £141 700

40 The 'money measurement' convention means that
  a. only transactions involving cash movements are recorded
  b. the importance of transactions is measured by their money values
  c. only transactions on which money values can be placed are recorded
  d. accountants are only interested in the money aspects of transactions

PART FIVE

Being Realistic

UNIT 14 ACCOUNTING FOR WEAR AND TEAR

Before you read this unit, try activity 14.1.

> **Activity 14.1**
>
> Ben started business with £1000 cash and an ice-cream van worth £24 000. During the following year, he sold ice-cream for £28 000 cash. His running expenses, all paid in cash, were £6000. At the end of the year, his van was worth £16 000. He had no other assets or liabilities.
>
> (i) What was his capital at the beginning of business?
> (ii) What was his cash balance at the end of the year?
> (iii) By how much had his cash balance increased?
> (iv) What was his capital at the end of the year?
> (v) How much 'better off' was he at the end of the year compared with at the beginning?

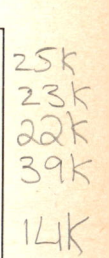

14A. The Nature of Depreciation

By the end of his first year of business, Ben (activity 14.1) had increased his cash balance from £1000 to £23 000—an increase of £22 000. But it would be misleading to say he had 'made' £22 000 because, in order to make it, his van had suffered considerable wear and tear, and was worth £8000 less than it had been at the start. Therefore, to be realistic about it, one has to say that Ben was only £14 000 (i.e. £22 000 − £8000) 'better off'. Although the drop in value of the van is not an expense that has to be paid in cash, it is still a real cost in earning the income, and therefore one that must taken into account in calculating the true profit of the business.

The drop in value of any asset as a result of normal wear and tear is known in accounting as **depreciation**. If a true calculation of profit is to be made, then the depreciation of all of the assets must be listed—along with the actual cash expenses—in the profit and loss account.

Two main problems arise with depreciation. The first is the book-keeping procedure by means of which the amount concerned is to be brought into the accounts. The second is the method of calculating the amount concerned.

14B. Accounting Methods

There are two ways of dealing with depreciation in the accounts. One is by means of a simple depreciation account; the other is by means of a depreciation provision account. The two methods are *alternatives* to each other, and one would not find the two methods in the same set of accounts.

Being realistic

1. Simple depreciation account

The procedure here is simple. The following entries are made in the ledger at the end of each year:

Debit Depreciation account.
Credit Asset account(s) concerned, with the amount of depreciation for the year.

The depreciation account is then transferred to the profit and loss account and closed. In the balance sheet, the asset is shown at its value at the start of the year, less the depreciation written off during the year, giving the net 'written-down' figure. At the end of the third year, the asset disappears from the ledger and does not appear in the balance sheet.

Example 14.1

A hotel purchased garden furniture for £9000 on 1 Jul 19-1. The furniture is expected to have a working life of three years and will have no residual or 'scrap' value at the end. It is decided to write off the depreciation at the rate of £3000 in each of the three years. Show the appropriate accounts. The accounting year is to 31 December.

Garden furniture account

1 Jul 19-1	Bank		9000	31 Dec 19-1	Depreciation		3000
				31 Dec 19-1	Balance	c/d	6000
			9000				9000
1 Jan 19-2	Balance	b/d	6000	31 Dec 19-2	Depreciation		3000
					Balance	c/d	3000
			6000				6000
1 Jan 19-3	Balance	b/d	3000	31 Dec 19-3	Depreciation		3000

Depreciation account

31 Dec 19-1	Garden furn.	3000	31 Dec 19-1	P&L	3000
31 Dec 19-2	Garden furn.	3000	31 Dec 19-2	P&L	3000
3 Dec 19-3	Garden furn.	3000	31 Dec 19-3	P&L	3000

Notes
1. The sum of £3000 each year will appear in the P&L.
2. The written-down balance of the asset will appear in the balance sheet each year.
3. A full year's depreciation is written off in the first year. Depreciation can be calculated on a *pro rata* time basis if this is thought more appropriate, such as, for instance, in the case of leases. Normally, however, the convention of prudence (unit 7, page 74) suggests that it is better to allow a full year's depreciation.

---

2. Depreciation provision method

A more sophisticated way of entering up the depreciation is to keep the asset account at its original balance, but to build up against it a depreciation provision account. The entries at the end of each year are:

Debit Profit and loss account.
Credit Depreciation provision account, with the depreciation for the year.

The balance is not transferred, but is carried down to the next period when the next year's depreciation is added to it.

Accounting for wear and tear

In the balance sheet, the asset is shown at its original value less the accumulated depreciation (i.e. the balance of the depreciation provision account) to date. A separate depreciation provision account must be opened for each asset, or group of assets. Following the provision method, the accounts of the hotel in respect of the garden furniture would appear as in example 14.2.

Example 14.2

Garden furniture account

| 1 Jul 19-1 | Bank | | 9000 | | | | |

Depreciation provision (garden furniture) account

31 Dec 19-2	Balance	c/d	6000	31 Dec 19-1	P&L		3000
				31 Dec 19-2	P&L		3000
			6000				6000
31 Dec 19-3	Balance	c/d	9000	1 Jan 19-3	Balance	b/d	6000
				31 Dec 19-3	P&L		3000
			9000				9000
				1 Jan 19-4	Balance	b/d	9000

Balance sheet (extract)

Fixed assets:	Cost	Depreciation	Net
at 31 Dec 19-1			
Garden furniture	9000	3000	6000
at 31 Dec 19-2			
Garden furniture	9000	6000	3000

Notes
1. The charge to the profit and loss account is the same no matter what book-keeping procedure is employed.
2. The provision account method has the advantage that the final accounts show clearly the original cost of the asset, the depreciation charged for the year, the accumulated depreciation to date, and the current written-down value of the asset.

A simple depreciation account only contains the depreciation for the current year; this is transferred to profit and loss, thus closing the account.

A depreciation provision account, on the other hand, carries its balance forward from year to year, and thus records the *accumulated* depreciation to date.

14C. Calculating the Depreciation

There are a number of different ways in which the amount to be charged for depreciation, in any one year, can be calculated. Each tends to be suitable for a particular type of asset. The *straight-line method* and the *diminishing-balance method* are by far the most common.

1. Straight-line depreciation

Straight-line depreciation consists of the same figure for each year and is calculated as a percentage of the *original* value of the asset. The garden furniture above was an example of this, with one-third ($33\frac{1}{3}\%$) of the original cost being written off each year. The straight-line method:

(i) is simple to understand;
(ii) is easy to calculate;
(iii) results in the total cost of the asset being eventually written off;
(iv) reflects the actual depreciation pattern of *some* assets—leases of premises is an example.

2. Diminishing-balance depreciation

Diminishing-balance depreciation is calculated as a percentage of the original cost of the asset less the accumulated depreciation to date, i.e. the written-down value of the asset.

If it had been decided to depreciate the garden furniture in example 14.1 on a diminishing-balance method at the rate of 60% per annum, the depreciation and written-down values of the asset would be:

Original value	9000
Depreciation, year 1	5400
Written-down value, end year 1	3600
Depreciation, year 2	2160
Written-down value, end year 2	1440
Depreciation, year 3	864
Written-down value, end year 3	576

The example demonstrates the major differences between the straight-line and the diminishing-balance methods. Whereas an equal amount is charged to depreciation each year under the straight-line method, the amount charged under the diminishing-balance method reduces each year. Also, under the diminishing-balance method, the asset will never disappear completely from the books.

A further point that is not always appreciated as fully as it might be is that, if the diminishing-balance method is chosen, a far higher percentage rate—with very much heavier depreciation charges in the earlier years—has to be charged to reduce an asset to a given value in a stated number of years.

The diminishing-balance method is particularly suitable for motor vehicles and machinery. These assets do, indeed, depreciate much more rapidly in the earlier years than the latter. Also, the cost of repairs tends to increase as these assets become older. So the charge for depreciation taken together with that for repairs tends to give a more-or-less constant charge to the profit and loss.

A summary of the depreciation provision procedure is shown in display 6 in unit 15 (page 153), where it is compared with the procedure for bad-debts provision (discussed in unit 15).

14D. Sale of a Depreciated Asset

When partly depreciated assets are *sold*, it is necessary to open a sale-of-asset account. The procedure is as follows:

Debit Sale-of-asset account.
Credit Asset account concerned, with the original value of the asset being sold.

Debit   Depreciation provision account.
Credit   Sale-of-asset account, with the relevant amount of depreciation.

Debit   Sale-of-asset account.
Credit   Cash account (or appropriate expenses account), with any expenses incurred in the sale.

Debit   Cash account.
Credit   Sale-of-asset account, with the proceeds of the sale.

There will usually be a small balance left on the account, which will represent a profit (if a credit balance) or a loss (if a debit balance) on the sale. This is usually written off to profit and loss account. The ledger procedure should be followed through carefully in the next example.

Example 14.3

The balance of the motor vehicle account of a particular firm at 1 January 19-1 stood at £300 000, and the balance of the depreciation provision (motor vehicles) account at £170 000.

On 5 May, one of the vehicles, which had originally cost £40 000 and against which a provision of £22 000 had been built up, was sold for £1640. Advertising and other expenses amounted to £320. Show the appropriate accounts.

Motor vehicles account

Jan 1	Balance	b/d	300 000	May 5	Sale of asset		40 000
				May 5	Balance	c/d	260 000
			300 000				300 000
May 5	Balance	b/d	260 000				

Depreciation provision account

May 5	Sale of asset		22 000	Jan 1	Balance	b/d	170 000
May 5	Balance	c/d	148 000				
			170 000				170 000
				May 5	Balance	b/d	148 000

Sale-of-asset account

May 5	Motor vehicles	40 000	May 5	Depreciation prov.		22 000
May 5	Bank (expenses)	320	May 5	Bank (proceeds)		16 400
			Dec 31	P&L: loss on sale		1 920
		40 320				40 320

14E. Examination Questions

Questions are often asked that involve the writing up of the depreciation or depreciation provision accounts, and the related asset accounts. But, very commonly, depreciation procedures are included in questions asking for final accounts drawn up from a given trial balance. The trial balance will have been drawn up after the posting of normal transactions, but *before* the adjustments for depreciation have been made. This means that the figures in the trial balance will be the balances brought forward from the previous year.

Directions for the calculation of the depreciation will be given in the notes following the trial balance, and candidates are expected to adjust the trial balance figures accordingly.

Being realistic

Where depreciation provision accounts are concerned, the balance sheet should show:

(i) the original cost of the asset or group of assets concerned;
(ii) the accumulated depreciation to date (i.e. the amount in the trial balance plus the current allocation);
(iii) the current written-down (net) value of the asset.

Example 14.4

The following trial balance was extracted from the books of Mathus & Co. on 31 December 19-2 after the preparation of the trading account and refers to the year ended on that date.

You are required to draw up the profit and loss account for the year, and the balance sheet as at 31 December, from the following information:

	£000	£000
Capital		130
Gross profit		150
Motor vehicles	260	
Equipment	80	
Depreciation provision (motor vehicles)		120
Depreciation provision (equipment)		30
Sundry expenses	60	
Sundry current assets	55	
Sundry current liabilities		25
	455	455

Take into account:

(i) Depreciation of motor vehicles is at 25% p.a. (per annum = per year), on a diminishing-balance basis.
(ii) Depreciation of equipment is at 20% on a straight-line basis.

Profit and loss account for the year to 31 December 19-2

	£000		£000
Sundry expenses	60	Gross profit	150
Depreciation provisions:			
Motor vehicles (note 1)	35		
Equipment (note 2)	16		
Net profit	39		
	150		150

Balance sheet as at 31 December 19-2

	£000	£000	£000		£000	£000
Fixed assets	Cost	Depreciation	Net	Capital		
				As at 1.1.19-2	130	
Motor vehicles	260	155	105	Profit	39	169
Equipment	80	46	34			
	340	201	139	*Current liabilities*		
Current assets				Sundry		25
Sundry			54			
			194			194

Notes

1. Calculation of depreciation, motor vehicles (£000)

Original cost	260
Accumulated depreciation to 1.1.19-2	120
Written-down value, 1.1.19-2	140

146

Accounting for wear and tear

```
                Current depreciation, 25% of £140           35
                Written-down value, 31.12.19-2             105
              (Accumulated depreciation to 31.12.19-2
                        £120 000 + 35 000 = £155 000)
  2.   Calculation of depreciation equipment (£000)
                Original cost                               80
                Current depreciation, 20% of £80      16
                Accumulated depreciation at 1.1.19-2   30
                                                            46
                Written-down value, 31.12.19-2              34
```

Activity 14.2

Depreciation calculations are based on the historical cost of the asset.

To what extent do you think this reflects the real cost of using the asset?

Check Your Understanding

Fill in the gaps in the following passages.

1 The main ways of calculating depreciation are the s___straight line___ method and the d___iminishing___ b___alance___ method. Each is suitable for particular types of assets. The first is particularly suitable for use in connection with ___leases___, while the latter is particularly suitable for ___vehicles/machinery___.

2 The annual figure for depreciation may be brought into account either by the simple depreciation account method, or by the ___Provision___ method. These are alternatives, and would not both appear in the same set of accounts. The ledger entries in respect of simple depreciation are *debit* ___Dpn acc___ and *credit* ___Assets acc___ with the year's depreciation.

The final balance of the depreciation account is transferred to the ___P+L___ account at the end of the accounting year. In the case of the alternative system, the ledger entries are *debit* ___P+L___ and *credit* ___Dpn p'ov___. The accumulated depreciation to date is shown in the ___B.S___ as a _____ from the _____ of the asset concerned.

3 When a partly depreciated asset is sold, a *sale-of-asset* account is opened and debited with ___Dep'n___ and credited with ___orig___. A final credit balance on the account indicates a ___profit___ on the sale, while a debit balance indicates a ___Loss___. It is usually of a relatively small amount and is transferred to the ___P+L acc___.

Practical Assignments

1 Distinguish carefully, with examples, between a depreciation account and a depreciation provision account. What is the advantage of the provision method?

2 Two assets are purchased for £30 000 each. Depreciation on asset 'A' is charged at 20% per annum for five years on a straight-line basis, and on asset 'B' at 20% on a diminishing balance method over the same period.
   a. Explain what is meant by the straight-line method of depreciation.
   b. Explain what is meant by diminishing balance depreciation.
   c. Does accounting for depreciation involve:
      (i) a reduction in profit for the year,
      (ii) a reduction in the cash balance at the end of the year?
   d. Calculate the annual charges for depreciation in the case of both asset 'A' and asset 'B' over the five-year period concerned.
   e. What will be the difference in the written-down value of the two assets at the end of the fifth year?

147

Being realistic

3 An articulated lorry is bought on 30 June 19-1, for £120 000. It is depreciated at the rate of 25% on a diminishing balance method. Show the asset account, the depreciation provision account and the appropriate extracts from the trading and profit and loss accounts for each of the years ending 31 December 19-1, 19-2 and 19-3, and the extracts from the balance sheet as at those dates.

In March 19-4, the lorry was sold for £45 000 cash. Advertising and other expenses amounted to £150. Show the relevant accounts.

4 Plant is purchased for £220 000 that has an anticipated working life of five years and an expected residual value of £20 000.
  a. State the annual percentage rate at which it will have to be written down on a straight-line basis to arrive at the residual value at the end of the fifth year.
  b. Show *in statement form* the written-form value at the end of five years if it is depreciated at a rate of 40% diminishing balance.
  c. If the plant is, in fact, depreciated at 40% diminishing balance, and is sold at the end of that time for £31 698, state with reasons how you would deal with the balances.

5 'Depreciation is a fair charge against profits.' Discuss this statement with particular reference to:
  a. the fact that the charge is never paid in cash,
  b. the position of non-profit-making organisations such as charities.

6 The following balance appeared in the books of Hepworth and White at the close of business on 31 March 1990 before any adjustments and the final accounts for the year were prepared.

	£
Motor vehicles	600 000
Equipment	450 000
Loose tools	15 000
Depreciation provision (motor vehicles)	360 000
Depreciation provision (equipment)	180 000

It is the policy of the firm to depreciate motor vehicles at the rate of 25% of the net value of vehicles held at 31 March each year, and equipment at the rate of 10% on a straight-line basis. Loose tools are revalued each year; at 31 March 1990, they were valued at £15 500.
  a. Show:
    (i) the two provision accounts as they would appear after the preparation of the firm's final accounts for the year ended 31 March 1990;
    (ii) the extract from the profit and loss account for the year to 31 March 1990, and the extract from the balance sheet as at that date.
  b. Give a statement, backed by reasons, explaining for which types of assets each of the three methods of depreciation is particularly suitable.

7 The following accounts appeared in the books of Tango Ltd at 31 March 1990, the end of the company's accounting year, immediately before the preparation of the balance sheet as at that date.

Fixtures and fittings A/c

1988				1990			
June 5	Bank		50 000	Jan 1	Disposal of asset		10 000

Depreciation provision (F & F) A/c

1990				1989			
Jan 1	Disposal of asset		2 000	Apr 1	Balance	b/d	10 000
				1990			
				Mar 31	P & L		6 400

Disposal of asset A/c

1990							
Jan 1	Fixtures and fittings		10 000	Jan 1	Depreciation provision		2 000
				Jan 10	Foster Ltd		7 500

  a. Which subsidiary book or books would have been used for each of the transactions in the three accounts?
  b. Which method and percentage rate of depreciation has been used by the company in connection with fixtures and fittings?
  c. On which side of the trial balance will the balance of the depreciation provision (F & F) account appear?
  d. What alternative methods of depreciation could have been used for this asset? Do you think that they would have been more suitable?
  e. Rewrite the provision for depreciation account as it would appear *after* the completion of the balance sheet.
  f. What entries, if any, would be made in the balance sheet in respect of fixtures and fittings and depreciation?
  g. Assuming that the company maintains its depreciation policy, and that there are no further sales or disposals, what will be the amount charged to profit and loss for the year ending 31 March 1991 in respect of fixtures and fittings?
  h. What entries are necessary in order to close the account for the disposal of the asset?

8 The following balances appeared on the books of Ambrose and Co. at 31 December 1989 and refer to the year ending on that day.

	£
Capital at 1 January 1989	952 387
Rent	80 500
Premises	250 000
Motor vehicles	30 000
Motor expenses	9 230
Salaries	55 718
Proprietor's drawings	9 000
Insurances	60 820
Depreciation provision (motor vehicles)	9 000
Equipment (purchased during the year)	35 246
Loose tools at 1 January 1989	8 248
Purchases	900 000
Sales	1 138 761
Sundry debtors	228 120
Sundry creditors	120 678
Lighting and power	120 928
Cash-in-hand and at bank	13 346
Returns-in	920
Returns-out	1 250
Stock: at 1 January 1989	420 000

Additional information:

	£
Stock at 31 December 1989	530 400
Prepayments: Insurance	111
Rent	500
Accrued charges: Lighting and heating	10 000
Salaries	5 121

Depreciation provision on motor vehicles is to be allowed at 20% per annum diminishing balance. A provision is to be created in respect of equipment at 10% straight-line.

Loose tools were revalued at 31 December 1989 at £9516.

From the above information, prepare a trading and profit and loss account for the year ended 31 December 1989, and a balance sheet as at that date.

9 In balance sheets, assets are usually written down from their original cost according to certain set procedures, and the figures at which they finally appear often seem to have little significance.

Do you consider that balance sheets should attempt to show the 'real' value of the assets concerned? What difficulties can arise in attempting to do this?

UNIT 15 PROVIDING FOR BAD DEBTS

Before you read this unit, try activity 15.1.

Activity 15.1

At the end of year 1, a mail-order company had debtors on its books amounting to £2 900 600. Of these, the company considered that debts for £900 should be regarded as 'bad'.

Of the remaining 'apparently good' debts, the company anticipates that some 5% will prove to be bad, though it has no idea which ones these will be.

(i) What action should be taken regarding the debts regarded as definitely 'bad'?
(ii) What will be the total of the debtors that the company should carry forward in its ledger to year 2?
(iii) What figure do you think will appear in the balance sheet for debtors? Do you think this is the figure that should appear, bearing in mind that the purpose of the balance sheet is to summarise the true value of the firm's assets and liabilities as at a certain date?

15A. Potential Bad Debts

1. The problem

There are two distinct problems in accounting arising from bad debts: the first is dealing with present bad debts as such; the second is making an allowance for those likely to prove bad in the future.

As regards the first problem, unit 11 explained (on pages 111–112) that known bad debts are transferred to a bad-debts account. At the end of the accounting period, the total is transferred to P&L as a trading expense for the period concerned. In activity 15.1, therefore, the mail-order firm would transfer the known bad debts of £900 to its bad-debts account, and this would be 'written off' to the profit and loss account. This leaves a total of £2 899 700 for debtors—all of which are 'good' as far as the company knows.

It is unlikely that every penny of debts of nearly £3m will be paid. Most firms will be able to state fairly accurately what proportion of their book debts at any one time are likely to prove bad. What they will not be able to say is precisely *which* of the debts they will be. This, then, is the problem:

(i) On the one hand, the firm must keep a record of each individual debt on its book unless and until it has some definite indication that it is likely to be bad.
(ii) On the other hand, the firm knows that the total of the debtors is more than their true worth because some of them (and it does not know which) are likely to prove bad.

2. Creating a bad-debts provision

The answer to the problem is to create a **bad-debts provision account**. The object of the provision is to reduce the figure for debtors to a

Providing for bad debts

realistic one for balance sheet purposes only. The procedure to create the provision in the first place is to *debit* the profit and loss account, and to *credit* the bad-debts provision account, with an amount equal to an agreed percentage of the 'apparently good' book debts at the end of the accounting year. The amount of this provision is shown as a deduction from the debtors in the balance sheet, and is carried forward in the books to the following year. In the case of the mail-order firm in activity 15.1, therefore, a bad-debts provision of £144 985 (i.e. 5% of £2 899 700—the book debts after the known bad debts have been cleared) would be created. The balance sheet would then show:

	£	£
Debtors	2 899 700	
less bad-debts provision	144 985	2 754 715

Thus, the ledger shows the full record for all debtors, while the balance sheet shows what they are estimated to be actually worth.

3. Maintaining the provision

The balance of the bad-debts provision account is carried forward from year to year as a credit balance in the ledger. Once it has been created, it is only necessary to *adjust* it (either increasing it slightly or decreasing it) at the end of each financial year in order to keep it at the agreed percentage of the debtors at that time. It may also be necessary to adjust the percentage from time to time.

Example 15.1

Show the bad-debts provision account and the extracts from the profit and loss accounts and the balance sheets, for the mail-order firm described in activity 15.1, for each of the years 1–3, bearing in mind that debtors (after bad debts had been cleared) at the end of year 2 amounted to £3 564 780 and at the end of year 3 to £3 222 160.

Bad-debts provision account

Year 1
Dec 31   Profit and loss   144 985

Year 2
Dec 31   Balance   c/d   178 239   Dec 31   Profit and loss   33 254
                                178 239   178 239

Year 3
Dec 31   Profit and loss   17 131   Jan 1   Balance   c/d   178 239
         Balance   c/d   161 108
                                178 239   178 239

Year 4
                                             Jan 1   Balance   b/d   161 108

Profit and loss (extract)

Year 1
  Bad-debts provision   144 985
Year 2
  Bad-debts provision   33 254
Year 3
                                             Bad-debts provision   17 131

Being realistic

> *Balance sheet* (extract)
> Current assets
> Year 1
> Debtors 2 899 700
> *less* provision 144 985   2 754 715
> Year 2
> Debtors 3 564 780
> *less* provision 178 239   3 386 541
> Year 3
> Debtors 3 222 160
> *less* provision 161 108   3 061 052
>
> Note: The adjustment at the end of year 3 entailed a reduction in the provision since the total of debtors was less than the previous year's; hence the credit entry in profit and loss account.

4. Comparison with depreciation provision

> ***Activity 15.2***
>
> Before reading the next section, draw up a table of (i) the similarities and (ii) the differences between bad-debts provisions and depreciation provisions. Then check your list with what follows.

There are two particular similarities in the principles relating to depreciation provisions and bad-debts provisions. These are:

(i) Both exist in the ledger as credit balances, which are carried forward to the next accounting period. Consequently, both appear in the balance sheet—each as a deduction from the asset account to which it refers.

(ii) Each involves an annual entry in the profit and loss account. That in respect of depreciation is always a debit one; that in respect of bad-debts provision may, however, be either a debit entry (if the provision is to be increased) or a credit entry (if the provision is to be decreased).

There are also two significant differences:

(i) Depreciation provision is increased similarly up to the full value of the asset, while bad-debts provision is simply adjusted each year to keep it at an agreed percentage of debtors.

(ii) Depreciation provision is an alternative to a simple depreciation account: the two do not appear in the same set of accounts. Bad-debts account and bad-debts provision account, however, are aimed at two different problems—the first at dealing with actual bad debts; the second at reducing apparently good book debts to a realistic figure for balance sheet purposes. The two will therefore appear in the same set of accounts.

15B. Bad-debts Provision and the Trial Balance

1. Procedure summary

Adjustments for the bad-debts provision, like those for depreciation, are usually carried out *after* the extraction of the trial balance, and *before* the preparation of the final accounts. A common form of examination question is to give a trial balance together with notes listing the adjustments to be made in respect of depreciation and bad-debts provision. There may also be a note regarding actual bad debts to be cleared before the provision is adjusted. The question requires the preparation of the final accounts.

The trial balance will probably already contain figures for depreciation and bad-debts provisions—these will be the balances brought forward from the previous year. It may also contain a figure for bad debts—these will be actual bad debts written off during the current year.

The procedure is set out step by step in display 6. Follow the procedure through, entry by entry, in the example set out in example 15.2.

Display 6: Procedure With Regard to Provisions

ADDITIONAL BAD DEBTS

1. *Add* the additional bad debts to the figure for bad debts in the trial balance.
2. *Deduct* the total from the figure for debtors.

(Note: The ledger entries are: *debit* bad-debts account, *credit* debtors accounts.)

DEPRECIATION PROVISION (see unit 14)

1. *Calculate* the amount for the year.
2. *Add* this amount to the depreciation provision in the trial balance and *debit* the figure to profit and loss.
3. Show the *new* total for the provision as a deduction from the asset concerned in the balance sheet.

(Note: In the P&L there appears only the amount for the current year, while in the balance sheet there appears the trial balance figure *plus* the amount in the P&L. The ledger entries are: *debit* P&L, *credit* depreciation provision.)

BAD-DEBTS PROVISION

1. Calculate the *new* balance required for the bad-debts provision and find the difference between this and the existing figure in the trial balance.
2. If the new balance is *more* than the trial balance figure:
    (i) *debit* the difference to the P&L;
    (ii) *add* the difference to the provision in the trial balance;
    (iii) show the *new* provision as a deduction from debtors in the balance sheet.

(Note: The ledger entries are: *debit* P&L, *credit* bad-debts provision account.)

3. If the new balance is *less* than the trial balance figure:
    (i) *credit* the difference to the P&L;
    (ii) *deduct* the difference from the provision in the trial balance.

(Note: The ledger entries are: *credit* P&L, *debit* bad-debts provision.)

4. The *new* balance for the provision should be shown as a deduction from debtors in the balance sheet.

Example 15.2

The following trial balance was extracted from the books of Anthony Adamson after the preparation of his trading account (hence opening stock, purchases and sales are replaced by gross profit, and the stock item is the closing stock) on 31 December 19-1.

Being realistic

	£	£
Gross profit, from trading account		35 250
Capital, at 1.1.19-1		115 000
Motor vehicles	20 000	
Stock at 31.12.19-1	42 000	
Debtors	21 000	
Cash	3 000	
General expenses	8 000	
Premises	82 000	
Creditors		15 000
Bad debts provision at 1.1.19-1		750
Depreciation provision (motor vehicles) at 1.1.19-1		12 000
Bad debts	2 000	
	178 000	178 000

Notes

1. After an examination of the closing balances for debtors, it was decided to write off a further £1000 of book debts as bad.
2. Depreciation on motor vehicles is at the rate of 20%, straight line.
3. Bad-debts provision is to be maintained at 5% of book debts.
4. Since the trading account was drawn up *before* this trial balance was extracted (note the item 'gross profit' in the list), the item for stock must refer to the closing stock.

You are asked to draw up Anthony Adamson's profit and loss account for the year to 31 December 19-1 and his balance sheet as at that date.

A. Adamson: Profit and loss account for year to 31 December 19-1

	£	£		£	£
Bad debts		3 000	Gross profit b/d		35 250
General expenses		8 000			
Depreciation provision (motor vehicles)		4 000			
Bad-debts provision		250			
Net profit		20 000			
		35 250			35 250

Balance sheet as at 31 December 19-1

Fixed assets				Capital		115 000	
Premises			82 000	Add net profit		20 000	135 000
Motor vehicles		20 000					
Less accumulated depreciation		16 000	4 000	Current liabilities			
			86 000	Creditors			15 000
Stock			42 000				
Debtors	20 000						
Less bad-debts provision	1 000	19 000					
Cash		3 000	64 000				
			150 000				150 000

2. Alternative procedure

In the procedure outlined above, the accounts for bad debts, and for bad-debts provision, are kept completely separate. There are strong arguments for this: they deal with different problems, and, by keeping them apart, it is possible to see clearly how much is having to be written off by way of actual bad debts as opposed to how much is being allocated to the provision. Not only is this useful for management purposes, but it is helpful from a taxation point of view because actual bad debts are a deductible expense for tax assessment purposes, while provisions are not. But despite these arguments some organisations combine the bad debts and the bad-debts provision into one account, taking only one figure to the profit and loss account. Example 15.3 shows how this could be done in the accounts of Anthony Adamson in example 15.2. Note how, under both procedures, the net effect is the same—a *total* charge of £3250 to the P&L. Under the first procedure it is possible to see immediately how this charge is made up in terms of actual bad debts and the provision; under the alternative procedure, it is not.

Example 15.3

Bad-debts provision account

—	Debtors (bad debts)		2000	Jan 1	Balance	b/f	750
Dec 31	Debtors (bad debts)		1000	Dec 31	P&L		3250
Dec 31	Balance	c/d	1000				
			4000				4000
				Jan 1	Balance	b/d	1000

Activity 15.3

Return to example 15.2. Open ledger accounts with the balances listed in the trial balance for bad debts, bad-debts provision, depreciation provision and debtors. Make the entries in those accounts in respect of the items in notes 1–3 and then balance the accounts. Circle—or otherwise identify—the figures in those accounts which correspond with items appearing in (i) the profit and loss account, and (ii) the balance sheet.

Rewrite the bad debts and the bad-debts provision account as a combined account following the principles shown in example 15.3.

Which procedure do you prefer, and why?

Check Your Understanding

1. Prepare a table listing the differences between bad-debts provision and depreciation provision.

2. In what way (or ways) does (do) the purpose and function of a bad-debts provision account differ from that of a bad-debts account?

3. State, with reasons, whether one is likely to find the following in the same set of books:
   (i) bad debts and bad-debts provision accounts;
   (ii) depreciation and depreciation provision accounts.

4. Is it possible to find entries on the *credit* side of profit and loss account in respect of:
   (i) depreciation provision;
   (ii) bad-debts provision?

5. What is the main advantage in:
   (i) combining bad-debts provision and bad-debts account into one account;
   (ii) keeping them separate?

Practical Assignments

1. a. What is the function of the bad-debts account?
   b. At the last day of her financial year, the ledger of Betty Brooke had debtor accounts for A. Andrew £500, C. Charles £360, R. Robinson £680, T. Tomkins £240 and W. Whistler £45.
      Notice has been received that Tomkins has been declared bankrupt and is unlikely to be able to pay any of his debts. W. Whistler's debt has been outstanding for so long that it is decided to write it off as bad.
      (i) What ledger entries will be made in respect of Tomkins and Whistler?
      (ii) In what subsidiary record would these entries have initially been recorded?
      (iii) Assuming that no other debts have been written off as bad, what entries will be made when the final accounts are prepared?

2. a. What is the purpose of the bad-debts provision account, and how does it differ from a bad-debts account?
   b. The ledger of Fantastic Fashions Ltd at the end of its last accounting year showed a balance of debtors of £246 796 and a balance on bad-debts provision account of £12 257. The policy of the firm is to maintain the provision at 5% of book debts.
      (i) In which column of the trial balance will the balance of the provision account appear?
      (ii) What entries will be made at the end of the accounting year in order to maintain the provision?
      (iii) What would have been the entries had the balance of debtors stood at £216 792.

3. At 31 March last, the end of its accounting year, the balance of sundry debtors account in the books of Comely Cosmetics Ltd stood at £150 336 and the balance of bad-debts provision account stood at £14 050. After an examination of the balances, it was decided to write debts amounting to £306 off as bad, and to maintain the provision at 10% of current book debts.
   Give the following:
   a. The sundry debtors account, bad-debts account and the bad-debts provision account as they would appear in the books of the company after the above adjustments had been made and the final accounts completed.
   b. The relevant extract showing sundry debtors and the bad-debts provision as they would have appeared in the balance sheet of the company as at 31 March last.

4. For each of the items listed below, explain how each would be entered in the firm's ledger and the effect of each entry on the firm's balance sheet:
   a. bad debts written off,
   b. decreasing the bad-debts provision,
   c. bad-debts recovered,
   d. increasing the bad-debts provision,
   e. adjusting a rent receivable account for an amount in arrears at the end of the year.

5. The following is the trial balance of the Timely Clock Co. at 31 December last:

	£	£
Capital		759 087
Sales		248 926
Stock	40 000	
Purchases	360 124	
Bad debts	1 200	
Debtors	48 246	
Bad-debts provision		1 346
Creditors		63 211
Sundry fixed assets	600 000	
Cash and bank	14 600	
General expenses	8 400	
	1 072 570	1 072 570

Prepare the trading and profit and loss account for the year to 31 December last, and the balance sheet as at that date, taking into account the following:
a. Stock at 31 December was valued at £46 000.
b. An additional debt of £540 is to be regarded as irrecoverable.
c. Bad-debts provision is to be maintained at 5% of book debts.

6. From the following trial balance of Tick and Co., prepare the trading and profit and loss account for the year ended 31 December 1989 and the balance sheet as at that date:

	£00	£00
Capital		14 413
Drawings	1 260	
Premises	5 000	
Sundry debtors and creditors	1 860	1 310
Loan		1 500
Stock	2 520	
Factory wages	11 600	
Office salaries	810	
Carriage on purchases	302	
Carriage on sales	640	
Factory expenses	1 813	
Office expenses	218	
Purchases and sales	6 780	22 830
Returns	120	230
Interest on loan to 30 June	150	
Advertising	86	
Bad debts	22	
Rent received		150
Office furniture and equipment	390	

Plant and machinery		8 800	
Cash-in-hand		27	
Bank overdraft			745
Depreciation provisions:			
office furniture			20
plant and machinery			1 200
		42 398	42 398

Take the following into account:

a. Stock at 31 December 1989 was valued at £400 750.

b. Wages due but unpaid, £24 000.

c. The figure for sundry debtors includes an amount for £8000 which should be regarded as bad.

d. It is decided that a provision for bad debts of 5% should be created.

e. Depreciation should be allowed for at the following rates:
   (i) office furniture, 10% straight line;
   (ii) plant and machinery, 15% diminishing balance.

f. Loan interest at 20% per annum for the period 1 July–31 December is owing.

7 The following was the balance sheet of John Morris at 1 January 1989:

	£	£	£		£
Fixed assets:				Capital	200 200
Land and buildings	130 000	—	130 000		
Equipment	20 000	14 000	6 000	*Long-term liabilities:*	
Motor vehicles	30 000	9 000	21 000	Loan	55 000
	180 000	23 000	157 000		
Current assets:					
Stock		40 000		*Current liabilities:*	
Debtors	22 900			Trade creditors	40 100
less provision	1 100	21 800			
Bank		73 900			
Cash		2 600	138 300		
			295 300		295 300

During the year, his transactions were:

	£
Goods purchased on credit	70 360
Returns to suppliers	120
Sales of goods on credit	150 640
Returns from customers	2 090
Paid for advertising by cheque	800
Paid salaries by cheque	22 100
Paid rent by cash	2 500
Cash drawings from bank for office use	5 000
Electricity charges paid by cheque	1 500
Sundry expenses paid by cheque	1 200
Cash drawings for personal use of proprietor	4 000
Credits paid by cheque	80 100
Cheques received from debtors	126 680
Bad debts written off	2 340
Purchase of equipment from Office Supplies Ltd on 1 October	5 000

You are required to:

a. Open the ledger at 1 January 1989 and post the transactions.

b. Draw up a trial balance.

c. Prepare the appropriate final accounts, taking into account:
   (i) closing stock £45 000;
   (ii) bad-debts provision to be maintained at 5% of book debts;
   (iii) provisions for depreciation on the value of assets held at 31 December: equipment 20% diminishing balance, motor vehicles 25% diminishing balance;
   (iv) rent includes a prepayment of £300;
   (v) salaries accrued amount to £1200.

d. Draw up a table showing the liquidity ratios at the beginning and end of the year, and the profitability ratios for the year.

e. Add a comment summarising the financial position of the firm as shown by the accounts and tables.

UNIT 16 A FURTHER LOOK AT BUSINESS TRANSACTIONS CAPITAL AND REVENUE TRANSACTIONS

Before you read this unit, try activity 16.1.

Activity 16.1

Consider the following situations and decide, giving reasons, whether or not the firms concerned had a successful year from a business point of view.

Business A is a private school. Its income during its last financial year was £302 000, which included a bequest (gift) under the will of the late Major General Bulldog CBE DSO, an old-boy of the school, of £50 000. The rest of the income was from fees. The school's running expenses for the year amounted to £283 000.

Business B is a manufacturing company producing plastic components for the toy industry. Its trading income during its last financial year was £2 230 000. Its business expenses were £1 920 000.

Business C is engaged on exactly the same type of work as Business B and its trading income was the same (£2 230 000). Its expenses were £2 420 000, which included £500 000 for the construction of extensions to its factory so that it could expand production in the future.

16A. Types of Transactions

1. Capital and revenue transactions

So far, we have studied two completely different types of transactions. First have been those directly connected with setting up the firm or organisation, or with expanding it, such as

Bought machinery by cheque, £10 000

the ledger entries for which are:

Debit Machinery account.
Credit Bank account.

Note that with this type of transaction *both* accounts concerned always appear, at the end of the trading period, in the balance sheet. They are *not* transferred to the trading or P&L.

Secondly, there are those transactions primarily concerned with the normal everyday work of the organisation—that is, with earning income or with the payment of routine expenses. One example would be:

Sold goods for cash, £40

the ledger entries for which are:

Debit   Cash account.
Credit   Sales account.

Another would be:

Paid rent by cheque, £50

the ledger entries for which are:

Debit   Rent account.
Credit   Bank account.

Note that with both of these transactions, *one* entry is made in a balance sheet account and *one* entry in a trading and P&L account.

Activity 16.2

The ledger entries (first example above) for the purchase of machinery are:

Debit   Machinery account.
Credit   Bank account.

If the transaction had been purchased goods (for re-sale) by cheque, the entries would have been:

Debit   Purchase account.
Credit   Bank account.

Prepare a brief but clear note explaining why the purchase of the machinery was not also debited to purchases account.

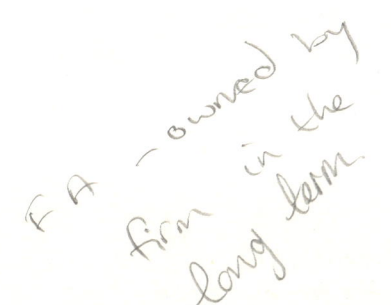

The first group of transactions dealt with above are known, in accounting, as **capital transactions**. A capital transaction is one that is aimed at increasing or decreasing the permanent assets of an organisation in order to improve its *ability* to make a profit or to do its work. Capital transactions are *not* concerned with actually earning the everyday income of the firm, or with paying the routine business expenses.

The second group are known as **revenue transactions**. A revenue transaction is one that is directly concerned with the normal everyday work of the organisation. In a trading organisation, this would refer to the income from selling goods, and the expenses of producing and marketing them. In a club or society, it would refer to income from subscriptions and normal club activities, and the expenses of providing the club's normal services.

It is extremely important to distinguish between capital and revenue. In order to see why, look back at activity 16.1.

What did you decide concerning the school (Business A)?

The school's total income was £302 000; its expenses £283 000. Without doubt, it was 'better off' at the end of the year than at the beginning, the cash reserves having increased by £19 000.

But does this really mean it had enjoyed a successful *business year*? On its *normal* operations—that is, leaving out the effect of the bequest—it made a £31 000 loss—quite a substantial figure. And this is what we *should* look at if we want to know how efficiently the business is running. After all, if the school continues in the same way in future years when old-boys may not happen to make generous bequests, it will not be long before it is in serious financial trouble. Unless bequests of the sort given by the Major General count as 'regular' income (as they would do with charities like Oxfam, for instance), then they should not be included as 'revenue' income.

The same principle applies to the two plastic factories. It would be nonsense to suggest that factory C made a loss—and that it had a poorer year than factory B—*because* it had the good sense to plan for the future and to expand. The cost of the factory extensions must be considered a 'capital' expense, and not included in the profit calculation.

2. Capital and revenue: ledger procedure

Because capital transactions must be kept separate from revenue ones, great care must be taken to make sure that proper postings are made in the ledger. If the transaction is a *capital* one, then both entries must be made in balance sheet accounts, the balances of which are carried forward from one period to the next—that is, in one of the asset or liability accounts. Almost all of these accounts refer to things that actually exist—you could actually touch the machinery, the land and buildings, and the cash, if you wished. For this reason, they are known as either **real accounts** or (in the case of debtors and creditors) **personal accounts**. Personal accounts are really only a special case of real accounts.

With revenue transactions, one entry is made in a balance sheet account (i.e. either a real or a personal account); the other is made in an account which, at the end of the trading period, is transferred to the trading or profit and loss.

Example: *Paid rent for the previous month by cash, £500.*

Entries: *Debit*   Rent account.
          Credit Cash account.

Cash account is obviously the real account concerned; rent account is the P&L account. The 'rent', in this case, does not have any independent existence of its own. After paying it, we could not go and touch it, and cut it up, and give a piece to one person and a piece to someone else. It exists only as a *description* of what the money was spent on. It is therefore termed a **nominal account**. This is the job of nominal accounts—namely, to *describe* where revenue income has come from, or what revenue expenditure has been spent on. By transferring them to the trading and profit and loss, we obtain an alternative picture of the changes in the assets and liabilities.

There are what may appear to be two exceptions to the above rule. The first concerns the purchase and sale of trading goods. These are considered as revenue transactions, and purchases and sales accounts as nominal accounts, although an argument could be put up for considering them as real accounts.

The second consists of payment of a creditor for trading goods previously bought on credit.

Example: *Paid Neptune Wholesalers Ltd cheque, £1200, in respect of trading goods bought last month on credit.*
Entries: *Debit*   Neptune Wholesalers Ltd.
          Credit Bank account.

This is, of course, a revenue transaction because it is directly within

A further look at business transactions

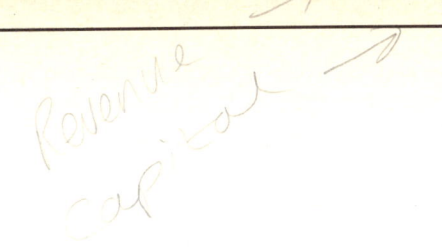

the course of trade; but both entries are made in accounts that appear in the balance sheet—one a real account and one a personal account. The answer is that this transaction must really be seen as a continuation of the credit purchase the month before, when the entries would have been:

Debit   Purchases account.
Credit Neptune Wholesalers Ltd.

Purchases account is, as described above, a revenue account and, as we saw in the previous unit, is transferred to the trading account. In other words, if both parts of the transaction are put together, the entry in the nominal account is, in fact, there.

A similar situation arises where payment is made to a debtor for trading goods previously bought on credit.

Activity 16.3

Discuss the following transactions, which refer to a small greengrocery firm, and decide, giving your reasons, whether each one is a capital or a revenue transaction:
   (i) Purchase of new shop premises.
  (ii) Payment for advertising.
 (iii) Payment of salaries.
  (iv) Purchase of greengrocery for re-sale.
   (v) Cheques sent to trade creditors.
  (vi) Cost of shop fittings and fixtures.
 (vii) Sale of greengrocery.
(viii) Loan received from relative.
  (ix) Purchase of deep freezers.
   (x) Additional capital paid in by proprietor.
  (xi) Part repayment of the loan to the relative.

16B. Capital Gains and Losses

Activity 16.4

The capital invested in a farm is £300 000. The net income on ordinary farming activity for the year ended 31 December 1988 amounted to £20 000 and in the year ended 31 December 1989 to £18 000. In addition, the farm owner obtained planning permission for a field, which had cost him £5000 and was surplus to requirements. In August 1989 he sold the field to a property developer for £300 000. The costs of the sale amounted to £1000.

   (i) *What was his final profit for the year ended 31 December 1989?*
  (ii) *What was his return on capital?*
 (iii) *State, with reasons, whether the farmer had a better or a worse year in 1989 than in 1988.*

Profit arises from the normal everyday activity of a business organisation—that is, from its revenue transactions. Sometimes 'profits' (or 'losses') arise from transactions outside the normal scope of business, such as the sale by the farmer in activity 16.4 of part of his land. Such a 'profit' is known as a **capital gain** (or, if a loss, a **capital loss**). Unless they are for insignificant amounts, such gains and losses must be kept quite separate from normal trading profit. There are a number of ways in which capital gains and losses can be treated, but the simplest way at this stage is to take them direct to capital account.

Being realistic

In the case of the farmer in activity 16.4, the profit *on normal farming activities only* should be calculated in the profit and loss account in the normal way, and this transferred to capital. The cost of the land being sold should be transferred to the debit of a sale-of-land account, which should also be debited with any expenses. The proceeds of the sale credited to the account and the balance (capital gain on the sale of the land) should be transferred to capital and shown separately from the normal profit. The accounts would appear thus:

Capital account

Dec 31	Balance	c/d	612 000	Jan 1	Balance	b/d	300 000
				Dec 31	P&L (profit		18 000
				Dec 31	Land (capital gain)		294 000
			612 000				612 000

Land account (*extract*)

Aug 31	Sale-of-land a/c	5 000

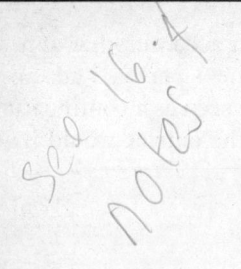

Sale-of-land account

Aug 31	Land a/c	5 000	Aug 31	Bank	300 000
Aug 31	Expenses	1 000			
Aug 31	Capital a/c	294 000			
		300 000			300 000

It should be clear now that, in activity 16.4, the profit was the net income arising from ordinary farming activities, namely £18 000, and that the calculation of return on capital invested should have been based on this figure.

In conclusion, can you provide the answer to activity 16.4?

16C. Materiality

During this book, we have come across the need to make many fine distinctions. If a trader wishes to know what he or she is spending money on, there has to be a separate account for each major expense. If amounts are owing or are pre-paid at the end of the year, adjustments have to be made. In this unit, we have seen the importance of drawing a distinction between capital and revenue transactions.

Despite all that has been said, however, accountants should avoid making distinctions that are *not* significant. In other words, they should only concern themselves with distinctions that are *material*.

If, for example, only a couple of pounds is owed for electricity, if a pre-payment only amounts to a few pence or a capital gain to a few pounds, then the amounts are best forgotten about and the total written off to revenue (i.e. to the profit and loss account). If a number of different expenses can just as well be grouped under one heading, then there is no point in separating them. If an item of capital expenditure—such as a ball-point pen compared with a cheque-writing machine—is so minor as not to justify inclusion in the balance sheet and a policy of depreciation, then it is best charged to P&L as an ordinary revenue expense.

The question is, of course, *what is material*? The answer will vary immensely from one organisation to another, depending upon its size and the sort of information it wants from its accounting system. The purchase of a specialised tool, for example, may be of insignificant cost (comparatively) to a multinational corporation, but could be an item of major expenditure to a self-employed garage owner. Even within an

A further look at business transactions

organisation, what is material for one purpose may not be so for another. Accounts submitted to members of a small club are usually 'rounded' to the nearest pound; those to shareholders of a largish commercial organisation to the nearest thousand pounds; those to shareholders of a multinational corporation to the nearest million pounds. There is no simple guide: one has to use one's common sense. This brings us to the last of our accounting conventions:

> ### Accounting Convention No. 8
> ### The Materiality Convention
>
> Despite accounting rules, trivial distinctions should not be drawn in the processing of accounting information.
>
> *Examples*
> (i) Minor items of expenditure should be written off the revenue even though, strictly speaking, they are capital.
> (ii) Accounting data may be suitably 'rounded' when reporting to management, shareholders, club members and similar groups.

But one final word of warning—if in doubt, draw the distinction and keep the information in separate 'boxes'. It is easier to combine separate data if, at a later date, the distinction is found not to be material, than it is to separate combined information when a distinction is found to be necessary.

Activity 16.5

The owner of a local factory is extremely upset because his accountant tells him that he made an excellent profit in the financial year just ended, and that he must expect a higher-than-normal tax bill in due course. He says that this cannot be the case because of the serious fire that burnt his factory to the ground just a few months ago, the insurance on which had expired. How can he, he argues, have made a big profit when he is virtually a ruined man?

How would you reply to him?

Check Your Understanding

1. State whether each of the following is a capital or a revenue transaction:
   (i) purchase of new machinery;
   (ii) purchase of goods for re-sale;
   (iii) payment of salaries;
   (iv) payment of wages in connection with the erection of new machinery.

2. Why is it important that capital transactions should be kept separate in the books from revenue transactions? What would be the ledger entries for each of the transactions in question 1 above?

3. Give an example of how (i) a capital gain and (ii) a capital loss can arise.

4. Is it possible for a trader to make a considerable amount of profit but yet be very much worse off financially at the end of a financial year?

5. Contrary to strict accounting principles as such, it is likely that a very small accrual (gain or profit) at the end of an accounting year would be ignored, and a small capital expense would be written off to revenue. Which accounting convention could be quoted in support of these procedures?

163

Being realistic

Practical Assignments

1. Explain, giving two examples of each,
   a. capital expenditure
   b. revenue expenditure.
   Why is it important to distinguish between them?

2. With respect to the various items of expenditure listed on right, state *with a reason* whether each should be treated as revenue or as capital, or whether the amount involved should be divided between the two. The firm concerned deals with motor car sales and repairs.

   a. Purchase of equipment for use within the business.
   b. The cost of the firm's own workers in installing the new equipment.
   c. Purchase of a breakdown lorry for use by the repairs division of the firm.
   d. Building costs resulting from necessary repairs to the existing workshop and the construction of a new paint shop.
   e. Expense of repainting of old premises and of the initial painting of new paint shop.
   f. Purchase of motor vehicles for resale.

3. Copy the table below into your work-file and indicate whether each item should be treated as a capital or revenue expenditure by placing a tick in the appropriate column.

	Item	Capital expenditure	Revenue expenditure
a.	Purchase of new equipment for office use		
b.	Cost of constructing new canteen		
c.	Painting and decoration of new canteen		
d.	Purchase of stocks for the factory canteen		
e.	Payment of rates for the year		
f.	Wages of factory employees		
g.	Purchase of new machinery		
h.	Wages of own staff in installing machinery		
i.	Directors' fees		
j.	Redecoration of canteen at end of year		

4. The following balances appeared on the ledger of the Standard Sports Club at 1 January 1989: premises £150 000; equipment £50 000; cash at bank £20 000; creditors £3000.

   The subscription income for the year to 31 December 1989 was £25 000 and expenses incurred amounted to £27 500. During the year, an anonymous donation of £5000 was received.

   Advise the club how the donation should be treated in the books of the club, and why you so advise.

5. a. The following balances appeared on the books of a small private nursery school at the end of its academic and financial year:

Debit balances	£
Premises	75 000
Purchases of:	
teaching materials	8 560
additional furniture	8 000
stationery	5 100
new buildings	32 000
Salaries	85 000
General expenses	17 500
Special expenses:	
rewiring of buildings	25 000
overhaul of drains	3 000
Investments (at cost)	50 000
Equipment (at cost)	20 000
Refund of fees	250
Cash in hand and at bank	22 650
Furniture (at cost)	30 000
Credit balances	
Fees	128 000
Bequests and donations	50 000
Interest:	
on deposit account	800
on investments	3 500
Annual garden fête	2 610
Capital	197 150

Additional information:
  (i) Overdue fees owing to the school, £1000.
  (ii) Owing by the school in respect of: salaries £2500, general expenses £1200.
  (iii) There is not expected to be any further rewiring needed for another 20 years.
  (iv) The drains cause trouble periodically and overhauls such as the one in the current year have to be undertaken every two or three years.
  (v) All the teaching materials were used during the year.

You have been asked by the school's governors to draw up appropriate final accounts from the above information. If you feel that any items need further explanation, comment or enquiry, you should add a note to that effect.

b. The chairman of the school governors has written to you as follows: 'I feel that the income now coming into the school is such that a definite allocation should be made out of revenue each year to provide for long-term capital development.' Write a memorandum in reply to him, basing your comments on your interpretation of the position shown in the school's accounts.

6 During the course of its trading year, an extensive fire destroyed a large part of the stock of the Tropical Trading Co. and seriously damaged their buildings. After the fire, it was found that the fire insurance had lapsed through failure to pay the annual premium, and therefore no compensation could be claimed. You, as the company's accountant, have prepared the final accounts, which show that a substantial profit was made. The managing director has complained, saying that surely you must be wrong since the fire has resulted in such a loss to the firm that it is doubtful whether it will be able to pay its creditors, let alone talk about a profit.

Write a memorandum setting out clearly your reply to this criticism.

UNIT 17 A LOOK BACK AT LEDGER POSTING

Before you read this unit, try activity 17.1.

Activity 17.1

(i) Without looking back, draw up a typical trading and profit and loss account and balance sheet, inserting (in their correct order) the names of the accounts that normally appear. You need not insert figures unless you wish.

(ii) When you have completed it, look back at previous examples of the accounts and see if you have left any items out.

17A. Ledger Posting: the Background

This unit summarises the ledger procedures covered so far. Many students become confused by the variety of ledger postings, but unless these are understood and carried out properly, the whole system breaks down. Also, it is impossible to apply your knowledge to unusual situations that might not have been met with before.

Understanding ledger posting becomes much easier if the following three important features of accounting are borne in mind:

1. The flow of information

Information flows from original documents through the day books to the ledger, and from there to the final accounts, as shown in figure 1.1 on page 5. The ability to 'visualise' this, and to understand where any particular procedure fits into the system, is essential.

Go back and revise figure 1.1 now, and make quite certain that you know the purpose of each part of the structure.

2. The purpose of each of the final accounts

(i) *Balance sheet* (unit 2): to summarise the net worth of an organisation at a particular point in time—hence ledger accounts for each main asset and liability are needed.

(ii) *Profit and loss account* (unit 6): to summarise the income and expenditure arising from normal business activities (other than those arising *directly* from the buying and selling of goods)—hence the need for ledger accounts for each income and expense item involved.

(iii) *Trading account* (unit 7): to show a detailed breakdown of the costs of goods sold, and the income earned from selling them—hence the need for stock and purchases accounts on the one side, and for sales on the other.

A look back at ledger posting

This structure of final accounts, and of the ledger accounts that spring from it, provides the framework into which the posting of transactions has to fit. Understand the framework, and you will more easily understand the posting.

3. The distinction between capital and revenue transactions

This is important because with capital transactions *both* entries are made in real or personal accounts, whereas with revenue transactions *one* entry is made in a nominal account (which appears in the trading or profit and loss account) and *one* is made in a real or personal account (see unit 16). The entry in the nominal account is necessary so that profit can be calculated; the entry in the real or personal account is necessary to record the change in asset or liability concerned.

17B. The Posting of Transactions

Helpful questions to ask when it comes to posting transactions are shown in figure 17.1. Correct answers to these questions are essential if correct information is to be fed through to the final accounts.

The postings for the main groups of transactions are summarised in display 7. Check through each one and relate it to the principles outlined above.

Figure 17.1
Questions to ask when posting transactions.

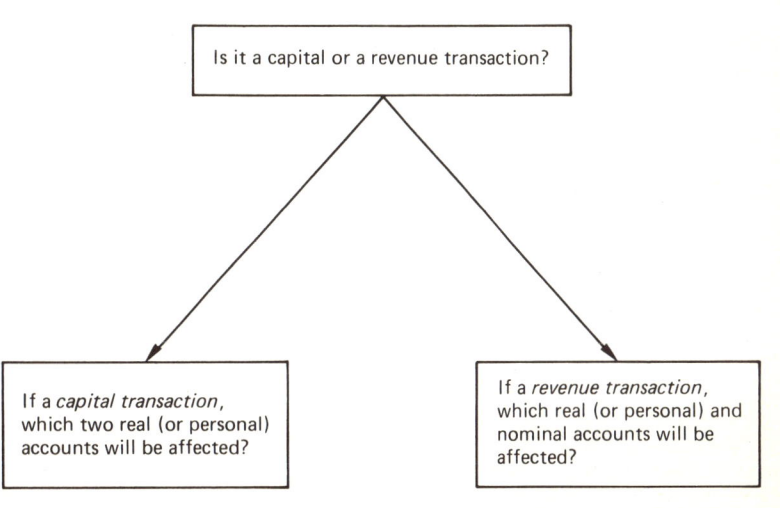

[Flowchart: "Is it a capital or a revenue transaction?" branching into two boxes: "If a *capital transaction*, which two real (or personal) accounts will be affected?" and "If a *revenue transaction*, which real (or personal) and nominal accounts will be affected?"]

Display 7: Summary of Ledger Postings

Note: Where the term *real account* is used in this display, it should be assumed to include personal accounts as well.

1. CAPITAL TRANSACTIONS

Objective: To record changes in the real accounts concerned.
Procedure: Debit the account which 'receives'.
   Credit the account which 'gives'.
Comment: Only balance sheet items affected.

Examples:	*Debit*	*Credit*
Bought premises by cheque	Premises	Bank
Purchased lorry from Ace Ltd	Vehicles	Ace Ltd
Paid Ace Ltd cash deposit	Ace Ltd	Cash

2. REVENUE INCOME

Objectives: (a) To record the change in the real account. (b) To show the amount and source of the income.

167

Procedure: Debit the real account which receives, e.g. cash, bank, debtors. *Credit* the nominal account describing source of income, e.g. sales, fees, subscriptions received, rent received.

Comment: Sales account transferred to credit or trading account. Other nominal accounts transferred to credit or profit and loss account.

Examples:	Debit	Credit
Sold goods for cash	Cash	Sales
Subscriptions received by cheque	Bank	Subscriptions
Received rent in cash	Cash	Rent received

3. REVENUE EXPENSES (GENERAL)

Objectives: (a) To record the change in the real account. (b) To show the amount and nature of the expenditure.

Procedure: Debit the nominal account describing nature of expenditure, e.g. rent, rates, insurance, advertising, salaries. *Credit* the real account concerned, e.g. cash, bank, creditor.

Comment: Normally transferred to debit of profit and loss. Those concerned directly with the cost of sales are a special case dealt with at items 4 and 5 below.

Examples:	Debit	Credit
Paid rent in cash	Rent	Cash
Insurance paid by cheque	Insurance	Bank
Salaries paid by direct debit	Salaries	Bank

4. COST OF SALES: THE BASIC COST OF STOCK

Objective: To show how the cost of the goods that have been sold during a particular trading period is made up.

Procedure: The cost of sales is made up of several components.
  (i) *Opening stock* will already be in the ledger 'stock account' and must be transferred to trading account at end of period. *Debit* trading. *Credit* stock.
  (ii) *Purchases of stock* during the period. *Debit* purchases. *Credit* cash, bank, creditor. Purchases account is transferred to the debit of trading account and added to opening stock at the end of the period.
  (iii) *Closing stock. Debit* stock. *Credit* trading—usually shown as a deduction on the debit side.

Comment: Since stock (a real account) appears in the trading account, it seems to be an exception to the normal rule. However, it is only shown there as part of the calculation of the *cost* of goods sold, which is a nominal item. The actual (i.e. closing) stock, as such, appears in its own right as an asset in the balance sheet. The *cost of sales* is also adjusted in respect of item 5.

Example: See unit 7.

5. COST OF SALES: OTHER ITEMS

Objective: To include within *cost of sales* all *direct* purchase costs of the goods sold. The common items that have to be allowed for are carriage-in and returns-out.

Carriage-in

Procedure: Debit carriage-in. *Credit* cash, bank, creditor.

Comment: Transport costs on purchases are regarded as an integral part of the cost of purchases and are therefore debited to trading account.

Notes
1. Carriage-out is not regarded as a direct cost, and is therefore debited to P&L.
2. Both carriage-in and carriage-out are expenses borne by the firm, and both are therefore debit balances.

Example:	Debit	Credit
Paid transport costs on purchases, by cheque £200	Carriage-in	Bank

Returns-out

Procedure: Debit creditor. *Credit* returns-out.

Comment: On transfer of the trading account, the credit balance for returns-out is *deducted* from purchases on the debit side.

Example:	Debit	Credit
Bought goods from J. Spring £2000	Purchases	J. Spring
Returned goods to Spring £100	J. Spring	Returns-out

6. OTHER TRADING ACCOUNT ITEMS: RETURNS-IN

Objective: To show sales at net value.

Procedure: Debit returns-in. *Credit* debtor.

Comment: On transfer to trading account, the debit balance for returns-in is shown as a deduction from sales on the credit side.

A look back at ledger posting

Example:

	Debit	Credit
Sold goods to L. Sim £5000	L. Sim	Sales
L. Sim returned goods £300	Returns-in	L. Sim

7. DISCOUNTS

Discount-allowed

Procedure: Debit discount-allowed. *Credit* debtor.

Comment: Discount-allowed is a trading expense and is transferred at the end of the period to the debit to P & L.

Example

	Debit	Credit
L. Sim pays cheque £4500	Bank	L. Sim
Discount-allowed £200	Discount-allowed	L. Sim

Discount-received

Procedure: Debit debtor. *Credit* discount-received.

Comment: Discount-received is a trading gain and is transferred at the end of the period to the credit of P & L.

Example:

	Debit	Credit
Paid cheque to J. Spring £1825	J. Spring	Bank
Discount-received £75	J. Spring	Discount-received

Notes

1. The above examples complete those given in items 5 and 6 above and the accounts of Spring and Sim end up with nil balance.
2. The discounts referred to here are *cash* discounts. *Trade* discount is ignored in accounting.
3. The titles of the accounts must be interpreted *specifically* from the point of view of the business concerned, i.e. discount-allowed *to* the business and discount-received *by* the business. Questions are often deliberately worded ambiguously. For example: (i) Paid F. Stamp (creditor) and was allowed discount (this is discount-*received*). (ii) B. Black (debtor) paid by cheque and received discount (this is discount-*allowed*).

8. ACCRUALS

Objective: To ensure that the full expenditure *incurred* on an item of expense, and not just the amount *paid*, is charged to P & L for the accounting period concerned.

Procedure: Debit expense account concerned (current period). *Credit* expense account concerned (new period).

Comment: The debit entry increases any amount already paid and enables the full cost for the period concerned to be written off to P & L. The credit in the new period must be shown in the balance sheet as a current liability.

Example:

	Debit	Credit
Paid rent by cheque £20 000	Rent	Bank
Owing for rent at year end £5000	Rent (current period)	Rent (new period)

Note that in the above account, £25 000 (the full rent for the year) would be charged to P & L although only £20 000 had been paid.

9. PRE-PAYMENTS

Objective: To ensure that any expense that has been paid in advance is carried forward to the following financial year, and not charged against the year in which the payment was made.

Procedure: Debit expense account concerned (new period). *Credit* expense account concerned (old period).

Comment: The pre-payment is, in effect, carried down from the old period to the new. This ensures that only the part of the payment which refers to the current year is charged against the P & L. The debit in the new period must be shown as a current asset in the balance sheet.

Example:

	Debit	Credit
Insurance paid by cheque £800	Insurance	Bank
Of the above payment, £200 referred to the subsequent year	Insurance (new period)	Insurance (current period)

Note that the charge to P & L in the above example will be the £600 remaining in the current period of the account, i.e. the amount that refers to the current year.

10. DEPRECIATION

Non-provision basis

Objective: To reduce an asset each year to its current book value (or, more strictly, writing the cost of an asset off to revenue over an agreed number of years).

Procedure: Debit depreciation. *Credit* asset.

Comment: The depreciation for the year is transferred to P & L, closing the depreciation account. The balance of the asset account shows the written-down value and appears as such in the balance sheet.

Example: *Debit*   *Credit*
Equipment
(current value
£7000) to be
depreciated by
£2000   Depreciation   Equipment

The balance of equipment would stand at £5000 after writing off the depreciation and this is the figure which would appear in the balance sheet.

Provision basis
Objectives: (a) To charge to P&L the depreciation for the current year. (b) To reduce the original cost of an asset to present book value by deducting the accumulated depreciation to date.
Procedure: Debit P&L with current depreciation. *Credit* depreciation provision (for the asset or group of assets concerned).
Comment: The balance of the provision increases each year and is shown as a deduction from the asset in the balance sheet (or in an attached note).
Example: Original cost of equipment £16 000. Depreciation provision brought forward from previous year £9000 (giving a written-down value at beginning of year of £7000). Current year's charge for depreciation £2000. The charge of £2000 to P&L will increase the existing balance of the provision to £11 000. The balance sheet will show equipment as £16 000 less £11 000, i.e. £5000.

If the examples for the non-provision method, and the provision method, are compared, it will be seen that they are *alternative* ways of achieving the same result.

11. BAD DEBTS

Actual bad debts
Objective: To write off from the books completely debts that are known to be bad.
Procedure: Debit bad debts. *Credit* debtor concerned. At the end of period, bad-debts account is transferred to the debit of P&L.
Comment: This procedure permanently reduces the total of debtors in the ledger as well as in the balance sheet. It does not prevent further administrative action to recover the debt.
Example: *Debit*   *Credit*
Debtors stand at
£34 000. Of these
it is considered
that debts for
£3000 must be
considered as   Debtors
bad   Bad debts   concerned

Note that the effect of this procedure will be to reduce both profit and the figure for debtors in the balance sheet.

Bad debts recovered
Procedure: Debit bank. *Credit* bad debts recovered. At the end of the period, bad-debts recovered account is transferred to the credit of P&L.

Bad-debts provision
Objective: To reduce the value of current (apparently good) debtors, after all known actual bad debts have been cleared, to a realistic figure *for balance sheet purposes only*. The provision is maintained at an agreed percentage of debtors.
Procedure: To establish or increase the provision: *Debit* P&L. *Credit* bad-debts provision. To decrease the provision: *Debit* bad-debts provision. Credit P&L.
Comment: The balance of the provision is carried forward from year to year and is shown as a deduction from debtors in the balance sheet.
Example: *Debit*   *Credit*
Debtors stand at
£31 000 after
writing off
known bad
debts. A
provision is
maintained at
10% of book
debts. Balance of   Bad-debts
provision b/f   provision
£2500   P&L (£600)   (£600)

The effect is that the provision will be increased to £3100 (i.e. 10% of book debts). Debtors will appear in balance sheet as £31 000 − £3100, i.e. £27 900.

Notes
1. The objective of the provision account is completely different from that of the bad-debts account. Therefore, one is not an alternative to the other.
2. A procedure exists which combines the accounting for both actual bad debts and bad-debts provision—see unit 15.

12. DRAWINGS

Objective: To record day-to-day cash and goods taken by the proprietor from the firm for his or her own personal use.

A look back at ledger posting

Procedure: Drawings of cash: *Debit* drawings. *Credit* cash, bank. Drawings of goods: *Debit* drawings. *Credit* purchases (if stock taken at cost price) *or* sales (if taken at selling price).

Comment: At the end of the period, drawings is transferred to the debit of capital account.

13. INTERPRETATION

Make sure you understand the following concepts and ratios:

Liquidity (pages 41–45)
  (i) Long-term solvency
  (ii) Short-term solvency
  (iii) Working capital
  (iv) Over-trading
  (v) Current ratio
  (vi) Quick ratio
  (vii) Cash ratio

Profitability (pages 125–131)
  (i) Return on capital invested
  (ii) Return on capital employed
  (iii) Return on total assets
  (iv) Return on sales

14. ACCOUNTING CONVENTIONS

Ensure you understand each of the following and can give examples of each:
  (i) Money measurement (page 12)
  (ii) Business entity (page 2)
  (iii) Continuity (page 73)
  (iv) Consistency (page 73)
  (v) Prudence (page 74)
  (vi) Matching (accruals) (page 108)
  (vii) Historical cost (page 131)
  (viii) Materiality (page 163)

Check Your Understanding

1 Complete the following table

Transaction	A/c to be debited	A/c to be credited
1 Drew cash from bank £1000		
2 Purchased office equipment for cash £700		
3 Bought filing cabinets from Omega Supplies Ltd £300		
4 Proprietor pays cash £10 000 into bank as additional capital		
5 Sent cheque for £300 to Omega Supplies Ltd		
6 Borrowed £5000 from Lenders Ltd. Repayable in two years		
7 Borrowed £1000 from Loans Inc. Repayable in six months		
8 Sold machinery at book value to Grant Ltd		
9 Purchased machinery from Alpha Ltd £20 000		
10 Bought stock from Omega Ltd £10 000		
11 Purchased goods for cash £500		
12 Cash sales £620		
13 Goods sold on credit to White Ltd £2000		
14 Returned faulty machinery to Alpha Ltd £500		
15 Returned goods not up to sample to Omega Ltd £20		
16 Paid transport costs on purchases, cash £50		
17 Paid transport costs on sales, cash £90		
18 Goods returned by White Ltd £40		
19 Closing stock at end of financial year £45 000		
20 Paid wages in cash £5000		
21 Salaries paid by cheque £25 000		
22 Paid insurance by cheque £2000		
23 Paid advertising, cheque £6000		
24 Received from White Ltd, cheque £1000		

Being realistic

25 Discount-allowed to White £50
26 Paid Omega Ltd cheque £8000
27 Discount-received from Omega £400
28 Paid Omega Ltd cheque £200 and was allowed discount £10
29 White Ltd paid us cheque £500 and received discount £25
30 Paid rent by cheque £500
31 Received rent, cash £60
32 Wages paid to own employees for assembling machinery £850
33 Debt owed by Jones, £500, written off as bad
34 At end of financial year:
   (i) insurance paid in advance £500
   (ii) owing for rent £100
   (iii) provide for depreciation provision on premises (cost £500 000; existing provision £100 000) at 20%, straight-line
   (iv) provide for depreciation provision on machinery (cost £800 000; existing provision £200 000) at 40%, diminishing-balance
   (v) provide for bad debts (debtors £300 000, existing provision £25 000) at 10% of book debts
35 Proprietor pays in additional capital, cheque £50 000
36 Goods taken by proprietor at cost, £300
37 Goods at selling price, £400, taken by proprietor for own use
38 Cash drawn from bank for office use £500
39 Cash drawn from bank by proprietor for own use £100
40 Surplus cash, £15 000 invested in short-term securities for two months
41 Purchased shares as long-term investment by cheque, £30 000

2 Assume the financial year ended immediately after each of the transactions listed in question 1. In respect of each account mentioned, state which final account(s), and where appropriate in which subgroup, each account would appear.

Revision Assignment

The following trial balance was extracted from the books of Robert Boulton on 30 September 1990:

	£	£
Capital, 1 October 1989		725 400
Loan (repayable 1998)		50 000
Rents	24 000	4 300
Motor vehicles at cost	300 000	
Depreciation provision (motor vehicles)		80 000
Salaries	50 000	
Carriage inwards	6 600	
Returns-out		4 840
Wages	80 000	
Debtors and creditors	62 000	89 600
Cash in hand and at bank	7 200	
General expenses	168 400	
Fixtures and fittings	106 800	
Commissions paid	70 200	
Motor van expenses	35 000	
Returns	7 300	
Stock	110 000	
Sales and purchases	850 300	1 474 460
Rates	12 200	
Equipment	539 100	
Bad debts	2 000	
Bad-debts provision		2 500
	2 431 100	2 431 100

Required:
a. A trading and profit and loss account for the year ended 30 September 1990, and a balance sheet at that date, taking into account:
   (i) wages owing amount to £6000,
   (ii) rates have been prepaid to the value of £3000,
   (iii) interest at the rate of 10% is owing on the loan for the full year,
   (iv) stock at 30 September 1990 was valued at £96 500,
   (v) the figure for wages includes £5000 spent on installing new equipment,

(vi) motor vehicles are depreciated at the rate of 20% per annum on a diminishing balance basis
(vii) bad-debts provision 5%.
b. A tabular statement showing the relevant liquidity and profitability ratios.
c. A calculation of the rate of stock turnover. What further information would you need in order to make a more accurate calculation?
d. Assuming that all the purchases and all the sales were on credit, calculate the rate of turnover of creditors and debtors, respectively.
e. Write a short comment on the position of the firm as revealed by the accounts and your calculations.

PART FIVE Multiple-choice test

In items 1–21, state which option best answers the question.

1. At the end of the financial year, the bad-debts account is transferred to the
   a. sundry debtors account
   b. trading account
   c. profit and loss account
   d. balance sheet

2. An asset is bought for £30 000 and is to be depreciated 10% per annum, diminishing balance method. Its written-down value after three years will be
   a. £8131
   b. £9000
   c. £21 000
   d. £21 870

3. Bad-debts provision will
   a. always have a credit balance
   b. have either a credit or a debit balance
   c. always have a debit balance
   d. never have a debit or credit balance

4. If a trader forgets to allow for depreciation
   a. gross profit will be increased
   b. net profit will be decreased
   c. gross profit will be decreased
   d. net profit will be increased

5. In respect of machinery, depreciation account and depreciation provision account are
   a. both likely to appear in the same set of accounts
   b. alternative procedures for accounting for the same problem
   c. accounting procedures in respect of different problems
   d. not alternative procedures for accounting for the same problem

6. The omission of bad debts from the accounts will
   a. increase gross profit
   b. decrease gross profit
   c. not affect gross profit
   d. decrease subsequent profit

7. Depreciation account
   a. will always have a debit balance
   b. will always have a credit balance
   c. may have either a credit or a debit balance
   d. will have neither a debit nor a credit balance

8. Bad-debts account and bad-debts provision account
   a. may both be found in the same set of accounts
   b. will not both be found in the same set of accounts
   c. are alternative ways of accounting for the same problem
   d. will always be found in the same set of accounts

9. If the amount of depreciation written off an asset is reduced each year, the method of depreciation is known as
   a. diminishing balance
   b. straight line
   c. revaluation
   d. progressive

10. Sundry debtors amount to £425 000 at the end of the financial year. The bad-debts provision stands at £40 000 and is to be maintained at 10%. In order to update it, the charge to profit and loss account should be
    a. £2500
    b. £25 000
    c. £40 000
    d. £42 000

11. In the trial balance, bad-debts provision account and the bad-debts account will appear as
    a. debit and credit balances respectively
    b. debit balances in both cases
    c. credit and debit balances respectively
    d. credit balances in both cases

12. The method of depreciation in which the same amount is written off an asset each year is known as
    a. straight line
    b. diminishing balance
    c. revaluation
    d. devaluation

13. It is decided to write off the debt owed by Acme Ltd as bad. The entries are

	Debit	Credit
a.	Acme Ltd	bad-debts account
b.	bad-debts provision account	Acme Ltd
c.	bad-debts account	Acme Ltd
d.	Acme Ltd	bad-debts provision account

14. In the trial balance, the bad-debts provision account will appear as a
    a. debit balance
    b. credit balance
    c. deduction from debtors
    d. deduction from creditors

15. Which of the following is most likely to appreciate in value:
    a. land and buildings
    b. motor vehicles
    c. office equipment
    d. plant and machinery

16. Which of the following is not a method of calculating depreciation:
    a. straight line
    b. revaluation
    c. provision
    d. diminishing balance

17. Depreciation is concerned with the reduction in the value of an asset from
    a. extraordinary cause
    b. normal usage
    c. any cause whatsoever
    d. obsolescence

175

18 If a trader's total sales are £600 000, his gross profit margin is 20% on cost and his average stock is £50 000, his rate of turnover is
   a. 8 times
   b. 10 times
   c. 12 times
   d. 20 times

19 On 31 December, year 1, the firm's balance sheet showed machinery account at £300 000 and depreciation provision account at £200 000. During year 2, machinery that had originally cost £10 000 and against which a depreciation provision of £7000 had been built up was sold, and new machinery costing £20 000 was purchased. The firm provides for depreciation at 20% diminishing balance on the value of assets held at the end of the year. The amount charged to profit and loss for depreciation of machinery in year 2 was
   a. £19 400
   b. £23 400
   c. £62 000
   d. £64 000

20 The cost of wages of a firm's employees engaged in installing new equipment would be debited to
   a. wages account
   b. profit and loss account
   c. equipment maintenance account
   d. equipment account

21 Provision for depreciation is made in order to
   a. provide a sum for the replacement of an asset
   b. reduce an asset to market value in the balance sheet
   c. charge against annual profit part of the capital cost of the asset
   d. show the true value of the asset concerned

In items 22–40, answer
A if option 1 *only* is correct
B if option 3 *only* is correct
C if *only* options 1 and 2 are correct
D if options 1, 2 and 3 are *all* correct

22 The purpose of allowing for depreciation is to ensure that
   1. a fair figure is obtained for profit for each period
   2. the cost of an asset is spread over its working life
   3. funds are available to replace the asset

23 Working capital is the amount by which
   1. current assets exceed current liabilities
   2. total assets exceed total liabilities
   3. current assets exceed total liabilities

24 Debit balances will be found in the
   1. carriage-in account
   2. carriage-out account
   3. returns-in account

25 Current assets, as listed in the balance sheet, include
   1. closing stock
   2. trade debtors
   3. cash at bank

26 Net profit is overstated if
   1. closing stock is overvalued
   2. depreciation on plant is omitted
   3. prepaid rates are excluded

27 A company maintains a provision for depreciation account in order to
   1. set aside funds for replacement of the asset
   2. pay for repairs as assets increase in age
   3. ensure that assets appear at a realistic figure in the balance sheet

28 If, at the end of the year, expenses that have been incurred are not included in the final accounts, the effect will be that
   1. profit will be overstated
   2. current liabilities will be understated
   3. the balance sheet will not balance

29 The ability of a firm to pay its current liabilities is indicated by its
   1. current ratio
   2. cash ratio
   3. profit/sales ratio

30 At the end of each financial year, closing stocks are shown in the
   1. trading and profit and loss accounts
   2. profit and loss account and the balance sheet
   3. trading account and balance sheet

31 The fixed assets plus the current assets less the total liabilities equals the
   1. proprietor's capital
   2. working capital
   3. capital employed

32 Credit balances are normally found in
   1. returns inwards account
   2. drawings account
   3. provision for depreciation account

33 A decrease in the provision for bad debts would result in
   1. an increase in net profit
   2. an increase in gross profit
   3. increases in both net and gross profit

34 A capital gain
   1. increases the profit for the period
   2. decreases the profit for the period
   3. does not affect the profit for the period

35 The balance of bad-debts provision
   1. is increased annually
   2. is always kept at a constant percentage of debtors
   3. may be decreased

36 An instalment allowed for straight-line depreciation provision is
   1. a charge against revenue
   2. included in items shown in the balance sheet
   3. based on the original cost of the asset

37 Reduction in value of uninsured stock as a result of flood
   1. is a capital loss
   2. is charged against revenue
   3. may result in a net loss

38 The wages of a firm's own employees engaged in redecorating and extending the firm's premises should be
   1. added to the capital value of the asset
   2. charged to revenue in the year concerned
   3. apportioned between capital and revenue

39 Loss arising from the sale of a depreciated asset is normally
   1. treated as a capital loss
   2. written off to trading account
   3. charged against profit and loss account

40 Provision for bad debts is calculated
   1. after allowing for bad debts
   2. before allowing for bad debts
   3. independently of bad debts

PART SIX
Some Routine Applications

UNIT 18 LOOKING AFTER THE POUNDS
ANOTHER LOOK AT CASH

Before you read this unit, try activity 18.1.

Activity 18.1

(i) How many reasons can you think of why it is useful to have the bank and cash accounts in a separate ledger?

(ii) All accounting records should be kept in a safe and secure place, but this is especially true of the cash and bank accounts. Why do you think that is so?

(iii) Discuss, in a group, the rules that you think should be laid down to ensure the proper security of *both* the cash and bank *balances* and the cash and bank *records*.

18A. Specialised Cash Books

In unit 3, we looked at the basic rules for recording cash and bank transactions, and also at the importance of cash security.

You should revise that unit at this point.

One special characteristic of cash and bank accounts is that almost every transaction we post to the ledger involves, either immediately or eventually, the payment or the receipt of cash. For instance, with cash sales and cash purchases, money changes hands immediately. With credit sales, payment will eventually be made (it is hoped) by the debtor, while in the case of credit purchases, the day will come when we have to pay our creditors. Loans can be received—and later they have to be repaid. Assets can be purchased—and sold. Although transactions do occur that will never involve the movement of money—depreciation and bad debts are examples—they are very few in number.

This means that there will be far more entries in the cash and bank accounts than there will be in any other account, and therefore it is convenient to take the cash and bank accounts out of the normal ledger. Each may then be kept in a book of its own or—as often happens with small firms—they can be put together in a book of their own—the **cash book**. Be careful that you are not confused by the name. Although it is simply called the 'cash' book, it nevertheless contains *both* the cash *and* the bank accounts.

1. Two-column cash books

There are several forms that a cash book can take. One of these is the **two-column cash book**. Unlike the ordinary ledger account ruling,

Some routine applications

which has one debit cash column and one credit cash column, the two-column cash book has *two* columns on each side. The two columns on the left-hand side of the page make up the debit columns for cash and for bank, respectively; and the two columns on the right-hand side represent the credit columns. The accounts are posted in the normal way, but at the end of the page or of the accounting period, the debit column for cash is balanced against the credit column for cash, and the debit column for bank with the credit column for bank. Each balance is then carried down in the normal way. The following example shows the working of a two-column cash book—in a real-life situation there are likely to be far more entries than those in the example.

Example 18.1

A firm starts the month of March with cash-in-hand of £200 and cash-at-bank of £15 000. During March, the following transactions take place:

			£
March	4	Cash sales	300
	10	Paid cash into the bank	350
	11	Cheque received from Wilkinson Ltd	600
	15	Paid cheque to Roma Ltd	420
	18	Cash sales	530
	18	Cash paid into bank	500
	28	Withdrew cash from bank	480
	31	Paid wages in cash	480

The entries in the two-column cash book are the following:

			Cash £	Bank £				Cash £	Bank £
Mar	1	Balances b/d	200	15 000	Mar	10	Bank	350	
	4	Sales	300			15	Roma Ltd		420
	10	Cash		350		18	Cash	500	
	11	Wilkinson Ltd		600		28	Cash		480
	18	Sales	530			31	Wages	480	
	18	Bank		500		31	Balances c/d	180	15 550
	28	Bank	480						
			1510	16 450				1510	16 450
Apr	1	Balances b/d	180	15 550					

Activity 18.2

Discuss with classmates whether there was any point in the firm in the above example paying money into the bank on 18 March, when they knew they would need to withdraw most of it on the 28 March in order to make up the wages.

2. Three-column cash books

A variation of the two-column cash book is the **three-column cash book**. As the name suggests, this has *three* columns on each side of the page. Two of these are for cash and bank as before, but the third one is for recording the discounts associated with any of the payments or receipts. This means a slight complication. The discount associated with money received from creditors (which will be debit entries in the cash and bank columns) will amount to *discount-allowed*, whereas the discount associated with the payments of cash and bank (which will be credit entries in the cash and bank columns) will be *discount-received*. In other words, the two columns refer to different things, and for this reason they cannot be balanced. The two columns must be totalled individually, and the totals taken to the appropriate accounts—i.e. the total of the debit discount column in the cash book will go to the debit of *discount-allowed account* in the ledger, while the total of the credit column will go to the credit of the *discount-received account* in the ledger. Check through each item in the following example.

Example 18.2

Post the following to the three-column cash book of the firm concerned and balance the book at the end of the month:

		£
Feb	1 Balances:	
	Cash	250.25
	Bank	7800.40
	4 Received cash from Extel Ltd	95.50
	Allowed Extel discount	4.50
	5 Paid cash for stationery	5.75
	7 Paid Younger Ltd by cheque	330.25
	Discount allowed by Younger Ltd	2.75
	9 Benger Ltd settled their account for £250, by cheque, less 10% cash discount	
	17 Paid sundry expenses in cash	83.25
	19 Withdrew cash from bank	250.00
	20 Paid wages in cash	148.85
	22 Received cheque Ozo Ltd	25.50
	Discount received by Ozo Ltd	1.50
	24 Purchased goods by cheque	50.00
	26 Paid Anson Ltd by cheque	95.00
	Discount received	2.50
	27 Cash sales	20.75

Preliminary explanations:

(i) Be careful of the wording used as regards the discounts. In each case, ask yourself whether, despite the wording, it is *discount allowed* by the firm concerned or *discount received* by them.

(ii) The transaction of 9 February involves a credit entry in the bank column, and a debit entry in the cash column—both in the same book. For this reason, it is sometimes known as a *contra* entry. In the case of the other transactions, the double entry would be completed by an entry in an account in the main ledger.

(iii) The total of the discount-allowed column (£31) and the total of the discount-received column (£5.25) would be posted to the debit of the discount-allowed account and to the credit of the discount-received account, respectively, in the main ledger.

The entries in the three-column cash book are the following:

		Disc't all'd £	Cash £	Bank £			Disc't rec'd £	Cash £	Bank £
Feb					Feb				
	1 Balance		250.25	7800.40		5 Stationery		5.75	
	4 Extel	4.50	95.50			7 Younger	2.75		330.25
	9 Benger	25.00		225.00		17 Expenses		83.25	
	19 Bank		250.00			19 Cash			250.00
	22 Ozo	1.50		25.50		20 Wages		148.85	
	27 Cash		20.75			24 Purchases			50.00
						26 Anson	2.50		95.00
						28 Balances c/d		378.65	7325.65
		31.00	616.50	8050.90			5.25	616.50	8050.90
Mar	1 Balances b/d		378.65	7325.65					

3. Cash analysis columns

Cash books are often ruled with additional 'analysis' columns across the page; example 18.3 shows a typical case. The analysis columns allow the entries in the main column to be split up, or 'analysed', under one of several subheadings. There can be analysis columns—as many as are needed—on either or both sides of the book. Most large stationers stock a good range of cash analysis books, which can be bought 'off the shelf'. Large organisations, of course, can afford to have books specially printed for them, which are designed to meet their specific needs.

When planning a cash analysis book, some thought has to be given to the headings for the analysis columns. Once they are chosen, it is best to keep them in the same order across the following pages of the cash book, as otherwise mistakes can easily occur through carrying balance figures forward to the wrong columns.

A suitably ruled and headed cash analysis book has several advantages:

(i) Only the totals of the columns need be posted to the respective accounts in the main ledger in order to complete the double entry.
(ii) Every time a transaction occurs, the entry in the analysis column (known as the *extension*) can be done immediately. There is no need to turn pages and pages in the ledger to find the right account for the double entry. It is quicker and reduces the risk of error.
(iii) Note that in this example the columns cross-cast (add across as well as downwards). This is an invaluable check, since it means that—arithmetically at least—all the posting is correct. It is, in a sense, a 'mini trial balance'.

Often, with organisations such as small clubs and societies, where the accounting problem is fairly simple and straightforward, a suitably ruled cash analysis book is the only accounting book that is needed, and all of the information needed for their final summaries—the profit and loss account (or income and expenditure account as it is usually called in the case of such organisations) and the balance sheet—can be picked up from the analysis columns.

Activity 18.3

(i) Think of an organisation with which you are familiar, and plan out a suitable cash book for it, with suitably headed analysis columns.

(ii) Refer back to the information in example 18.3. It was stated that all receipts were paid into the bank, and all payments were by cheque. What do you think is the value of such a procedure, particularly where small clubs and similar organisations are concerned?

---

4. Separate cash-payments and cash-receipts books

If the amount of work makes it worth while, it may be possible to split the cash book into a *cash-payments book* and a separate *cash-receipts book*. This lets two different people work on each 'subsidiary' book at the same time, so speeding up the work considerably. Such a system increases security: if a person has access to only one of the books, it is more difficult to cover up fraud than if one person is handling the whole book.

Obviously, where the books are split in this way, it is not possible to balance them in the normal way and it becomes necessary to have, in the main ledger, a 'cash totals' account to which the individual totals

Looking after the pounds

Example 18.3

Below are the transactions for a small commercial college for September 19—, and the college's cash book with analysis columns. All receipts are paid into the bank, and all payments made by cheque.

Sep		£	Cheque No.
1	Bank balance	7341.28	
2	Cheque to Office Supplies Ltd for stationery	30.50	78661
7	Paid staff wages	250.42	662
9	Canteen sales	360.34	
10	Fees received by cheque	1320.00	
11	Stamps purchased	20.00	663
13	Canteen sales	104.30	
14	Paid wages	261.74	664
15	Fees received by cheque	2560.00	
16	Cheque to Office Supplies Ltd for stationery	250.00	665
17	Bank charges	40.00	
18	Envelopes purchased	26.00	666
20	Fees received by cheque	5670.00	
21	Paid wages	240.78	667
23	Canteen receipts	326.84	
28	Wages paid	250.80	668
30	Staff salaries paid by cheque	2670.50	669–675

The entries in a cash analysis book are the following:

		Total	Canteen	Fees	Miscell.		Cheque No.	Total	Supplies	Wages & Sals	Post, etc.	Bank charges
Sep		£	£	£	£	Sep		£	£	£	£	£
1	Balance b/d	7341.28			7341.28	2	661	30.50	30.50			
9	Sales	360.34	360.34			7	662	250.42		250.42		
10	Fees	1320.00		1320.00		11	663	20.00			20.00	
13	Sales	104.30	104.30			14	664	261.74		261.74		
15	Fees	2560.00		2560.00		16	665	250.00	250.00			
20	Fees	5670.00		5670.00		17	—	40.00				40.00
23	Sales	326.84	326.84			18	666	26.00			26.00	
						21	667	240.78		240.78		
						28	668	250.80		250.80		
						30	669–675	2670.50		2670.50		
		17682.76	791.48	9550.00	7341.28			4040.74	280.50	3674.24	46.00	40.00
						30	Balance c/d	13642.02				
		17682.76						17682.76				
Oct												
1	Balance b/d	13642.02										

183

from each of the two subsidiary books—the cash-payments book and the cash-receipts book—are transferred.

For example, in addition to the main column in which all payments are entered, the cash-payments book of a youth club may have other columns for payments to suppliers, rent, cleaner's wages, cleaning expenses, heating and lighting, stationery and postage. There is usually a column at the end for miscellaneous items that do not fit into any of the other columns. An example would look like this:

CASH-PAYMENTS BOOK

Date	Payment details	Total £	Suppliers £	Rent £	Wages £	Cleaning £	Heat & light £	Stationery & postage £	Miscell. £
Apr 1	Stamps	14.20						14.20	
5	Slimline Ltd	120.50	120.50						
7	Polish, etc.	5.60				5.60			
8	Cleaner	20.00			20.00				
12	Electricity Co.	78.20					78.20		
14	Brasso	1.20				1.20			
15	Cleaner	15.00			15.00				
23	Rent of rooms	120.00		120.00					
25	Van hire	30.00							30.00
		404.70	120.50	120.00	35.00	6.80	78.20	14.20	30.00

(The total of the 'totals' column would be credited to bank account; the totals of the analysis columns would be debited to the ledger accounts for the items concerned.)

18B. Cash Flows

Not only must the cash *balance* be watched and recorded, but also expected **cash flows** must be monitored. This takes us into the field of *cash management*—i.e. estimating the likely receipts and payments, and ensuring that there will be enough in the cash box to meet needs. It means drawing up a table divided into weeks, or months, for the foreseeable future, and for each period setting down the cash receipts expected and the cash payments that will have to be made. At the end of each period, there will be an anticipated cash balance to be carried forward.

Cash-flow tables will involve making estimates. It is better to under-estimate likely receipts and to over-estimate expenses—an example of the *prudence convention* (see page 74). They are usually prepared for several periods ahead on a 'rolling' basis, i.e. as one period is ended, so an estimate for a further period is added.

Watching the cash flow enables a manager to anticipate difficulties before they arise and to take action in good time.

Example 18.4

A firm has a balance of cash at 1 May of £5200. The anticipated cash incomes for May and the four months after are £26 000, £20 000, £14 000, £12 000 and £28 000, respectively. Rent for premises will amount to £500 a month until 1 July, when it will increase to £600 a month. Payments to suppliers are expected to be £10 000, £13 000, £14 000, £13 000 and £9000, and wages £5500 a month until 1 August, and £6500 a month after. General expenses are expected to be £3000, £2500, £4100, £2000 and £1500.

SOLUTION

Anticipated cash flow, 1 May–30 September, 19--

	May	Jun	Jul	Aug	Sep	Oct
	£	£	£	£	£	£
Opening balance	5 200	12 200	10 700	500	(9 600)	
Cash receipts	26 000	20 000	14 000	12 000	28 000	
Total	31 200	32 200	24 700	12 500	18 400	
Cash payments						
Rent	500	500	600	600	600	
Suppliers	10 000	13 000	14 000	13 000	9 000	
Wages	5 500	5 500	5 500	6 500	6 500	
Other expenses	3 000	2 500	4 100	2 000	1 500	
Total payments	19 000	21 500	24 200	22 100	17 600	
Balance c/f	12 200	10 700	500	(9 600)		

Activity 18.4

Refer to the cash-flow table in example 18.4.

(i) *What anticipated cash balance would be carried forward to October on the basis of present information?*

(ii) *A major problem is likely to face the firm at one point during the period. What is it? What action will have to be taken in respect of it? When will the action have to be taken?*

(iii) *What other action would a wise manager consider during the period?*

18C. Looking after the Pence: Petty-cash accounting

Another way in which cash accounting can be modified is to take out of the main cash account the very small payments. The need to do this often arises when someone other than the accountant or treasurer has to make the payments, and when it would be inconvenient for the person to pass all these small items through to the main accounts office for payment in the normal way. The caretaker of a youth club, for instance, may be given a small sum of money for the purchase of minor items such as tins of polish, washers for a dripping tap and felt pens for notices.

Such a fund is known as **petty cash** ('petty' comes from the French word *petit* meaning 'small'), and the holder of such a fund is usually expected to keep a record, known as a *petty-cash account*, of the amounts he or she spends and of the balance in-hand. Each payment should be backed by some form of receipt, or by a signed 'voucher' describing the payment.

From time to time, the person holding the petty cash will need additional cash to 'top up' the fund. Unless there is some form of control over the amount of the 'top-up', there is a danger that the petty-cash balance could steadily mount, leading to a situation where there could be a security risk and a serious risk of theft. In order to avoid this, the **imprest** system is usually followed.

The 'imprest' is the *maximum* amount that the person responsible for the petty-cash fund is allowed to hold at any one time. When the amount in the fund needs topping up, the holder presents his or her

Some routine applications

receipts and vouchers to the main cashier. The cashier then pays to the holder of the fund the amount necessary to restore the original imprest—this will be equal to the amount that has been paid out.

Petty-cash books are often provided with analysis columns on the expenditure side. The following is an example.

Example 18.5

A caretaker at a youth club is provided with a petty-cash fund from which to make small payments. The account is opened on 1 October with an imprest of £50. During October, the following payments are made from it. At the end of the month the imprest was restored:

			£
Oct	2	Purchase of stamps	7.00
	4	Purchase of envelopes	2.50
	5	Cleaning materials bought	5.30
	6	Payment to casual cleaner	6.00
	8	Payment for milk	1.25
	10	Purchase of glue	0.60
	11	Purchase of coloured felt pens	1.20
	12	Payment to casual cleaner	6.00
	14	Purchase of tea-bags	2.13
	15	Large sheets of cartridge paper for notices	3.60
	20	Bus fares	1.20
	22	Telephone call from call-box	0.20
	25	Ball of string	0.80
	26	Electric light bulbs, replacements	5.30

SOLUTION

		Total			Total	Postage	Cleaning	Wages	Sundries
Oct		£	Oct		£	£	£	£	£
1	Cash (imprest)	50.00	2	Stamps	7.00	7.00			
			4	Envelopes	2.50	2.50			
			5	Cleaning mats.	5.30		5.30		
			6	Cleaner	6.00			6.00	
			8	Milk	1.25				1.25
			10	Glue	0.60	0.60			
			11	Felt pens	1.20	1.20			
			12	Cleaner	6.00			6.00	
			14	Tea-bags	2.13				2.13
			15	Paper	3.60	3.60			
			20	Bus fares	1.20				1.20
			22	Telephone	0.20	0.20			
			25	String	0.80	0.80			
			26	Bulbs	5.30				5.30
		50.00			43.08	15.90	5.30	12.00	9.88
			26	Balance c/d	6.92				
		50.00			50.00				
26	Balance b/d	6.92							
	Cash	43.08		(This entry represents the restoration of the original imprest.)					

186

Looking after the pounds

Activity 18.5

(i) Refer to example 18.5. What was the balance that the caretaker had in-hand immediately after the restoration of his imprest on 26 October?

(ii) What entries would the accountant have made in the main ledger on creating the imprest of £50 on 1 October; and on restoring the imprest on 26 October?

(iii) What entry would have appeared in the trial balance had one been extracted on 15 October.

Check Your Understanding

1 What accounts are shown in a two-column cash book?

2 In what ways does a three-column cash book differ from a two-column cash book?

3 Why is it incorrect to say that a three-column cash book contains the accounts for discount-allowed and for discount-received?

4 What are the advantages of having the cash records in a separate book?

5 To which ledger account is the discount column on the debit side of the cash book transferred?

6 To which ledger account is the discount column on the credit side of the cash book transferred?

7 What are *cash analysis* columns, and what is their purpose?

8 What is meant by the term *imprest*?

9 What is the advantage of the imprest system of petty cash?

10 Jot down a list of suggestions for improving cash security in a busy bar with sales that are entirely 'cash over the counter'.

11 What is a cash-flow forecast and what are its main functions? Why does it have to be regularly up-dated?

Practical Assignments

1 a. Why is it necessary that special care be taken as regards the handling and recording of cash transactions?
   b. Why is it advantageous to have a separate cash book? What data are recorded in a
      (i) two-column cash book,
      (ii) three-column cash book,
      (iii) petty-cash book?
   c. Why is it *not* correct to say that the three-column cash book contains the discount-allowed and the discount-received accounts?
   d. What procedures are followed in order to 'close' the cash book at the end of the accounting period?

2 Judy Johnson commenced business on 1 March with a capital of £24 000 divided into cash-in-hand £4000 and cash-at-bank £20 000. Open a two-column cash book with the appropriate balances and then record, in the cash book, the following transactions:

			£
Mar	2	Cash sales paid directly into the bank	3500
	3	Paid wages in cash	2050
	5	Cash sales £3000 of which £2000 was paid into the bank	
	6	Sundry expenses paid in cash	190
	9	Paid George Martin by cheque	950
	10	Paid carriage by cheque	260
	16	Johnson drew cheque for private use	600
	17	Transferred £500 from bank to office cash	
	19	Received a cheque from W. Brown	540
	20	Cash sales paid directly into bank	2150
	28	Paid all cash except £200 into the bank	

Balance the cash book at 31 March.

3 The firm for which you work maintains a three-column cash book. On 23 November, the balances were cash-in-hand £86, bank overdraft £380. During the week 24–30 November, the following transactions occurred:

Nov 24 Paid cash for stationery £8 and stamps £11
25 Paid the amount owing to R. Green, £300, less 2½% cash discount, by cheque
25 Received the sum of £190 cash from E. Brown in settlement of her account less 5% discount
26 Paid £150 cash into the bank account
27 Paid cash for fares £12 and stationery £15
28 Paid cash for window cleaning £17
29 Banked a cheque received from M. White for £114 in settlement of her account less 5% discount
30 Cash sales £545
30 Paid cash into the bank £540
30 Drew cheque for wages £320

187

Some routine applications

You are required to:
a. Write up the cash book and balance at 30 November.
b. Give *three* reasons why the amount of the cash-in-hand may not agree with the balance stated in the cash book.
c. State where the totals of the discount columns will be posted to, and what will be their effect upon the net profit of the organisation.

4 At the start of business on 15 April, the three-column cash book of J. Farrell contained the following balances:

	£
Cash-in-hand	500
Bank	3600 (overdrawn)
Discount allowed	40
Discount received	75

The following transactions then took place:

April 18 Amory Ltd paid its debt of £240 by cheque less 5% cash discount
      23 Cash sales £1000
      24 Paid cheque to Anderson Ltd having been allowed discount from the debt of 10%, £450
      25 Paid wages in cash £358
      28 Paid cash into bank £500

You are required to open the cash book of Farrell with the balances given, to enter the above transactions, and to balance the cash book at 30 April, the end of Farrell's accounting year.

5 State
(i) the effect of each of the transactions listed below, and
(ii) the net effect of all the transactions,
on the cash flow position of the firm concerned:
a. Drew cash from bank £500
b. Paid creditors by cheque the amount owed to them, £6900, less 10% cash discount
c. Purchased stock on credit from Cumbers Ltd £5450
d. Cash sales £740
e. Paid rent by cheque £1000
f. Credit sales £9460
g. Full payment received from debtors who owed £4840. Discount at the rate of 5% was allowed
h. Bank charges £98
i. Payment by bank of standing orders £2400
j. Allowed for depreciation of motor vehicles, £1296
k. Direct debits collected by the bank £3560
l. Creation of a bad-debts provision of 10% of the current book debts of £245 890

6 Robert and Gwenda Jenkins keep a careful record of their personal receipts and payments in a cash book with cash and bank columns, and with analysis columns for the payments covering food, medical, travel, clothing and housing. Write up their cash book for the first fortnight of June from the following information, and balance it.

			£
June 1	Cash in house		5.38
	Cash at bank		506.50
2	Drew from bank, cash		100.00
4	Paid the following:		
	grocer		50.00
	butcher		18.70
	greengrocer		9.54
5	Rates paid by direct debit		352.96
9	Drew from bank, cash		120.00
10	Paid cash for petrol		18.00
11	Paid the following:		
	milkman		24.42
	grocer		10.00
	butcher		17.40
	chemist		5.60
12	Paid for dry cleaning		9.00
14	Bank receives salary by credit transfer		450

What would be the implications for the cash book balances if Mr Jenkins were to pay for his week's groceries at the supermarket £54.86, by credit card.

7 Julie, Janice and Jill plan to set up a secretarial agency after they have completed their secretarial course next July. They have arranged to borrow £1000 from various relatives to give them a start. Half of this will be received when they commence work on 1 September, and half on 1 October.

Careful enquiries have been made into possible sources of work and the costs that will be involved. Their research indicates the following:

	August £	September £	October £	November £
Anticipated earnings each month	600	800	900	1000
Stationery expenses:				
cash purchases	100	50	30	30
credit purchases	500	100	100	150

The earnings are expected to be received in the month following that in which they are earned, and two months' credit will be taken as regards stationery expenses.

In addition, three Amstrad word processors will be ordered at a cost (with software) of £1500. The bill will be payable at the end of October. Fixed costs each month will amount to £200 and the wages of the part-time cleaner to £40 a month. It is expected that the bill for the telephone installation and other costs will amount to £300 and be payable at the end of November. Electricity and other costs are expected to amount to an average of £60 a month, payable monthly.

The following are required:
a. A cash-flow forecast for the months of August to November inclusive.
b. A statement of any potential problems that the forecast discloses together with a note of the nature and timing of any courses of action that could be taken.

8 a. Post the following to the three-column cash book of Skint Productions Ltd and balance the books at the end of the month.

			£
Feb	1	Balances b/f from January	
		cash	250.25
		bank	1800.40
	4	Received cash from T. Jones	95.50
		Allowed him discount	4.50
	5	Paid cash for stationery	5.75
	7	Paid B. Wilson by cheque	330.25
		Discount allowed by Wilson	2.75
	9	Blackstones & Co. settled their account for £250 less 5% discount by cheque	
	17	Paid sundry expenses by cash	83.45
	19	Withdrew cash from bank	250.00
	20	Paid wages in cash	148.65
	22	Received cheque from Zoom Ltd	25.10
		Discount received by Zoom Ltd	1.50
	24	Purchased goods by cheque	50.00
	26	Paid Andrews & Co. by cheque	95.00
		Discount allowed by Andrews	2.50
	27	Cash sales	20.75

b. What are the principal advantages of the three-column cash book compared with normal ledger accounts?

9 a. (i) For what purposes does a firm keep a petty cash book?
(ii) What is meant by the 'imprest'?
(iii) Explain the system of keeping an imprest petty cash book.
(iv) Why is it better to operate petty cash on the imprest system?
(v) Describe what happens to the totals of the postage and cleaning expenses columns.

b. A firm maintains a petty cash book with analysis columns for postage, stationery, wages, cleaning and miscellaneous expenses. The amount of the imprest is £50. Post the following transactions to the petty cash book and restore the imprest.

October			£
	1	Received opening balance, cash	50.00
	1	Paid for stamps	10.00
	2	Purchased envelopes	2.50
	3	Paid for 'Vim' cleaner	1.50
	3	Paid wages to casual cleaner	5.00
	4	Paid milk bill for office tea	1.25
	5	Bought glue	1.00
	8	Refunded taxi fare to office manager	5.50
	9	Purhcased tea	2.50
	10	Cost of telegrams	3.05
	11	Purchase of stamps	2.50
	11	Purchase of miscellaneous office supplies	2.75
	12	Bought sugar for office tea	0.75
	16	Wages for cleaner	2.75
	17	Bus fares	0.80

10 a. Describe the main differences between a cash account and a profit and loss account.
b. Explain why it is possible to make a substantial loss although there has been a considerable increase in cash balances.

11 Consider the situation of a business that receives daily a considerable amount of cash both through the post and 'over the counter' for which change often has to be given. Describe the system that you would advise setting up in order to cope with the accounting and security problems involved.

UNIT 19 RECONCILING THE BANK BALANCE

Before you read this unit, revise unit 3 and try activity 19.1.

Activity 19.1

1. (i) You make a loan of £20 cash to a friend. Later, she repays £12. What entries would you make in your personal ledger (if you were keeping one) to record the two transactions?
   (ii) What entries would your friend make in *her* personal ledger to record the same transactions?
   (iii) Do you see any similarities or differences in the pattern of the entries in the two sets of books?

2. (i) You pay £100 cash into your current account at the bank. You later withdraw £30. Enter these two transactions in your personal ledger.
   (ii) Now try to look at the same two transactions from the point of view of the bank—who *receive* your cash. How would *they* post the two transactions?
   (iii) What similarities or differences do you see in the pattern of entries in your ledger compared with those in the bank's ledger?

19A. Bank Statements

1. Comparisons of statements and cash books

If you have a current account at a bank, you will from time to time receive a **bank statement**. In unit 3 we saw that this document is set out in running-balance format, and that it is a copy of *your* account in the books of the bank. If you have money in the bank, you will have recorded (quite rightly) the bank in your own books as a debtor. From the bank's point of view, you will be *their* creditor, and this is what the statement will show.

What this means is that the bank account as it appears in a firm's ledger, and the firm's account as it appears in the books of the bank, *should* contain exactly the same entries, but on opposite sides. So, if a check is to be made of one against the other, then the debit side of the bank account in the firm's ledger has to be checked against the credit column of the bank statement—and the credit side of the bank account in the firm's books checked against the debit column of the bank statement.

Also, it is very important that a check of the two should be made each time a statement is received. This is because mistakes sometimes occur—even by banks! A deposit (i.e. a payment into the bank) may have been entered in someone else's account by the bank, or someone else's cheque wrongly charged to your account. Also, of course, *you* may have made the mistake—by mis-casting (i.e. adding up wrongly) your cash book—and you may be quite happily thinking that you have far more money in the bank than you actually have.

Unfortunately, this checking is not as easy as it sounds, because there are inevitably differences (discrepancies) between the bank account and the bank statement. The main reasons for these are shown in display 8.

Display 8: **Common Reasons for Discrepancies between a Bank Statement and the Customer's Own Cash Book (Bank Columns)**

1 Recent deposits paid into the bank (and *debited* in the cash book) may not have been passed through by the bank—and so will not appear on the bank statement.

2 Cheques drawn by the customer (and *credited* in the cash book) may not have been presented for payment—and so will not appear on the statement.

3 The bank may have collected amounts on behalf of the customer (and *credited* them on the bank statement) without the customer's knowledge—and so they will not have been entered in the cash book. (Examples include direct debits and standing orders paid into the customer's account, and items such as dividends on shares owned by the customer collected by the bank on behalf of the customer.)

4 The bank may have made various payments on behalf of the customer (and *debited* them on the bank statement) of which the customer was unaware or about which he or she had forgotten—and so they will not have been entered in the cash book. (Examples include direct debits and standing orders chargeable to the customer, and bank charges.)

Activity 19.2

Four customers of a bank open current accounts and deposit £200 each, which is correctly recorded in their respective cash books, and in the records of the bank.

What is the amount and the nature of the balance of each: (i) in their respective cash books and (ii) in the records of the bank?

Immediately before the customers receive their bank statements, the following transactions take place:

Customer A pays a further £50 into the bank. This is recorded by him in his cash book, but does not appear on his bank statement.

Customer B draws a cheque for £60 and posts it to a creditor to whom she owes money. She enters it in her cash book but it does not appear on her bank statement.

Customer C finds, on receipt of her statement, that the bank has deducted £15 'bank charges'. These have not been entered in her cash book.

Customer D has forgotten to enter up a standing order for £25 subscription to his sports club. The bank has paid the money out and deducted it on his bank statement.

In each of the above cases, state:

(i) *the balance that will appear in the cash books and on the bank statements in respect of each of the customers;*
(ii) *what each customer will have to do to the cash book balance in order to make it agree with the bank statement balance;*
(iii) *what each customer will have to do to the bank statement balance in order to make it agree with the cash book balance.*

2. Reconciliation statements

Not only is it essential for both the bank account in the cash book and the bank statement to be correct, but also it is equally important that *they are seen to be correct*. So, when the balance of a statement that has been received does not agree with that in a firm's (or an individual's) bank account, it is necessary to draw up what is called a **bank reconciliation statement** (or, for short, a *bank rec*). This attempts to show that, if all the reasons for the differences are taken into account, then the two balances agree. The main steps involved are as follows:

(i) Check both the cash book and the bank statement in order to identify items that are not common to both. (It is usual to tick the items that *do* correspond lightly in pencil.)
(ii) Take the balance of one of the documents (either the cash book or the bank statement) and show that, by allowing for the unticked items, the balance of the other is obtained.

Some routine applications

In step (ii), considerable *care* is necessary. If you start with the cash book balance and end with the bank statement balance, it is necessary to:

add   (i) the unticked items in the credit column of the bank statement,
      (ii) the unticked items on the credit side of the cash book;

deduct   (i) the unticked items in the debit column of the bank statement,
        (ii) the unticked items on the debit side of the cash book.

This all sounds rather confusing, but it has a logical basis. Remember what you are doing—namely, trying to show that, if you allow for the unticked items, the cash book balance is the same as that of the bank reconciliation statement.

Therefore, if you start with the cash book figure, anything that has been added to the cash book but not to the bank statement should be deducted, and anything deducted from the cash book but not from the bank statement should be added back. Similarly, anything added to the bank statement balance should also be added to the cash book balance, and anything deducted from it should also be deducted from the cash book.

If you start with the bank statement figure, the items added above will have to be deducted, and the items deducted will have to be added.

Activity 19.3

Compare your answers in activity 19.2 with the framework of additions and subtractions set out above.

Do they agree?

The reconciliation statement can be simplified by up-dating the cash book immediately after checking the bank statement, and before preparing the reconciliation. This involves taking the 'unticked' items on the bank statement and entering them in the cash book. This is the normal procedure in practice, but examination questions often require reconciliation statements to be drawn up without up-dating the cash book.

Example 19.1

From the following cash book and bank statement, a bank reconciliation statement is to be prepared. Note that the 'common' items have already been ticked.

Cash book (bank columns only)

				£						£
Apr	1	Balance	✓	6 000	Apr	2	Motor expenses	49244 ✓		300
	3	Cash	✓	2 000		14	Advertising	49245 ✓		1 080
	30	A creditor		3 100		28	Insurance	49246		500
						30	Balance	c/d		9 200
				11 100						11 100
Jun	1	Balance	b/d	9 220						

Bank statement

			Debit £	Credit £	Balance £
Apr	1	Balance			✓ 6000
	3	Sundries		✓ 2000	8000
	10	49244	✓ 300		7700
	15	Dividends received		600	8300
	20	49255	✓ 1080		7220
	30	Bank charges	20		7200

(i) *Bank reconciliation statement without up-dating the cash book*

	£	£
Balance as per cash book at 30 April 19--		9 220
Add:		
Dividend received	600	
Unpresented cheque	500	1 100
		10 320
Deduct:		
Bank charges	20	
Deposit not yet credited	3 100	3 120
Balance as per bank statement of 30 Apr 19--		7 200

(ii) *Bank reconciliation statement from up-dated cash book*

Cash book (bank columns, up-dated)

				£						£
Jun 1	Balance	b/d		9 220	Jun 1	Bank charges				20
1	Dividend received			600	1	Balance		c/d		9 800
				9 820						9 820
1	Balance	b/d		9 800						

	£
Balance as per up-dated cash book	9 800
Add: Unpresented cheque	500
	10 300
Deduct: Deposit not credited	3 100
Balance as per bank statement of 30 Apr 19--	7 200

Activity 19.4

(i) One advantage of preparing a reconciliation statement from an up-dated cash book is that there are fewer items to deal with. Can you think of another reason why it is advisable to up-date the cash book as soon as possible?

(ii) Rewrite the first reconciliation statement in example 19.1 starting with the balance of the bank statement.

19B. Further Complications

In practice, a number of complications arise. These are as follows:

(i) There may be many more 'unticked' items than shown in the example above. In particular, there are often a large number of unpresented cheques. It is usual to prepare an additional list of these, which is attached to the reconciliation, with only the total being entered in the statement itself.

(ii) Banks often use a confusing variety of symbols on their statements, which replace the more explicit written terms.

Some routine applications

(iii) Particular care has to be taken if credit balances in the cash book are involved, or debit balances on the bank statement. These, of course, represent 'minus' figures, indicating that the account is overdrawn. If you start with such a balance, it is advisable to take the 'deductions' first, since these increase the minus amount (and therefore have to be added to the overdrawn balance). Also, since the use of the words 'debit' or 'credit' is confusing because of the different meaning in the 'other' document, it is better to avoid them and simply add *overdrawn* to the balance concerned.

Two complications sometimes appear in examinations:

(iv) The cash book and the bank statement may start with different balances. This can only mean that one or more items shown on one of the documents appear on a previous page (not shown) of the other document. These items should be ignored completely and the reconciliation started from a point where the two balances do agree.

(v) In order to save space and to prevent students from fitting the pieces together like a jigsaw, questions sometimes do not give copies of the two documents as shown in example 19.1. Instead, just one balance is given together with a list of items to be included in the reconciliation. The student then has to decide whether the items should be added or subtracted from the given balance, and the balance of the other document calculated. An example of this is shown in example 19.2.

Example 19.2

At 30 June, the cash book of Alpha Ltd showed a credit balance of £1086. A check of the cash book and bank statement showed the following:

	£
(i) Standing orders, paid by the bank, not entered in the cash book	200
(ii) Deposits not credited by the bank	1122
(iii) Bank charges not entered in the cash book	40
(iv) Cheques drawn but not presented	2560
(v) Dividends and interest collected by the bank, not entered in the cash book	200

Prepare a bank reconciliation statement, showing the balance of the bank statement.

Bank reconciliation statement as at 30 June 19--

	£	£
Balance of cash book at 30 June		1086 (overdrawn)
Deduct:		
Standing orders	200	
Deposits not credited	1122	
Bank charges	40	1362
		2448 (overdrawn)
Add:		
Unpresented cheques	2560	
Dividends	200	2760
Balance as per bank statement		312

Activity 19.5

Do you think it is reasonable or unreasonable for an auditor to insist on seeing a bank reconciliation statement? Give your reasons.

Reconciling the bank balance

Check Your Understanding

1. Explain the reasons why, when a firm has 'money in the bank', it is represented by a debit balance in the firm's cash book but a credit balance on its bank statement.

2. Prepare a list of the reasons why the balance in the firm's cash book may differ from the balance shown on the bank statement.

3. What is the *main* purpose of a bank reconciliation statement?

4. List *two* advantages in up-dating the cash book before preparing the bank reconciliation statement.

5. In going from the cash book balance (not up-dated) to the bank statement figure when preparing a reconciliation statement, which of the following should be added and which subtracted:
   (i) unpresented cheques;
   (ii) deposits not yet credited;
   (iii) bank charges not recorded in the cash book;
   (iv) standing orders not entered in the cash book;
   (v) direct debits recorded as having been paid out by the bank, but not entered in the cash book;
   (iv) credit transfers received by the bank.

6. Why does particular care have to be exercised when preparing a bank reconciliation statement in which some or all of the balances are overdrawn?

Practical Assignments

1. a. Explain the *two* principal ways in which the form of a bank statement differs from the conventional 'T' type ledger account to which it refers. Why does it take this different form?
   b. Give as many reasons as possible why:
      (i) the debit column of the bank statement and the credit column of the cash book, and
      (ii) the credit column of the bank statement and the debit column of the cash book,
      may differ.
   c. What is the purpose of the bank reconciliation statement?

2. From the following cash book and bank statement, prepare
   a. a bank reconciliation statement (without up-dating either the cash book or the bank statement),
   b. a calculation of the up-dated cash book balance,
   c. a reconciliation of the bank statement to the up-dated cash book balance.

Cash book

Mar		£	Mar		Cheque no.	£
1	Balance	210.20	6	Baker	753	20.46
8	Cash	3546.28	7	Charles	754	348.91
13	Dividends	620.71	9	Dodge	755	38.39
15	Cash	2970.39	10	Smith	756	892.91
22	Cash	1248.15	10	Apex Insurance	757	56.78
			10	Jones	758	540.60
			14	Blue Peter	759	20.00
			15	Tom Bola	760	89.90
			18	Ackroyd	761	40.00
			25	Wages	762	3448.20
			25	National Insurance	763	1246.60

Bank statement

March		Dr	Cr	Balance
1	Balance b/f			220.00
2	966750	9.80		210.20
8	SDS		3546.28	3756.48
13	Divi		620.71	4377.19
14	966753	20.46		4356.73
15	SDS		2970.39	7327.12
17	966754	348.91		6978.21
18	966759	20.00		6958.21
19	966757	56.78		6901.43
19	Divi		346.48	7247.91
20	966761	40.00		7207.91
26	966762	3448.20		3759.71

195

Some routine applications

3 Early last June, Joanna Ranger received the following statement of her account at the bank.

			Dr	Cr	Balance
May					
1	Balance	b/f			211.40 OD
5	Sundries			600.00	388.60
10	Sundries			20.00	408.60
12	Abbey National DD		300.00		108.60
18	Sundries			800.00	908.60
24	558776		64.40		844.20
30	Sundries			740.00	1584.20
30	Chs		41.00		1543.20
June					
5	558777		60.00		1483.20

Her cash book, at this stage, was as follows:

			Disc £	Cash £	Bank £				Disc £	Cash £	Bank £
May						May					
1	Balance	b/d		60.00		1	Balance				211.40
3	Sales				600.00	9	Bank			20.00	
9	Cash				20.00	16	Wages			21.00	
13	Sales				800.00	17	Insurance				64.40
19	Withers		7.40		192.60	21	Holbein		3.40		196.60
24	Foukes		2.40		97.60	29	Bank			740.00	
27	Sales			800.00							
29	Cash				740.00						

Joanna requests you to up-date her cash book and to reconcile the balance with the bank statement.

4 Phil Oddie does not keep proper accounting records since he does not understand 'all that figures stuff'. In July last, he received the following bank statement:

		Dr	Cr	Balance
June 1	Balance			30.00
3	Sundries		1800.00	1830.00
19	Sundries		294.00	2124.00
24	842397	93.00		2031.00
30	Rates DD	180.00		1851.00
30	Commission	51.00		1800.00

Phil has asked you whether this statement represents the correct position. You ask him for details of his cash and bank transactions since a check was later carried out, and he produces this list:

Balances at June 1: cash in office £90 and at bank £30 (checked and found correct)

June 3 Paid cash into bank from cash sales, £1800
19 Paid into the bank a cheque from Foster & Co. in settlement of their account for £300 (discount of £6 was allowed)
20 Wages paid to casual worker, cash £30
21 Drew a cheque payable to the insurance people for £93
29 Cash received from market sales £1050
20 Sent a cheque to Rambo Ltd for £351
30 Received a cheque from J. Thompson for £434.50
30 Paid into bank all cheques and cash apart from £50 retained for office use

Calculate an up-dated figure for his bank balance at 1 July, and reconcile the figure with the balance of the bank statement.

5 Ragdolls Ltd received a bank statement dated 30 September 1990 indicating that the company had a credit balance at the bank of £1409. A check of the statement and of the firm's cash book revealed the following:

	£
a. Cheques drawn but not presented to the bank	13 420
b. Deposits paid into the bank, but not shown on the statement	10 215
c. Standing orders paid by the bank, but not entered in the cash book	5 300
d. Bank charges not entered in the cash book	300
e. Dividends received by the bank on the company's behalf, but not entered in the cash book	4 300
f. Cheque, previously paid in and recorded as such in the cash book, now dishonoured. No entry for the dishonour had been made in the cash book	200

You are required to prepare a bank reconciliation statement showing the balance that would have appeared in the cash book before any adjustments were made in respect of the above. Your statement should indicate whether the balance would have been a debit or a credit one.

6 On 31 May last, the cash book (bank columns) of the firm Greenmark Ltd showed a debit balance of £1180.20. The bank statement of the same date showed a credit balance of £2068.65.

A comparison of the cash book with the bank statement showed the following:
   a. Cheques totalling £229.35 had been paid into the bank on 31 May, but were not credited until the following day.
   b. Cheques for £853.05 had been drawn, but had not been presented for payment.
   c. Bank charges of £16.50 appeared on the bank statement, but had not been entered in the cash book.
   d. A standing order in respect of a trade magazine, £15, which had been paid by the bank on 16 May had been omitted from the cash book.
   e. Dividends amounting to £296.25 had been collected by the bank and credited to the account, but had not been entered in the cash book.

Prepare a bank reconciliation statement as at 31 May last.

7 A check of a firm's bank statement, and of its cash book after it had been balanced at 31 March, showed the following:
   a. Deposits at the bank on 31 March amounting to £250.26 had been entered in the cash book but did not appear in the bank statement.
   b. Cheques amounting to £1130.74, which had been drawn during the month, had not been presented.
   c. Dividends for £250 on stock had been received by the bank and credited on the statement, but no entry had been made in the cash book.
   d. Bank charges of £30 had been entered on the statement but no entry had been made in the cash book.
   e. An advice regarding a dishonoured cheque for £100 had gone astray in the post and the item had therefore not been entered in the cash book.
   f. A standing order paid by the bank on 20 March for £150 had not been entered in the cash book.
   g. The debit side of the cash book had been overcast by £1000.

You are required:

(i) to prepare a reconciliation statement, given that the bank statement had a credit balance of £104.32, showing the balance of the cash book at 31 March *before* any adjustments were made;
(ii) to calculate the balance of the cash book after updating had been completed.

UNIT 20 PAYING THE WAGES

Before you read this unit, try activity 20.1.

Activity 20.1

A new contracting firm plans to employ 150 'shop-floor' workers in three different workshops, each 50 miles away from the others. The rates of pay and the hours of the workers are expected to vary greatly. Wages will be paid weekly in cash.

What problems may arise when setting up the wages system? How can they be tackled?

20A. The Wages System

1. Some of the problems

All organisations that employ staff have to pay wages. This means not only recording the amounts in the accounts but also tackling a number of other problems. These include keeping the basic records from which the payroll is made up, calculating and recording the wages and then organising the actual wage payments—and all the time making sure that no fraud takes place. Unfortunately, the payroll is one of the areas in accounting that is particularly vulnerable to fraud.

Wage accounting involves a lot of detailed calculations and routine book-keeping. In most firms of any size, the work is now computerised, and suitable programs can be bought quite cheaply 'over the counter' to meet the needs of most organisations. But manually prepared payrolls can still be found in small firms, clubs and societies; in any case, it is important to understand the mechanics of what the computer is doing for us.

Payroll accounting covers both wages and salaries. The accountant is not concerned with the purely *social* distinction between these two—for example, the fact that people usually consider themselves socially superior if their income is classified as 'salary' rather than as 'wage'. Nevertheless, a distinction *is* drawn between them in accounting—and this distinction will become more important when we deal with manufacturing accounts (see unit 26). **Wages** are usually paid to non-managerial staff and tend to vary with output. In the past, they have usually been paid weekly rather than monthly, though this is rapidly changing. **Salaries** consist of a regular fixed payment to supervisory and management staff, normally paid monthly, and usually do not vary with output. Of the two, wages are the more complicated to deal with: they usually concern many more workers, are paid more often and involve more detailed calculations. In the past—though to a lesser extent today—they have been paid in cash 'on-site', and this can give rise to major security-related problems.

Activity 20.2

What advantages—and what problems—do you see in paying *all* employees by cheque?

What are the advantages and disadvantages to both the employee and the employer of wages being paid monthly instead of weekly?

---

2. The 'back-up' records

Wages can be calculated in a number of different ways. Many workers are paid on a 'time-rate' basis, with the actual wage being based on the number of hours worked. Others, such as salesmen, may be paid on a 'commission' basis—or on a basic fixed wage plus a commission ('commission' means a percentage of sales). Another basis is the quantity of work done or of goods produced—in other words, a 'piece-rate' basis. Whatever the system, proper basic records have to be kept so that the wages due can be correctly calculated.

If workers are paid on a time-rate basis, a record must be kept of the hours actually worked. This record is known as a **time sheet** and it forms the 'original document' from which the wages of time-rate workers are prepared. The time sheet shows the times each day the employee started and finished work, and, from this, the total hours worked can be calculated and the 'gross' wage calculated. The gross wage is the wage before any deductions are made.

Example 20.1

Below is a typical time sheet. Make a list of the details that it contains. Alison, the worker concerned, is contracted to work a 35-hour week, spread over five days, but occasionally she works overtime, which is paid for at the rate of time-and-a-half during the week, and double-time for any work on Saturdays. Note how this is shown in the end column indicating the number of hours to be paid for.

Midland Traders Ltd

				Name		BARRETT, Alison
				Works No.		92 06
Week commencing		19.6.89		Department		Warehousing

| DAY | AM | | PM | | HOURS | | | |
	In	Out	In	Out	Total	Normal	Overtime	Net
Mon	0900	1200	1300	1700	7	7	–	7
Tue	0900	1200	1300	1800	8	7	1	8½
Wed	0900	1200	1300	1700	7	7	–	7
Thu	0900	1200	1300	1800	8	7	1	8½
Fri	0900	1200	1300	1900	9	7	2	10
Sat	0900	1200			3	–	3	6
Sun								
Week's Total					42	35	7	47

---

3. Wage sheets

The information on the time sheets—or similar documents for workers paid on some other basis—is transferred to the wage sheets, or payroll. The wage sheets form a specialised subsidiary book, which feeds summarised totals into the main ledger.

From the gross wages, various deductions are made in order to obtain the net wages—which are the amounts actually paid over to the individual employees. These deductions consist of the following:

(i) **Statutory deductions** have to be deducted by law and paid

Some routine applications

over to the State by the employer. The main examples are income tax and national insurance.

(ii) **Voluntary deductions** can only be deducted with the permission of the employee concerned. Examples often include private health and insurance schemes, superannuation (i.e. pension) contributions, and trade union subscriptions.

Some deductions, such as approved pension contributions, are deducted from pay before income tax is calculated. So there is a distinction between *gross pay* and *taxable pay*. The tax itself is found by looking up, in special tables issued by the Inland Revenue, each worker's wage in relation to that individual's 'code number' previously issued by the tax office. It is a cleverly designed system, which enables employees to receive certain 'tax-free' allowances as well as having the tax deducted from pay as and when it is earned. It is thus known as the PAYE (pay-as-you-earn) tax deduction system.

Activity 20.3

Before the introduction of PAYE, workers paid tax on their wages in the year *following* that in which money had been earned.

What advantages and disadvantages do you see in the present system?

National insurance contributions (NIC) are also deducted by referring to special tables. The system differs from that of income tax in that the employer as well as the employee is required to pay towards the 'total' contribution. National insurance is complicated and involves several different rates depending on a worker's circumstances. Guidance on the matter should be obtained from the Department of Social Security (DSS).

Example 20.2

Below is part of the payroll of Midland Traders Ltd. The hourly rates of pay of the workers concerned are listed on the wages sheet.

Notes
1 The hours of Alison (see example 20.1)—and of other workers—have been transferred from the time sheets to the wage sheet, and then multiplied by the rate per hour to give the gross wage.
2 Amounts in some of the columns have been calculated from previous columns. Can you spot which?
3 Certain of the columns cross-cast. Can you identify which?
4 The wage sheet (dated week beginning 26 June) has picked up the hours from Alison's time sheet for the week beginning 19 June. Why do you think there is a difference of a week?

Week beginning *26 June 1989*

1 Works No.	2 Name	3 Hours	4 Rate (£/hr)	5 Gross wage £	6 NIC £	7 Taxable pay £	8 Tax £	9 Union £	10 NET WAGE £	11 Employer's NIC £
92 06	Barrett A.	47	4.00	188.00	16.92	171.08	30	0	141.08	21.53
84 08	Cassell J.	36	4.00	144.00	12.96	131.04	20	0	111.04	16.49
72 88	Frank C.	28	4.00	112.00	10.08	101.92	13	0	88.92	12.83

98 05	Miller C.	48	4.00	192.00	17.28	174.72	24	5	145.72	21.98
43 56	Wood G.	40	5.00	200.00	18.00	182.00	26	5	151.00	22.90
				836.00	75.24	760.76	113	10	637.76	95.73

20B. Ledger Postings

The wage sheet shown in example 20.2 is a subsidiary book and provides 'totals' figures for posting into the ledger. In practice, there would probably be several wages sheets and the totals would be carried forward. Only the cumulative totals of all the sheets would be posted to the ledger.

In the more general examples described earlier in this book, the distinction between gross and net wages, and the various deductions from pay, have been ignored. Wage payments have been posted simply by *debiting* wages account and *crediting* cash or bank. The complications that now arise are as follows:

(i) Not one but several payments will have to be made out of the bank. These will include:
— net wages payable to the employees;
— payments to the Inland Revenue for the tax deducted;
— payments to the DSS for national insurance—both the amounts deducted from the employees and the employer's contributions;
— payments to trade unions or any other bodies in respect of voluntary deductions.

(ii) Not all the payments will be made at the same time.

(iii) The charge to P & L account must be the gross wage (without allowing for deductions) plus any additional payments by the employer such as the employer's share of the national insurance contributions.

The ledger entries that will have to be made are:

Debit Wages account.
Credit Bank account, with the net wages paid to employees.

Debit Wages account.
Credit Accounts for Inland Revenue (re income tax), DSS (re national insurance), pension, and trade union(s) concerned, with the amounts deducted from the employees' wages.

Debit Wages account.
Credit Accounts for DSS, and pension, with the employer's contributions.

When payments are made in respect of the various deductions and contributions, the account concerned will be debited and the bank will be credited. At the end of the accounting period, wages account will be transferred to P & L account.

20C. Wage Payment Procedures

1. Methods of payment

Wages and salaries may be paid either in cash, by cheque, or directly into the employee's bank account by credit transfer. Payment by cheque and credit transfer prevent any danger of 'wage snatches' and greatly

Some routine applications

reduce the risk of fraud. But there is the disadvantage of the employees having to have bank accounts. Some may find it difficult to get to the bank during its opening hours in order to obtain cash.

Payment in cash involves the preparation of wage packets and the actual payment of them to the workers concerned. This means a considerable amount of cash being transported and handled, with the associated risks of fraud and theft. Every possible step must be taken to ensure that neither mistakes nor stealing takes place. Display 9 lists the steps that should be followed in preparing wage packets.

Display 9: Wages Procedures

PREPARATION OF THE WAGE PACKETS

1 Write out the wages cheque for the *exact sum* required for the wages, and draw this from the bank. This means that if any money is left over after making up the wages, or if there is a shortage of cash, it is immediately known that a mistake has been made.
2 The sum should be brought from the bank under proper security protection. If a security firm cannot be employed, the time at which the money is collected and the route to and from the bank should be varied. The money should *never* be left in the sole care of one person.
3 Before drawing the money from the bank, a *note and coin analysis* should be made. This ensures that each wage due is made up from the smallest number of notes and coins, thus reducing bulk. It also provides an additional check against mistakes.
4 At least two persons, and not always the same two, should be involved in making up the wage packets. Interruptions should be avoided if possible; in particular, the staff should not allow themselves to be called away during the operation.
5 Sufficient time should be allowed in making up the wages to search for mistakes—if, for example, 4000 wage packets have been prepared and there is a shortage of £5 at the end, it means that *at least* one packet is wrong, and it may take a considerable while to find which one(s). Remember that you cannot rely on employees complaining if they have been paid £5 too much, even if you can be certain that they will complain if they have been paid £5 too little.

PAYMENT OF THE WAGES

1 A signature should be obtained for all wages collected by employees. The wages for sick employees should only be released against an authorisation signed by the sick person. Uncollected wages should be listed and the packets returned to the safe; in the absence of a satisfactory reason, enquiry should be started.
2 At least two wages staff should be present at the pay-out and should sign or initial the wage sheets on completion of the task. Each employee collecting the wages should be known by sight to at least one of the supervisors: in the case of a large organisation where this is impossible, a responsible person from the department concerned should also be present at the pay-out. Alternatively, proof of identity should be required.
3 The times at which the staff of different departments collect their wages should be staggered. Consideration should be given to whether or not it is better for staff to collect wages from the wages office, or from a point within their own departments.
4 Wage payments should be made in a room with good security, preferably from behind a screen.

---

2. Note and coin analysis

A *note and coin analysis* involves calculating from the wage sheets the minimum numbers of each coin and note required in order to pay each employee the exact wages to which he or she is entitled.

The procedure is simpler than it sounds. It means looking at the amounts on the wage sheet and noting the coins that will be required. This can be done by analysing the amounts to be paid, one at a time. The analysis for the wages in the example above thus becomes:

Wage (£)	£20	£10	£5	£1	50p	20p	10p	5p	2p	1p
141.08	7			1				1	1	1
111.04	5	1		1					2	
88.92	4		1	3	1	2				1
145.72	7		1			1	1			1
151.00	7	1		1						
637.76	30	2	2	6	2	3	–	1	5	1

An experienced wages clerk will *not* need to analyse each individual payment, but will be able to run his or her eye down the 'wage due' column and count up the number of 1p, 5p, 20p, 50p and £1 coins—and also the number of £5, £10 and £20 notes—required simply by looking down each column in turn.

Activity 20.4

(i) It is usual to list the coins and notes needed on the back of the wages cheque.
   Why do you think this is a helpful practice?
(ii) Check through the ledger postings, which are made from the wages book. Then post the relevant items from the wages book in example 20.2 to the appropriate accounts (and extracts of accounts) in the ledger for Midland Traders Ltd.
(iii) Return to Activity 20.1.
   Can you now improve the suggestions you made?

Check Your Understanding

1. What problems arise when wages are paid *in cash*? What are the alternatives?

2. Why do some employees object to being paid by cheque. To what extent, if at all, does payment by credit transfer overcome this?

3. What are the advantages to the firm of paying wages by credit transfer rather than in cash?

4. Do you think it reasonable that employees should be required, as a condition of their employment, to have a bank account and to accept the payment of wages or salary by cheque or credit transfer?

5. Why is it desirable that a cheque should be drawn for the *exact* amount of the wages to be paid out?

6. What is a note and coin analysis, and what is the purpose in preparing one?

Practical Assignments

1. a. What is the principal difference between statutory deductions and voluntary deductions in connection with payroll accounting? Give one example of each.
   b. Explain precisely the information that would be found on a time sheet.
   c. What is meant by a 'note and coin analysis' and why is it used?

Some routine applications

d. Prepare a note and coin analysis for the following wage payments:

136.56	463.19
269.41	242.23
453.63	258.89
263.10	369.86
325.58	473.34
225.41	339.11
321.76	421.78

2. a. Calculate the total gross pay in each of the following cases:
   (i) Employee A works a basic week of 42 hours at £2.20 an hour.
   (ii) Employee B works a basic week of 39 hours at £2.30 an hour.
   (iii) Employee C works a basic week of 40 hours at £2 an hour plus an additional six hours at time-and-a-quarter.
   (iv) Employee D works a basic week of 40 hours at £2 an hour, plus an additional four hours at time-and-a-quarter plus two hours at double time.
   b. An employee works a standard week of 46 hours for which her gross wage is £103.50.
   (i) What is her rate per hour?
   (ii) What would her gross salary be if she worked an additional six hours at time-and-a-half?
   c. An employee is paid 9p for every handle he fixes to an electric iron up to 200 per day, 10.5p for every handle over 200, and 12p for every handle over 300. What will be his daily gross earnings if he fixes:
   (i) 180 handles,
   (ii) 220 handles,
   (iii) 360 handles.

3. A shop assistant is paid a basic wage of £50 per week plus a commission of 5% on sales in excess of £500 a week. What will her gross earnings be if she sells goods worth:
   a. £480,
   b. £500,
   c. £600?

4. a. Freda Burrows is a secretary in an estate agent's office. Her weekly wage is £160 gross. She contributes 5% of her gross wage to the firm's superannuation (i.e. pension) scheme. After allowing for her personal allowances, the required tax deduction on this wage is £25 and the national insurance is £11. Calculate her net wage for the week.
   b. What does the employer do with the income tax and national insurance contributions that it deducts from employees' wages each week?

5. The following workers are paid at £7.50 an hour, with time-and-a-half for hours in excess of 40 each week. The hours worked in the week ended 7 July were:

Johnson	40	Cox	41
McBeth	46	Daley	40
Singh	40	Hart	45
Lee	40	Patel	42
Campbell	48	Hamid	43
Suleman	42	Stokes	44

All workers except Daley, Lee and Patel contribute to a voluntary contributory pension scheme: the worker contributes 5% of income and the employer 10%. Deductions for income tax contributions, as given by the official tax tables in conjunction with the individual's code number, are:

	£		£
Johnson	68	Cox	70
McBeth	76	Daley	68
Singh	65	Hart	73
Lee	64	Patel	72
Campbell	80	Hamid	(20 *refund*)
Suleman	70	Stokes	71

The employees McBeth, Patel, Suleman and Stokes have agreed to the deduction of their trade union subscription, £1.50, from their wages.

Required:
a. A suitably ruled wages sheet entered up for each employee. The sheet should include columns for the employer's contributions to the pension fund.
b. A note and coin analysis.
c. A schedule of the ledger entries that would be made from the wages sheet, and a note of the amount that would appear in the profit and loss account in respect of these wages.
(Ignore national insurance contributions by both employer and employee.)

6. Assume you have taken over as Chief Accountant in charge of 16 staff. Your company employs some 1750 employees who are paid their wages in cash, and these workers are spread between six different sites, each some miles apart. The company has grown considerably in recent years and the system of wage preparation and payment, designed in the days when the total labour force was only 32, is no longer adequate.

Draw up a report setting out clearly how you think the system of wage preparation and payment should be organised.

UNIT 21 PAYING TAX

Before you read this unit, try activity 21.1.

Activity 21.1

(i) List as many different taxes as you can think of.

(ii) How many of the taxes you have listed affect, in some way, the operation of businesses.

21A. Tax and the Business Organisation

All firms and organisations are directly responsible to the State for the payment of any tax due from them, for the collection and remittance of (i.e. sending off payment for) certain taxes for which their employees (and in the case of companies, their shareholders) may be liable, and for the collection and remittance also of certain taxes for which their customers are liable. The courts can impose heavy penalties if the job is not done properly, and it is not surprising that many business people feel considerable resentment at being unpaid tax collectors for the benefit of the Government—at considerable expense to their firms.

The taxes with which a business organisation is primarily concerned are the following ones.

1. Schedule E income tax

This is often known as PAYE (pay-as-you-earn) because it is the employer's responsibility to deduct the tax from wages and salaries *at source* (i.e. before paying it over to the employees concerned). The employer has to calculate the amount to be deducted according to the system of PAYE code numbers and relevant tax tables. Although it is the employer's duty to deduct and remit the tax, the worker remains liable should the employer fail to do so.

Tax must also be deducted at source from any interest payments on loans, including that on debentures (see page 241).

2. Schedule D income tax

This tax is payable on the profits of sole proprietorships and partnerships. The tax for any one year is based, in general, upon the profits made in the previous year.

3. Corporation tax

Corporation tax has to be paid on the profits of companies (see units 24 and 25), and replaces income tax. For small companies, the rate is the same as the standard rate of income tax; but for larger companies, it is appreciably higher. As with schedule D tax, it is not possible to assess the tax until some while after the end of the company's tax year. If dividends are paid out of the profits before the tax assessment has been made—which is usually the case—then what is known as *advance corporation tax* (ACT) must be deducted and remitted to the Inland

Some routine applications

Revenue immediately. The amounts paid by way of ACT are deductible from the corporation tax eventually payable.

4. Consumption taxes

Commercial organisations are also responsible for collecting and remitting a number of taxes that are payable by consumers on their purchases. Examples include the taxes on petrol, tobacco, alcohol, gambling and new motor cars. In addition, there is the 'general' consumption tax, namely value added tax (VAT). This is a very wide-ranging tax with considerable implications for accounting. Questions are often asked on it at GCSE level; therefore, a special section must be devoted to it.

21B. VAT: the General Idea

When goods are sold, they are often subject to **value added tax** (VAT)—that is, a tax based upon and additional to the selling price. VAT is a complicated tax: it does not apply to all goods, the rate at which it is charged can be changed by Parliament, and many traders can reclaim the tax that they have to pay on their purchases. Consequently, the purchase price as such, and the amount of VAT that might be payable, are kept separate and often only the former quoted in advertisements.

So, if you are buying goods—particularly from a catalogue or in response to an advertisement—check whether VAT is likely to be added to the price you are being asked to pay. Otherwise, you may find yourself having to pay more for the goods than you anticipate (currently, 15% more, which can be quite a lot).

Activity 21.2

Sheila decided to purchase a portable electronic typewriter and some notepaper with printed address in order to improve the look of her job applications. She saw a typewriter advertised in an office equipment catalogue for £250. The local Snazziprint office quoted her £38.50 for printing 250 letterheads, and £6.50 for matching envelopes. She decided that she could just—but only just—afford the amounts, and so she placed orders.

She did not realise that the quotes did not include VAT. When the invoices arrived, she was dismayed to find that VAT at 15% had been added in each case.

How much was the extra amount that Sheila had to pay?

VAT is a tax that most business people—whether they are manufacturers, wholesalers or retailers—are required to add to their own price of the goods or services they are selling. They are then responsible for paying the amount to the Customs and Excise department.

The general principle is that every company or person in the distribution chain, from the producer of the raw materials right down to the retailer who sells the goods to the consumer, charges a tax on the 'value they have added' to the goods—hence its name 'value added' tax. The amount of this tax is based on the difference between the purchase price and the selling price, at each step in the chain. This is achieved, in practice, by the business people concerned having to pay tax on the full selling price of their goods (known as the **output tax**) but being able to reclaim the tax paid when the goods are bought (the **input tax**).

Paying tax

Although this system seems unnecessarily complicated, it does mean that, by the time the goods are eventually sold to the final consumer, the Government has received tax on the full, final selling price. A simple illustration will make this much clearer.

Example 21.1

The following summarises the steps in the manufacture of a product from raw material through to sale to the final consumer:

(i) The supplier sells the raw materials to the manufacturer for £80. ('Value added' at this stage is £80.)
(ii) The manufacturer makes a product from the raw materials and sells it to a wholesaler for £200, not including tax. ('Value added' at this stage is £(200 − 80) = £120.)
(iii) The wholesaler sells it to a retailer for £600, not including tax. ('Value added' at this stage is £(600 − 200) = £400.)
(iv) The retailer sells the product to a consumer for £1400, not including tax. ('Value added' at this stage is £(1400 − 600) = £800.)

The tax payable—and reclaimable—at each stage is set out below.

Notes
1. A VAT rate of 15% is assumed in all examples in this unit.
2. Although the full 15% of the selling price is payable, traders registered for VAT may reclaim what they themselves have paid (the input tax *element*). *Unregistered* traders do not have to levy (i.e. include) the tax on their sales, but they are unable to reclaim what they themselves have had to pay.

SOLUTION

	Basic selling price (not incl. tax)	Value added	Total tax to be added (15% of basic selling price)	Selling price (incl. tax)	Net tax payable at each stage
	£	£	£	£	£
Raw materials supplier	80	80	12	92	12 − 0 = 12
Manufacturer	200	120	30	230	30 − 12 = 18
Wholesaler	600	400	90	690	90 − 30 = 60
Retailer	1400	800	210	1610	210 − 90 = 120
Total tax received by government (15% of £1400)					= 210

21C. Book-keeping Procedures

When recording the purchase of goods in a trader's books, it is essential to keep the VAT separate from the basic cost of the goods as debited to purchase account. Similarly, in recording the sale of the goods, it is equally important to keep the VAT separate from the sale price of the goods as credited to sales account. But in both cases the entry in the personal account of the creditor or debtor can be of the combined figure. If, for example, goods were bought from Flix Ltd for a price of £300 plus £45 VAT (total £345), the entries would be:

		£
Debit	Purchases account	300
Debit	VAT account	45
Credit	Flix Ltd	345

This shows the amount in full that must be paid to Flix Ltd; also it shows the amount that can later be reclaimed from the Government (the *input tax*), together with the true cost of the purchases.

Similarly, if the goods are then re-sold to Ambient Temperature Ltd for £460 plus £69 VAT (total £529), the entries would be:

		£
Debit	Ambient Temperature Ltd	529
Credit	Sales account	460
Credit	VAT account	69

The amount of the VAT is the gross amount due to the Government (the *output tax*).

The *balance* of the VAT account shows the net figure payable by the trader to the Government as far as these two particular transactions are concerned. In the example given, this amounts to £(69−45), i.e. £24. It represents the tax on the 'value added' by the trader, namely £(460 − 300), i.e. £160.

In order to pick up the correct information for the ledger, the sales and the purchases day books should each have an additional column for recording the VAT as distinct from the price of goods. If a firm is not able to reclaim the VAT, then it is usual for it to be included in the purchase price as part of the basic cost of the goods.

It should be remembered that goods other than those intended for re-sale are subject to VAT. If a firm purchases office equipment, for example, it will find that VAT will be added. This should be posted in the normal way as part of the input tax and deducted from the total output tax on general sales in order to arrive at the net amount due to the Government.

In addition to the book-keeping records, a VAT return has to be completed every quarter (every three months).

21D. Complications

This brief account of VAT is deceptively simple. In practice, VAT is a very complicated tax indeed, and anyone going into any form of business would be well advised to obtain detailed advice from their local VAT office. Some of the complications that arise are now dealt with.

1. Differing rates of tax

Not all goods and services bear the same rate of tax. Although most are *standard-rate* (currently 15%), some are *zero-rated*, while a few are *exempt*.

Exempt goods are those which by law are exempt from the tax. These include the lease and hire of most buildings, insurance services, betting and gaming (so schools, colleges and clubs do not have to worry about VAT on raffles), provision of credit, certain education and training services, services of doctors and of *some* related occupations, certain services of undertakers (this makes dying cheaper) and entry to certain sports competitions.

Zero-rated goods are those which currently bear VAT of 0%—which is another way of saying that no tax is chargeable on them. This sounds much the same as being exempt—but the procedure for changing the situation is different. Also, there is a complication in the amount of input tax a supplier can claim back if the goods or services he produces happen to be exempt as opposed to zero-rated. Examples of goods that are currently zero-rated include mobile homes and houseboats, dispensing of prescriptions, sales of new buildings, books and newspapers, clothing and footwear for young children, and most food. However, some fine distinctions are drawn—for example, as regards food from take-aways, only cold food (such as sandwiches) is zero-rated; but hot food (such as burgers and fish and chips) are standard-rated. Also, if fitted kitchen units are built into a new house, they are zero-rated; if they are added later, they are standard-rated.

2. Exempt firms

Not all firms are 'taxable firms', i.e. required to charge VAT on their products. Firms do not *have* to register unless their taxable turnover (that is, total sales of goods subject to VAT) is much larger than £20 000—the precise figure is announced in each year's budget, and tends to increase each year (the exemption limit for 1987–88 was £21 000, having risen annually from £5000 in 1973 when VAT was first introduced).

If a firm does not register, it means that it does not have to add VAT to its goods and is therefore able to sell them appreciably cheaper to its customers than a registered firm is able to. However, such a firm cannot claim back its input tax.

Activity 21.3

Two joinery firms have been asked to quote for the same job—the supply and erection of fitted bedroom furniture. Firm 'A' has a turnover slightly below the VAT limits and is not registered; firm 'B' is slightly over, and is registered. The house concerned is not a new one.

The raw materials for the work will cost £800 plus VAT of 15%. Each firm requires to make a gross profit margin of 20% of the basic cost of materials (not including VAT). Other costs may be ignored.

(i) *What is the lowest price that each firm will be able to quote for doing the work?*
(ii) *Which firm is in the most 'competitive' position?*
(iii) *What difference would it make to the situation if the furniture was to be fitted in a 'brand new' house?*

---

3. Trade and cash discounts

VAT is charged on the invoice price of goods net of both trade and cash discounts (i.e. after they have been deducted). Since the VAT must be mentioned on the invoice, it means that it has to be assumed that the cash discount will, in fact, be allowed. Even if the cash discount is not taken up—and the customer pays the full amount—the VAT is not altered.

4. Bad debts

VAT has to be stated on the invoice for goods, and it is from this that the VAT records must be made up. This means that as soon as a supplier invoices the goods to the customer, the supplier has to pay the VAT irrespective of how long it takes to get the money from the customer.

All traders face the prospect of bad debts—that is, customers who do not pay at all. In such cases, suppliers remain liable to pay the VAT on the sale: the regulations do not allow the suppliers to avoid the payment, or to deduct it from future VAT payments, on the grounds that they have been unable to obtain it from the customer.

5. Cost to traders

Traders are required by law to maintain 'adequate and proper' records to support their VAT returns, and VAT officers have the power to call and inspect them. Traders are also responsible, as we have seen, for the collection of the VAT from their customers, and for the payment of this to the VAT office—all of which involves time, trouble and considerable paperwork.

All of this makes VAT an expensive business for traders, and many of them complain bitterly about being unpaid tax collectors for the Government.

Activity 21.4

Form yourselves into groups. Bearing in mind that the Government *must* obtain the money for the services that it provides (e.g. health, education, defence, social security) from *somewhere*, debate whether or not you think VAT is a fair tax, pointing out what improvements you think should be made, or what alternatives you would offer.

Check Your Understanding

1. An accountant of a company is likely to be concerned with three types of taxes. What are they?

2. What are the differences between schedule E and schedule D taxation?

3. Which groups of people connected with a firm or a company are affected by each form of taxation?

4. What does VAT stand for?

5. What is the current rate of VAT?

6. What are the differences between:
    (i) zero-rated goods and exempt goods;
    (ii) exempt goods and exempt firms;
    (iii) input tax and output tax?

7. Which government department would you contact for guidance and information concerning:
    (i) schedules E and D income tax;
    (ii) corporation tax;
    (iii) value added tax?

8. What effect does being registered for VAT have upon the price that a trader charges customers for his goods?

9. What are the book-keeping entries when goods are (i) purchased, (ii) re-sold, with VAT added in both cases?

10. Why would a person about to establish a new business be well advised to take advice from the local office of the Customs and Excise regarding his VAT position?

11. What is the *current* figure for VAT exemption? By what percentage has it increased since the tax was introduced in 1973? To what extent does this tax correspond with the increase in the general level of prices?

12. How frequently does a VAT return have to be made?

Practical Assignments

1. a. List the different types of taxes that a business firm will be concerned with.
   b. What do the abbreviations:
      (i) PAYE
      (ii) VAT
      stand for?
   c. What is the difference between:
      (i) zero-rated goods
      (ii) exempt goods
      (iii) an exempt firm.

2. During the month of June last, a firm's sales were as follows:

	£		£
G. Rowlands	230	T. Williams	540
B. Smith	40	K. Etchley	620
D. Younger	120	W. Forsyth	380

   All sales are subject to VAT at current rates.
   Show the appropriate ledger accounts and extracts.

3. Post the following transactions to the ledger, taking care to calculate correctly the amount that should be posted to the customer's account, to the VAT account and to the sales account.
   a. Sale of goods to T. Robson at list price of £300.
   b. B. Tooks bought goods at list price of £590 less trade discount of 25%.
   c. Goods sold to Harry Andrews at list price of £450 less 20% trade discount and 10% cash discount one month.
   VAT should be allowed for at the current rate.

4. Mollinson and Co. purchased the following goods during the month of July last:

July	1	Office Supplies Co.	320	standard rate
	5	Bletchley and Crossly	450	standard rate
	10	Morton and Mersey	230	exempt goods
	15	Go-Go-Go Ltd	790	standard rate
	20	Farnley & Co.	190	zero-rated goods
	24	Pennine Contractors	880	£600 of these goods at standard rate; balance zero-rated
	28	Office Supplies Co.	742	standard rate

   Calculations should be based upon the *current* standard rate.
   You are required:
   a. to make the postings to the appropriate ledger accounts;
   b. to state the total amount of the input tax suffered by Mollinson and Co.;
   c. to calculate
      (i) the total amount of the output tax in respect of the above transactions,
      (ii) the amount that will be payable to HM Customs and Excise,
   assuming that Mollinson and Co. work on a standard mark-up of 30%.

PART SIX Multiple-choice test

In items 1–30, state which option best answers the question.

1. Which of the following ledger accounts can never have a credit balance:
   a. personal accounts of customers
   b. cash account
   c. discount account
   d. bank account

2. If a firm has made a profit, it means that the cash and bank balances
   a. will be greater than previously
   b. will be less than previously
   c. are likely to be unaffected
   d. may be either greater or less than previously

3. Sums of money received by a trading organisation in respect of selling goods are referred to in accounting as
   a. extraordinary income
   b. non-revenue income
   c. capital income
   d. revenue income

4. If, at the end of a trading period, a firm's cash and bank balances are low, it means that the firm
   a. has purchased a lot of goods
   b. is making a profit
   c. is making a loss
   d. may be making either a profit or a loss

5. Which of the following is a real account:
   a. wages account
   b. cash account
   c. capital account
   d. West End Productions Ltd

6. In the pay-as-you-earn system, the amount of tax deducted is based upon the
   a. gross wage
   b. gross wage less statutory deductions
   c. gross wage less voluntary deductions
   d. gross wage less all deductions

7. A credit balance in a bank statement means that
   a. the account is overdrawn
   b. money is owed to the bank
   c. the bank owes money to the customer
   d. the bank is the creditor of the customer

8. Bank reconciliation statements should be prepared
   a. as often as is practicable
   b. the last business day of every month
   c. every time a bank statement is received
   d. whenever a trial balance is extracted

9. A bank reconciliation statement is concerned with the difference between the firm's
   a. bank account and cash account
   b. cash book and the ledger
   c. account at the bank and the bank statement
   d. bank statement and bank account in the ledger

10. The cash book is
    a. a book of original entry but not a ledger account
    b. a ledger account but not a book of original entry
    c. both a ledger account and a book of original entry
    d. neither a book of original entry nor a ledger account

11. A tax deduction card
    a. certifies the amount of tax deducted
    b. shows the calculation of tax deducted
    c. authorises an employer to deduct tax
    d. indicates net wage payable

12. The main purpose of a bank reconciliation statement is to
    a. show that there are differences
    b. demonstrate that there are no differences
    c. explain the differences
    d. remove the differences
    between the bank account in the customer's ledger and the customer's account in the books of the bank

13. A firm's bank statement shows a credit balance of £24 960. A check against the cash book showed that cheques for £320 and £410 had not been presented and that a deposit of £300 had not been credited. The balance of the cash book should therefore be
    a. £23 930
    b. £24 530
    c. £25 390
    d. £25 990

14. The imprest system is primarily aimed at controlling the
    a. minimum balance held by the cashier concerned
    b. number of disbursements made
    c. maximum balance held by the cashier concerned
    d. average amount held

15. Which of the following would appear on a bank statement?
    a. unpresented cheques
    b. deposits not credited
    c. dishonoured cheques
    d. lost cheques

16. The total of the cash book column listing the discounts allowed by creditors is posted to the firm's

Some routine applications

a. discount-allowed account
b. discount-received account
c. profit and loss account
d. balance sheet

17 Overtime is
a. a regular part of a normal worker's wage
b. a payment for hours above an agreed minimum
c. a payment above the national time minimum
d. an allowance over normal time wage

18 A bank statement contains a deposit paid in by a third party which does not appear in the cash book. In order to reconcile the balance of the statement to that of the cash book, the item would be
a. added to the bank statement balance
b. deducted from the cash book balance
c. deducted from the bank statement balance
d. added to the cash book balance

19 A three-column cash book will not contain details of
a. cash transactions
b. trade discount allowances
c. bank transactions
d. cash discount allowances

20 The receipt of an amount by cheque should be
a. debited to bank account
b. credited to cash account
c. debited to cash account
d. credited to bank account

21 Voluntary deductions include
a. private insurance premiums, trade union subscriptions, private pension contributions, holiday fund
b. trade union subscriptions, national insurance contributions, holiday fund contributions, private insurance contributions
c. pension contributions, tax deductions, private insurance premiums, trade union subscriptions
d. trade union subscriptions, tax deductions, holiday fund, private insurance contributions, pension contributions

22 Entries in the credit columns of the cash book should be posted to the
a. credit of the personal or nominal accounts concerned
b. debit of the personal or nominal accounts concerned
c. debit or credit of the personal accounts as appropriate
d. credit of the nominal accounts concerned

23 A separate cash book does not
a. speed up ledger posting
b. ensure current cash balances are always available
c. enable more than one clerk to be employed on the same set of books
d. reduce the size of the ledger

24 The payment of a debt by cheque should be
a. debited to bank account
b. credited to bank account
c. debited to cash account
d. credited to cash account

25 Cash received in settlement of credit transactions means that
a. profits will be increased
b. losses will be reduced
c. the rate of turnover will be increased
d. the cash flow will be improved

26 The entries in the debit columns of the cash book should be posted to the
a. credit of the personal or nominal accounts concerned
b. debit of the personal or nominal accounts concerned
c. debit or credit of the personal or nominal accounts concerned
d. credit of personal accounts only

27 The 'pay-as-you-earn' system
a. means that wages cannot be paid without tax being deducted
b. is the only means through which tax is now paid
c. allows tax due to be deducted from wages before payment
d. applies to everyone irrespective of income

28 A bank statement indicates a debit balance of £2300. This includes bank charges of £400, which have not been recorded in the cash book. Examination shows that cheques to the value of £5600 have not been presented for payment, and that a deposit of £8000 cash has not yet been cleared. The balance of the cash book should, therefore, be
a. £500 credit
b. £500 debit
c. £5100 credit
d. £11 700 debit

29 The statement of account received by a firm from its bank would include
a. cheques sent to creditors but not yet presented
b. deposits that have not yet been cleared
c. cheques from customers that have been dishonoured
d. a payment made from the petty cash account

30 Payment by commission is usually made to
a. operatives on the basis of an amount stipulated in their contract of employment
b. salesmen on the basis of sales made by themselves
c. managers on the basis of sales made by the firm
d. directors on the basis of the commissions they obtain for the firm

In questions 31–40, answer
A if option 1 *only* is correct
B if option 3 *only* is correct
C if *only* options 1 and 2 are correct
D if options 1, 2 and 3 are *all* correct

31 A worker's net wage is the amount
1. he receives in his pay packet
2. he has earned
3. before deductions have been made

32 Under the heading *Current assets* in a balance sheet, one would find
1. trade debtors
2. closing stock
3. bank overdraft

33 Wages and salaries may be paid by
1. credit transfer
2. cheque
3. cash

34 Wages may be calculated on the basis of
1. a fixed and agreed amount each week
2. the quantity produced
3. hours worked each week

35 A bank statement shows the
1. cleared deposits
2. direct debits
3. credit transfers

36 A distinction is made in accounting between wages and salaries because
1. wages tend to vary with turnover
2. wages and salaries are paid to persons with different social backgrounds
3. wages are considered to be direct costs, and salaries indirect costs

37 A petty cash book is always
1. based on an imprest
2. ruled with analysis columns
3. for the disbursement of small amounts

38 The difference between gross and net wages equals the
1. sum of both statutory and voluntary deductions
2. difference between earnings and 'take-home' pay
3. amount added in respect of overtime

39 PAYE
1. is a method for deducting tax from wages and salaries
2. permits tax allowances to be coded into the tax deductions
3. does not apply to traders and self-employed workers

40 Wage slips contain information concerning
1. net pay
2. deductions
3. gross pay

PART SEVEN

Accounts of Particular Organisations

Receipts + Payments acc
— summarised cash + bank acc.
receipts - debits
payments - credits
not part of double entry system

UNIT 22 ACCOUNTING FOR CLUBS AND SOCIETIES

Before you read this unit, try activity 22.1.

> **Activity 22.1**
>
> Imagine that you are a member of a fair-sized club. The treasurer has said to you that, since the club is a non-profit-making organisation, there is no point in preparing a profit and loss account.
>
> *How would you answer him?*

Accounting practice should always reflect the actual and likely needs of the organisation concerned and—for the most part—*only* those needs, since it is a waste of time to produce information that no one wants. This is as true of clubs and societies, and other non-profit-making organisations, as it is of any other organisation. If all that is needed is a record of cash currently available, then simple cash and bank accounts are sufficient.

However, the members of an organisation—even quite a small one—may feel that they need something more than just a cash balance at the end of the day, week, month or year. They may want to know, for example, exactly where the money has come from over the past year, and on what it has been spent.

Also, a club or society does not have to be larger for its members to see the importance of knowing what *income*, such as subscriptions for the year, has been 'earned' (whether received or not) by the club, and what *expenditure* has been incurred (again, whether actually paid or not). In other words, they may well see a need for an account that follows all the principles of a profit and loss, though not described as such.

22A. Receipts and Payments Accounts

For many small clubs and societies, nothing more is needed than an accurate record of cash and bank transactions. It is normal, once a year, to prepare a year-end summary of these transactions, and this is known as a **receipts and payments account**. A receipts and payments account is nothing more nor less than a summarised cash and bank account, and it follows all the rules of cash and bank accounts. This means that the summarised receipts are listed as debits and the summarised payments as credits—either in normal ledger format or as a vertical statement. Whichever way it is presented, a receipts and payments account starts with the opening balances of cash and bank at the beginning of the year, and ends with the closing balances at the end of the year. If cash has been drawn from, or paid into, the bank account, there will be corresponding entries in both cash and bank accounts.

Accounts of particular organisations

These will, or course, be self-cancelling when the accounts are combined and will not appear in the receipts and payments account.

The title 'receipts and payments' account is important since this is exactly what it is—a summary of actual *cash* receipts and actual *cash* payments. The account is not concerned with accruals or pre-payments; neither does it include 'notional' expenses such as depreciation and bad-debts provisions, or take any note of whether transactions are capital or revenue. Although called an 'account', it is *not* part of the double-entry system, and nothing is transferred to it or from it.

In order to draw up a receipts and payments account, it is necessary to do the following:

(i) Combine similar items—such as the various payments for rent. This may involve combining entries in both the cash and the bank accounts.
(ii) Exclude transfers from bank to cash, and from cash to bank.
(iii) Ignore any reference to the dates that items refer to, and concentrate solely on the actual sums received, and the actual payments made.
(iv) Remember that a receipts and payments account, although a summary for the year, follows the same basic rules as a cash account, with receipts on the debit side and payments on the credit side. It starts with the opening balance and ends with the closing balance of both cash-in-hand and cash-at-bank.

Example 22.1

The following are the bank and cash accounts of the Fortuna Social Club for the year ended 31 December 1989. Show the receipts and payments account for the year.

1989						1989			£
		Bank account							
					£				£
Jan 1	Balance		b/f	1000		Feb 1	Rent (Apr–Jun '89)		300
Feb 14	Cash			1440		14	Electricity (July–Dec '88)		240
Mar 15	Bequest from late President			4000		June 20	Rent (July–Sep '89)		300
Aug 10	Cash			1600		30	New disco equipment		3000
Nov 20	Cash			500		Aug 15	Insurance (July '89–Jun '90)		2400
						Sep 14	Rent (Oct–Dec '89)		300
						Oct 5	Electricity (Jan–Jun '89)		320
						Dec 7	Rent (Jan–Mar '90)		600
						31	Bank charges		40
						31	Balance c/d		1040
					8540				8540

1990				
Jan 1	Balance	b/d	1040	

Cash account

1989				£					£
Jan 1	Balance	b/f	92		Feb 14	Bank			1440
31	Subscriptions		1448		May 20	Refreshments costs			160
May 20	Refreshment receipts		200		Aug 10	Bank			1600
Aug 1	Subscriptions		1652		Sept 3	Refreshments costs			180
Oct 3	Refreshment receipts		240		Nov 20	Bank			500
Nov 15	Subscriptions		590		Dec 31	Balance c/d			342
			4222						4222

1990				
Jan 1	Balance		b/d	342

SOLUTION

Receipts and payments account for year ended 31 December 1989

Receipts		£	Payments		£
Balances at 1.1.89			Rent		1500
Cash	92		Electricity		560
Bank	1000	1092	Refreshments		340
Subscriptions		3690	Disco equipment		3000
Bequest		4000	Insurance		2400
Refreshments		440	Bank charges		40
			Balances at 31.12.89		
			Cash	342	
			Bank	1040	1382
		9222			9222

The cash and bank accounts shown in example 22.1 were very simple ones, and it was not difficult to combine and summarise the items concerned. Normally, even with quite a small club or society, the accounts for the year will be spread over a number of pages. So it makes the task considerably easier if a cash book with analysis columns is used, similar to those described in unit 18. Or a full set of ledger accounts can be maintained, but this is not usually necessary, except for large clubs and societies.

Activity 22.2

(i) Rewrite the receipts and payments account in the above example in the vertical format. Which of the two forms is better if the information is to be circulated to club members at the annual general meeting?

(ii) What do you regard as the main disadvantages of a receipts and payments account as a way of reporting the financial position of a club to the members?

22B. Income and Expenditure Accounts

1. General principles

In unit 6, we saw that profit and loss accounts take the *income earned* in a trading period (whether or not it has been received) and charges against it all items of *expenditure incurred* (no matter whether they have been paid or not). It is only by doing this that a fair view of the operating efficiency—measured by 'profit' or 'loss'—of the organisation can be obtained. As we saw, profit is something quite different from money received.

Strictly, P&L accounts only refer to commercial businesses. But exactly the same principles can be applied to non-profit-making organisations—the only real difference is a change in name. Instead of being known as a *profit and loss account*, it is called an **income and expenditure account**; and in place of the terms *profit* and *loss*, the terms **surplus** and **deficit** are used. These terms are considered to be more suitable for non-profit-making organisations.

Accounts of particular organisations

As with a P&L account, adjustments are made when preparing an income and expenditure account for pre-payments and for accruals (see unit 10). In addition, any 'capital' receipts or expenditure (see unit 16) are excluded. 'Notional' charges, such as depreciation, are also allowed for. Also, income will appear on the credit side and expenditure on the debit side.

The detailed figures for each of the items can be picked up either by keeping a full system of ledger accounts in the normal way, or by adjusting (where necessary) the data obtained from the cash book. An income and expenditure account may be drawn up either instead of a receipts and payment account, or in addition to it.

2. The problem of subscriptions

Care has to be taken with club subscriptions. It must be remembered that these are payable *to* a club, unlike expenses, which are payable *by* a club. If there are subscriptions owing at the end of the financial year, these will be subscriptions owing *to the club*. The amount is *added* to subscriptions for the year, and will appear as an asset in the balance sheet alongside the pre-paid expenses.

If a ledger account is being kept for subscriptions, then the old period will be credited (thus increasing the amount to be transferred to income and expenditure), and the new period will be debited.

If, on the other hand, subscriptions have been received during the year in advance for the following year, then the amount must be deducted from the actual subscriptions received for the current year and carried forward—appearing as a liability in the balance sheet. The ledger entries for this will be to debit the old period of the account with the amount paid in advance, and to credit the new period.

Activity 22.3

A club keeps full ledger accounts. By December 31—the end of its first financial year—it had actually received subscriptions in cash of £900. Included in this were subscriptions of £100 that had been paid in advance for year 2. Subscriptions of £300 for year 1 were owing to the club.

During year 2, the club received £1500 in cash by way of subscriptions. This included the £300 owing from year 1; it also included subscriptions of £200 that had been paid in advance for year 3. Subscriptions of £50 were owing to the club at the end of the year.

(i) *Show the subscriptions account as it would appear in the club's ledger for years 1 and 2, including the appropriate amounts carried forward at the end of each year.*
(ii) *What amounts would appear in the club's balance sheet at the end of each of the two years?*

Example 22.2

Change the receipts and payments account in example 22.1 into an income and expenditure account, taking into account:

(i) Rent of £260 for the first quarter of 1989 had been paid in advance in December 1988.

(ii) Depreciation of £200 is to be allowed on the new disco equipment.
(iii) Subscriptions of £700 due to the club for 1988 were received during 1989. Overdue subscriptions at the end of 1989 amounted to £680, but subscriptions for 1990 amounting

to £80 had been paid in advance and were entered in the cash account during 1989.
(iv) Amount owing for electricity for the period July–December 1989 was estimated at £300.
(v) Insurance for the period January–June 1989, £960, had been paid in advance during 1988.

Notes
1. Further information regarding accruals and pre-payments can be picked up from the data given in the cash and bank accounts of the original example.
2. The bequest from the late President, and the purchase of the new disco equipment, should both be regarded as capital transactions.
3. Where an item involves both income and expenditure (e.g. refreshments in the example), the two elements can be brought together and a net figure worked out and entered—showing, of course, the surplus or deficit on that particular item.

Preliminary calculations

	£	£
Subscriptions		
Cash received during 1989	3690	
Add: owing at end of 1989	680	4370
Less: 1988 subscriptions received in 1990	700	
1990 subscriptions received in 1989	80	780
		3590
Electricity		
Cash paid during 1989	560	
Add: owing at end of 1989	300	860
Less: 1989 payments for 1988		240
		620
Insurance		
Cash paid during 1989	2400	
Add: pre-payment in 1988 for 1989	960	3360
Less: pre-payment in 1989 for 1990		1200
		2160
Rent		
Cash paid in 1989	1500	
Add: pre-payment in 1988 for 1989	260	1760
Less: pre-payment in 1989 for 1990		600
		1160

Income and expenditure account for year ended 31 December 1989

Expenditure			Income		
Rent		1160	Subscriptions		3590
Electricity		620	Refreshments	440	
Depreciation		200	*less:* costs	340	100
Insurance		2160	Deficit for year		490
Bank charges		40			
		4180			4180

22C. Other Final Accounts of Clubs and Societies

1. Trading accounts

Many clubs, societies and similar organisations, although non-profit-making as such, sometimes undertake trading activities for the purpose either of providing a service to members or of making a profit to subsidise their normal work. Many clubs, for example, provide a bar for their members, and many charities sell a range of merchandise (goods) for the purpose of raising funds. With these activities, it is possible to prepare a conventional trading account, the profit (or loss) of which is taken either to the income and expenditure account, or direct to the balance sheet (see below).

2. Balance sheets

Provided the appropriate information concerning assets and liabilities is available, it is possible to draw up balance sheets for clubs and societies. If the club concerned is maintaining (keeping) a full set of accounts, then the data required for the balance sheet will be available in the ledger in the normal way. If such accounts are not maintained, the data will have to be calculated from such information as may be available. Provided the source information is adequate and reliable, a perfectly satisfactory balance sheet can usually be constructed. The following points should be noted:

(i) The term *capital* is considered unsuitable for a non-profit-making organisation; the expression **accumulated fund** (or sometimes *consolidated fund*) is used instead.

(ii) It is common in examination questions to provide a list of the balances of assets and liabilities as they stood at the beginning of the period, plus the actual cash and bank accounts. The list of assets may well *not* include the following:
— The cash and bank balances. Candidates are expected to obtain these from the cash and bank accounts.
— The opening balance of the accumulated fund. This has to be calculated by finding the difference between assets and liabilities at that date.
— The amount to be charged in respect of depreciation. This can be calculated by comparing the opening and closing balances of the assets concerned after allowing for any assets bought or sold.

(iii) The surplus or deficit on income and expenditure account will be added to, or subtracted from, the accumulated fund in the same way that profit (or loss) is taken to capital account in a commercial firm.

Example 22.3

The assets and liabilities of the Parkside Sports Club at 1 January 1989 were: premises £50 000; subscriptions-in-arrears £96; equipment £6400; bank balance £3792; bar stocks £1840; subscriptions-in-advance £58.

Receipts during the year were: subscriptions £3388; bar takings £14 400; disco evenings £640; sub-letting of room £400.

Payments during the year were: new equipment £2000; equipment maintenance £1520; light and heating £440; insurance £172; general expenses £108; bar purchases £13 600; rates £1400.

Further information available at 31 December 1989:

(i) Equipment at year end was valued at £8200 and bar stocks at £1642.
(ii) Subscriptions-in-arrears amounted to £90 and in-advance £40.
(iii) Insurance had been pre-paid in the sum of £28.
(iv) It was estimated that £100 was owing for heat and electricity.

Draw up a receipts and payments account, a bar trading account and an income and expenditure account for the year to 31 December 1989, and a balance sheet as at that date.

Parkside Sports Club
Receipts and payments account for the year to 31 December 1989

	£		£
Bank balance 1.1.89	3 792	Equipment	2 000
Subscriptions	3 388	Maintenance	1 520
Sub-letting of rooms	400	Light and heat	440
Bar takings	14 400	Insurance	172
Disco evenings	640	General expenses	108
		Bar purchases	13 600
		Rates	1 400
		Bank balance 31.12.89	3 380
	22 620		22 620

Bar trading account for year to 31 December 1989

	£	£		£
Stocks 1.1.89		1 840	Bar takings	14 400
Purchases	13 600	15 440		
less stocks 31.12.89		1 642		
Cost of sales		13 798		
Bar profit		602		
		14 400		14 400

Income and expenditure account for the year to 31 December 1989

	£	£		£
Depreciation (note 2)		200	Subscriptions (note 3)	3400
Insurance	172		Disco evenings	640
less pre-paid	28	144	Sub-lets of room	400
Maintenance		1520		
Rates		1400		
Light, heating	440			
add accrued	100	540		
General expenses		108		
Surplus for year		528		
		4440		4440

Balance sheet as at 31 December 1989

	£	£		£	£
Fixed assets			Accumulated fund at 1.1.89		
Premises	50 000		(note 1)		62 070
Equipment	8 200	58 200	*Add:* bar profit	602	
			club profit	528	63 200
Current assets			Current liabilities		
Stock	1 642		Subs. in advance	40	
Subs. owing	90		Light, heat accrued	100	140
Insurance prepaid	28				
Bank	3 380	5 140			
		63 340			63 340

Note 1. Accumulated fund at 1.1.98

		£	£
Assets:	Premises	50 000	
	Equipment	6 400	
	Stock	1 840	
	Subscriptions owing	96	
	Bank	3 792	62 128
	Less: subscriptions in advance		58
			62 070

Accounts of particular organisations

Note 2.

	£	£
Depreciation		
Equipment at 1.1.89	6 400	
Purchases	2 000	8 400
Equipment at 31.12.89		8 200
		200

Note 3. Subscriptions

	£	£
Cash received	3 388	
Add: in advance at 1.1.89	58	
in arrears at 31.12.89	90	3 536
Less: in arrears at 1.1.89	96	
in advance at 31.12.89	40	136
		3 400

(The bar profit could have been carried to the credit of the income and expenditure account so that the balance of the income and expenditure showed the surplus for the club as a whole. The advantage of transferring the surpluses to the accumulated fund separately is that it is possible to monitor the success (or failure) of each aspect of the club's activities.)

Activity 22.4

(i) Assume that you are the treasurer of the Parkside Sports Club (example 22.3) and that you feel the formal presentation of the accounts is not very suitable for circulation to club members, many of whom do not have any knowledge of accounts. Re-draft them in a form which you think would be more suitable.

(ii) State *with reasons* whether or not you consider the profit on the bar to be satisfactory. Do different considerations crop up here than with the operation of a bar on a purely commercial basis?

Check Your Understanding

1 *Complete the following passage by selecting words from the list given below. Each word may be used once only. The list contains more words than you will need.*

At the end of the last financial year, the honorary treasurer of the Albany Tennis Club drew up a _R+P acc_, which was a summary of his cash book for the year. A friend, who had recently passed his GCSE in accounting, converted the summary into an _I+E acc_ by allowing for the _p. pay_ and the _accr._ and excluding the _Capital_ transactions such as the 'one-off' grant of £500 from the local authority. The treasurer had been in some difficulty in knowing how to modify subscriptions in order to obtain the club's true _Income_ for the year. His friend advised him that subscriptions paid in advance at the beginning of the year should be _added_ to the amount actually received in cash, whereas the subscriptions pre-paid at the end of the year should be _deduct._. His friend also advised him that accruals at the beginning of the year should be _added_ to the expense item concerned, whereas accruals at the end of the year should be _deduct_. The credit balance of this account he termed the _Profit_ for the year.

The friend also drew up a _B/S_ summarising the financial worth of the club as at the last day of the financial year. The difference between the assets and the liabilities he called the _accumulated fund_.

[*accumulated fund; added; deficit; capital; loss; profit; balance sheet; pre-payments; receipts; profit and loss account; cash summary; accruals; income; payments; deducted; income and expenditure account; surplus; receipts and payments account.*]

2 Clubs sometimes prepare a trading account in addition to the other final accounts. There are two alternative ways of dealing with the profit. What are they, and what factors are borne in mind in deciding which to follow:

Practical Assignments

1 a. List the main features that distinguish:
   (i) a cash account;
   (ii) a receipts and payments account;
   (iii) an income and expenditure account.
  b. How does an income and expenditure account differ from a profit and loss account?
  c. List the additional information that might be required in order to convert a receipts and payments account into an income and expenditure account.

2 At 1 January 1989, the Selby Stonewallers Cricket Club possessed cricketing equipment valued at £5200. Subscriptions owing at that date amounted to £80, and subscriptions in arrears to £80. Insurance prepaid was £60 and £10 was owing for electricity. The following accounts had been kept throughout the year:

Cash account

1989			£	1989			£
Jan 1	Balance	b/f	58	Jan 15	Dance tickets, etc.		30
5	Dance tickets sale		20	Feb 24	Postage		115
10	Subscriptions		80	Mar 3	Envelopes		30
Feb 14	Dance:			Apr 5	Wages: casual cleaner		50
	Sale of refreshments		150	Apr 10	Bank		250
	Sale of tickets		200	May 29	Postage		145
Mar 15	Subscriptions		350	Jun 5	Typewriter ribbons		30
Dec 6	Bingo tickets		120	Aug 10	Casual cleaner, wages		30
				Dec 31	Balance	c/d	298
			978				978
1990							
Jan 1	Balance	b/d	298				

Bank account

1989			£	1989			£
Jan 1	Balance	b/f	4 720	Jan 1	Rent		300
31	Subscriptions		560	5	Dance—room hire		30
Feb 5	Five-year loan		5 000	Feb 10	Sports equipment		7 000
Apr 12	Cash		250	15	Dance prizes		80
Jun 30	Subscriptions		720	Apr 15	Electricity		120
				Apr 20	Music centre		580
				May 5	Redecoration, club house		300
				May 10	Printing letterheads		120
				June 30	Rent		300
				Aug 31	Insurances		300
				Oct 30	Electricity		180
				Nov 30	Bingo prizes		150
					room hire		40
				Dec 16	Bank charges		50
				Dec 31	Balance	c/d	1 700
			11 250				11 250
1990							
Jan 1	Balance	b/d	1 700				

Further information:
a. At 31 December 1989, £40 was owing for electricity, £100 on insurance was prepaid, subscriptions in arrears stood at £120 and subscriptions prepaid amounted to £60. It was decided that subscriptions amounting to £35 should be regarded as bad.
b. It is the club's policy to depreciate equipment at 25% on a straight-line basis.

Required: A receipts and payments account and an income and expenditure account for the year ended 31 December 1989, and a balance sheet as at that date.

Accounts of particular organisations

3 On 1 September of last year, you were elected treasurer of the Nomad Sports Club. No proper accounts had previously been kept, but the retiring treasurer gave you the following information regarding the Club's position at the date of his handing over to you. You make the necessary checks, and satisfy yourself that the information is correct.

Club pavilion £8000; equipment £3500; bank deposit account £4000; bank current account £1000; debt owed to the club by Jones, a member, for sports equipment purchased £60; owed to Sporting Supplies Ltd £250; loan to the club by Midtown Bank (the Club's sponsor) £2000.

From this information, you open the Club's ledger.

During the year following, the (summarised) transactions listed below took place:

	£
Subscriptions received from members	15 400
Travelling expenses paid by the Club	1 500
Costs of maintaining the pavilion	2 500
Auditor's honorarium	25
Cost of printing fixture cards	175
Postage costs	850
Proceeds from raffle	360
Costs of raffle	120
Received from the member Jones	60
Stationery and secretarial expenses	550
Rents paid during the season	600
Part-repayment of loan	500
Payments by the Club for insurance	250
Income from Club Annual Dinner	840
Purchase of additional major equipment	8 500
Costs of Annual Dinner	2 200
Purchase of second-hand Transit van	4 500
Additional subscriptions received from members	2 100

Post the transactions to the ledger, bearing in mind that you had paid all receipts into the Club's current account, and that you paid all costs immediately by cheque.

Extract a trial balance; then draw up the Club's income and expenditure account for the year ended 30 September last, and a balance sheet as at that date.

4 The position of the National Club on 1 January 1989 was that, in addition to their credit at the bank, the Club owned equipment to the value of £64 000 and investments of £30 000. Subscriptions owing to the Club amounted to £5100 and bills owing by the Club for sundry expenses to £2200. The following is the Club's bank account for the year.

Bank account

				£
Jan	1	Balance	b/d	35 500
	3	Sale of equipment (at book value)		100
	30	Subscriptions (for 1988)		5 050
Mar	1	Subscriptions (for 1989)		5 300
May	10	Subscriptions (for 1989)		4 800
Aug	10	Raffle receipts		4 600
Nov	30	Subscriptions (for 1989)		8 600
Dec	20	Dance receipts		1 950
	21	Subscriptions (for 1990)		1 200
	30	Donation		1 000
	31	Sale of investments (book value)		1 200

			£
Jan 20	Expenses		3 200
Feb 14	Insurances		5 210
Apr 2	Hire of premises		1 130
May 5	Electricity		1 413
June 30	Hire of premises		1 130
Jul 1	Purchase of equipment		2 000
8	Premises hire		1 130
9	Electricity		2 380
15	Heating oil		3 800
Sep 10	Sundries		1 340
Oct 2	Hire of premises		3 390
Dec 23	Dance expenses		1 855
29	Electricity		2 500
30	Telephone		870

Additional information: Equipment is to be depreciated at the rate of 25% of the book value at 31 December 1989. The remainder of the subscriptions owing in respect of 1988 are to be written off as irrecoverable. £850 is owing in respect of hire of premises. Dance expenses amounting to an estimated £250 are still owing. Owing for electricity (estimated) £200.

Required:
a. A receipts and payments account for the year.
b. An income and expenditure account for the year.
c. A balance sheet as at 31 December 1989.
d. A report to members on the financial position of the club. Particular attention should be drawn to matters not immediately obvious from the cash book or the receipts and payments account.

5 At the start of its last full accounting year, a rugby league football club had the following balances, among others, in its ledger: insurance account, debit £948; wages account, credit £960; subscriptions account, debit £540, credit £320.

During the year that followed, it paid on account of insurance £2400 and on account of wages £60 594. It received by way of members' subscriptions £180 240. At the end of the year, the insurance prepaid for the current year amounted to £760 while the wages owing amounted to £680. Subscriptions due but not received amounted to £420, and those paid in advance for the current year to £410.

Required:
a. A statement describing the meaning of the balances above, which were on the books at the beginning of the year.
b. The insurance, wages and subscriptions accounts written up for the full year showing clearly the amounts transferred to income and expenditure account, and any balances carried down to the current year.

UNIT 23 ACCOUNTING FOR PARTNERSHIPS

Before you read this unit, try activity 23.1.

Activity 23.1

Joanna and Nick have decided to go into business as partners selling computer systems. Nick will be putting up most of the capital, but has little knowledge of computers and will not be doing a great deal of work within the firm. He has also agreed to make a loan to the partnership independent of the capital he is subscribing.

Joanna is a computer specialist and will be doing most of the work, but she has only a very small amount of capital that she can put into the business. She has three children, who, she hopes, will one day follow her into the business and also become partners in it.

Consider the matters over which Joanna and Nick should agree before they start the partnership in order to avoid arguments later.

23A. General Considerations

A number of commercial and professional organisations operate as partnerships. These are firms that have at least two joint proprietors (owners). Unlike 'one-man' businesses, partnerships are subject to a specific law—namely, the Partnership Act 1890. But this act only lays down a bare framework of working relationships between the partners, who would be well advised to draw up—or better still have drawn up by a solicitor—a properly thought-out partnership agreement. The most important clauses (i.e. items) that should be included within such an agreement are shown in display 10.

Activity 23.2

Check through the items listed in display 10.

(i) How many did you think of in connection with Joanna and Nick in activity 23.1?

(ii) Which ones are particularly important in relation to the accounts?

In the absence of a clear partnership agreement, the Partnership Act lays down that no interest should be allowed on partners' capitals, even if the amounts they invest are considerably different. But interest is allowed on loans, and this is at the rate of 5%—modest by today's standards, but remember the date when the Act was passed! No salary is payable, irrespective of how much more work one partner does than the others, and profits—or losses—have to be divided among the partners equally. Remember, these provisions apply *only in the absence of a partnership agreement*. The point is that, if the partners are not happy with what the Act lays down, then it is up to them to agree to other arrangements beforehand.

Each partner is personally liable for the full amount of the firm's debts and, as with sole proprietors (i.e. single owners), partners' private

> **Display 10: Partnership Agreements—The Most Important Items to be Included**
>
> 1. The amount of capital to be contributed by each partner.
> 2. The rate of interest (if any) to be allowed to the partners on capital.
> 3. The procedure for partners making loans to the partnership.
> 4. The rate of interest (if any) to be allowed on loans.
> 5. A specific statement of the duties and responsibilities of each partner.
> 6. The salaries (if any) to be paid to each partner.
> 7. The ratio in which the profits and losses are to be divided between the partners.
> 8. The procedure for partners to draw money out of the firm, or to take goods (i.e. procedure for drawings).
> 9. The interest (if any) to be charged *to the partners* on drawings.
> 10. The involvement of each partner in the management and decision-making processes.
> 11. Accounting provisions and the rights of the partners to inspect the books.
> 12. Procedure to be followed on the death, retirement or withdrawal of a partner.
> 13. Procedure in the event of sickness or incapacity of a partner.
> 14. To what extent a partner is to be restrained from undertaking similar work should he withdraw from the partnership.
> 15. Procedure to be followed as regards the admission of new partners.
> 16. Rules to be followed in the event of the winding-up of the partnership, including the division of surpluses or deficits after the realisation of the assets and the payment of the liabilities.
> 17. Procedure—arbitration or otherwise—for resolving disputes between the partners.

assets can (and will!) be taken in settlement if the assets of the firm are not enough to pay the creditors.

It is the unlimited liability of each partner for the full amount of the debts that is the biggest disadvantage of this form of business organisation. It did become possible in 1907 to form a 'limited partnership', which enables some of the partners to have their liability limited, but such partners cannot take any part in the running or management of the firm. Also, there must be at least one partner with unlimited liability. This, together with the development shortly afterwards of the idea of a 'private' limited company, in which limited liability is extended to all, has meant that very few limited partnerships have been formed.

The full trading profits of a partnership are subject to income tax and it is up to each partner to claim whatever personal allowances he or she might be entitled to. Each partner is also liable for national insurance as a self-employed person.

23B. Accounting Procedures

Because of the general nature of partnerships, normal accounting procedures have to be modified. In some cases, procedures have to be followed that are contrary to true accounting principles. This arises, for example, in the case of salaries due to partners, and of interest on loans by them to the firm.

1. Capital and loan accounts

It is essential that a separate capital account be maintained for each partner. It is also vital that separate loan accounts be kept. This is not only because they may carry a different rate of interest than capital accounts but also because, in the event of winding-up, a loan from a partner has to be repaid in full before any of the capital is returned.

Accounts of particular organisations

2. Appropriation account

In the case of a sole trader, the net profit is transferred from the P&L account directly to the capital account, and the drawings are then deducted (see page 114). Where a partnership is concerned, the net profit is carried down to the credit of a further section of the account, which is known as the **profit and loss appropriation account**. The main purpose of this account is to split (i.e. appropriate) the profit between the partners, though in fact it goes a little further than this and it records any item that affects the financial relationship between the partners. So, the interest (if any) payable to the partners on their capitals or loans and any salary that may be due to them appear on the debit side. On the credit side, in addition to the trading profit brought down, there will appear any interest chargeable to the partners on their drawings.

The appropriation account is closed by dividing the balance between the partners in their agreed profit-sharing ratio. In the absence of such a partnership agreement, the balance is divided equally.

The corresponding double entries for the items in the appropriation account are shown either in the individual partners' capital accounts, or in their current accounts (see below).

Activity 23.3

Firm A is a sole partnership. The owner has a loan from the bank and has a staff of ten employees.

Firm B is a partnership. It has a loan for a similar amount as Firm A, but the loan has been made by a partner, not by a bank. Also, Firm B has a staff of only four employees. The rest of the work is undertaken by the partners, who are paid salaries.

In all other respects, the firms are identical.

Why is it necessary to be careful when comparing the net trading profits of the two firms?

---

3. Current accounts

The various amounts that become due to a partner—such as salary, interest on profits and loans, share of profits—which appear as debits in the P&L appropriation account, can be credited to the individual partners' capital accounts. Alternatively, they can be credited instead to each partner's **current account**. This is an account that records all the items due to, or by, a partner and allows his or her original capital to remain as a fixed amount on the books.

Where current accounts exist, the partner's actual drawings for the year are transferred to the debit side of his or her current account and not to the capital account.

The final balances of the current accounts are carried forward from year to year. A *credit* balance means that an amount is due *to* the partner *by* the firm, whereas a debit balance indicates that a debt is due *to* the firm *by* the partner.

4. A summary of entries

The ledger entries for the items commonly appearing in partnership appropriation and current accounts are shown in display 11.

Display 11: Partnership Accounts—Ledger Procedures

1. Partners' salaries (if any).
   Interest due to partner on capital or loan (if any).
   Share of profits.

   Debit P&L appropriation account.
   Credit Current account of the partner concerned.

2. Interest chargeable to partners on loans and on drawings.
   Share of losses.

   Debit Current account of the partner concerned.
   Credit P&L appropriation account.

3. Drawings:
   When initially made.

   Debit Drawings account of the partner concerned.
   Credit Cash/bank (if of cash) or purchases (if goods at cost price) or sales (if goods at selling price).

   At end of financial year.

   Debit Current account.
   Credit Drawings account.

Example 23.1

The following trial balance was extracted from the books of White and Black after the preparation of their profit and loss account for the year ended 31 December 1989:

	£	£
Net trading profit		68 000
Premises	81 000	
Other fixed assets	65 500	
Current assets	68 000	
Current liabilities		40 000
Capital accounts		
J. White		40 000
S. Black		80 000
Current accounts		
J. White		4 500
S. Black	3 000	
Drawings		
J. White	15 000	
S. Black	50 000	
Loan		
S. Black		50 000
	282 500	282 500

Draw up the P&L appropriation account and the partners' current accounts for the year to 31 December and the balance sheet as at that date, taking into account the following:

(i) Interest on capital is to be allowed at 10%.
(ii) Interest on loan is to be allowed at 20%.
(iii) A salary of £30 000 is payable to J. White.
(iv) Interest on drawings is to be charged:
    J. White £2000
    S. Black £3000.
(v) The partners share profits and losses equally.

SOLUTION

P&L appropriation account for year to 31 December 1989

		£	£	£			£
Partners' current accounts					Net profit b/d		68 000
	J. White	S. Black					
Salary	30 000		30 000				
Interest on capital	4 000	8 000	12 000				
Interest on loans		10 000	10 000				
Share of profit	8 000	8 000	16 000				
	42 000	26 000	68 000				68 000

233

Accounts of particular organisations

Current account—J. White

Drawings		15 000	Balance	b/f	4 500
Balance	c/d	1 500	Interest on capital		4 000
			Share of profit		8 000
			Salary		30 500
		16 500			46 500
			Balance	b/d	1 500

Current account—S. Black

Balance	b/f	3 000	Salary		30 000
Drawings		50 000	Interest on capital		8 000
Balance	c/d	3 000	Interest on loan		10 000
			Share of profit		8 000
		56 000			56 000
			Balance	b/d	3 000

Balance sheet as at 31 December 1989

Fixed assets				Capital	Current	
Premises	81 000		J. White	40 000	1500	41 500
Other fixed assets	65 600	146 500	S. Black	80 000	3000	83 000
Current assets				120 000	4500	124 500
Sundry		68 000	*Long-term liability*			
			Loan (S. Black)			50 000
			Current liabilities			
			Sundry			40 000
		214 500				214 500

Note: There are various other ways in which the detailed data concerning the partners can be shown in the appropriation account and in the balance sheet. What is shown in this example is only one possibility.

23C. Goodwill in Partnership Accounts

Goodwill is a payment that is made in respect of the value of a business as a 'going concern'—obviously a well-established firm with plenty of regular customers is of more value than a new one struggling to make its mark in the market-place. Accountants prefer not to have it recorded in the books for various reasons—one of which is that it can disappear overnight. Nevertheless, occasionally it does have to be brought into account.

There are two main occasions when goodwill arises in partnership accounts. These are, first, on the admission of a new partner, and, secondly, on the death or retirement of an existing partner.

1. Admission of a new partner

When a new partner is admitted to an existing, successful partnership, he or she may be expected to purchase a share of the goodwill. This payment will be in addition to any capital that he or she has to contribute. The book-keeping for the goodwill is simple. The amount due will be credited to the existing partners (either their capital accounts or their current accounts), usually in their profit-sharing ratio. If paid immediately on admission, the debit will be to bank account. If not paid immediately, the debit will be to the new partner's current account. The new partner will then either pay the amount in cash at some later date, or it will be set against his or her share of the profits.

Accounting for partnerships

Activity 23.4

What are the advantages and the disadvantages to (a) the new partner and (b) the existing partners of the payment for goodwill being credited to the existing partners' (i) current accounts or (ii) fixed capital accounts?

2. Retirement and death of partners

On retirement or death, a partner is entitled to be credited with his or her share of the goodwill as at that date. The procedure is simple: the retiring (or deceased, i.e. dead) partner's current account is credited, and the current accounts of the continuing partners are debited.

There is one snag, however. A retiring partner—or the 'estate' of a deceased partner—is entitled *in the absence of agreement to the contrary* to have the full amount due (i.e. the balance of current and capital accounts after the addition of goodwill) paid immediately. The payment involved may be a very large sum—more, in fact, than the partnership has available in ready cash at the time in question, and the only way of finding it would be to realise some of the fixed assets—which could well mean winding-up the business. So, it is wise to set out a procedure in the partnership agreement which will avoid the winding-up of the firm—for example, such that the retiring partner will remain a cash creditor of the firm and that the amount due will be paid in instalments over a period of time.

Example 23.2

The following is the balance sheet of White, Green and Black immediately before S. Black's death:

	£	£		£ Capital	£ Current	£
Fixed assets						
Premises	80 000		J. White	45 000	10 000	55 000
Equipment	100 000	180 000	A. Green	45 000	15 000	60 000
			S. Black	90 000	25 000	115 000
				180 000	50 000	230 000
Current assets						
Stock	60 000					
Cash	10 000	70 000	*Current liabilities*			
			Creditors			20 000
		250 000				250 000

S. Black's share of the goodwill at date of death was estimated at £40 000, the amount to be charged equally to J. White's and A. Green's current accounts. It is agreed that the amount due to S. Black will be paid in five annual instalments starting in two years' time.

The following is the balance sheet after the adjustments arising from S. Black's death:

	£	£		£ Capital	£ Current	£
Fixed assets						
Premises	80 000		J. White	45 000	(10 000)	35 000
Equipment	100 000	180 000	A. Green	45 000	(5 000)	40 000
				90 000	(15 000)	75 000
Current assets						
Stock	60 000		*Long-term liability*			
Cash	10 000	70 000	S. Black (note 1)			155 000
			Current liabilities			
			Creditors			20 000
		250 000				250 000

Note 1

The amount due to S. Black is made up of the balance of capital (£90 000) and current (£25 000), and the goodwill at valuation (£40 000).

235

Accounts of particular organisations

Activity 23.5

Consider the balance sheet in example 23.2 after the adjustments have been made in respect of S. Black's death. If no arrangement had been made to spread the repayments due to S. Black over a period of time, and the executors of his estate demanded the money immediately, how could the debt have been met?

Check Your Understanding

1. Jot down the items of importance *from an accounting point of view* that the partners should agree about before commencing business.
2. What are the main accounting provisions of the Partnership Act 1890? In what circumstances do they apply?
3. In what way or ways is the *structure* of accounts modified to meet the needs of partnerships?
4. What are the main items that appear in the appropriation section of a partnership profit and loss account?
5. What particular item commonly appears in partners' current accounts which does not appear in the appropriation account?
6. In what ways does the accounting procedure for the payment of salaries to the partners differ from that for the payment of salaries to the senior employees? Do you agree that there should be such a distinction?
7. In what circumstances can goodwill arise in partnership accounts?
8. For what reasons should a partner's loan account be kept separate from his or her capital account?
9. How is:

    (i) interest on a bank loan,
    (ii) interest on a partner's loan,
    (iii) interest on a partner's drawings,

    dealt with in partnership accounting?
10. Why are there so few limited partnerships?

Practical Assignments

1.
   a. List the ways in which the structure of partnership accounts differs from those of a sole proprietor.
   b. What are the advantages of maintaining current accounts in addition to capital accounts for the partners?
   c. Why is it essential that a partner's loan to the firm should be recorded in a different account from his capital?
   d. What item or items may appear:
      (i) in both the profit and loss appropriation account and a partner's current account;
      (ii) in a partner's current account but not in the profit and loss appropriation account?
   e. The Partnership Act 1890 sets out certain rules which, *in the absence of agreement between the partners to the contrary*, must be followed in preparing partnership final accounts. What are they?

2. Jack and Jill are partners sharing profits and losses in the ratio of 2:1. The following trial balance was extracted from their books on 31 December 1986:

	£	£
Capital accounts: Jack		26 500
Jill		14 200
Current accounts: Jack		5 000
Jill		3 000
Drawings: Jack	6 450	
Jill	4 200	
Motor vehicles	10 000	
Depreciation provision (motor vehicles)		2 000
Sales		237 864
Salaries	26 192	
Rates	500	
Discounts allowed and received	4 264	2 146
Purchases	179 465	
General expenses	10 261	
Bank	2 694	
Premises	17 500	
Furniture and equipment	1 650	
Debtors and creditors	17 042	13 149
Stock	23 641	
	303 859	303 859

You are given the following information:
a. Stock in trade at 31 December 1987 was £24 780.
b. Rates paid in advance at 31 December 1987 amounted to £120.
c. It was decided to write debtors for £478 off as bad.
d. Salaries owing at 31 December amounted to £514.

e. Depreciation on motor vehicles is to be provided at 25% p.a. diminishing balance.
f. The partners are to be allowed interest on capital at 10%. Jill is to be allowed a salary of £1000.

Required: a trading, profit and loss account and profit and loss appropriation account for the year ended 31 December 1987, and a balance sheet as at that date.

3 Jackson and Johnson are partners in a firm specialising in the supply of fitted kitchens and bedroom furniture in kit form. Their partnership agreement states that profits and losses are to be divided in the ratio of their capitals and for interest of 10% to be allowed on both capitals and loans.

On 31 December 19-1, the following balances were extracted from their ledger:

	£		£
Bank overdraft	4 002	Motor vehicles	24 000
Cash-in-hand	1 310	Discount allowed	1 130
Sundry debtors	25 952	Discount received	2 840
Sundry creditors	18 888	Repairs to fittings	236
Buildings, at cost	65 500	Wages and salaries	19 840
Depreciation provisions:		General expenses	702
		Bad debts	2 540
Fixtures and fittings	5 400	Current a/cs at 1 Jan 19-1:	
Motor vehicles	6 000	Jackson (credit)	2 750
Stock at 1 Jan 19-1	58 650	Johnson (debit)	290
Fixtures and fittings	18 000	Drawings:	
Purchases	140 600	Jackson	10 720
Sales	200 840	Johnson	7 950
Returns-in	2 310	Capitals:	
Returns-out	1 890	Jackson	60 000
Carriage-in	468	Johnson	30 000
Carriage-out	912	Loan:	
Bad debts provision at 1 Jan 19-1	1 000	Jackson	10 000
		Bank	40 000
Rates	2 500		

Required: the trading and profit and loss account for the year ended 31 December 19-1, and the balance sheet at that date, taking into account the following, for which no entries have yet been made:

	£
a. Stock at 31 December 19-1	64 032
b. Accrued expenses—repairs to fittings	152

c. The rates have been paid through to 31 March 19-2
d. A salary is due to Johnson of £4000
e. An examination of debtors revealed that a further debt of £50 should be regarded as bad
f. Interest chargeable on drawings has been calculated at:

| Jackson | 390 |
| Johnson | 220 |

g. Jackson has taken goods for his private use worth £400 at cost price.
h. Depreciation is to be allowed on fixtures and fittings at 10% straight line and on motor vehicles at 20% diminishing balance.
i. Bad-debts provision is to be maintained at 5% of book debts.
j. Interest of £6500 is owing to the bank.

4 Jean and John are partners. On 31 December 19-1, the following balances were extracted from their ledger:

	£		£
Bank	44 002	Carriage-in	468
Cash in hand	300	Discount-allowed	1 300
Sundry debtors	26 620	Discount-received	6 526
Sundry creditors	63 016	Repairs to fittings	250
Buildings, at cost	60 000	Salaries	4 000
Depreciation provision on fittings	4 400	Wages	5 840
		General expenses	702
		Bad debts	2 540
Fixtures, at cost	20 000	Current accounts at 1 Jan 19-1	
Stock at 1 January 19-1	58 400	Jean (credit)	2 740
Purchases	154 400	John (debit)	290
Sales	192 840	Drawings	
Returns-in	2 310	Jean	11 470
Returns-out	1 890	John	7 950
Carriage-out	1 570	Capitals	
Bad debts provision at 1 January 19-1	1 000	Jean	50 000
		John	80 000

Required: the final accounts for the year ended 31 December 19-1, taking into account the following for which no entries have yet been made in the accounts:

	£
a. Stock at 31 January 19-1	65 000
b. Accrued epenses: repairs to fittings	150
c. Salary due to Jean	4 000

d. An examination of the debtors revealed that a further £150 should be regarded as bad.
e. Interest on capitals at 10% is to be allowed.
f. Interest chargeable on drawings has been calculated at:

| Jean | £390 |
| John | £228 |

g. John has taken goods from the firm for his private use worth £400 at cost price.
h. Depreciation on fittings is to be allowed at 10% straight line.
i. Bad debts provision is to be maintained at 5% of book debts.
j. Profits shared equally.

5 A and B are partners in a very successful firm, and share profits and losses in the ratio of their capitals. At 31 December 19-1, their balance sheet showed: assets (other than cash) £70 000; cash £30 000; current accounts,

A £20 000, B £40 000; capitals, A £10 000, B £10 000; sundry liabilities £20 000.

It was agreed to admit C as from 1 January 19-2 in consideration of a contribution of capital of £20 000, and payment in respect of goodwill of £80 000. The amounts concerned were paid in cash into the firm. Profits and losses are to continue to be shared in the ratio of the capitals.

Advise the partners how the payments might be treated, and the implications involved for each of them of the alternative possibilities.

6 X, Y and D are in partnership with capitals of £20 000, £40 000 and £60 000 respectively. They share profits and losses in the ratio of their capitals. D dies. Under the Partnership Agreement, a deceased partner is entitled to a share of the goodwill as at the date of death, as well as the return of his capital. Under the formula given in the Agreement, the goodwill of the firm is calculated at £24 000.

How may this be brought into account? What problems are likely to arise?

UNIT 24 ACCOUNTING FOR COMPANIES: 1
THE BACKGROUND

Before you read this unit, try activity 24.1.

> *Activity 24.1*
>
> Most of those who form companies do so in order to obtain *limited liability*. This means that, if the company is would up and the assets are not sufficient to pay the debts, the shareholders are only liable for a limited amount (none, in fact, if their shares are fully paid). It is the creditors themselves who suffer the loss.
>
> *What are the advantages and the disadvantages to both those running companies, and those trading with them, of this arrangement?*

24A. General Considerations

1. The idea of a 'company'

The word *company* can be used to indicate any group of people, and many firms refer to themselves broadly as 'companies'—e.g. Smith & Co.—although legally they are partnerships. The description can have a very precise meaning—namely, it refers to a 'joint stock' company, which is registered as such under the Companies Act. Such companies have emerged as the most significant of all forms of business enterprise.

The most important feature of such companies is that each exists as a separate legal 'person' quite distinct from those who formed it and who are responsible for running it. This means that a company owns its own assets—they are *not* the property of the shareholders—and is for the most part responsible for its own liabilities. It can sue and be sued in its company name, and, although *controlled* by its managers and shareholders, it is not *owned* by them or by anyone else.

Although companies had existed as a type of organisation for many years prior to the nineteenth century, it was the invention of the idea of limited liability in 1855 that was to result in their tremendous growth. Limited liability companies as we know them today emerged as a response to basic changes in industrial society, and in particular to the need for industries to be able to obtain huge sums of capital, sometimes from all over the world, without the investors being held back because of fear of the liability for huge debts should their company fail.

2. Types of companies

Under present company law, there are two main types of companies. The first consists of **public limited companies** (which have the abbreviation *PLC* after their names); the second are **private limited companies** (which have *Ltd* after their names). It is also possible to register as a company with unlimited liability, but these are few in number and are not significant from a commercial point of view.

Accounts of particular organisations

The Companies Act 1985 laid down that public limited companies must have issued to the public, and have had paid up, shares to the value of at least £50 000—since increased to £500 000. They are allowed to advertise their shares without restriction, but are subject to very stringent (i.e. tight) rules and regulations. They may be **quoted** companies, which means that their shares can be bought and sold on the stock exchange, or they may be **unquoted**.

There is no minimum share-issue requirement for private companies, but they are not allowed to offer their shares to the general public by advertisement. This means that they can only be sold to immediate contacts. The requirements of the Companies Acts for private companies are not as stringent as those for public companies.

In order to form a company, it is first necessary to file a number of documents, i.e. to send them to the appropriate authorities. The most important of these from an accounting point of view are the **memorandum of association** and the **articles of association**. The memorandum is a short document, its most important clause being a statement of the **authorised capital**, which is the maximum number and value of shares that a company is *allowed* to issue—it does not necessarily have to issue them all. The articles consist of the 'internal working' procedures of the company, and define among other things the rights of the different classes of shareholders and the procedures to be followed at meetings.

3. Capital

(a) Share capital

A problem arises with the use of the word *capital*, as it may mean a number of different things. First, there is **share capital**. Share capital is that amount which can be raised by the issue of shares. The *authorised share capital* is the maximum that can be issued and is the amount stated in the memorandum. The *called-up share capital* is the amount that has actually been issued; the *called-up capital* is the amount of the issued capital for which payment has been requested—companies sometimes allow their shares to be paid for in instalments—whereas the *paid-up capital* is the amount of the called-up capital that has actually been paid for. Once shares have been paid for in full, the company can turn them into *stock*. This means that, instead of shareholders owning so many individually numbered shares of a specific value (rather like five-pound notes), they own instead an 'amount' (rather like a bank balance) which can be sold in portions of any size.

No interest is allowed on shares. But if profits are sufficient to justify it, a **dividend** can be paid at the end of the financial year. In the case of *ordinary shares* (sometimes known as 'equity' shares), there is no fixed rate for the dividend and the amount each year will depend entirely upon the amount of the profits, and what proportion of this the company is prepared to distribute. Ordinary shareholders have a right to vote at the company's general meetings—including the annual general meeting, where the individual dividend for the year has to be approved.

In the case of *preference shares*, a percentage will be quoted (e.g. they will be described as (say) $7\frac{1}{2}\%$ preference shares) and—provided profits are sufficient—this must be paid before any dividends are paid to the ordinary shareholders. Most preference shares are, in fact, cumulative preference shares, which means that if profits are insufficient to pay the preferred dividend in any one year, it is held over to the future and

Accounting for companies: 1

all arrears of preference dividend must be paid before the ordinary shareholders receive anything. We shall see later that dividends amount to an appropriation of profit and therefore appear in the appropriation account. Preference shareholders have no voting rights at company meetings.

The price at which shares are listed in the memorandum is known as their *authorised* or *nominal* value. If issued at this price, they are said to be issued **at par**. If issued for more than the par value, the excess is called a **premium**. Since 1983, it has been illegal to issue shares at a discount—i.e. for less than their par value. But shares can be allotted to existing shareholders for free, subject to certain conditions. This is known as a **bonus** issue of shares. Also, companies often offer shares to existing shareholders at a much smaller premium than would normally be payable; this is known as a **rights** issue.

(b) Loan capital

Quite contrary to accounting principles, money that has been obtained by means of long-term loans is often known as **loan capital**. These loans may be in the form of **debentures**—which is an old-fashioned word meaning *document*—or they may be simple loans. Debentures tend to be the more formal type of loan, often secured against a mortgage of one of the company's assets. Loan capital items, whether in the form of debentures or not, are long-term liabilities, and are not capital at all. They carry a legal right to a fixed rate of **interest**, which *must* be paid when due whether the company is making a profit or a loss. Interest is a trading expense, which is charged to the normal P&L; it is *not* an appropriation, as in the case of dividends. Since debentures are a form of loan, they are normally redeemed after an agreed period of time.

(c) Other uses of the term 'capital'

The term *capital* can also be used to refer to the following:

 (i) *Capital invested*—this is the issued share capital together with any reserves and retained profits, which are listed separately from the share capital.
 (ii) *Capital employed*—which is the share capital, plus the reserves and the undistributed profits, plus also the long-term liabilities (loan capital).
 (iii) *Total assets*—which, of course, are the capital employed plus the current liabilities (or, in other words, the total capital being employed from all sources).

24B. When Not to Form a Company

Limited liability, and the opportunity to persuade potential shareholders to invest in the organisation, are the great attractions in forming a company. But there is another side of the coin.

The directors of a company may find it very difficult to obtain credit or loans in the early days of their company—precisely because they *do* have limited liability. In addition, directors may find that their tax liabilities are greater than they would have been as partners or sole proprietors. This is because the profits of a company are subject to corporation tax, whereas income stemming from a partnership or a sole proprietorship is assessable under schedule D income tax—from which various personal and other allowances are deductible. Also, schedule D tax is not payable, as was explained in unit 21, until a year or more after it has been earned, whereas both salaries and dividends paid to directors are taxed immediately—one under schedule E (PAYE) and the other under what is known as advance corporation tax. The national insurance contributions that directors have to pay are much more than those which they would pay as partners or sole proprietors.

A company is much more expensive to form than other types of enterprise. Also, the procedures regarding meetings, filing of resolutions, preparation of accounts and all the other other stringent requirements of the Companies Acts have to be followed to the letter throughout the life of the company.

Capital from outsiders—without any liability to repay it—sounds a particularly attractive proposition. But dividends out of profits will have to be paid, and this will be not just for one or two years, but for the rest of the life of the company. It will be a constant drain on the profits—and those actually doing all the work running the company may well come to feel resentment. Finally, ordinary shares carry voting rights—if more than half of the ordinary shares get into the hands of 'other people', then control of the company is lost.

Activity 24.2

There is a confusing variety of terms listed above. Go back over them and make sure you understand them. Pay particular attention to the rules governing the payment of dividends on ordinary shares, and interest on debentures.

Then decide, with reasons, which of the three types of investment it is best to hold:

(i) *in a company that is almost certain to make losses for the foreseeable future;*
(ii) *in a company not likely to make more than small profits;*
(iii) *in a company that is doing extremely well, and shows every sign that it will continue to do so.*

Check Your Understanding

1 A person has paid £3 on each of the 100 ordinary shares of £5 each that she owns in a company. What is the maximum she could be asked to contribute in the event of the company being wound up as insolvent?

2 In what ways do companies differ from sole proprietorships and partnerships?

3 What are the two main types of company that can now be formed? How can they be distinguished by the abbreviations that follow their names?

4 Two clauses of the memorandum of association of a company are of particular importance from a financial point of view. What do the clauses state?

5 In what way or ways does the memorandum differ from the articles of association?

6 What is the legal difference between dividends and interest? How do the accounting procedures in respect of each differ?

7 What is meant by stating that shares have been issued at:
   (i) par,
   (ii) a premium?

8 What is the difference between a rights issue and a bonus issue of shares?

9 In what way or ways does the position of an ordinary shareholder differ from that of a preference shareholder?

10 How do debentures differ from shares? Can either or both be issued at a discount?

Practical Assignments

1. John Worth has run a successful catering business for a number of years. He now has several restaurants, and trade continues to expand. His present annual turnover is in excess of £80 000, and he reckons to achieve a net profit margin of about 25%.

   He is considering turning his business into a company and has asked your advice on the following points:
   a. The difference between a company and a sole proprietorship as a form of business undertaking.
   b. The principal advantages and disadvantages of being a company.
   c. The initial steps that will have to be taken, and the decisions that will have to be made, if he goes ahead with forming a company.

2. Jennie Clark has recently won £15 000 in a *Spot the Ball* competition. She will be completing her A-level studies next year, and hopes then to enter university or polytechnic. She realises that money is going to be 'tight', so she is anxious to do the sensible thing as regards her windfall.

   She has been looking at the financial pages of various papers and has come across various references to preference shares, ordinary shares and debentures. She also knows that building societies offer various schemes for investment. Someone has also suggested that she might like to invest in a private company rather than a public one.

   Explain, in a letter to her, what the various forms of investment are and compare their pros and cons in relation to her plans.

   (Students should note that if, in the practical situation, an approach is made for advice of this nature, caution should be exercised as the Financial Services Act now restricts the right to give advice to certain individuals.)

UNIT 25 ACCOUNTING FOR COMPANIES: 2 ACCOUNTING PROCEDURES

Before you read this unit, try activity 25.1.

Activity 25.1

Companies are required by law to publish various items of information concerning their financial affairs. Assume that most of your savings are invested in a nation-wide supermarket company.

What information would you expect the company to release about their financial affairs each year?

(Bear in mind that what is available to you, will also be available to your company's competitors—and retailing is a highly competitive industry!)

In principle, the accounting procedures of companies differ little from those of other organisations. But there are certain transactions that only happen in companies, and students must be familiar with the book-keeping in respect of them. Also, the law lays down rules regarding the ways in which the final accounts must be presented, and the information that must be disclosed (i.e. shown).

25A. Ledger Procedures

Although examination questions concentrate on the presentation of company final accounts from trial balance stage, it is essential to understand a few particular ledger procedures so that their effect on the final accounts can be appreciated.

1. Share issue

If shares are issued at par, the entries are simply:

Debit Bank
Credit Issued share capital account (a separate account will be maintained for each class of share, as this detail must be in the balance sheet).

If shares are issued at a premium, the entries will be the same as in the above as far as the nominal value is concerned, but the amount of the premium must be credited to a share premium account—in other words, it must be kept quite separate from the issued share capital account.

2. Debenture issue

The book-keeping for an issue of debentures is similar to that for shares—except that the credits go to a debentures account and a debentures premium account. Debentures will be shown as a long-term liability in the balance sheet, except in the year in which they are due for repayment.

3. Dividend procedure

If a company has been trading successfully, the directors have the power to recommend the payment of an *interim dividend* during the course of the trading year. The entries for this are quite simply:

Debit   Interim dividend account.
Credit Bank account.

At the end of the year, the interim dividend account would be transferred to the P&L appropriation account.

The procedure for the *final dividend* is not as straightforward, since the directors can only *recommend* it; they cannot pay it until it has been *approved* by the shareholders at the annual general meeting. Since the final accounts have to be presented to the same meeting, this means that the dividend can only appear as a proposal. It cannot be paid until after the meeting. So the book-keeping is done in two stages. The entries for the dividend proposed by the directors are:

Debit   P&L appropriation account.
Credit Proposed final dividend account. (The balance of this account will be carried forward to the following year.)

When, after the meeting and approval by the shareholders, the dividend is paid, the entries are:

Debit   Proposed final dividend account.
Credit Bank account.

Notice that the full amount for the dividend for the whole year is charged to appropriation. Also, the proposed dividend will appear as a current liability in the balance sheet.

4. Interest

If interest on debentures and other loans is paid before the final accounts are made up, the entries are the normal ones:

Debit   Interest account.
Credit Bank account. (The interest account is transferred to the P&L—*not* to the appropriation.)

If any interest is owing at the end of the financial year, then this must be treated as an accrual. The entries are:

Debit   P&L.
Credit Interest owing account. (The amount of the interest owing will appear, of course, as a current liability in the balance sheet.)

Accounts of particular organisations

Example 25.1

Jan 1 Suntours Ltd is incorporated and issues 25 000 ordinary shares of £1 for £1.50 each payable in full on application.
Apr 1 Suntours issues 20 000 10% preference shares of £5 at £8.75 each.
Jun 30 The directors declare and pay an interim dividend of 5% on the ordinary shares.
Jul 1 Suntours issues 150 000 12% debentures of £1 at par repayable in July 2030.
Dec 31 The directors propose a final dividend of 10%, making a total dividend of 15% for the year.

The journal entries for the above are required, including those at 31 December for the preference dividend owing and the interest due on the debentures. Assume all sums due are received immediately.

			£	£
Jan 1	Bank account	Dr	37 500	
	Ordinary share account			25 000
	Share premium account			12 500
	Issue of 25 000 ordinary £1 shares at £1.50 each.			
Apr 1	Bank account	Dr	175 000	
	Preference share account			100 000
	Share premium account			75 000
	Issue of 20 000 10% preference shares of £5 at £8.75 each.			
Jun 30	Interim dividend account	Dr	1 250	
	Bank account			1 250
	Payment of interim dividend of 5% on ordinary shares.			
Jul 1	Bank account	Dr	150 000	
	Debenture account			150 000
	Issue of 150 000 12% debentures of £1 at par.			
Dec 31	P&L appropriation account	Dr	2 500	
	Proposed ord. dividend account			2 500
	Proposed final dividend of 10% on ordinary shares making 15% for the year.			
Dec 31	P&L appropriation account	Dr	7 500	
	Proposed pref. dividend account			7 500
	Dividend due on preference shares for the period April–December 19--.			
Dec 31	Profit and loss account	Dr	9 000	
	Interest due account			9 000
	Interest due on debentures for the period July–December 19--.			

Activity 25.2

Post the journal entries in example 25.1 to ledger accounts. Note how they build up a picture of what is going on.

25B. Company Final Accounts

As with any other organisation, the final accounts of a company consist of a suitable revenue summary (such as a trading and profit and loss account), an appropriation account and a balance sheet. But a number of complications creep in, with the result that the accounts tend to become very complicated documents, and it is only necessary to know the basic framework at this stage.

The Companies Act 1985 requires public limited companies to use one of a number of specific formats for their published P&L (which includes an abbreviated trading account as well as the appropriation), and for the published balance sheet. While these are mandatory (i.e. compulsory) only for public limited companies, the Act strongly recommends other organisations to follow one of the suggested patterns.

With both the P&L and the balance sheet, it is permissible to present the information either in vertical format or in the more conventional horizontal format, provided assets are listed on the left and capital plus liabilities on the right. The former (i.e. the vertical format) is now being followed in practice by almost all companies, and students are advised to get into the habit of presenting accounts in this form.

1. Profit and loss accounts

The published profit and loss account of a company really consists of three sections, though the information is usually presented as one statement. The first section is an abbreviated trading account, showing the turnover (i.e. sales) less the cost of sales to give the gross trading profit. This leads into the proper P&L section in which the usual expenses are deducted from the gross profit in order to give the net trading profit (or, as it is usually listed, the *profit on ordinary activities before taxation*). The expenses are usually grouped into those for selling, distribution and administration, and further details of these are often given in notes following the account. Selling and distribution costs are sometimes grouped under one heading.

This brings us to the appropriation section. By law, the first item to be deducted must be the provisions for taxation, and the profit has to be shown both before and after this item. At GCSE level, it is usual to ignore taxation and the complications that arise from it.

After providing for taxation, deductions are then made for the year's dividends and for any transfers to reserves. It is common for a balance to be 'left over' and this is known as the *retained earnings for the year*. This is added to any retained earnings brought forward from previous years.

A basic typical profit and loss account for a company is shown in display 12. Note that it is necessary for comparative information to be given for the previous year, and that figures have been rounded. In the company's actual accounting books, they would have been recorded in full detail.

2. Balance sheets

(a) Format

The required format for the vertical presentation of a company balance sheet is a particularly complicated document to understand. It helps to remember the basic accounting equation. Take as an example:

		£000
	Assets	40
less	Liabilities	15
equals	Capital	25

Broken down into subheadings, this could become:

		£000	£000
	Assets		
	Fixed	22	
	Current	18	40
less	Liabilities		
	Long-term	10	
	Current	5	15
equals	Capital		
	at 1.1.19--	19	
	Profit	6	
			25

In company balance sheets, these subheadings are then moved around a little in order to give figures that are important in the interpretation of the accounts. The current liabilities are shown as a deduction from current assets in order to show the *working capital*, and this figure is added to that for fixed assets to give the *total assets less current liabilities*. From this, the long-term liabilities are deducted, and this gives a figure for *total net assets* (which, of course, is the same as the total for capital).

Although the total net assets is the same figure as the total for capital, it is customary to show how the capital figure is made up in a separate statement. This separate statement is sometimes preceded by the phrase *Financed by* or *Represented by*.

The above balance sheet recast in order to meet the requirements of the Companies Act would appear as:

	£000	£000
Fixed assets		22
Current assets	18	
less Current liabilities	5	
Working capital		13
Total assets less current liabilities		35
less Long-term liabilities		10
Net total assets		25
Financed by		
Capital at 1.1.19--		19
Profit		6
		25

Activity 25.3

(i) Check back to the initial simple balance sheet in the above example, and note that, apart from the subtotals, there is nothing in the latest form that is not in the original.

(ii) What do you consider to be the value of presenting a balance sheet in this form?

(iii) From the following information, write up the balance sheet in 'company form'—without referring to the balance sheet above and working out for yourself whether items should be added or subtracted.

Fixed assets £220m.
Current assets £360m.
Long-term liabilities £200m.
Current liabilities £150m.
Capital at beginning of year £200m.
Profit £30m.

Be extremely careful when deciding whether to add or subtract items—it is very easy to make mistakes.

(b) Content

A number of complications arise as regards the actual content of company balance sheets. The information that must be included is given below:

(i) Comparative information must be given for the previous year, just as in the case of a company P&L.
(ii) The subtitle 'Long-term liabilities' is usually replaced with the term *Creditors: amounts falling due after more than one year*, and the subtitle 'Current liabilities' with the term *Creditors: amounts falling due within one year*.
(iii) Both the current and the accumulated depreciation must be shown, together with the original cost of the assets concerned. In order to keep the balance sheet fairly simple, this detail may be given in a note attached to the balance sheet. We can now appreciate the value of accounting for depreciation through the 'provision' method (see pages 142–143), since the above information is automatically fed into the final accounts.
(iv) The amounts of all payments made to directors must be clearly displayed.
(v) The amount of investments held by the company must be shown. If it is intended to hold them for more than a year, they must be included under fixed assets. If it is intended to hold them for less than a year, they would be included under current assets.
(vi) The section showing the make-up of capital (or more accurately, the *Total shareholders' interest*) has to be broken down into the following:
— Issued capital. If this is less than the authorised capital, then there also has to be a statement of this. It is usually given as a note attached to the balance sheet.
— Capital reserves. These are reserves that cannot be distributed to shareholders as dividends. The most common examples are share premiums, and amounts arising from the upwards revaluation of assets—such as land, for example.
— Revenue reserves. These are amounts set aside out of profits but which can be 'taken back' and used for dividend purposes if the company wishes.
— Retained earnings. This consists of the balances of the current and of previous profit and loss accounts that have not been 'appropriated' for any particular purpose (e.g. for dividends or for reserves) and are being carried forward.
— Finally, details of any contingent liabilities have to be stated in a note. A *contingent liability* is one that may—but also may not—arise. An example would be guarantees that the company may have given in respect of loans to its subsidiary companies.

The full format for a company balance sheet is therefore shown in display 12.

Accounts of particular organisations

Display 12: Company profit and loss accounts and balance sheets—a recommended format

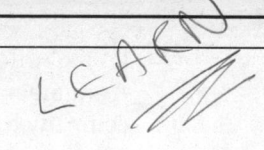

LEARN

Profit and Loss Account for year ended ——

Previous year £000	£000		Current year £000	£000
203		Turnover		317
138		Cost of sales		222
65		Gross profit		95
	9	Administration	10	
	5	Selling	9	
	6	Distribution	8	
20				27
45		Profit before tax		68
27		Taxation		41
18		Profit after tax		27
	12	Dividends	15	
	5	Reserves	10	
17				25
1		Balance (i.e. retained earnings for the year)		2

Balance Sheet as at:

Previous year £000	£000		Current year £000	£000
100		Fixed assets		120
	140	Current assets	160	
		less Liabilities due within		
	60	one year	50	
80		Net current assets		110
		Total assets less current		
180		liabilities		230
		Liabilities due in more		
20		than one year		20
160		Net total assets		210
Financed by:				
80		Issued share capital		80
10		Capital reserves		20
40		Revenue reserves		60
30		Total retained earnings		50
160				210

Note: Detail of main items would be given in notes attached to the balance sheet together with a statement of authorised capital.

Example 25.2

Copycat Ltd is incorporated, with an authorised capital of 1 000 000 ordinary shares of 50p and 100 000 8% preference shares of £5. The following trial balance was extracted from their books at 31 March 1990:

	£000	£000
Sales (turnover)		565
Stock at 1 April 1989	175	
Purchases	400	
Issued capital: 520 000 ordinary shares of 50p		260
20 000 8% preference shares of £5		100
Share premium		20
Debenture issue: 80 000 10% debentures of £1 (1999)		80
Equipment at cost	80	
Depreciation provision (equipment) at 1 April 1989		48
Premises at cost	343	
Bank	16	
General administrative costs	51	
General selling and distributive	20	

250

Accounting for companies: 2

Interim dividend of 5% (paid, 30 September 1989)	13	
General reserve as at 1 April 1989		18
Debtors and creditors	33	30
Retained earnings at 1 April 1989		10
	1131	1131

It is required to draw up a profit and loss account for the year to 31 March 1990, and a balance sheet as at that date, satisfying the requirements of the Companies Act 1985, and taking the following into account:

(i) Stock at 31 March 1990, £180 000.
(ii) Depreciation on equipment is charged at 20% per annum on a straight-line basis.
(iii) A final dividend of 10% is to be allowed for, making a total of 15% for the year.
(iv) The preference dividend is to be allowed for.
(v) The interest due on debentures is to be allowed for.
(vi) Tax is to be provided for in the sum of £13 000.
(vii) The sum of £6000 is to be transferred to general reserve.

SOLUTION

Copycat Ltd: Profit and loss account for year to 31 March 1990

1988-9		1989-90	
	£000	£000	£000
Turnover			565
Cost of sales (note 1)			365
Gross profit			170
Administrative expenses:			
General	51		
Depreciation provision			
(equipment)	16	67	
Selling and distribution		20	
Debenture interest		8	95
Profit before tax			75
Provision for tax			13
Profit after tax			62
General reserve		6	
Dividends:			
Ordinary: interim	13		
proposed	26	39	
Preference, owing		8	53
Retained earnings for current year			9

Balance sheet as at 31 March 1990

31 March 1989		31 March 1990	
	£000	£000	£000
	Cost	Depreciation	
Fixed assets			
Premises	343		343
Equipment	80	64	16
	423	64	359
Current assets			
Stock	180		
Debtors	33		
Bank	16	229	
Liabilities due within one year			
Creditors	30		
Debenture interest owing	8		
Dividends owing: preference	8		
ordinary	26		
Provision for taxation	13	85	
Net current assets (working capital)			144

Accounts of particular organisations

		£000	£000
Total assets less current liabilities			503
Liabilities not due within one year			
80 000 10% debentures (1999) of £1			80
Net total assets			423
Financed by:		£000	£000
Issued share capital (note 2):			
520 000 ordinary shares of 50p		260	
20 000 8% preference shares of £5		100	360
Capital reserve: share premium			20
Revenue reserve			24
Retained earnings			19
			423

Note 1: Cost of sales

	£
Stock at 1 April 1989	175
Purchases	400
	575
Stock at 31 March 1990	180
	395

Note 2: Authorised capital
The authorised capital of the company consists of:

	£
1 000 000 ordinary shares of 50p	500
20 000 8% preference shares of £5	500
	1000

Activity 25.4

Refer back to activity 25.1. How well does your list of the information your felt the supermarket should disclose coincide with what the law does, in fact, require companies to publish.

Do you feel any change in the law is called for?

Check Your Understanding

1. It is the practice in company balance sheets to group items under one of various specific subheadings. Under which subheadings will the following appear:
   (i) issued shares,
   (ii) debentures,
   (iii) share premium,
   (iv) retained earnings,
   (v) tax provision,
   (vi) dividend provision?

2. In what ways do interim dividends differ from final dividends? What are the accounting provisions in respect of each?

3. What is the order of the main items in a company profit and loss account?

4. What are the titles of, and the order of, the main sections of a vertical balance sheet? Is each section added to, or subtracted from, the balance being carried down? How does this form of presentation aid interpretation?

5. List at least four items that must be disclosed in company final accounts or in notes attached to them.

Practical Assignments

1. Flimbo Ltd had a registered capital of £250 000 divided into 400 000 ordinary shares of 50p each and 100 000 8% preference shares of 50p each. The following balances remained in the accounts of the company after the trading and profit and loss accounts had been prepared for the year ended 31 May 1990:

	£	£
Ordinary share capital, fully paid		50 000
8% preference shares, fully paid		15 000
Premises at cost	65 000	
Light and heat		420
P & L balance, 1 June 1989		9 600
Bank		4 100
Debtors and creditors	2 900	560
Net profit, year ended 31 May 1989		12 800
Machinery and plant at cost	25 000	
Provision for depreciation on machinery and plant		15 000
Stock	11 670	
Insurance	410	
Interim dividend at 5%	2 500	
	107 480	107 480

The directors have recommended: (i) a transfer of £2000 to reserve; (ii) a final dividend of 7%, making 12% for the year; (iii) the payment of the year's preference dividend.

You are required

a. To prepare the profit and loss appropriation account for the year ended 31 May 1990 and the balance sheet as at that date in a form that clearly shows the shareholders' funds and the working capital.

b. To explain the term 'interim dividend' and to give *two* differences between an ordinary share and a preference share.

2 Selby Quicksales Ltd has an authorised capital of £60 000 divided into 100 000 ordinary shares of 50p each, and 2000 10% preference shares of £5 each. On 31 March 1987, the following balances appeared on the books:

	£
Ordinary share capital (fully paid)	40 000
Preference share capital (fully paid)	5 000
General reserve	7 500
Profit and loss for year ended 31 March 1978 (credit)	30 980
Premises at cost	20 000
Machinery, at cost	48 000
Depreciation provision (machinery)	16 000
Office equipment (at cost)	10 000
Depreciation provision (office equipment)	2 500
Stocks	29 700
Debtors	8 200
Creditors	10 300
Cash at bank and in hand	6 500
Bank loan (repayable in 1990)	5 000
Appropriation account at 1 April 1986 (credit)	5 120

You are required to prepare the profit and loss appropriation account for the year ended 31 March 1987, and the balance sheet as at that date in a form that conforms with the requirements of the Companies Act 1985 taking into account the following:

a. the provision of the preference dividend;

b. the directors have recommended a dividend of 20% on the ordinary shares;

c. the transfer of £10 000 to a provision for taxation account.

3 a. Tolstoy & Co. Ltd have an authorised share capital of 100 000 £1 ordinary shares and 50 000 8% £5 preference shares. The following information was taken from the company's ledger at 31 March 1990.

Issued share capital: 80 000 ordinary shares of £1 and 10 000 preference shares of £5, all fully paid; premises £130 000; share premium £140 000; retained earnings £20 000; stocks £90 000; trade creditors (including accrued debenture interest) £56 000; cash-at-bank £26 000; debtors £55 000; dividend provision on ordinary shares £16 000; 10% debentures (redeemable 2010) £40 000; machinery £101 000.

Required: a balance sheet drawn up in a form to show clearly the working capital and the total of the shareholders' interests.

b. During April 1990, the following were among the transactions that took place:

(i) The dividend for which provision had been made was paid.

(ii) The accrued debenture interest—which represented interest on the debentures for one full year—was paid.

(iii) The remainder of the ordinary shares were issued and paid for at a price of £3 per share.

(iv) Advertising costs of £2000 were paid.

Required: a table setting out the effect of each transaction on working capital and on cash for the year ending 31 March 1991.

c. The provision for the ordinary dividend arose from a recommendation of the directors to the annual general meeting of the company that a first and final dividend of 20% be paid. Would it have been in order, had the directors wished, for a dividend of 30% to be recommended and subsequently paid?

d. If a dividend of 25% is paid in April 1991, how much will be paid on each of the shares issued in January 1990 at £3 per share?

Accounts of particular organisations

4 Stan Leach runs a small company engaged in engineering contract work. The issued share capital consists entirely of £1 ordinary shares and is held by himself (41 000 shares), his wife (20 000 shares) and his son (1186 shares). After the preparation of his profit and loss account for the last financial year, Stan had an argument with his accountant.

He demanded the return of all books and papers, and decided to draw up the balance sheet himself. He produced the following:

Assets	£		£
Agreed profits for the year *cap*	5 184	Capital as authorised *not used* *cap*	90 000
Debtors *CA*	5 600	Bank loan *L.T.L.*	2 000
Stocks (paid for) *C.A.*	13 260	Stocks (not paid for) *L.A.*	1 200
Cash in hand and at bank *CA*	2 686	Expenses (paid in advance) *C.A.*	1 394
Provision set aside against bad debts *c.A.*	180	Creditors *L*	1 998
Premises *FA*	50 000	P & L credit balances b/f from last year	12 460
Plant and machinery *FA*	21 000		
Provision set aside against depreciation of plant *F.A*	11 000		
Accruals *C.L*	132		
	109 042		109 042

Someone has told Stan, in as kind a way as possible, that he has not got it quite right, and he has therefore asked you to sort it out for him.

Prepare his balance sheet as it should be. You may assume that the figures themselves are correct.

5 At 31 March 1990, General Traders Ltd had the following balances on their books:

	£		£
Freehold premises at cost *BS*	500 000	Carriage-in	27 000
Sales *T*	1 500 000	Stock at 1 April 1989	160 000
Wages: administration *P+L*	40 000	Purchases	860 000
distribution *P+L*	80 000	Vehicle running costs	22 000
Directors' fees *P+L*	40 000	Returns-in	36 000
Administrative costs *P+L*	18 000	Returns-out	50 000
Retained earnings at 1 April 1989 (credit)	520 000	Audit fees	5 000
Vehicles at cost *BS*	80 000	Discounts allowed	5 000
		Interim dividend	60 000
		Depreciation provisions:	
		Premises	80 000
		Vehicles	32 000

Required: the trading, profit and loss and profit and loss appropriation account of the company for the year to 31 March 1989, taking into account the following information:

a. The closing stock was valued at £180 000.
b. The directors proposed a final dividend, making the dividend for the year on ordinary shares 11%.
c. The authorised capital of the company consisted of three million £1 ordinary shares of which two million had been issued and were fully paid.
d. It was decided to transfer £200 000 to a general reserve.
e. The following expenses were owing at 31 March 1988:
    Vehicle running expenses   £2200
    Commissions to sales staff   £6000
    Administrative expenses paid in advance at the same date   £3000
f. It is company policy to depreciate freehold premises at 4% per annum straight line and motor vehicles at 20% on a diminishing balance basis. The figures include a vehicle that cost £16 000 two years ago and had been sold for £5000 on 1 April 1987. There were no other purchases or sales.
g. The motor vehicles had been used as follows:
    for sales and distribution   60 000 miles
    for administrative reasons   20 000 miles

6 The following is the trial balance for Boomkar Ltd at 31 December 19-1.

	DR £	CR £
Authorised and issued share capital:		
80 000 ordinary shares at £3 each		240 000
80 000 10% preference shares of £2 each		160 000
Debentures: 100 000 12% at £1 each		100 000
Freehold property at cost	350 000	
Furniture and fittings at cost	20 000	
Stock at 1 Jan 19-1	127 250	
Provision for bad debts at 1 Jan		2 250
Depreciation provision (furniture and fittings) 1 Jan		5 000
Salaries: office staff	30 000	
warehouse staff	10 000	
sales staff	15 000	
Other distribution and selling expenses	4 450	
Purchases	700 200	
Sales		903 500
Trade debtors	75 000	
Trade creditors		49 400
General administrative expenses	36 450	
Bad debts	4 250	
Directors' fees	10 000	
Bank	87 300	
Debenture interest paid to 30 June	6 000	
Rates of office premises	1 000	
Rates of warehouse	750	
Retained earnings at 1 Jan		17 500
	1 477 650	1 477 650

Draw up the trading and profit and loss for the year and the balance sheet at 31 December 19-1 in a form that satisfies the Companies Act 1985 taking into account:

a. Stock at 31 Dec £142 750.
b. Provision for bad debts to be maintained at 2.5% of debtors.
c. Depreciation on furniture and fittings at 5% straight line.
d. A dividend of 10% to be provided for on ordinary shares.
e. Tax on profits to be provided for at 25%.
f. Accrued salaries at 31 December: sales staff £2000, warehouse staff £1000, office staff £7246
g. Rent for premises that have been sub-let is owing to the company in the sum of £2500.
h. No entry has been made for goods of £300 which had been returned to the supplier in December as not being up to sample.
i. Accrued for carriage-in £500 and for carriage-out £350.
j. The sum of £10 000 is to appropriated to revenue reserve.

UNIT 26 THE ACCOUNTS OF MANUFACTURERS

Before you read this unit, try activity 26.1.

Activity 26.1

A retailer purchases stocks of *finished* goods, and debits the full invoice price of them to the purchases account. That price will have been made up of a number of separate costs that the manufacturer will have incurred, together with the manufacturer's profit.

(i) *Prepare a list of as many cost items as you can think of which will have gone into the 'purchase price' paid by the retailer.*
(ii) *Look at your list carefully, and see if you can sort the list into two main groups—as a clue, think of how each one would vary if the manufacturer were to double output.*

26A. The Problem

Trading accounts are concerned, as the name would suggest, with *trading*—that is, with the simple buying and re-selling of goods without processing them or changing them in any major way. The retailer, as we have seen, can calculate the *cost of goods sold* simply by taking the cost of purchases, and adjusting it for opening and closing stocks. This is as far as the retailer is concerned with their cost.

The purchase price that the retailer pays for goods, and which appears as one figure for 'purchases' in the accounts, is not really the start of the story. Before the retailer receives them, the goods will have gone through a (perhaps long) process of manufacture, and the figure for 'purchases' is the total of a wide range of costs that have already been incurred. These will include:

(i) the cost of the raw materials used;
(ii) the cost of power for the machines;
(iii) wage costs of the workers directly involved in production;
(iv) wage costs of supervisors;
(v) factory lighting and heating costs;
(vi) factory and related insurance and similar costs;
(vii) factory rates and rent;
(viii) depreciation of machinery and factory buildings;
(ix) possibly a share of management costs.

All of these will have to be included in the basic price of goods charged out to any purchaser.

Activity 26.2

(i) How many of these costs did you get in activity 26.1? Did you think of any others—for instance, returns and carriage? Returns-out and carriage-in are both allowed for in calculating the manufacturing cost of goods, but returns-in and carriage-out are not.
    Can you think why?

(ii) Which of the manufacturing costs listed above are likely to vary with the level of *output* (i.e. not of *sales*)?

The accounts of manufacturers

A manufacturer not only produces goods, but also sells them. This means that, as well as being concerned with all the separate costs of manufacturing, a manufacturer is also concerned with trading in the same way as a retailer.

So, a manufacturer's first task is to calculate the *cost of goods manufactured*. This is a direct replacement for the simple item 'purchases' in a retailer's accounts. This calculation is undertaken in the **manufacturing account**, which is an additional 'final' account. It is prepared immediately *before* the trading account, and the cost of goods manufactured is transferred to the trading account, where it replaces the item 'purchases'.

26B. Form and Content of Manufacturers' Accounts

1. The structure of manufacturing accounts

A manufacturing account is divided into three subsections. In the first, the **prime costs** are listed. These are costs that vary directly with output.

The second subsection lists the other costs that can be attributed to the manufacturing process but tend not to vary with output. These are known as the **factory overheads**.

The last section deals with a further complication that arises in manufacturing—namely the variation in the stocks of **work-in-progress**. This is described in more detail below.

The prime costs, plus the factory overheads, plus (or minus) the variation in work-in-progress, gives the **cost of goods manufactured**.

(a) Prime costs
Prime costs consist of:

(i) the cost of raw materials used—this is obtained by adding together the opening stock and the purchases, and deducting the closing stock, of raw materials; carriage-in on raw materials should be added to the purchase cost;
(ii) direct labour costs;
(iii) direct power for the machines.

(b) Factory overheads
Typical overheads include:

(i) indirect labour (such as supervisors' wages);
(ii) factory lighting and heating;
(iii) factory rent, rates and insurance;
(iv) machinery repairs;
(v) depreciation of machinery and of factory buildings.

Examination questions sometimes state that other costs—such as a share of management salaries—should be split between the manufacturing account and the profit and loss account. The items concerned, and the basis on which they have to be split, will be stated in the question.

(c) Work-in-progress
At the end of the accounting year, most manufacturing firms will have partly manufactured goods on the production lines. These amount to the work-in-progress, and have to be valued on the basis of the lesser of cost or net realisable value (see unit 12).

To find the true cost of goods that have been manufactured, it is

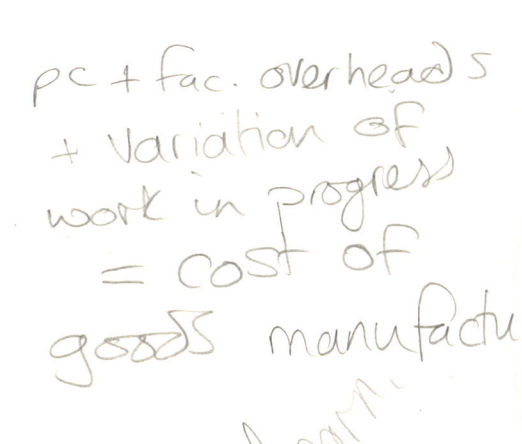

Accounts of particular organisations

necessary to allow for the difference between the opening and the closing stocks of work-in-progress. If the opening stock is the greater figure, then the difference has to be added to the other costs; if the closing stock is the greater, then it has to be deducted.

2. The trading and profit and loss accounts

The cost of goods manufactured (sometimes called the *factory cost of goods produced*) is transferred to the trading account, where it replaces purchases. The opening stock of finished goods is added and the closing stock is deducted in the normal way. This gives the *cost of goods sold*.

The profit and loss account follows the normal structure, except that some of the items may have been split with the manufacturing account. It is usual to group costs into subtotals for administrative, selling and distribution costs.

Example 26.1

From the following information, draw up the manufacturing, trading and profit and loss account of A Producer for the year ended 31 December 19-1.

	£000		£000
Stocks at 1 January 19-1		*Electricity*	
Raw materials M	32	Factory power M	18
Work-in-progress M	39	Factory lighting M	7
Finished goods T	46	Office lighting: P+L	
		administrative	2
Stocks at 31 December 19-1		selling and distribution P+L	1
Raw materials M	24		
Work-in-progress M	32	*Depreciation*	
Finished goods T	42	Machinery M	36
		Buildings (see note 2) M, P+L	6
Wages and salaries			
Direct factory wages M	46	*Other items*	
Works manager's salary M	16	Purchases of raw materials M	116
Administrative staff salaries P+L	25	Carriage-in M	1
Selling and distributive staff salaries P+L	20	Carriage-out P+L	2
Directors' fees (see note 1) M, P+L	60	Returns-out of raw materials M	3
		Returns-in T	2
		General expenses:	
		Administration P+L	100
		Selling P+L	150

Income earned from sales amounted to £740 000.

Notes
1. Directors' fees should be divided up as half to manufacturing and half to administrative costs.
2. Two-thirds of the depreciation for buildings refers to the factory and one-third to the administrative offices.

SOLUTION

A Producer: Manufacturing account for the year to 31 December 19-1

	£000	£000		£000	£000
Prime costs			Factory cost of goods		
Stock, 1.1.19-1		32	manufactured c/d		286
Purchases		116			
Carriage-in		1			
		149			

258

Less Returns-out	3		
Stock, 31.12.19-1	24	27	
Cost of materials used		122	
Direct wages		46	
Factory power		18	
Prime cost		186	
Factory overheads			
Works manager's salary	16		
Directors' fees, share of	30		
Factory lighting	7		
Depreciation:			
Machinery	36		
Buildings, share of	4		
Factory overheads		93	
Work-in-progress			
Stock, 1.1.19-1	39		
Less Stock, 31.12.19-1	32	7	
		286	286

Trading and profit and loss account for year to 31 December 19-1

Factory cost of goods			Sales		740
manufactured	b/d	286	*Less* Returns-in	2	738
Stocks of finished goods:					
At 1.1.19-1	46	332			
Less at 31.12.19-1		42			
Cost of goods sold		290			
Gross profit	c/d	448			
		738			738
			Gross profit	b/d	448
Administrative					
Salaries	25				
Directors' fees, share	30				
Lighting, share	2				
Depreciation:					
buildings, share	2				
General	100	159			
Selling and distribution					
Salaries	20				
Lighting	1				
Carriage-out	2				
General	150	173			
Net profit		116			
		448			448

Activity 26.3

(i) Note the position of the apostrophe in the expressions *works manager's salary* and *directors' fees* in example 26.1 above. Why should it be before the 's' in the first case, and after the 's' in the second case?

(ii) Manufacturing accounts are particularly difficult documents to show in vertical format because of the number of subtotals. Rewrite the manufacturing account in the above example in vertical format, using your

Accounts of particular organisations

(iii) It has been stated a number of times that *cost of goods manufactured* replaces the item

initiative to present the figures in the most easily understood way you can think of.

purchases of a conventional retailer's trading account. But the calculation of the amount still omits one vital element that would be included in the *cost of the purchases* of a retailer. *What is it?*

26C. Alternative Structure

The item *cost of goods manufactured* differs from a retailer's cost of purchases in that it does not include a profit element. Therefore, in example 26.1, the gross profit included *both* the profit (or loss) on manufacturing as well as that on trading. The trading account of manufacturers who are selling the goods they make is therefore not directly comparable with the trading account of a retailer who is buying-in the goods to sell, and whose price includes the profit element of the manufacturer.

If the goods that are being manufactured are a standard product that can also be bought on the open market, no great problem arises, since the normal purchase price of the goods can be compared with the cost of manufacturing them, and it can be clearly seen how much of the profit originated from the manufacturing activity, and how much from the selling activity.

This distinction can easily be brought into the accounting system. Instead of transferring the *cost of goods manufactured* to the trading account as was done in example 26.1, the manufacturing account is credited with the *market price* of the goods produced (i.e. what it would have cost to buy them on the open market). This gives either a profit or a loss on the manufacturing activity, and this is transferred directly to the profit and loss account.

The value of the market price of the goods is debited to trading account in place of cost of goods manufactured, and there added to opening stock of finished goods in the normal way. We then have an account that is directly comparable to a normal retailer's, and which will show the profit (or loss) on the trading activity.

Example 26.2

Broadbent Ltd manufacture nuts and bolts of a standard design, which could alternatively be bought on the open market. For the year to 31 December 19--, prime costs amounted to £6m and factory overheads to £4m. Opening stocks of finished goods were valued at £20m and closing stocks at £18m. Administrative costs were £4m, selling £2m and distributive £1m. Sales amounted to £23m.

The goods manufactured could have been bought from other producers for £15m.

Prepare the manufacturing, trading and profit and loss accounts, showing separately the gross profits on manufacturing and on trading.

SOLUTION

Broadbent Ltd: Manufacturing, trading and profit and loss accounts, year to 31 Dec. 19--

	£m	£m		£m	£m
Prime costs	6		Market price of goods manufactured,		
Factory overheads	4	10	c/d to trading account		15
Profit on manufacturing, c/d to P&L account		5			
		15			15

260

Market price of goods manufactured b/d	15		Sales		23
Finished goods, At 1.1.19--	20	35			
Less At 31.12.19--		18			
Cost of goods sold		17			
Profit on trading		6			
		23			23
Administrative costs		4	Gross profit on:		
Selling costs		2	manufacturing	5	
Distribution costs		1	trading	6	11
Net profit		4			
		11			11

The procedure is not as straightforward if the goods produced could not have been bought elsewhere. In such cases, a fictitious 'market price' has to be taken—such as manufacturing cost plus a percentage.

Activity 26.4

(i) Prepare a manufacturing, trading and profit and loss account from the following information in the format shown in example 26.1: Prime costs £200 000. Factory overheads £40 000. Finished goods—opening stock £60 000, closing stock £92 000. Sales revenue £360 000.

(ii) Rewrite the accounts in the format shown in example 26.2, given that the goods could have been bought on the open market for £206 000.

(iii) What do you think is the main advantage of following the format in example 26.2?

(iv) What is the value, if any, of assuming a fictitious market price in circumstances where one is not actually available?

Check Your Understanding

1 What does a manufacturing account attempt to show?
2 What is the distinction between *prime costs* and *factory overheads*?
3 Give the order in which the items in a manufacturing account should be listed.
4 If the closing stock of work-in-progress is (i) greater than, (ii) less than, the opening stock, is the difference added to, or subtracted from, the total of other costs in the account?
5 (i) The normal practice when preparing manufacturing accounts is to show the *cost of goods manufactured* and to transfer this to the trading account. Is there an alternative procedure?
   (ii) What is the purpose of the alternative procedure?
   (iii) Can the alternative procedure still be followed if a market price for the goods produced is not available? Why would you be cautious in accepting the value of any results in such a case?

Practical Assignments

1 The following balances were taken from the books of the Highrise Manufacturing Co. at 31 December 1989:

	£
Stocks at 1 January 1989:	
Raw materials	17 000
Work in progress	10 000
Finished goods	12 000
Stocks at 31 December 1989:	
Raw materials	13 000
Work in progress	13 960
Finished goods	16 000
Carriage on raw materials	560
Carriage on sales	900
Manufacturing wages	41 000

Accounts of particular organisations

Purchase of raw materials	60 000
Returns inwards	4 000
Office rent and rates	1 820
Sales	196 000
General expenses	9 000
Discount allowed	800
Discount received	1 120
Depreciation, factory machinery	1 800
Factory expenses	16 000
Selling expenses	18 000
Office salaries	10 600

Required: a manufacturing, trading and profit and loss account for the year ended 31 December 1989.

2 Memphis Ltd manufacture components. At 31 March 1990, the following balances appeared in their ledger:

	£
Ordinary share capital: 100 000 shares of £1	100 000
Stocks at 1 April 1989	
Raw materials	22 000
Work in progress	32 000
Finished goods	40 180
Stocks at 31 March 1990	
Raw materials	34 000
Work in progress	36 000
Finished goods	36 080
Wages	
Direct manufacturing	406 160
Factory supervisors	26 650
General office	20 400
Warehouse	36 600
Direct factory power	190 000
Heating and lighting	18 000
Purchase of raw materials	512 000
Carriage outwards	1 972
Plant and machinery	160 000
Premises	240 000
Returns inwards	840
Office equipment	30 000
Rates	12 000
Administrative expenses	3 600
Debtors	28 000
Creditors	24 000
Cash in hand	7 324
Sales	1 600 580
Bank overdraft	63 146

The following are required:
a. The manufacturing, trading and profit and loss account of Memphis Ltd for the year to 31 March 1990, and a balance sheet as at that date. Heating, lighting and rates should be apportioned one-half to the factory, one-third to the warehouse and one-sixth to the office.
b. An explanation why it is important in manufacturing to distinguish between variable and fixed expenses. What are the shortcomings of the distinction?

3 From the following data, draw up the manufacturing, trading and profit and loss accounts of Omega Manufacturing Ltd for the year to 31 August 1990.

Stocks at 1 September 1989: raw materials £108 000; work-in-progress £130 200; finished goods £150 486.

Stocks at 31 August 1989: raw materials £80 100; work-in-progress £140 100; finished goods £140 286.

Wages: direct wages £152 230; works manager's salary £45 320; office salaries £159 114; warehouse staff wages £50 420; directors' emoluments (fees) £280 000; salesmen's commissions £82 124.

Electricity: factory power £68 112; factory lighting £29 133; office lighting £15 200.

Depreciation: machinery £120 000; lease on buildings £20 000.

Other: purchases of raw materials £386 500; sales £1 646 840; carriage in £5120; carriage out £4120; advertising £40 000.

Additional notes:
a. Directors' emoluments should be apportioned half to manufacturing account and half to P&L.
b. Three-quarters of the depreciation charge for buildings relates to the factory, one-quarter to the office block.
c. The amortisation of the lease is to be divided equally between office buildings and the warehouse.

4 The following summarised information refers to the affairs of Chemi-Con Ltd, which produces and markets a standard chemical preparation under a trade name, for the year ended 30 September last:

	£		£
Prime costs	50 000	Stocks of finished	
Factory overheads	10 000	goods:	
Sundry office costs	20 000	opening	15 000
		closing	23 000
		Sales	90 000

The same product could alternatively have been purchased on the open market at a trade price of £49 000.
a. (i) Prepare the manufacturing, trading and profit and loss account in the conventional manner, carrying the cost of goods manufactured to the trading account.
   (ii) On the basis only of the information disclosed in this set of accounts, do you consider the profit to be satisfactory?
b. (i) Rewrite the accounts to show the profit or loss on manufacturing separately from that on the trading operation.
   (ii) Have you any further comment to make on the situation now revealed?
c. Under what circumstances and for what reasons might a manufacturing firm decide to continue to manufacture its own product even though it could be bought more cheaply on the open market?

The accounts of manufacturers

5 The O.K. Engineering Co. has been offered a fixed-price contract to manufacture 100 000 standard components at a price of £5 per component. The company accountant has produced the following information relating to the possible costs of the operation:

	£
Raw materials required	198 750
Power	18 750
Heating and lighting	8 300
Carriage in	4 950
General and factory expenses	2 750
Direct labour	50 000
Maintenance labour	19 750
Factory rent and rates	15 000
Depreciation of machinery	17 500
Other indirect factory costs (non-variable)	8 600

At the same time, the company received an enquiry for 50 000 of the components in respect of which only £3.50 per component could be charged.

It is the policy of the company to accept only work that will yield a profit on manufacturing of at least 22.5% of the contract price.

The major trade union of the firm is pressing for a major pay award, which could increase direct labour costs by as much as 60%.

Required: an accounting statement summarising the proposals and their implications, together with a recommendation (with reasons) whether or not the company should accept only the first contract, only the second, or both first and second. You may assume that the company has the capacity to undertake this.

6 Judith has been unemployed since leaving full-time education but she believes that she 'could make a go' of designing and producing dresses, and selling them direct to local retailers.

Preliminary enquiries with samples among local retailers indicate marked interest. Sales could amount to 600 dresses a year provided the price is right, and that the product is up to sample. Other enquiries reveal the following possible costs:

a. Premises could be obtained in an enterprise development estate at a cost of £1000 a year inclusive of rent and rates.
b. The necessary equipment is likely to cost £8850 and to have a working life of five years.
c. The costs of materials for the production of 600 dresses is likely to be in the region of £15 000. Reasonable credit terms will be available from the suppliers.
d. Wage costs for assistants will be limited to £6000 a year.
e. Transportation costs are estimated at £5000 for the year. Two-fifths of this will relate to collecting materials from suppliers; three-fifths to transporting the finished dresses to retailers.
f. The estimate for electricity costs is £1200 for the year. Four-fifths of this will be incurred by the workshop, the balance by the office section.

Judith has asked you

(i) to advise her on the significance for her business of the various types of costs involved;
(ii) to calculate her selling price per dress, assuming that she requires a net profit of 30% on cost;
(iii) to prepare a draft of the projected final accounts for her first year of operation, assuming that she sells 600 dresses as expected. A note should be added explaining the significance of each section of the accounts.

If Judith found that her dresses proved popular and that production could possibly increase to 800 dresses in the full year, what advice would you give her regarding her pricing and production policy?

7 The Malvern Engineering Co. Ltd produce, among other products, two types of boiler component—the *Malvern Standard* and the *Malvern Super*. During the year to 31 December last, the following apportioned costs were allocated to the production section concerned:

	Standard £	Super £
Stocks of materials: opening	21 000	31 000
closing	22 800	32 600
Purchases of materials	35 645	88 400
Wage costs: direct labour	46 800	62 100
maintenance staff	1 500	2 200
Factory rent and rates	3 500	5 800
Number of boilers produced during the year	22 000	28 000

There was no work-in-progress at either the beginning or the end of the year.

The following are required:

a. A manufacturing account with analysis columns for the two products showing distinctly the prime cost and the factory cost of production of each.
b. (i) A calculation of what the minimum selling price of the boilers would have had to be in order to give a return of 20% on the factory cost of production.
(ii) Assuming that the prices you have just calculated were, in fact, charged, prepare an analysed trading account assuming that, at the end of the year, there were 10 000 *Malvern Standard* and 15 000 *Malvern Super* boiler components in stock.

PART SEVEN

Multiple-choice test

In items 1–33, state which option best answers the question.

1. A club
   a. never prepares a trading account
   b. always prepares a trading account
   c. sometimes prepares a trading account ✓
   d. prepares an income and expenditure account instead of a trading account

2. The total of debentures issued appears in the balance sheet as a
   a. capital reserve
   b. revenue reserve
   c. current liability
   d. long-term liability ✓

3. A partner's account has a debit balance. This means that
   a. a mistake could have been made, but the balance could be correct
   b. a mistake has been made and the balance is incorrect
   c. a mistake has not been made and the balance is correct
   d. a mistake is not likely to have been made and the balance is probably correct

4. A credit balance in an income and expenditure account indicates the
   a. profit
   b. surplus
   c. deficit ✓
   d. loss
   for the period

5. Dividends are calculated on the basis of the amount of share capital
   a. authorised
   b. issued
   c. called-up
   d. paid-up

6. Which of the following would appear in a company profit and loss appropriation account?
   a. directors' emoluments
   b. interest on debentures
   c. provision for bad debts
   d. dividends on shares

7. An income and expenditure account takes account of
   a. accruals and prepayments
   b. capital receipts and payments
   c. income from all sources
   d. all types of expenditure

8. A receipts and payments account is
   a. another name for a cash account
   b. a form of profit and loss account suitable for clubs
   c. a summarised cash account
   d. a combined cash and bank account

9. The fixed assets must be shown in a company's balance sheet or attached notes at the
   a. original cost less accumulated depreciation to date
   b. net written-down value
   c. value at beginning of year less depreciation
   d. value at beginning of year less accumulated depreciation

10. The accumulated (or consolidated) fund of a non-profit-making organisation refers to the
    a. total of the reserves and provisions
    b. difference between assets and liabilities
    c. total of cash, bank and reserves
    d. total of cash and bank

11. The main purpose of manufacturing accounts is to find out the
    a. gross cost of manufacturing
    b. prime cost of goods manufactured
    c. factory overhead
    d. factory cost of goods produced

12. A credit balance in a partner's current account shows that the partner
    a. owes money to the firm
    b. has contributed capital to the firm
    c. is owed money by the firm
    d. has made a loan to the firm

13. The balance of a receipts and payments account shows the
    a. profit or loss for the period
    b. surplus or deficit for the period
    c. increase in cash holdings during the period
    d. cash and bank balances being carried forward to the next period

14. In company accounts, machinery is depreciated
    a. by the diminishing-balance method
    b. by the straight-line method
    c. at a rate agreed with the tax authorities
    d. at such rate as the company thinks fit

15. Factory overheads include
    a. direct manufacturing wages
    b. works manager's salary
    c. work-in-progress
    d. carriage on purchases of raw materials

16. An interim dividend may be paid by directors
    a. with the approval of all shareholders
    b. with the approval of a general meeting
    c. at their discretion
    d. with the approval of the auditor

Accounts of particular organisations

17 The difference in the stock of raw materials at the beginning and end of a period, plus the cost of raw materials purchased, is part of the
   a. prime cost
   b. work-in-progress
   c. cost of goods produced
   d. cost of raw materials consumed

18 Work-in-progress is an item that appears in the
   a. manufacturing account and balance sheet
   b. trading account and balance sheet
   c. manufacturing and trading account
   d. manufacturing account only

19 Shareholders own
   a. the assets of the company
   b. the capital of the company
   c. certain dividend and voting rights
   d. the company itself

20 If a partner is entitled to a salary, the ledger entries are
   Debit   *Credit*
   a. salaries account   bank account
   b. profit and loss account   current account
   c. profit and loss appropriation capital account
   d. profit and loss appropriation current account

21 Cost of goods manufactured is calculated by taking account of
   a. prime costs, direct expenses, factory overheads
   b. prime costs, direct expenses, work-in-progress
   c. prime costs, factory overheads, work-in-progress
   d. prime costs, work-in-progress, indirect expenses

22 A and B are in partnership. B is entitled to a salary of £3000. Under the agreement, profits and losses are shared in the ratio of two-thirds to A, one-third to B. If the profits before appropriation are £21 000, A's share will be
   a. £12 000
   b. £14 000
   c. £7000
   d. £6000

23 Voting rights at company general meetings are usually given to
   a. preference shareholders only
   b. debenture holders only
   c. ordinary shareholders only
   d. both debenture holders and shareholders

24 A company's profit calculation takes into account
   a. retained earnings brought forward
   b. allocations to general reserves
   c. debenture interest for the year
   d. proposed dividends on shares

25 Issued share capital is the total amount
   a. issued to and paid up by shareholders
   b. authorised to be issued to shareholders
   c. authorised and paid up by shareholders
   d. issued to but not necessarily paid up by shareholders

26 A company has an issued share capital of 1000 10% preference shares of £5 and 5000 ordinary shares of £10. The company's profits amount to £55 000. Assuming all profits are distributed, the actual amount that will be paid on each ordinary share will be
   a. £1
   b. £1.09
   c. £109
   d. £10.90

27 If a shareholder sells his shares in a company, the capital of the company
   a. will be increased
   b. may be increased
   c. will remain unchanged
   d. will be decreased

28 Debenture holders have a right to
   a. interest whether profit has been made or not
   b. dividends provided profits have been made
   c. interest provided profits have been made
   d. dividends whether profits are being made or not

29 Goodwill is classified in accounting as
   a. a circulating asset
   b. a fixed asset
   c. a current asset
   d. an intangible asset

30 Depreciation of machinery is
   a. an indirect cost appearing in the profit and loss account
   b. a direct cost forming part of the prime cost
   c. a factory overhead cost
   d. a direct manufacturing cost

31 The book-keeping entries in respect of a proposed dividend are
   Debit   *Credit*
   a. profit and loss appropriation   dividend account
   b. dividend account   bank account
   c. profit and loss appropriation   dividend provision account
   d. bank account   profit and loss appropriation

32 Which item will appear on the credit side of the profit and loss appropriation account of a partnership?
   a. interest on capital
   b. interest on drawings
   c. salaries owing
   d. partners' drawings?

33 Which of the following items would be included in the current liabilities of a limited company?
   a. retained profits
   b. debenture interest paid
   c. proposed dividends
   d. depreciation provisions

In items 34–40, answer
- A if option 1 *only* is correct
- B if option 3 *only* is correct
- C if *only* options 1 and 2 are correct
- D if options 1, 2 and 3 are *all* correct

34 In the absence of a partnership agreement
1. interest is allowed at 5% on loan accounts
2. partners are not credited with salaries
3. profits are shared between partners in the ratio of their capitals

35 Revenue reserves
1. can be used for any purpose
2. are appropriations of profit
3. can only be used for certain purposes

36 Goodwill can arise on the
1. admission of a new partner
2. death of an existing partner
3. retirement of a partner

37 Final dividends are
1. paid at the discretion of the directors but only if profits have been made
2. charges against profits and not appropriations of profit
3. payments that have to be approved by the company in a general meeting

38 A partner's current account shows
1. profits due to him for the accounting year in question
2. interest due to him on loans and on capital
3. salary due to, and drawings made by, him during the year concerned

39 The current liabilities of a limited company include
1. retained profits being carried forward
2. debenture interest paid during the year
3. proposed final dividend for the year

40 Prime cost of manufacturing includes
1. direct wages
2. carriage on purchases of raw materials
3. factory lighting and heating

PART EIGHT

Checking Up, Summing Up and Selling Up

UNIT 27 GETTING THE BOOKS RIGHT: 1 THE CORRECTION OF ERRORS

Before you read this unit, try activity 27.1.

Activity 27.1

1. Revise pages 33–35 of unit 4 and particularly activity 4.3. Check on the different examples of errors that you listed.
2. What effect on the accuracy of the ledger, the final accounts, and the trial balance, would the following have?
   (i) The loss of an invoice for £540 before posting to the purchases day book.
   (ii) An invoice for £540 incorrectly entered in the purchases day book as £450.
   (iii) The correct entry of an invoice for £540 in the purchases day book, but the posting of the amount to the personal account as £450.
   (iv) An invoice for £540 correctly entered in the purchases day book and posted to the ledger, but the purchases day book over-cast by £1000.
   (v) The omission of a creditor for £5789 from a list of balances extracted from the purchases day book for the purpose of obtaining a total of creditors for the trial balance.
   (vi) The total of creditors, £128 945, is inadvertently entered in the balance sheet as £182 945.

   What action (if any) will need to be taken in each case?

27A. Errors and Their Effects

Unit 4 summarised the rules for the correction of errors when nothing more than the immediate correction of a figure is required. Often, more is needed, either because the error is complicated or because it has remained undetected for so long and its correction would mean the alteration of many figures after it. In these cases, it is usual to pass a 'correcting entry'. This is an entry that will put the accounts right without altering the wrong entry as such.

In order to understand the nature of the right 'correcting entry', it is necessary to see how the error is likely to affect the ledger, the trial balance, the profit calculation and the balance sheet. This means being able to:

(i) *visualise* the 'map' of the accounting system;
(ii) *identify* at what point in the map the error occurred;
(iii) *decide* what effect the error would have had from that point on in the cycle of accounting operations.

For example, if a purchases invoice is lost before it is posted to the day book, the transaction will not be entered into the books *at all*. It will not show up in the trial balance, but the profit calculation, and the creditors in the balance sheet, will both be wrong.

Checking up, summing up and selling up

But if it is entered correctly in the day book, and simply not posted to the personal account, the personal account will be wrong—but the purchases account will be correct (since that will have been posted from the *total* of the day book). So the trial balance will not balance and the figure for creditors will be wrong—but the profit calculation will be correct.

If the invoice was entered correctly in both the day book and the ledger, but the purchases day book simply over-cast, then the trial balance will be wrong, but the figure for creditors will be correct. The purchases account will be wrong and so will the profit.

Activity 27.2

(i) If the purchases book is over-cast, how will the purchases account and the gross profit be affected?

(ii) How will gross profit be affected if the closing stock is over-valued?

27B. The Correction of Errors

1. Types of errors

It helps to understand the correcting entry that has to be passed if the *type* of error is understood. The usual classification is into errors of *omission*, *commission* and *principle*; there are also *compensating errors*. This division is not entirely satisfactory, as some errors do not fit neatly into these prescribed 'boxes'.

2. Error correction

(a) Errors of omission

This is where a transaction has been completely omitted from the books, either by leaving out a posting or by losing an invoice before it has even been entered in the day book. Obviously, the correction that must be made is the complete posting—both the debit and the credit entries—for the transaction concerned.

Where there has been *complete* omission, the error will not show up in the trial balance. But if there has been partial omission, with only one of the entries not having been posted, then the error will show up and the correction will involve the posting necessary to complete the record.

(b) Errors of commission

This error arises when an entry has been made in the wrong account by mistake, although the book-keeper knows what entry *should* have been made. For instance, if sales were made to D. Smith, and the debit entry was made in P. Smith's account, then there would have been an error of commission. This error is not likely to show up in a trial balance, and the correction will be a straightforward transfer from the wrong account to the right account.

A further common example arises when the wrong amount is entered in one or both accounts. An example would be the payment of cash expenses for £395 posted as £359. Here, the correcting entry would be an additional entry for £36 in each of the two accounts concerned, on the same side as the original entry. If the correct amount had been £359, but it had been mistakenly posted as £395, then the correcting entries would have been £36 on the other side of the account to the original entries.

(c) Errors of principle

An error of principle arises when an entry is made in the wrong *type* of account—intentionally, not mistakenly—through poor knowledge of the accounting principles involved. An example would be the payment of motor vehicle running expenses intentionally debited to motor vehicles account in the belief that that was the correct account. The debit entry should have been made in a nominal account, which will be transferred to the profit and loss, and not to a real account, whose balance will appear in the balance sheet. Again, this error will not show up in the trial balance, but obviously it will lead to the wrong figure for profit.

(d) Compensating errors

If there have been at least two errors (which may be any of the above types) that happen to balance each other out, there is said to have been a compensating error. An example would be the omission of a debit in the cash account for £200, together with the under-casting of the sales account by the same amount. Given the existence of the *two* errors together, then the trial balance will not show them up. The errors are unconnected and each will be corrected independently.

Activity 27.3

What correcting entry or entries would have to be made in order to 'put the books right' in the following cases?

(i) The payment of rent had been credited to *both* cash and rent account.
(ii) Cash received from S. Smith had been credited to cash and debited to S. Smith.
(iii) The sale of goods to F. Oppenheimer for £782 had been posted to the credit of his account as £728.
(iv) The sale of goods to F. Oppenheimer in (iii) had been posted, by mistake, to the credit of D. Oppenheimer's account.

Be careful, there is a hidden catch in questions (iii) and (iv).

27C. Correction through a Suspense Account

If errors cannot be located speedily, the trial balance difference can be posted to a suspense account until such time as a thorough search of the books can be made. This confirms and records the net effect of the errors as at that particular date. It balances the books at that point and the routine work can continue. Subsequent checking can then concentrate on the postings up to the date of the entry and can safely ignore the later ones.

The entry in suspense account represents the net effect of the errors that affected the trial balance—and *only* those errors. The correction involves making one entry to correct the error, and a corresponding double entry in the suspense account. When all the errors have been found, the suspense account will balance.

Checking up, summing up and selling up

> **Example 27.1**
>
> Imagine that a payment for stationery of £90 is correctly credited to the cash book, but is debited to stationery account as £70.
>
> The effect on the trial balance will be that the credit column will be £20 greater than the debit column. This is the amount that will be entered in the suspense account—on the debit side in order to make the books balance.
>
> The correcting entry will be:
>
> Debit   Stationery account.
> Credit Suspense account.
>
> The accounts will appear thus:
>
> *Cash account (extract)*
>   –   Stationery   90
>
> *Stationery account (extract)*
> –   Cash   70
> –   *Suspense*   *20*
>
> *Suspense account*
> –   Balance   20   –   *Stationery*   *20*
>
> Note: The correcting entries are shown in *italics*. Note how the double entry for the correction in suspense account cancels out the original balance inserted when the error was first discovered.

Errors that do not affect the trial balance must still be corrected, but the correction will not involve the balance in suspense. All correcting entries, whether involving a suspense account or not, must be backed by a journal entry and narrative.

27D. Errors and Examination Questions

Questions concerning the correction of errors, both directly and through a suspense account, are common in examinations. The questions usually look for a knowledge of:

(i) the correcting entries to be made—the questions may ask for the journal entries that would have to be made, or for the writing up of the suspense account;
(ii) a statement of the effect on profit.

Care must be taken regarding the wording of the question. The question may require a statement of the direct effect of the error on profit (in the case of the error illustrated in example 27.1, this would be an increase of £20). Alternatively, it may require a statement of how the original draft profit will be affected when the error is corrected (in the above case, it will be reduced by £20). If it is not clear which the examiner wants, give both!

Where the question involves the writing up of the suspense account, the following complications are usually introduced:

(i) Usually included, in the list, are some errors whose correction will *not* involve an entry in suspense account. These should be ignored as far as the suspense account is concerned.
(ii) The amount of the original discrepancy (error) in the trial balance—and therefore the initial entry in the suspense account—may not be given. This is to prevent students 'juggling' with the sides on which to put correcting entries in order to make the account balance out. The amount of the original discrepancy will always be the same as the balance of the correcting entries.

Example 27.2

At the end of its accounting year, there was a discrepancy (error) in a firm's trial balance, which was entered in a suspense account. A draft profit and loss account showed a profit of £45 500. The following errors were then discovered:

(i) Sale of goods to Memphis Ltd for £2000 had been completely omitted.
(ii) Payment of rates, £500, had been debited to rent account.
(iii) Purchase of machinery for £10 000 had been debited to machinery repairs account.
(iv) Cash received from J. Jamieson, £450, had been entered in his account as £540.
(v) The discount-allowed column in the cash book had been under-cast by £100.
(iv) A receipt of £680 from J. Jones had been debited to her account as £860.

The following are required: (1) the journal entries required to correct the errors; (2) the suspense account, showing the discrepancy originally entered; and (3) a statement of the revised profit.

SOLUTION

(1) *Journal entries*

		Dr	
(i) Memphis Ltd		2 000	
Sales account			2 000
Transaction omitted from ledger.			
(ii) Rates account		Dr 500	
Rent account			500
Payment of rates wrongly debited to rent account.			
(iii) Machinery account		Dr 10 000	
Machinery repairs account			10 000
Purchase of machinery wrongly debited to machinery repairs account.			
(iv) J. Jamieson		Dr 90	
Suspense account			90
Receipt of £450 wrongly credited to J. Jamieson's account as £540.			
(v) Discount-allowed account		Dr 100	
Suspense account			100
Discount-allowed column in cash book under-cast by £100.			
(vi) Suspense account		Dr 1 540	
J. Jones			1 540
Receipt of £680 from J. Jones incorrectly posted: (i) to the debit of her account; (ii) posted as £860 and not £680.			

Note that (vi) actually consists of two errors, both of which are corrected by the entry shown—what has to be corrected is the wrong entry on the *debit* side for £860 by a *credit* entry for the *same* account. There then has to be a *credit* entry for the *correct* amount, i.e. £680. The two items together mean a credit entry of £1540.

(2) *Suspense account*

	£		£
(vi) J. Jones	1540	(iv) J. Jamieson	90
		(v) Discount-allowed	100
			190
		Amount of original discrepancy	1350
	1540		1540

Note that errors (i), (ii) and (iii) would not have affected the trial balance and therefore are not corrected through suspense account.

(3) *Statement of revised profit*

		£	£
Original calculation of profit			45 500
Add	re error (i)	2 000	
	(iii)	5 000	7 000
			52 500
Deduct	re error (v)		100
			52 400

Note that errors (iv) and (vi) do not affect profit.

Checking up, summing up and selling up

27E. Other Uses of Suspense Accounts

The correction of errors is not the only use for a suspense account. Very often items arise for which the proper entries cannot be made immediately. Banks, for instance, may receive a draft in respect of a person for whom they have no record; or a commercial firm may receive a personal cheque from someone who ordered the goods in the name of a firm—consequently causing difficulty in tying the two up. In such cases, it is convenient to place the receipts in an easily identified suspense account until such time as the problems can be sorted out.

Activity 27.4

1 Return to activity 27.1 and check on the answers you gave then.
2 When a trial balance does not balance, the following steps may be taken to locate the error:

  (i) look for a figure equal to the difference;
  (ii) look for a figure equal to half the difference;
  (iii) check whether the difference will divide exactly by 9.

  Explain the reasons why each of the above steps is taken. Could they be misleading as a guideline to the location of errors?

Check Your Understanding

1 List the main types of errors that can arise in accounting.

2 Give *two* examples of errors that *do not* show up in a trial balance.

3 Give *two* examples of errors that *do* show up in a trial balance.

4 When an error has occurred but some time has passed before it is discovered, why is it usually better to correct it by a 'balancing' entry rather than by altering the original figures?

5 Which of the two types of errors mentioned in questions 2 and 3 can be corrected through a suspense account?

6 If there is a suspense account in a set of accounts, does it necessarily mean that errors exist?

7 List, in order, the steps that should be taken when it is found that a trial balance does not balance.

8 If the sales day book has been over-cast, what effect (if any) will there be on:
  (i) sales account;
  (ii) gross profit;
  (iii) net profit;
  (iv) the total of the debtors' accounts?

9 If the cost of a TV advert has been entirely omitted from the accounts, what will be the effect upon:
  (i) gross profit;
  (ii) net profit;
  (iii) the total of the creditors' accounts?

10 The purchase of goods from Albion Ltd for £4356 has been correctly entered in the purchases day book but has been credited to the account for Albion Ltd as £4536.
  What effect will the error have on:
  (i) the trial balance;
  (ii) gross and net profits:
  (iii) the total for sundry creditors?
  What correcting entries will be required assuming that the difference has been entered in a suspense account?
  What would be the answers to each of the above questions if the account for Albion Ltd had been *debited* with the figure of £4536?

… Getting the books right: 1

Practical Assignments

1 The trial balance of William Holdsworth failed to agree and the following errors were subsequently discovered:

The total of returns outward book, £250, had not been posted to the ledger.

An invoice received from Dacra Ltd, £180, had gone astray and no entries for the transaction had been made.

A payment for repairs to a word processor, £124, had been entered in the office equipment account as £142.

When balancing the ledger account of Rowlands Ltd, the debit balance had been brought down in error as £526 instead of £652.

Required:
a. (i) Journal entries, with suitable narrations, to correct each of the above errors.
    (ii) A suspense account indicating the nature and extent of the original difference in the books.
    (iii) The total of the credit column of the incorrect trial balance if the total of the debit column in that trial balance had been £22 246.
b. *Four* types of errors that do not affect the agreement of the trial balance, giving an example of each.

2 Celia Heffer runs her own secretarial bureau. At 31 October last, her trial balance failed to agree, but draft final accounts were drawn up which indicated a net profit of £6400. A check of her books subsequently revealed the following errors:
a. Her 'Fees Day Book' had been undercast by £1000 although the individual amounts had been posted correctly to the accounts of her clients.
b. An invoice for £120 from Office Supplies Ltd in respect of stationery had been mislaid and the transaction completely omitted from the books.
c. A charge of £45 for overhaul and cleaning of her typewriter had been debited to the typewriter account.
d. A payment of £60 for office rent had been entered on the wrong side of rent account, although the correct entry had been made in the cash account.

Required:
(i) A statement of the precise effect of each error upon the trial balance figures, indicating which account or accounts would have been affected, and by how much.
(ii) The final figure for net profit after correction of the errors.

3 Alison Goodrich runs a small sports shop and on 31 March 1990, the end of her financial year, the following balances appeared in her ledger:

	£		£		£
Fittings	1240	Stock	6400	Motor van	5000
Sales	1840	Returns-in	138	Bank	5200
Cash	360	Purchases	7000	Drawings	60
Creditors	4380	Capital	19518		

Her trial balance did not agree and a check revealed the following errors: Goods at £170 (cost price) that Alison had taken for her personal use credited to the drawings account. Stock to the value of £1600 had been overlooked when taking stock at the year end. No entry had been made for bank charges of £20.

Required:
a. A corrected trial balance as at 31 March 1990 after the correction of the above errors.
b. An explanation of the uses of a trial balance.
c. A statement of the limitations of a trial balance.

4 At the completion of its last accounting year, the trial balance of Hester Ltd did not agree. The difference was entered in a suspense account. Draft final accounts prepared before any corrections were made indicated a gross profit of £332 460 and a net profit of £164 670. The following errors were subsequently discovered:
a. The purchase of a second-hand delivery van for £6000 had been debited to motor vehicle expenses account.
b. An account from the florist for £60 in respect of flowers for the reception area had been debited to plant and machinery account.
c. No entry had been made in respect of the theft of £300 from the business by a (now) former employee. The insurance company have refuted liability on the grounds of negligence by the company, and the money will not be recovered.
d. The total of the discount received column in the cash book had been overcast by £100.
e. The balance on the account of Hoot Ltd, a creditor, £298, had been carried forward as £289.
f. The return of goods for £500 to Ajax Ltd, the supplier, had been correctly entered in the day book but no posting had been made in respect of it to Ajax's account.
g. A sale to Penrose Ltd for £458 had been correctly recorded in the sales day book, but was posted to the credit of Penrose's account as £485.
h. A resolution of the Board to create a general reserve of £10 000 had not been put into effect.

Required:
(i) Journal entries to correct each of the errors above. Narratives are not required.

(ii) The completed suspense account, showing clearly the balance.
(iii) A calculation showing the revised gross and net profits.

5   The draft balance sheet of George Unwin, a trader, showing his position at 31 December 1987, was as follows:

Fixed assets		Capital as at	
Leasehold premises	6 080	1 Jan 87	52 160
Fixtures and fittings	5 120	Profit for year (Drawings)	5 440 (3 200)
			54 400
Current assets			
Stock at cost	32 000	Current liabilities	
Debtors	35 200	Creditors	25 600
Bank	1 280		
Cash	320		
	80 000		80 000

Unwin felt some concern at the picture presented by the accounts and an investigation revealed the following:
a. In taking stock at the year end, some stock had been included at its selling price of £9000. It is Unwin's policy to add a 50% mark-up to cost.
b. In order to cover embezzlement, Sykes, an employee, had inserted the figure of £120 as cash purchases. These purchases had never been made.
c. The same employee had also stolen a payment of £3000 received from a customer. The payment had been subject to a cash discount of £75. No entries had been recorded for the payment.
d. No adjustment had been made for the payment of rent, £500, for the first quarter of 1988.
e. A cheque for £42, paid into the bank, had been inadvertently debited to cash account.

In order to escape prosecution, Sykes agreed to repay the sum of £25 per month to Unwin for a period of one year, the first payment to be 31 January 1988.

Required:
(i) Journal entries to correct the books for the year ended 31 December 1987. Narratives are not required.
(ii) The corrected net profit figure for the year.
(iii) A redrafted balance sheet as at 31 December 1987.

6   Don Lowry is in need of extra capital for his business and he recently produced the following figures for the consideration of his bank manager, from whom he is hoping to obtain a loan:

Net profits, 1985–89, as calculated by Lowry

	£		£
1985	10 000	1986	15 000
1987	14 000	1988	18 000
1989	38 000		

Lowry pointed out to the bank manager that, since his profits had shown a steady and persistent increase, his application for a loan was a reasonable one.

The bank manager was not happy with Lowry's figures and carried out an investigation into Lowry's books. The following facts emerged:
a. Stock that Lowry had taken for his own personal use amounting to £16 000 (at selling price) per year had, in each of the years 1987–89 inclusive, been credited to sales account.
b. In 1987, Lowry had decreased the rate of depreciation on his machinery from 25% straight line, to 5%. This lower rate had been applied in each of the subsequent years. The amount actually charged in 1987 was £8000.
c. Of the closing stock in 1989, certain items had been valued at their cost of £15 000. Their realisable market value was £11 000. (Profit margin 25%.)
d. A loan had been obtained from a relative at the beginning of 1988 of £40 000 at 12% per annum. It was agreed that the payment of interest could be delayed until the firm was in a better financial position. No interest had, in fact, been paid and no entries had been made in respect of it.

Required:
(i) A revised profit figure for each of the years 1984–89 on the basis of the information provided.
(ii) A comment on each of the items a to d explaining why, from an accounting point of view, the original treatment has been queried.

UNIT 28 GETTING THE BOOKS RIGHT: 2 CONTROL ACCOUNTS

Before you read this unit, try activity 28.1.

Activity 28.1

A mail-order firm has 50 000 customers spread throughout the country, and nearly a thousand suppliers. In addition, it has the usual accounts for expenses, assets and liabilities.

How do you suggest the ledger could be 'split up' so that a number of staff could be employed on the work at the same time. Do you see any other advantages that could result from a split?

28A. General Principles

The ledgers of large and busy firms can become extremely bulky things—a problem not made easier by paper-producing computers. In order to overcome the difficulties that arise, the ledger is often split into a number of different 'sub-ledgers', each containing a particular group of accounts.

In a typical commercial organisation, the majority of the accounts refer to debtors, creditors and general expenses. So it is common to find separate sub-ledgers for each of these and for the real accounts. The debtors (or sales) ledger and the creditors (or purchases) ledger are often divided further, such as alphabetically (e.g. purchases ledgers A–M and N–Z), geographically (e.g. sales ledgers for the south, north, east and west regions), or numerically (e.g. where each customer has a number—this can also involve a code to indicate region or credit status). In such cases, the day books are usually ruled with analyses columns referring to each of the divisions.

In complex accounting systems of this type, another problem arises—namely the time it takes to locate errors. It is one thing to take out a trial balance and to know that there are errors *somewhere* among several thousand accounts, but it is of far greater help if it is known that the errors are in a particular sub-ledger of just a few hundred accounts. One way in which this can be achieved is by making each sub-ledger 'self-balancing' by what are called **control accounts**.

The procedure is basically quite simple. Assume that all the personal accounts for debtors are taken out of the 'general ledger' and placed in their own sub-ledger called the *sales* (or *debtors*) *ledger*. The normal entries for credit sales will then be:

Credit Sales account in the general ledger.
Debit Debtors' accounts concerned in the sales ledger.

In a busy firm, there will be several such 'posting runs' every week, if not every day.

Checking up, summing up and selling up

From this, it follows that *if* a credit entry is made in the sales ledger equal to the total of all the debit entries, then the sub-ledger will be 'self-balancing'. In addition, if a debit entry for the total is made in the general ledger, that also will balance.

These 'total' entries are made in control accounts. The one in the sales ledger is known as the *general ledger control account*, and the one in the general ledger is called the *sales ledger control account*.

The sales ledger consists of all the personal accounts of the debtors. The purchases ledger consists of all the personal accounts of the creditors. If the control accounts are to do their job, all entries in the personal accounts must be matched by balancing entries in the corresponding control accounts. This means that, in addition to the transactions involving actual sales and purchases, entries must also be recorded in the controls for payments, discounts, returns, bad debts and any expenses charged.

For example, when goods are returned, the initial entries will be:

Debit Returns-in account in the general ledger.
Credit Debtor's accounts concerned in the sales ledger.

The entries in the controls will be:

Credit Sales ledger control in the general ledger.
Debit General ledger control in the sales ledger.

Similar entries will be made for payments received from debtors.

Work out for yourself what entries must be made in respect of discounts allowed.

Example 28.1

A firm enters up its control accounts monthly. The relevant transactions for June last year were:

Credit sales

Week ending:	Customer:	£	£
June 8	A Ltd	2 000	
	B Ltd	3 300	5 300
June 15	A Ltd	4 100	
	C Ltd	3 500	7 600
June 22	B Ltd		5 600
June 29	A Ltd	1 500	
	C Ltd	6 700	8 200
			26 700

Returns-in

Week ending:	Customer:	£
June 22	A Ltd	750
	C Ltd	100
		850

Payments received

Week ending:	Customer:	Cash (£)	Discount (£)
June 29	A Ltd	5 795	305
	C Ltd	2 325	175
		8 120	480

Show the relevant accounts.

SOLUTION

GENERAL LEDGER

Sales account

			£				£
Jun 30	Balance	c/f	26 700	Jun 8	Sundry debtors		5 300
				15	Sundry debtors		7 600
				22	Sundry debtors		5 600
				29	Sundry debtors		8 200
			26 700				26 700

				Jul 1	Balance	b/f	26 700

Cash account (extract)

Jun 30	Sundry debtors		8 120				

Discount-allowed account

Jun 30	Sundry debtors		480				

Returns-in account

Jun 22	Sundry debtors		850				

Sales ledger control account

Jun 30	Sales		26 700	Jun 30	Returns-in		850
					Cash		8 120
					Discount allowed		480
					Balance	c/d	17 250
			26 700				26 700
Jul 1	Balance	b/d	17 250				

SALES LEDGER

General ledger control account

Jun 30	Returns-in		850	Jun 30	Sales		26 700
	Cash		8 120				
	Discount allowed		480				
	Balance	c/d	17 250				
			26 700				26 700
				Jul 1	Balance	b/d	17 250

A Ltd

Jun 8	Sales		2 000	Jun 22	Returns-in		750
15	Sales		4 100	29	Cash		5 795
29	Sales		1 500		Discount		305
				30	Balance	c/d	750
			7 600				7 600
Jul 1	Balance	b/d	750				

B Ltd

Jun 8	Sales		3 300	Jun 30	Balance	c/d	8 900
22	Sales		5 600				
			8 900				8 900

C Ltd

Jun 15	Sales		3 500	Jun 22	Returns-in		100
29	Sales		6 700	29	Cash		2 325
					Discount		175
				Jun 30	Balance	c/d	7 600
			10 200				10 200
Jul 1	Balance	b/d	7 600				

Activity 28.2

Prepare a trial balance for the general ledger accounts in example 28.1, and one for the sales ledger accounts. Then prepare a consolidated trial balance for both ledgers together. Note how the two control accounts balance each other out.

Checking up, summing up and selling up

Purchases ledgers (sometimes called *creditors' ledgers* or *bought ledgers*) contain the personal accounts of creditors in respect of trading goods bought on credit. The procedure is the same as for sales ledgers, with a *purchases ledger control account* in the general ledger and a *general ledger control account* in the purchases ledger.

From time to time totals for purchases on credit will be entered on the credit side of the purchases ledger control in the general ledger, and returns-out, payments made and discounts received will be debited there.

The general ledger control in the purchases ledger will contain the same entries, but on the opposite side. In order to get the operation clear in your mind, work carefully through activity 28.3.

Display 13: Control Accounts—Five Important Points

1 Each of the control accounts is a complete summary of the ledger to which it refers.

2 The general ledger control account in the sub-ledger is a 'mirror image' of the corresponding control account in the general ledger

3 A clue to posting—note that an entry in an account (e.g. sales account in main ledger) is matched by one on the *opposite* side in control in the same ledger, and on the *same* side in control in the other ledger. (This rule *always applies*. Think of the 'normal' entry: entry in control in the same ledger will be on the opposite side, in control in the other ledger on the same side.)

4 The sales and purchases ledgers, and therefore their respective controls, are only concerned with entries that appear in the personal accounts of those to whom trading goods are sold on credit, or from whom credit purchases of trading goods are made. (In questions involving the posting of transactions to control accounts, cash purchases and sales are sometimes included, as are also credit purchase or sale of fixed assets. These transactions should be ignored.)

5 When required to write up a control account in an examination, double-check to make certain you are thinking of the right account. Their names are confusing. (If asked to write up the sales ledger control, for example, it is easy to think of it as the control that appears in the sales ledger—in actual fact, of course, it is the control (for the sales ledger) that appears in the general ledger. If you think 'wrongly', you can easily end up putting all the entries on the wrong sides.)

Activity 28.3

The following relates to the affairs of A. Trader during the month of March 19--. Show his general ledger (including sales ledger control account and purchases ledger control account), his purchases ledger (including the general ledger control in that ledger) and the sales ledger (including the general ledger control in that ledger). Check accuracy by taking out a trial balance for each ledger.

(i) *Credit sales during month*

			£
Mar	5	Ambrose & Co.	1 500
	11	Beauchamp Ltd	12 000
	16	C&M Ltd	16 000
	27	Hunt Hotels	10 000
			39 500

(ii) *Credit purchases during month*

			£
Mar	6	Wingate & Co.	6 000
	12	C.X. Ltd	8 000
	18	Yenston Ltd	4 000
			18 000

(iii) *Returns-in during month*

			£
Mar	25	C&M Ltd	100
	30	Hunt Hotels	200
			300

(iv) *Returns-out during month*

			£
Mar	15	Wingate Ltd	100
	20	C.X. Ltd	20
			120

(v) *Cash received during month*			(vi) *Cash paid during month*		
	Cash £	Discount £		Cash £	Discount £
Mar 29 C & M Ltd	15 110	790	Mar 25 Wingate Ltd	5 408	492
30 Hunt Hotels	9 310	490	26 Yenston Ltd	2 400	–
	24 420	1 280		7 808	492

What should the entries be if one of the debtors had to be written off as bad?

28B. Complications

1. Credit balances in the sales ledger

Although the sales ledger consists of the accounts of *debtors*, an account with a *credit* balance may occasionally be found. This may arise, for example, when a customer has inadvertently overpaid his or her account, or has returned faulty goods after payment has been made. The amount in question can be settled in cash, or it can be carried forward on the account against future orders.

At balancing time, the total of the credit balances should be carried down in the control account, as only in this way can the correct *total* of debit balances be shown.

Example 28.2

A firm sells goods on credit to A Ltd for £5000, to B Ltd for £7000 and to C Ltd for £3000. By mistake, C pays the firm £4000. Show the sales ledger.

General ledger control account

– Cash		4 000	– Sales		15 000
Balances	c/d	12 000	Balance	c/d	1 000
		16 000			16 000
Balance	b/d	1 000	Balance	b/d	12 000

A Ltd

– Sales		5 000			

B Ltd

– Sales		7 000			

C Ltd

– Sales		3 000	– Cash		4 000
Balance	c/d	1 000			
		4 000			4 000
			Balance	b/d	1 000

Note that it is only by bringing down the balances independently that a correct picture of the ledger is retained. This would not be obtained if the net balance (£11 000) only of the control were brought down.

Just as credit balances can arise in the sales ledger, so debit balances can occur in the purchases ledger. The procedure is the same.

Checking up, summing up and selling up

Activity 28.4

A firm started the month of April with credit balances in its purchases ledger brought forward from March of £15 000.

During the month of April, the firm purchased more goods on credit for £120 000 from various suppliers. Goods for £2300 were returned. Payments made during the month amounted to £64 000 with a discount of £2500 being allowed. A check on 30 April showed that there were debit balances amounting to £560 in the purchases ledger.

Write up the purchases ledger for the month, showing the total of the credit balances existing in the ledger as at 30 April.

2. Transfer of balances

A more complicated situation arises when one person or organisation both sells to, and buys from, a firm. This means that the person or organisation has accounts in both the purchases and the sales ledgers.

The best way of sorting out this situation is to keep the two separate, with cheques in settlement being sent both ways in the post. This greatly reduces the risk of confusion.

But it may be decided that the accounts should be merged and only the balance paid one way or the other. This means that the balance of the small account has to be transferred and set against the larger account, and only the net figure paid over. The transfer has to be recorded:

(i) in the personal accounts of the individual concerned in both the purchases ledger and the sales ledger;
(ii) in the general ledger control accounts in both the sales ledger and the purchases ledger; and
(iii) in both the purchases ledger control account and the sales ledger control account in the general ledger.

Only by making *all* of these entries will all the controls continue to reflect the balances in the individual ledgers to which they refer.

The stages of the operation are best seen in an example. Work through example 28.3 now, and trace each entry that is made. Note how, at the end of the example, the relevant control accounts continue to be a mirror of each other, and how they reflect the position in the actual ledger accounts concerned.

Example 28.3

Wellesley Ltd sell wellington boots to Macintosh Ltd and buy raincoats from them. During April, Wellesley sold boots to Macintosh for £2000, and bought raincoats from them for £3000. In May, it was decided to merge the accounts and for Wellesley to remain on the books of Macintosh as a debtor for the net figure of £1000. Show the entries in the books of Macintosh Ltd.

SOLUTION

(To make things clear and simple, the entries in the controls are limited to those relevant to the above transaction. The entries relating to the transfer are shown in *italics*.)

Books of Macintosh Ltd

PURCHASES LEDGER

General ledger control account

April	Creditors	2000	May	Sales ledger control, transfer		2000

Wellesley Ltd

May	Wellesley (sales ledger)	2000	April	Purchases		2000

SALES LEDGER

General ledger control account

May	Purchases ledger control, transfer	2000	April	Sales		3000

Wellesley Ltd

April	Sales	3000	May	Wellesley (purchases ledger)		2000

GENERAL LEDGER

Purchases ledger control account

May	Sales ledger, transfer	2000	April	Purchases		2000

Sales ledger control account

April	Sales	3000	May	Purchases ledger, transfer		2000

Activity 28.5

(i) Refer back to example 28.1. How would you *now* plan the accounting system of the mail-order company?

(ii) Refer to example 28.3 and write up the relevant accounts in the books of Wellesley Ltd.

(iii) Bonus point to anyone who knows the connection between Wellesley and wellington boots.

Check Your Understanding

1. How does a system of control accounts work in order to make ledgers 'self-balancing'?
2. Are control accounts listed in the trial balance?
3. What is the primary purpose of control accounts?
4. Name the control accounts commonly found in the books of a commercial firm. In which ledger would each be found?
5. How can a debit balance arise in a purchases ledger, and a credit balance in a sales ledger?
6. Why is it important that debit balances in the purchases ledger, and credit balances in the sales ledger, should be entered and 'carried down' in the respective control accounts instead of simply carrying down the net balance?
7. What are the two alternative courses of action that can be taken when an account for the same customer appears in both the purchases ledger and the sales ledger? Which of the two procedures is likely to cause the least confusion?

Checking up, summing up and selling up

Practical Assignments

1 Aztec Ltd commenced business on 1 November last and decided to maintain control accounts on its purchases and its sales ledgers. During November, the following transactions took place:

	£	£
Sales to Albion Ltd	5 678	
Benson & Co.	2 890	
Cloud Ltd	1 000	
D. Dent	4 390	
		13 958
Cash sales		26 500
Purchases from Cloud Ltd	3 500	
Darwin Ltd	2 990	
Errant Ltd	3 442	
		9 932
Cash purchases		5 467
Returns from Albion Ltd	200	
Benson & Co.	150	
		350
Returns to Cloud Ltd		400
Cheques received from Albion Ltd	2 000	
Benson & Co.	1 000	
		3 000
Discount allowed to Albion Ltd		100
Cheques paid to Darwin Ltd		2 000
Discount allowed by Darwin Ltd		50
Dent's debt written off as bad		

Required: the sales and purchases control accounts as they would appear in the general ledger, and the general ledger control accounts as they would appear in the sales and the purchases ledgers.

After the control accounts had been balanced, the following took place:
a. Aztec then paid Errant Ltd a cheque for £4332, the overpayment being in error. It was agreed that the balance should remain on the books against further purchases.
b. It was decided to transfer the balance of Cloud Ltd's account from the sales ledger to the purchases ledger.
 Required: a statement of the balances of the control accounts after the above amendments had been entered.

2 D. Walsh Ltd maintains control accounts for its purchases and sales ledgers. Balances at 1 April 1989 were:

	£	£
Purchases ledger	1 457 (Dr)	23 694 (Cr)
Sales ledger	27 419 (Dr)	512 (Cr)

The summarised transactions for the year to 31 March 1990 were:

	£
Sales	223 410
Purchases	175 803
Payments to suppliers	187 510
Cash sales	80 524
Receipts from customers	234 829
Returns outwards	221
Returns inwards	855
Cash purchases	1 998
Discounts received	284
Bad debts written off	3 705
Refund of overpayment to creditor	886
Balances in sales ledger set off against balances in purchases ledger	97

At 31 July 1987, credit balances in the sales ledger amounted to £423 and debit balances in the purchases ledger to £148.
 Required: the sales ledger control account and purchases ledger control account for the year to 31 March 1990.

3 The firm Selby Quick Sales Ltd maintains a separate sales ledger in respect of its credit customers. Transactions of the firm for the month of May 1990 included the following:

		£
May 1	Balances: debit	25 000
	credit	1 250
May 31	Credit sales	290 000
	Cash sales	348 269
	Returns in	1 800
	Returns out	240
	Credit purchases	98 546
	Cash received from customers	281 000
	Discount allowed	1 700
	Discount received	3 246

At 31 May, there was one credit balance in the sales ledger amounting to £540.
 Required: using such of the above information as you may need, prepare the sales ledger control account of the firm, showing clearly the balances carried forward to 1 November.

4 The following balances were taken from the books of Alpha Ltd:

Balances at 1 June 1989	£
Credit balances in the purchases ledger	35 926
Credit balances in the sales ledger	3 134
Debit balances in the purchases ledger	1 056
Debit balances in the sales ledger	72 474
Totals for year to 31 May 1990	
Credit sales	423 504
Credit purchases	357 713
Remittances received from customers	386 723
Payments to suppliers	349 254
Sales ledger balances written off as bad	1 096
Purchases returns and allowances	2 202

	£
Discounts allowed	9 435
Discounts received	7 729
Purchases ledger credits transferred to the sales ledger	983
Legal expenses charged to customers	540
Balances at 31 May 1990	
Credit balances in the sales ledger	5 101
Debit balances in the purchases ledger	2 406

Required: the purchases ledger control account and the sales ledger control account as they would appear in the general ledger, showing clearly all balances carried forward to the following year.

5 The following figures relate to the year 1989 and have been extracted from the books of Universal Supplies Ltd.

	£
Sales ledger balances (debit) at 1 January 1989	150 728
Bought ledger balances (debit) at 1 January 1989	2 400
Bought ledger balances (credit) at 1 January 1989	130 480
Returns outwards	7 906
Returns inwards	6 485
Cheques received from customers	1 643 497
Cheques paid to suppliers	1 014 486
Discounts allowed	39 782
Discounts received	29 843
Credit sales	1 584 248
Credit purchases	1 024 581
Cheque paid in respect of a credit balance in the sales ledger	260
Bad debts written off during the year	24 952
Credit balances in the sales ledger at 31 December 1989	580

Required: the sales ledger control account and the bought ledger control account for the year to 31 December 1989.

6 The following relates to the loans made to the staff of a local authority to assist them with car purchases and removal expenses:

	£
Debit balances in the Personal Accounts (Staff Loans) Ledger at 1 April 1989	267 120
Loans made to staff during the year	635 412
Interest charged on overdue payments	6 205
Amounts transferred to the debit of the accounts in the Personal Accounts (Pensioners) Ledger	12 064
Debts considered irrecoverable and written of as bad	3 280
Legal expenses charged out to debtors	1 510
Loans cancelled	2 967
Cheques received from debtors during the year but subsequently dishonoured	1 258
Amount standing to the credit of a personal account as a result of an overpayment	65
Loan repayments received	643 200

Required: the general ledger control account as it would appear in the Personal Accounts (Staff Loans) Ledger of the Authority, showing the amount of the total debit balances in the personal accounts at 31 March 1990.

UNIT 29 INCOMPLETE RECORDS PUTTING THE PIECES TOGETHER

Before you read this unit, try activity 29.1.

Activity 29.1

A friend of yours started a small business a year ago. She needs an estimate of her profit but she has not kept proper accounting records other than a cash book. She comes to you with her problem.

What items in the cash book can give you an indication of what has been bought and sold on credit during the year? Is there any other information, not included in the cash book, that you will need in order to obtain an accurate figure?

29A. Statements of Affairs

It is often necessary to draw up accounting statements from incomplete information—incomplete in the sense that a full double-entry system of book-keeping has not been followed. This often arises with small-scale traders and with clubs and societies. The problem can also arise where records have been lost or destroyed.

The information available can range from little more than bank statements, to a fully analysed cash book with complete files of invoices, credit notes and other documents. How far it is possible to draw up statements, and how accurate they will be, will depend entirely on the adequacy of the information available. The task will need a thorough knowledge of accounting systems and procedures, plus an ability to apply that skill and knowledge to particular situations. It will involve identifying what *relevant* information already exists, what needs to be calculated, and how that calculation is to be carried out from the information available.

The term *single entry* is sometimes used where conventional double entry has not been followed. This is misleading because it suggests an alternative and perfectly acceptable system of accounting. This is *not* the case; single entry indicates the *lack* of a proper system rather than the existence of an alternative one.

Sometimes, the information available is so limited that all that can be done is a summary of the assets and liabilities at the date in question. The difference between the two will give the capital—or accumulated fund in the case of a club. If similar information is available for the previous year, then the variation in capital will present profit or loss—subject to allowances for capital receipts and expenditure, and for drawings. In view of the restricted information from which such summaries are usually drawn up, the term **statement of affairs** is usually used rather than balance sheet, which suggests the existence of a proper book-keeping system.

Example 29.1

From such records as exist, it appears that the assets of A. Trader on 1 January 19-1 consisted of buildings £20 000, stock £40 000, debtors £6000 and cash £5000.

At 31 December of the same year, the values of the assets were buildings £20 000, stock £70 000, debtors £7000 and cash £1600.

An estimate of profit for the year is required.

SOLUTION

A. Trader: Statement of affairs at 1 January and 31 December 19-1

	1 Jan £	31 Dec £
Assets		
Buildings	20 000	20 000
Stock	40 000	70 000
Debtors	6 000	7 000
Cash	5 000	1 600
	71 000	98 600

Estimate of profit for the year to 31 December 19-1

Capital at 31 December		98 600
at 1 January		71 000
Profit estimate		27 600

Activity 29.2

A Trader, in example 29.1 above, is very concerned when you show him the calculation of his profit. He is certain that he must have made a loss since he had less cash at the end of the year than at the beginning. Further enquiries reveal that during the year:

(i) he paid £10 000 cash into the firm as additional capital;

(ii) he withdrew £7500 cash by way of drawings;

(iii) there was £450 owing for rates at the end of the year, but insurance of £200 had been paid in advance for the following year.

1 *How will each of the above affect the profit calculation?*
2 *What is the recalculated profit?*
3 *How would you answer Trader's argument that he must have made a loss since he has less cash now than he had a year ago?*

29B. Preparation of Conventional Final Accounts

Even though double-entry rules may not have been followed, sufficiently detailed information may be available to permit the preparation of accurate accounts in conventional form. Commonly, this information consists of an analysed cash book (see pages 183–184), together with information concerning the valuations of assets and liabilities at both the beginning and the end of the accounting period concerned, and other 'non-cash-book' data such as depreciation rates, returns, bad debts and whether any accruals and pre-payments are to be brought into account. Given adequate information, then accurate summaries can be drawn up, and it is justified to use the normal terms such as *trading and profit and loss account* and *balance sheet* in respect of them. It is usually necessary to calculate certain items.

1. Purchases and sales

Unless full double-entry records have been maintained, it is unlikely that the amounts of purchases and of sales will be immediately available, and they will have to be calculated.

(a) Purchases

The payments for *cash* purchases should be available from the cash book. *Credit* purchases will not be listed as such, but a clue can be obtained from the amount paid to trade debtors during the current period—since what is purchased has to be paid for in the end. But this figure will have to be adjusted by *adding*:

(i) discounts received and returns-out (since these represent gross purchases not included in the payments to creditors);

(ii) creditors at the end of the period (since these represent purchases already made, but not yet paid for);

and *deducting*:

(iii) creditors at the beginning of the period (since these represent payments made for purchases during a previous period).

(b) Sales

Sales can also be obtained by adding the cash sales to the credit sales. Since goods sold on credit will eventually be paid for, the credit sales can be obtained by taking the receipts from debtors during the period and adjusting the amount by *adding*:

(i) discounts allowed, returns-in and bad debts written off (since these represent sales not included in the receipts from debtors);

(ii) debtors at the end of the period (since these represent sales already made but not yet paid for);

and *deducting*:

(iii) debtors at the beginning of the period (since these will represent receipts for sales made in the previous period).

Example 29.2

Calculate the figures for purchases and sales to be included in the trading account from the following information:

	£		£
Cash sales	100 000	Creditors:	
Receipts from debtors	854 000	at 1 January 19-1	190 000
Cash purchases	10 000	at 31 December 19-1	230 000
Payments to creditors	440 000	Debtors:	
Returns-out	8 200	at 1 January 19-1	150 000
Returns-in	6 500	at 31 December 19-1	112 000
Bad debts written off	9 100	Discount allowed	15 200
		Discount received	20 500

SOLUTION

	£	£		£	£
Purchases					
Cash purchases	10 000		*Sales*		
Payments to creditors	440 000		Cash sales	100 000	
		450 000	Receipts from debtors	854 000	
Returns-out		8 200			954 000
Discounts received		20 500	Discount allowed		15 200
Creditors at 31 December		230 000	Bad debts written off		9 100
		708 700	Returns-in		6 500

Less: Creditors at 1 January	190 000	Debtors at 31 December	112 000
	518 700		1 096 800
		Less: Debtors at 1 January	150 000
			946 800

The calculations in example 29.2 give the figures for *gross* purchases and sales. In the trading account, opening and closing stocks would be shown in the normal way. Returns would be shown as deductions, and carriage-in would be added to purchases (this payment does not affect the calculation of purchases). Discounts, bad debts and carriage-out would appear in the profit and loss account in the normal way.

2. Expenses

The actual payments for expenses need to be adjusted by:

(i) *adding* any pre-payments at the beginning of the period and any accruals at the end;
(ii) *deducting* any accruals at the beginning of the period and any pre-payments at the end.

Can you see why these adjustments have to be made? They are necessary in order to bring the figure going to P&L in line with the amounts incurred during the year.

Example 29.3

Check through the calculations for each of the expenses below. Note how, in each case, the calculation gives the amount incurred during the year.

Expense	Amount paid	1 January		31 December	
		Pre-paid	Accrued	Pre-paid	Accrued
	£	£	£	£	£
Insurance	6 000	1 000	–	2 000	–
Electricity	4 000	–	500	–	300
Rent	8 000	–	1 500	3 000	–
Advertising	12 000	2 000	–	–	3 500

SOLUTION

		£			£
Insurance			*Electricity*		
Amount paid		6 000	Amount paid		4 000
Add pre-payment, 1 Jan		1 000	*Add* accrual, 31 Dec		300
		7 000			4 300
Deduct pre-payment, 31 Dec		2 000	*Deduct* accrual, 1 Jan		500
		5 000			3 800
Rent			*Advertising*		
Amount paid		8 000	Amount paid		12 000
Deduct			*Add*		
accrual, 1 Jan	1 500		pre-payment, 1 Jan	2 000	
pre-payment, 31 Dec	3 000	4 500	pre-payment, 31 Dec	3 500	5 500
		3 500			17 500

Checking up, summing up and selling up

3. Depreciation

A slightly different calculation may be required for depreciation. Two separate situations can arise.

In the first case, the opening balances of the asset and of depreciation provision (if any) are given, plus directions regarding the rate of depreciation to be allowed. In this case, the normal procedure is followed.

Alternatively, in the second case, the values of the asset as at the beginning and the end of the period are given. From the cash book, it is possible to pick up any purchases or sales of the asset during the year. Without depreciation, the original value *plus* additions *less* disposals will equal the closing value. If there is a discrepancy, the difference must be regarded as depreciation.

Example 29.4

The value of machinery is listed at £200 000 at 1 January and at £250 000 at 31 December in the same year. During the year, additional machinery was purchased for £500 000 and machinery valued at £400 000 was sold at book value. Calculate the depreciation for the year.

SOLUTION

	£
Value of machinery at 1 January	200 000
Purchase of machinery during year	500 000
	700 000
Disposals during year	400 000
	300 000
Value as at 31 December	250 000
Depreciation for the year	50 000

29C. Conversion to Double Entry

Though it is often possible to prepare accurate final accounts from incomplete records, the system can become inadequate as the organisation concerned grows, and it then becomes desirable to convert to formal double entry.

If all that is required is to introduce double entry *for the future*, it is sufficient to prepare an accurate summary of assets, liabilities and capital as at the date at which the books are to be opened and, after the items have been passed through the journal—what are known as the **opening entries**—to open conventional ledger accounts in respect of them. Then normal double-entry principles are followed.

A more difficult task is to prepare accounts on a double-entry basis *in retrospect*, i.e. for a period that has already passed. It is then necessary to go back to a previous statement of affairs and, after opening the ledger as at that date, to build up the double entry for the past transactions from such information as may be available. The possibility of doing this will obviously depend upon the adequacy of the information available.

Activity 29.3

From the following information relating to the year to 31 December 19-1, prepare a trading and profit and loss account:

Cash book extracts

Payments for the year	£		£
Insurance	750	Advertising	3 700
Electricity	1 500	Rent	2 300
Creditors	85 600	Cash purchases	5 400
(Discount received	4 560)	Carriage-out	1 200
Carriage-in	3 400		

Receipts for the year			Extracts from balance sheet at 31 December 19-1			
			Assets		Liabilities	
Cash sales	30 500		Stock	50 560		
Debtors	110 620		Debtors	32 444	Creditors	15 670
(Discount			Pre-payments:		Accruals:	
allowed	3 240)		Insurance	450	Electricity	760
			Advertising	2 000	Rent	150

Extracts from balance sheet at 1 January 19-1

Assets		Liabilities	
Stock	45 540		
Debtors	20 991	Creditors	23 700
Pre-payments:		Accruals:	
Insurance	300	Electricity	300
Rent	800	Advertising	1 000

Credit notes received during the period totalled £2249 and credit notes issued totalled £1496. Bad debts written off amounted to £4723.

Check Your Understanding

1. In what circumstances is a summary of assets and liabilities called a *statement of affairs* instead of a balance sheet?

2. How can:
   (i) credit sales,
   (ii) credit purchases,
   be calculated if the conventional information is not available?

3. What information additional to that contained in the cash book is necessary for the calculation of expense items to be included in the profit and loss account?

4. How may depreciation be calculated if the conventional information is not available?

5. A friend has been asked to be treasurer of a small club. It is not proposed to maintain a full ledger. How would you advise your friend to plan her cash book, and what additional information would you tell her she will need if a proper income and expenditure account is to be drawn up?

Practical Assignments

1. a. In what ways do statement of affairs and statements of profit and loss differ from balance sheets and profit and loss accounts?
   b. (i) If it is not possible to draw up an account or a statement of profit and loss based on income and expenditure during a given year, what other way exists of estimating the profit for the year?
      (ii) What items may have to be allowed for in calculating profit in this way?

2. a. At the beginning of 1989, Alpha Co. had creditors of £40m. Their purchases during 1989 amounted to £90m and their payments to creditors to £96m. In addition, cash purchases were £8m and returns out £5m. Discount received was £4m. What was the value of creditors at the end of the year?
   b. At the close of 1989, Omega Ltd's debtors stood at £56m. Their sales on credit had amounted to £104m and for cash to £10m. Returns in had been £4m and discount allowed £7m. Receipts from debtors £73m. What was the value of debtors at the beginning of the year?

3. Andrew has not been in the habit of keeping conventional accounts. The Inland Revenue has complained and is not willing to accept the figures he has submitted. You are asked to prepare his accounts from the following information:

   Position at 1 January of last year (£000): trading stock £14; creditors £11; mortgage £15; debtors £10; cash in hand and at bank £2; owing for stationery £3; owing for insurance £1; machinery £16; land and buildings £20.

   Position at 31 December last (£000): machinery £30; mortgage—to be calculated; stock £20; creditors £10; debtors £15; cash—to be calculated; land and buildings £20; owing for stationery £4; insurance prepaid for the current year £2.

   A check of his bank statements and other information revealed the following cash receipts and payments:

   Receipts (£000): received from debtors £36 (including £5 for machinery sold at book value); additional capital from Andrew £50; cash sales £4; loan from Andrew's brother John £2.

Payments (£000): payments to creditors £20; payment for stationery £6; cash purchases £4; payment for insurance £9; cost of new machine £20; Andrew's private drawings £6; payment to mortgage company: capital repayment £13 (plus £7 interest).

You are also able to ascertain the following (£000): discount allowed during year £1; discounts received £3; returns in £5; returns out £1; drawings of stock by Andrew for his own use (at cost) £2.

Required: a calculation of (i) the profit by reference to the two balance sheets only; (ii) the items necessary for a trading and profit and loss account.

4 John Gilpin, a family friend, recently set up in business as a retailer. Unfortunately, he did not appreciate the importance of keeping proper books of account, and is now worried because the Inland Revenue is demanding a statement of his profits for the year ending 31 March 1990. He has heard that you are studying accountancy, and he has approached you to prepare, for him, the appropriate accounts. You agree, and he gives you the following information:

Summary of bank account for the year to 31 March 1990

	£
Opening balance	1 560
Closing balance	6 598
Receipts in respect of	
sales	60 326
loan from brother	5 000
Payments in respect of	
trade expenses	6 240
repainting of private house	360
stock purchased for resale	47 248
repainting of shop	240
purchase of store rooms	1 200
private expenses	5 000

Other information	at 1 May 1989	at 31 Mar 1990
	£	£
Value of stock	15 672	14 846
Trade debtors	465	762
Trade creditors	1 460	1 280
Delivery van	5 200	to be calculated
Expenses owing	246	341

John tells you that he withdrew £650 worth of stock for his own use. No motor vehicles were either bought or sold during the year and depreciation of the existing delivery van should be allowed at 25% of its value at the beginning of the year.

Required:
a. John's trading and profit and loss account for the year ended 31 March 1990, and his balance sheet as at that date.
b. *Four* reasons why John should, in the future, keep proper accounting records.

5 A retail trader has not kept proper accounting records, but he is able to produce the following information:

	at 31.12.88	at 31.12.89
	£	£
Cash in hand	500	3 000
Sundry creditors	15 400	16 000
Accrued expenses	10 000	5 000
Prepayments	6 050	4 200
Sundry debtors	22 200	21 600
Stock-in-trade	21 800	23 500
Bank overdraft	20 300	20 000
Fixtures and fittings	12 000	12 000
Motor van	17 800	17 800

Cash drawings for the year amounted to £3000 and he had taken goods from the firm, for his own personal use, which had cost £500.

Required: from the above information, calculate the profit or the loss for the year ended 31 December 1989, and a balance sheet as at that date, taking the following into account: (i) Fixtures and fittings are to be depreciated by 10% and motor vans by 20%. (ii) A debt of £250 is considered to be irrecoverable. (iii) A provision of 5% is to be made against doubtful debts.

6 Sara McDougal started business on 1 January 1989 with capital in cash of £6000, which she paid into the business's bank account. She drew cheques in respect of rent for the year in advance, £2400, and for fixtures and fittings costing £1800. Her summarised transactions for the year to 31 December 1989 were:

	£
Goods purchased (all on credit)	23 305
Sundry expenses paid	1 832
Goods that had cost £19 940 sold for	26 065
Cash received from debtors	22 497
Cash paid to creditors	19 186
Cash withdrawn by Sara for private use	2 500

Required: Sara's trading and profit and loss account for the year ended 31 December 1989 and a balance sheet at that date, taking into account:
a. Various business expenses amounting to £35 had been paid during 1989 but referred to 1990.
b. Expenses of £140 were owing at 31 December.
c. The fixtures and fittings should be depreciated by 10% on cost.
d. All cash receipts were paid into the bank, and all payments were made by cheque.

7 John Hawkins commenced practice as a private dental surgeon on 1 April 1989. At that date, he had cash at the bank of £700 and equipment valued at £23 000. During the year, the receipts from his practice totalled £152 600. In addition, various patients owed him a total of £460. He paid expenses during the year amounting to £124 560, which included an item for £240 referring to insurance for the

period 1 April to 30 June 1990. It is expected that his equipment will have a working life of no more than five years and should be depreciated over that period on a straight-line basis.

Required:

a. A calculation of his bank balance at 31 December 1989, bearing in mind that all expenses were paid by cheque, and all receipts were paid into the bank.
b. His profit and loss account for the year ended 31 December 1989, and his balance sheet at that date.

UNIT 30 SELLING UP THE BUSINESS

Before you read this unit, try activity 30.1.

Activity 30.1

A cousin of yours has a problem and has come to you for advice. He is treasurer of a school project, which has run into financial difficulties. He tells you that the intention was to make and sell jewellery for Christmas, but it seems—rather unfortunately—that no one wanted the sort of jewellery they made. Most of it has had to be scrapped.

There were 20 members of the project who put up £2.50 each. Loans were obtained from the school fund for £100, and a personal one from the headmaster—a fearsome individual at the best of times, who was always against the project anyway—of £50. A sum of £120 is owed to local firms for materials. Against these debts, the company has £80 cash-in-hand, and expects to sell the remaining stock (cost £200) for £50.

It has been decided to wind up the project but the members disagree how the remaining funds should be used. What would you advise?

30A. Winding Up

All good things must come to an end—and this is as true of businesses as of anything else—unless the business is a limited company enjoying what is called 'perpetual succession', which means, in theory at least, that it is immortal.

A business may simply 'cease to exist'. A large number of companies, for example, are deleted (removed) from the official files every year because all attempts to trace them have failed.

But many businesses are either wound up or sold off as going concerns. If a sole trader winds up, the procedure is much the same as with the sale of a single asset. All assets of the firm except cash are transferred to a realisation account and the expenses of the winding up are debited. Income from the sale of the assets is credited to the realisation account, and debited to cash, and any profit or loss transferred to capital account. There should then be just sufficient in cash account to meet the liabilities and to repay the capital.

Example 30.1

It was decided to wind up *Newsflash*, a college newspaper, at 30 June. The following is its summarised balance sheet at that date:

Sundry assets	290	Capital	260
Cash	20	Liabilities	50
	310		310

The assets realised £144 and the expenses of the winding up were £10. Show the realisation, cash and capital accounts.

SOLUTION

Realisation account

Mar 31	Sundry assets	290	Mar 31	Cash (proceeds)		144
	Cash (expenses)	10		Capital, loss on realisation		156
		300				300

Cash account

Mar 31	Balance b/d	20	Mar 31	Realisation expenses		10
	Realisation proceeds	144		Liabilities		50
				Capital		104
		164				164

Capital account

Mar 31	Loss on realisation	156	Jun 31	Balance	b/d	260
	Cash	104				
		260				260

If the capital in the *Newsflash* operation in example 30.1 had been wholly subscribed by one person—as is normal in many cases—then the sole proprietor would have to take the £104 realised in settlement of his or her capital. If the capital had been subscribed by a number of people on the basis of, say, 260 shares of £1, then the £104 available would have to be distributed according to shareholding. Each share would therefore rank for a repayment of £104 divided by 260, i.e. 40p.

The winding up of partnerships and of limited liability companies, particularly where there are insufficient funds to meet liabilities, is a complicated matter and is beyond the scope of this book.

30B. Sale of an Existing Firm

1. Vendor's books

When a business is sold as a going concern, the accounting procedures are no different in principle than when wound up. The proceeds of the realisation would, of course, be the purchase price paid by the purchaser.

It is common for a sole proprietorship or partnership to be turned into a company. Although it may well be that the same people will continue to run it and to enjoy the profits, the company exists as a separate legal 'person' (see page 239), and it means that, legally, the firm is wound up on being sold to the company. In such cases the purchase price is often wholly or partly settled by the issue of shares, the shares counting as 'fully paid' although they are in fact issued free. In such an event, the realisation account is credited with the share issue in place of cash, and the capital account debited.

2. Purchaser's books

On buying a business as a going concern, a situation not unlike conversion to double entry arises. The purchaser will prepare an opening balance sheet listing the assets—and the liabilities, if any—that are being taken over from the previous firm, together with any additional assets (such as cash) that are being put into the new organisation.

The purchase price will, in the first instance, appear as a liability. If settled in cash, the cash account will obviously be credited, and the

Checking up, summing up and selling up

liability account debited. If settled by shares, then the credit would go to the issued share capital account.

It is common for the purchaser to revalue the assets for his or her own books—this in no way concerns the realisation values in the vendor's books. Land is often revalued upwards but other assets such as equipment, stocks and debtors may well be brought into the purchaser's books at what he or she considers to be a more realistic value. It is also common for the purchaser to pay the vendor more than the revised book value of the assets being taken over. The difference between the net assets (i.e. assets less liabilities) at the values the purchaser places upon them for his or her own purposes, and the purchase price, has to appear in the purchaser's balance sheet as goodwill—an intangible fixed asset (see page 234). However, for many reasons it is considered undesirable to have goodwill 'on the books', and it is usually written off as quickly as possible against profits.

Example 30.2

Anne has decided to convert her secretarial bureau, which she has built up over a number of years, into a limited company with an authorised capital of 50 000 ordinary shares of £1. The balance sheet of the bureau immediately before the conversion was:

Fixed assets			Capital	23 100
Premises	10 000			
Equipment	12 500	22 500	Current liabilities	
Current assets			Creditors	200
Stocks	450			
Cash	350	800		
		23 300		23 300

It was agreed that the new company should take over all assets and the creditors of the bureau at an agreed price of £30 000 payable by the issue, as fully paid, of 30 000 ordinary shares at par. It was also agreed that 10 000 ordinary £1 shares should be issued to Anne's husband at £1.50, payable in cash.

The new company revalued the assets as follows:

	£
Premises	15 000
Equipment	9 000
Stocks	250
Cash	350
	24 600

Anne's realisation and capital accounts, and the opening balance sheet of the company, are required.

SOLUTION

ANNE'S BOOKS

Realisation account

Premises	10 000	Creditors	200
Equipment	12 500	Capital: shares issued	30 000
Stocks	450		
Cash	350		
Profit on realisation	6 900		
	30 200		30 200

Selling up the business

	Capital account		
Shares issued	30 000	Capital b/d	23 100
		Profit on realisation	6 900
	30 000		30 000

NEW COMPANY'S BOOKS

Balance sheet

Fixed assets			*Authorised capital*	
Goodwill (note 1)	5 600		50 000 ordinary £1	50 000
Premises	15 000		*Issued capital*	
Equipment	9 000	29 600	40 000 ordinary £1	40 000
Current assets			*Reserves*	
Stocks	250		Share premium	5 000
Cash (note 2)	15 350	15 600	*Current liabilities*	
			Creditors	200
		45 200		45 200

	£
Note 1. Calculation of goodwill	
Assets at company valuation taken over	24 600
Deduct: Creditors	200
Net assets taken over	24 400
Purchase consideration	
30 000 ordinary shares at par	30 000
Goodwill	5 600
Note 2. Calculation of cash balance	
Cash taken over from the bureau	350
Issue of 10 000 ordinary shares at £1.50	15 000
	15 350

Activity 30.2

(i) The balance sheet in example 30.2 included a heading for authorised capital, the figure for which was ruled off and not included in the column total. Why was this? Is there an alternative way in which the figure could have been shown?

(ii) Rewrite the balance sheet for the new company, which was set out in horizontal format in example 30.2, in vertical format in a style that satisfies the requirements of the Companies Act 1985.

Check Your Understanding

1. In what ways may a business come to an end?

2. What are the book-keeping entries for the winding up of the affairs of a firm through a realisation account?

3. If a firm is bought as a going concern and the value that it places on the assets is less than the agreed purchase price, how is the balance accounted for in the books of the purchaser?

4. Of what does the 'goodwill' of an existing firm consist and why might a purchaser be prepared to pay for it?

5. If an existing firm is converted into a company, in what ways may the purchase price of the firm be settled?

Checking up, summing up and selling up

Practical Assignments

1. a. In what ways may a firm 'cease to exist'?
   b. What is the purpose of a realisation account?
   c. What is the significance of a final
      (i) debit balance
      (ii) credit balance
      in the realisation account?
   d. To which account is the balance of the realisation account of a sole proprietorship transferred.

2. Howard Black decided to close his business at the end of December last year when his balance sheet stood as follows:

   Fixed assets
Premises		20 000	Capital	21 800
Fixtures		3 000		
		23 000		
Current assets				
Debtors	1 300		Trade creditors	4 000
Cash	1 500	2 800		
		25 800		25 800

   The premises realised £35 000, the fixtures £500 and the debtors £900. The expenses of the realisation were £500, which Black paid in cash. He also paid the creditors in full.
   Required: show the appropriate entries in the realisation and other relevant accounts.

3. John Sykes decided to retire at 31 March last. His balance sheet at that date was as follows:

   Fixed assets
Premises		60 000	Capital	115 240
Vehicles	75 000		*Long-term liability*	
less depreciation	60 000	15 000	Loan	5 000
Current assets			*Current liabilities*	
Stock	35 000		Creditors	15 400
Debtors	22 500			
Cash	3 140	60 640		
		135 640		135 640

   Sykes sold the premises for £110 000 and the motor vehicles for £2000. Most of the stock was obsolete and only fetched £3000. He managed to obtain £14 000 from the debtors; the rest had to be regarded as a loss. He then repaid the loan and settled the creditors in full. Expenses of the realisation amounted to £2500.
   Required: the realisation account and the ledger accounts as listed in the balance sheet showing all entries necessary to complete the winding-up.

4. Ann Crozier has built up a successful business as a hairdresser over several years, establishing and managing three separate unisex salons. She decided to form her business into a company to be known as Hair-e-Styles Ltd as from 1 May last. Her balance sheet at the close of business on 30 April was:

   Fixed assets
Unexpired leases on premises	20 000	
Equipment	8 000	28 000
Current assets		
Stocks	5000	
Bank	2750	7 750
less creditors		3 500
		4 250
Net assets		32 250

   The company took over all assets at book values, including the bank balances, and assumed responsibility for the creditors. Ann received 70 000 ordinary shares of 50p each at par, fully paid, in consideration of the purchase.
   Required:
   a. The realisation account of Ann's firm.
   b. The opening balance sheet of Hair-e-Styles Ltd. The company was formed with an authorised capital of 150 000 ordinary shares of 50p.

5. Greenveg Ltd was formed on 1 January 1990, with an authorised capital of 5000 ordinary shares of £1 and 3000 8% preference shares of £5, to take over the business of White and Swann, greengrocers. The final balance sheet of White and Swann at the close of business on 31 December 1989 was:

	£	£
Fixed assets		
Premises	120 000	
Fixtures and fittings	6 000	
Motor vehicles	12 000	138 000
Current assets		
Stock	160 950	
Debtors	2 500	
Bank	24 600	
	188 050	
less Creditors	45 600	
Current assets less current liabilities		142 450
Total assets less current liabilities		280 450
Long-term liabilities		
Bank loan		40 000
Net assets		240 450

Represented by:	White	Swann	
	£	£	£
Capital accounts	100 000	100 000	200 000
Current accounts	21 100	19 350	40 450
	121 100	119 350	240 450

The company agreed to purchase the premises at a valuation of £220 000 and the fixtures and fittings and motor vehicles at book values. The debtors were taken over at a revised figure of £1800. The partners remained responsible for settling the creditors and the bank loan. It was agreed that the purchase consideration would be the issue to each of the partners of 100 000 ordinary shares of £1 at par and 10 000 8% preference shares of £5 at par, all shares to rank as fully paid. Partners share profits equally.

Required:
a. The realisation account, capital and current accounts of the partnership.
b. The opening balance sheet of the company.

PART EIGHT Multiple-choice test

In items 1–30, state which option best answers the question.

1 A cheque is received from F. Martin but by mistake it is posted to E. Martin. The correcting entries would be

	Debit	Credit
a.	F. Martin	E. Martin
b.	bank account	F. Martin
c.	E. Martin	bank account
d.	E. Martin	F. Martin

2 If the entries for a transaction are entered on the credit side of both accounts concerned, the difference in the trial balance would be equal to
   a. half the amount
   b. the amount itself
   c. double the amount
   d. three times the amount

3 A trial balance indicates
   a. any type of error
   b. some but not all types of error
   c. none of the principal types of error
   d. all errors except compensating errors

4 In posting a transaction, a single entry is
   a. never made
   b. always made
   c. sometimes made
   d. made if possible

5 Errors are corrected by entries that are
   a. always passed through the journal and the suspense account
   b. always passed through the journal and sometimes through the suspense account
   c. always passed through the suspense account but seldom through the journal
   d. never passed through both the journal and the suspense account

6 Errors that a trial balance will disclose include
   a. omission of entries for a credit purchase due to the loss of an invoice
   b. overcasting of the rent account by £10
   c. cash sales for £50 credited to purchases account instead of sales
   d. the complete reversal of the debit and credit entries

7 A statement of affairs is
   a. an estimate of profit or loss for the period
   b. a summary of the firm's financial position as far as it is known
   c. a formal list of a firm's business interests
   d. an alternative term for a balance sheet

8 The primary purpose of control accounts is to
   a. prevent errors
   b. locate errors
   c. correct errors
   d. avoid errors

9 The term *single entry* is used to indicate
   a. accounting systems using single cash columns
   b. a speedier version of double-entry book-keeping
   c. a form of summarised accounting
   d. any system that is not double entry

10 In the general ledger, the total of discounts received would be entered on the
   a. debit of purchases ledger control account
   b. credit of purchases ledger control account
   c. debit of sales ledger control account
   d. credit of sales ledger control account

11 A firm's total credit purchases amounted to £220 000. The opening balance of creditors was £80 000 and the closing balance was £200 000. The amount paid to creditors during the period was
   a. £70 000
   b. £90 000
   c. £100 000
   d. £490 000

12 The balance of the purchases ledger control account in the general ledger
   a. normally has a debit balance
   b. normally has a credit balance
   c. may have either a debit or a credit balance
   d. normally has a nil balance

13 The total of discounts allowed is posted to the general ledger control in the
   a. sales ledger (debit side)
   b. sales ledger (credit side)
   c. purchases ledger (debit side)
   d. purchases ledger (credit side)

14 The value of debtors at the beginning of an accounting period was £125 000. Receipts from debtors during the period amounted to £465 000 and the value of debtors at the end of the period was £98 000. The credit sales for the period were
   a. £438 000
   b. £492 000
   c. £503 000
   d. £688 000

15. The balance of the general ledger control account in the sales ledger
    a. is normally a debit balance
    b. is normally a credit balance
    c. may be either a debit or a credit balance
    d. will be a nil balance since the ledger is self-balancing

16. A firm's credit sales for the year amounted to £210 000. The receipts from debtors were £200 000 and the balance of debtors at the end of the year was £50 000. The value of debtors at the beginning of the period was
    a. £250 000
    b. £160 000
    c. £150 000
    d. £40 000

17. The entries in the general ledger for the total of the sales day book are

Debit	Credit
a. sales ledger control account	sales account
b. sales ledger control account	general ledger control account
c. general ledger control account	sales account
d. respective accounts for debtors	sales account

18. A sole proprietor's statement of affairs summarised his current position as: cash £3800; machinery £28 000; creditors £50 000; vehicles £60 000; bank loan £40 000; stock £14 000; debtors £6800. His capital at this point is
    a. £22 600
    b. £45 700
    c. £86 200
    d. £102 600

19. The balance of the sales ledger control account shows the amount
    a. owing to suppliers
    b. of goods sold
    c. of goods purchased
    d. owed by customers

20. The amount of trade debtors at the beginning of the year was £220 000. Amounts received during the year from debtors were £1 080 000 and sales during the year were £1 200 000. The balance of closing debtors was:
    a. £100 000
    b. £340 000
    c. £2 060 000
    d. £2 500 000

21. The entries when posting transactions in the purchases day book to the purchases ledger are

Debit	Credit
a. purchases ledger control account	general ledger control account
b. general ledger control account	personal accounts concerned
c. personal accounts concerned	general ledger control account
d. general ledger control account	purchases ledger control account

22. A trader is able to supply the following information:

	1 January £	31 December £
Total assets	38 240	46 160
Total liabilities	19 199	20 400

    Drawings of £3000 were made during the year. The net profit for the year was
    a. £3719
    b. £6719
    c. £3179
    d. £9719

23. Which of the following items would appear on the debit side of the sales ledger control account?
    a. returns inwards
    b. discount allowed
    c. credit sales
    d. bad debts

24. A cheque received from A. S. Wilson was credited by mistake to the account of S. A. Wilson. This was an error of
    a. principle
    b. commission
    c. omission
    d. original entry

25. The draft profit and loss account of a business showed a net profit of £320 000. Subsequently, the following errors were discovered:
    (i) interest received, £3000, had been debited to interest account
    (ii) sales account had been overcast by £1000
    (iii) closing stock had been undercast by £500
    The correct net profit was
    a. £314 500
    b. £315 500
    c. £325 500
    d. £326 500

26. A firm increased its provision for bad debts at the end of the financial year from £2500 to £3750. This will be recorded in the sales ledger control account by
    a. a debit entry for £1250
    b. a credit entry for £1250
    c. a debit entry for £250
    d. no entry at all

27. Assuming no other figures are available, it would be possible to calculate the value of credit sales from
    a. opening debtors plus cash receipts from debtors less closing debtors
    b. cash receipts from debtors plus opening and closing debtors
    c. closing debtors plus cash receipts from debtors less opening debtors
    d. cash receipts from debtors less opening and closing debtors

28. The capital of a trader who does not keep conventional records was £240 000 at the beginning of the financial year and at the end of the year £320 000. During the year he paid into the firm £50 000 by way of extra capital, but made drawings amounting to £25 000. His profit or loss for the year was
    a. £55 000 profit
    b. £55 000 loss
    c. £1050 profit
    d. £1050 loss

29 The profit for a firm that has not kept conventional accounts may be obtained by calculating
   a. change in net assets
   b. change in total assets less total liabilities
   c. change in net assets plus drawings
   d. change in net assets less new capital plus drawings

30 Which of the following would cause an imbalance in the trial balance?
   a. a cheque for £960 received from F. Jones debited to S. Jones
   b. a sale for £438 posted in the sales day book as £483, and posted from there to the ledger
   c. payment of a cheque to T. Jones for £842 debited to G. Jones
   d. a purchase of office equipment, £500, debited to office supplies account

In items 31–40, answer
   A if option 1 *only* is correct
   B if option 3 *only* is correct
   C if *only* options 1 and 2 are correct
   D if options 1, 2 and 3 are *all* correct

31 Control accounts
   1. speed up the posting of transactions to personal accounts
   2. permit a trial balance to be drawn up for the general ledger only
   3. make each ledger self-balancing

32 A trial balance will disclose
   1. undercasting of equipment account by £3000
   2. the posting of the discount allowed column of the cash book, £589, as £598
   3. omission of the entries for a credit purchase through loss of invoice

33 A credit entry in the sales ledger control account may indicate
   1. an overpayment by a customer
   2. return of goods after the account has been settled
   3. purchase of goods by customers

34 If a purchaser pays more for an existing business than the net value of the assets, the difference is known as
   1. satisfaction
   2. consideration
   3. goodwill

35 A statement of affairs is
   1. a summary of business transactions and affairs
   2. a statement of assets, liabilities and capital as listed in the ledger
   3. an estimate of assets, liabilities and capital

36 Control accounts permit
   1. quicker location of errors
   2. ledgers to be self-balancing
   3. speedier posting

37 A trader's capital a year ago was estimated at £81 450 and this year at £76 380. He has taken drawings of £17 300. His estimated profit or loss is
   1. £15 230 loss
   2. £22 370 profit
   3. £12 230 profit

38 The purchases ledger control account contains
   1. credit entries for goods purchased on credit
   2. debit entries for the payments made to suppliers
   3. credit entries for discounts allowed to customers

39 Calculations of the credit sales of businesses involves taking account of
   1. returns in
   2. discounts received
   3. bad-debts provision

40 The term *bankruptcy*
   1. cannot be used in connection with limited companies
   2. can refer to partners and sole traders
   3. does not mean the same thing as insolvency

GENERAL REVISION MULTIPLE-CHOICE TEST

This test should be preceded by a thorough revision of the whole course.
In items 1–48, state which option best answers the question.

1. Reasons for giving special consideration to cash accounting procedures include all of the following except the
   a. security problems involved
   b. large number of transactions involved
   c. possibility of fraud
   d. reliance on different accounting principles rather than on non-cash transactions

2. The profit or loss for a bar operated by a social club would be calculated in the club's
   a. trading account
   b. profit and loss account
   c. receipts and payments account
   d. income and expenditure account

3. If shares are sold by a company for more than their par value, they are said to have been issued at a
   a. discount
   b. premium
   c. bonus
   d. surplus

4. The term *factory overheads* does not include
   a. factory lighting
   b. foremen's salaries
   c. depreciation of machinery
   d. cost of raw materials

5. Working capital is
   a. current assets minus current liabilities
   b. total assets minus total liabilities
   c. current assets minus total liabilities
   d. total assets minus current liabilities

6. Invoices received for goods purchased on credit from suppliers would first be entered in the
   a. purchases day book
   b. sales day book
   c. purchases account
   d. sales account

7. The total of the discount column on the credit side of a three-column cash book is taken to the
   a. debit of discount-allowed account
   b. debit of discount-received account
   c. credit of discount-allowed account
   d. credit of discount-received account

8. A trader buys goods for £500 less 20% trade discount and 10% cash discount one month. If he settles three months later, he would pay
   a. £500
   b. £450
   c. £400
   d. £360

9. John is paid £8 an hour for a forty-hour week. Overtime is paid at time-and-a-half and all work on Sundays at double time. Last week John worked six hours overtime plus two hours on Sunday. His gross earnings for the week were
   a. £450
   b. £430
   c. £424
   d. £384

10. A company's profit remaining after tax appropriations is usually
    a. added to capital in the balance sheet
    b. divided between the shareholders as dividends
    c. partly paid out as dividends, and the remainder credited to capital account
    d. partly paid out as dividends, and the remainder added to reserves

11. The object of a manufacturing account is to find the
    a. prime cost
    b. cost of production
    c. factory overhead cost
    d. profit on manufacture

12. Which of the following accounts is not a personal account?
    a. Mechanical Diggers Ltd
    b. A. Johnson
    c. Returns-in
    d. Scottish Trading Ltd

13. During its first year of operation, a company purchased stock as follows:

    10 Jan   1000 tonnes at £5 per tonne
    31 July   2000 tonnes at £10 per tonne
    30 November   500 tonnes at £20 per tonne

307

At 31 December the firm had 3000 tonnes in stock. The value of this stock on a FIFO basis is
a. £60 000
b. £32 500
c. £25 000
d. £22 000

14 A trader's book debts amount to £10 000 with an existing bad-debts provision of £1200. To adjust the provision to 10% of book debts, the trader would need to
a. debit profit and loss account with £200
b. credit profit and loss account with £1000
c. debit profit and loss account with £1000
d. credit profit and loss account with £200

15 A company's sales for the year amounted to £39 000 and this represented a mark-up of 30% on cost. If the average stock-holding was £12 000, the rate of turnover would be
a. 2.275
b. 2.5
c. 3.25
d. 4.225

16 Voting rights at company meetings are normally held by
a. ordinary shareholders
b. preference shareholders
c. debenture holders
c. ordinary and preference shareholders

17 The normal order of liquidity in listing the following is
a. vehicles, machinery, office equipment, premises
b. premises, machinery, office equipment, vehicles
c. office equipment, machinery, vehicles, premises
d. premises, vehicles, machinery, office equipment

18 A credit balance in the bank account in a firm's ledger indicates a
a. long-term liability
b. current asset
c. current liability
d. fixed asset

19 A trial balance will not show up
a. a casting error in cash account
b. the omission of a transaction from the day books
c. an entry on the wrong side of an account
d. a reversal of figures in a balance carried forward

20 A trader purchased goods for £1000 subject to 25% trade discount and 10% cash discount one month. If he pays within a week, the cash discount will be
a. £225
b. £100
c. £75
d. £10

21 The following entry appeared in the last balance sheet of a firm:

	Cost £	Accumulated depreciation £	Net £
Machinery	10 000	4 000	6 000

It is the practice of the firm to depreciate machinery at 20% per annum diminishing balance. The figure that will appear for accumulated depreciation in the next balance sheet will be
a. £1200
b. £4800
c. £5200
d. £6000

22 A credit balance in a partner's current account is part of the firm's
a. current liabilities
b. capital
c. long-term liabilities
d. assets

23 If a shareholder sells his shares, the capital of the company will be
a. increased
b. decreased
c. improved
d. unaffected

24 *Long-term liabilities* normally include
a. proprietor's capital
b. loan secured by debentures
c. bank overdraft
d. trade creditors

25 The main purpose of the day books is to
a. speed up the location of errors
b. provide a check on ledger postings
c. summarise entries of a similar type
d. provide totals for control accounts

26 Copies of credit notes issued would be entered in the
a. returns-in day book
b. sales day book
c. returns-out day book
d. purchases day book

27 Voluntary deductions from workers' wages do not include
a. trade union subscriptions
b. national insurance contributions
c. holiday fund
d. private pension scheme deductions

28 Debentures are normally listed in company balance sheets under
a. issued capital
b. reserves and provisions
c. long-term liabilities
d. current liabilities

29 If one partner is allocated a salary, the profits available for distribution will be
a. more than the net profit
b. less than the net profit
c. the same as the net profit
d. unaffected

30 A firm's liabilities include
a. prepaid rent
b. trade debtors
c. bank overdraft
d. trade investments

31 Which of the following require knowledge of subjects other than accountancy?
a. recording of financial transactions
b. calculation of profits and losses
c. summaries of financial position
d. guidance on financial policy

32 The totals of the bought journal are posted to the
   a. debit of purchases account
   b. debit of the personal accounts concerned
   c. credit of sales account
   d. credit of the personal accounts concerned

33 If fixed capital accounts are maintained for partners, a partner's salary would be entered in the
   a. debit of the profit and loss appropriation account
   b. credit of the partner's capital account
   c. debit of the partner's current account
   d. credit of salaries account

34 A person has bought 50 ordinary shares of £100 each at a purchase price of £200 half-way through a firm's financial year. The company subsequently declares a dividend of 10% for the year. The actual dividend received by the shareholder will be
   a. £10
   b. £20
   c. £500
   d. £1000

35 Discount allowed will appear on the
   a. debit side of trading account
   b. credit side of the profit and loss account
   c. credit sale of the trading account
   d. debit side of the profit and loss account

36 In the three-column cash book at the end of the accounting period
   a. cash, bank and discount columns are balanced
   b. cash and bank columns are balanced and the discount columns are totalled
   c. the cash column is balanced, and bank and discount columns are totalled
   d. cash, bank and discount columns are totalled

37 £2500 spent on a new snooker table for a social club would appear in the
   a. receipts and payments account and the balance sheet
   b. income and expenditure account and the balance sheet
   c. receipts and payments account and the profit and loss account
   d. income and expenditure account and the profit and loss account

38 Would you regard a cash ratio of 160%, in the normal run of events, as being
   a. too high
   b. satisfactory
   c. a little low
   d. dangerously low

39 The figure taken to manufacturing account as *work-in-progress* is the value of work-in-progress
   a. at the end of the year
   b. at the beginning of the year
   c. at the end of the year less that at the beginning of the year
   d. at the beginning of the year less that at the end of the year

40 Credit notes received are recorded initially in the
   a. returns-in day book
   b. returns-out day book
   c. sales day book
   d. purchases day book

41 The primary objective of the trading account is to show the
   a. overall trading profit or loss for the period concerned
   b. net trading profit or loss for the period concerned
   c. profit or loss on the turnover of goods sold in the period
   d. difference between income earned and expenditure incurred in the period

42 The main purpose of a bank reconciliation statement is to
   a. ensure the cash book (bank columns) and the bank statement show the same balance
   b. explain the difference between the cash book balance and the bank statement
   c. ascertain the correct balance at the bank
   d. update the cash book

43 A receipts and payments account shows the
   a. gross profit for the period
   b. net profit for the period
   c. surplus or deficit for the period
   d. variation in cash holdings during the period

44 A statement of affairs is similar to a
   a. bank statement
   b. statement of account
   c. bank reconciliation statement
   d. balance sheet

45 Manufacturing accounts do not include
   a. factory overheads
   b. prime costs
   c. direct manufacturing expenses
   d. apportioned selling expenses

46 The purchases day book records
   a. payments to customers
   b. credit purchases from suppliers
   c. credit purchases of fixed assets
   d. all purchases of goods for resale

47 A bank statement is a
   a. copy of the customer's account in the books of his bank
   b. copy of the bank's account in the books of the customer
   c. certified statement of the balance of the bank account
   d. warning to the customer that he is overdrawn

48 A possible liability that has not been taken into account is known as a
   a. coincidental liability
   b. contingent liability
   c. contiguous liability
   d. connected liability

General revision

In questions 49–60, answer
A   if option 1 *only* is correct
B   if option 3 *only* is correct
C   if *only* options 1 and 2 are correct
D   if options 1, 2 and 3 are *all* correct

49 A company's memorandum of association specifies the
1. total amount of shares it has power to issue
2. name of the company
3. voting rights of shareholders

50 A partner's current account shows
1. profits due to him for the accounting year in question
2. interest due to him on loans and on capital
3. salary due to, and drawings made by, him during the year

51 A business that maintains control accounts is able to
1. locate errors more quickly
2. obtain total figures for creditors and debtors
3. extract a trial balance on the general ledger alone

52 The disadvantages of partnership organisation include
1. unlimited liability
2. no perpetual succession
3. no legal entity for the business

53 A trial balance will not identify
1. transactions omitted from day books
2. undercasting of the debit side of bank account by £9 coupled with the posting of an amount for £4236 to the purchases account as £4326
3. a credit sale of £206 entered by mistake in the purchases day book

54 The term *limited liability* means that
1. the company is not fully liable for its debts
2. liability is limited to the shareholders
3. shareholders' liability is limited to amounts unpaid on shares

55 In its annual report and accounts, a company must disclose
1. depreciation written off during the year
2. the accumulated depreciation to date
3. the current value of each main group of assets

56 Distribution expenses include
1. office salaries
2. advertising
3. carriage outwards

57 A reduction in working capital will result from
1. an increase in bank overdraft used to pay for office equipment
2. a decrease in cash resulting from paying rates in advance
3. a receipt of cash from trade debtors

58 Which of the following can never have a credit balance?
1. personal accounts of customers
2. bank account
3. cash account

59 A credit entry in a cash account and a debit entry in the bank account indicate
1. payment of cash into the bank
2. payment of bank charges
3. drawing of cash from the bank

60 A firm's profitability is indicated by the ratio of
1. net profit to sales
2. expenses to sales
3. gross profit to net profit

APPENDIX A Coping with Percentages

Percentages are used a lot in accounting work and it is essential that you understand them. This appendix is meant for those who need to revise the processes involved.

Generally, you can calculate percentages by using a pocket calculator. Most examining boards now accept their use, but the regulations of your particular board should be checked before the examination. Also, you should understand how the calculation is done: this will help you to use the calculator more effectively. It will assist you in situations where you may not be able to use your calculator, and it will enable you to avoid some of the errors that can arise in calculator work, and to be able to guess if the answer a calculator gives is roughly correct or if you have pressed the wrong button.

Expressing One Number as a Percentage of Another

This is done by expressing the one number as a fraction of the other and multiplying by 100/1. If done arithmetically, cancel if possible before working out the answer, but remember that it is easy to divide by 10 or 100—the numbers simply move one or two places respectively to the right of the decimal point.

Example

Express 25 as a percentage of 300 (correct to one decimal place).

$$\frac{25}{300} \times \frac{100}{1} \% = \frac{25}{3} \% = 8.3\%$$

Accounting applications

Profit often needs to be expressed as a percentage of capital, and the various expenses as percentages of turnover.

Problems

1 Express the following as a percentage of 300 correct to one decimal place: (i) 15, (ii) 18, (iii) 30, (iv) 70, (v) 95, (vi) 120, (vii) 130, (viii) 200, (ix) 250, (x) 300.

2 The capital of a firm is £400 000. Its profits last year were £33 000. What was the percentage return on capital?

Appendix A

Note
If a calculator is used, and its capacity will allow it, always work out the numerator (the top number) of the fraction before dividing by the denominator (the bottom number) and do not round until the end.

Example

Express 35 as a percentage of 613 correct to one decimal place.

$$\frac{35}{613} \times \frac{100}{1}\% = \frac{3500}{613}\% = 5.7\%$$

Problems

3 Express the following as percentages of 613 (correct to one decimal place): (i) 36, (ii) 92, (iii) 111, (iv) 214, (v) 345, (vi) 390, (vii) (424), (viii) 516, (ix) 666, (x) 750.

4 A firm's turnover (sales) last year was £1 226 421 and wages amounted to £72 430. What percentage were wages of turnover?

5 In the list that follows, express the first number as a percentage of the second, giving your answer correct to one decimal place where appropriate—cancel or use a calculator, whichever is more suitable: (i) 25, 200; (ii) 20, 350; (iii) 25, 400; (iv) 25, 450; (v) 50, 500; (vi) 44, 240; (vii) 44, 220; (viii) 41, 900; (ix) 42, 1500; (x) 44, 4400; (xi) 31, 47; (xii) 137, 250; (xiii) 84, 700; (xiv) 330, 150; (xv) 1000, 400.

Finding a Percentage of a Given Number

Arithmetically, the given number is multiplied by the required percentage expressed as a fraction (of 100).

Examples

(i) Find 21% of £200.

$$\frac{\cancel{£200}^{2}}{1} \times \frac{21}{\cancel{100}_{1}} = £42$$

(ii) Use a calculator to find 34% of £82.64.

$$£82.64 \times 34\% = £28.097 = £28.10 \text{ (to nearest penny)}$$

Accounting applications

Profit is often expressed as a percentage of cost price (when it is known as the *mark-up*) or as a percentage of selling price (the *profit margin*).

Problems

6 Find 21% of the following amounts: (i) £150, (ii) £350, (iii) £500, (iv) £750, (v) £1000.

7 Find 34% of the following amounts: (i) £47, (ii) £63, (iii) £142.50, (iv) £273.25, (v) £816.42.

8 What is the profit if:
  (i) the cost price of an article is £24 and mark-up is 20% of cost;
  (ii) the selling price is £360 and the profit margin is 15%?

Note

Often, in accounting work, figures like $12\frac{1}{2}\%$ or $33\frac{1}{3}\%$ are used, which reduce to simple fractions, and the answers to problems are then easily found arithmtically. Remember that: $10\% = 1/10$; $12\frac{1}{2}\% = 1/8$; $20\% = 1/5$; $25\% = 1/4$; $33\frac{1}{3}\% = 1/3$; $50\% = 1/2$; $66\frac{2}{3}\% = 2/3$; $75\% = 3/4$.

Example

Find $33\frac{1}{3}\%$ of £150.

$33\frac{1}{3}\% = 1/3$. One-third of £150 = £50.

Problems

9 Find $12\frac{1}{2}\%$ of: (i) £16, (ii) £240, (iii) £130, (iv) £480, (v) £150.

10 Find $33\frac{1}{3}\%$ of: (i) £21, (ii) £45, (iii) £240, (iv) £330, (v) £422.

11 Find (i) $66\frac{2}{3}\%$ of 240; (ii) 50% of 160; (iii) 75% of 440; (iv) 20% of 910; (v) $133\frac{1}{3}\%$ of 480.

12 Find the profit if it is:
  (i) 50% of the cost price of £300;
  (ii) $33\frac{1}{3}\%$ of the selling price of £450.

Does anything significant strike you about your answers to 12(i) and (ii)?

Increasing or Decreasing a Number by a Given Percentage

When the percentage is given of a known figure

There are two basic methods. Either the percentage increase (or decrease) needed can be calculated and added to (or subtracted from) the original figure, or the given percentage can be added to (or subtracted from) 100% and *that* percentage found of the original figure.

Example

Increase £690 by 18%.
(i) 18% of £690 = £124.20. So increasing £690 by 18% gives £(690 + 124.20) = £814.20.
(ii) An increase of 18% means 118% of £690 has to be found. 118% of £690 = £814.20.

Accounting applications

It is often necessary to obtain selling price by increasing cost price by a given percentage, or to obtain cost price by reducing selling price by a given percentage.

Problems

13 Increase: (i) £140 by 10%; (ii) 3126 by 17%; (iii) 348 by 32%; (iv) £748 by 214%.

14 Decrease: (i) 429 by 5%; (ii) £12m by 42.5%; (iii) 333 by 25%; (iv) 412.39 by 37%.

15 Find selling price if profit is 40% of cost price of £35.

16 Find cost price if profit is 24% of selling price of £216.

When the percentage is given of an unknown figure

Questions are often set in accounting examinations in which the profit is given as a percentage of cost but only the selling price is given, or the profit is given as a percentage of selling price but only the cost price is given. *It is essential to appreciate that profit will NOT be the same percentage of cost as it is of selling price.*

Examples

(i) Cost price is £580 and profit is 24% of selling price. Find the selling price.

Since profit = 24% of selling price, the cost price (£580) must be 76% of the selling price. So selling price equals:

$$£580 \times \frac{100}{76} = £763.16 \text{ (to nearest penny)}$$

(ii) Selling price is £85, profit is $33\frac{1}{3}$% on cost. Find cost price.

Selling price = £85 000 = $133\frac{1}{3}$% of cost price.

$$\text{Cost price} = £85\,000 \times \frac{100}{133\frac{1}{3}} = £85\,000 \times \frac{300}{400}$$
$$= £63\,750$$

Note

If $133\frac{1}{3}$% is approximated to 133.3%, then the correct answer is not obtained. (Check it for yourself on a calculator!) Hence the arithmetic procedure should be followed using actual numbers and not decimal approximations, even on a calculator, i.e. multiply by 300 and divide by 400 (in effect × 3 and ÷ 4) in the above case.

Problems

17 Find selling price if the cost is £300 and the profit is 16% of selling price.

18 Find the cost price if the selling price is £52 and the profit is 25% of cost price.

19 If the mark-up is 25% and the selling price is £85, find cost price.

20 If the profit margin is 40% and the cost is £320, find selling price.

Answers to problems

1 (i) 5%, (ii) 6%, (iii) 10%, (iv) 23.3%, (v) 31.7%, (vi) 40%, (vii) 43.3%, (viii) 66.7%, (ix) 83.3%, (x) 100%.

2 8.25%.

3 (i) 5.9%, (ii) 15.0%, (iii) 18.1%, (iv) 34.9%, (v) 56.2%, (vi) 63.6%, (vii) 69.2%, (viii) 84.2%, (ix) 108.6%, (x) 122.3%.

4 5.9%.

Coping with percentages

5 (i) 12.5%, (ii) 5.7%, (iii) 6.3%, (iv) 5.6%, (v) 10%, (vi) 18.3%, (vii) 20%, (viii) 4.6%, (ix) 2.7%, (x) 1%, (xi) 66.0%, (xii) 54.8%, (xiii) 12%, (xiv) 220%, (xv) 250%.

6 (i) £31.50, (ii) £73.50, (iii) £105, (iv) £157.50, (v) £210.

7 (i) £15.98, (ii) £21.42, (iii) £48.45, (iv) £92.91, (v) £277.58.

8 (i) £4.80, (ii) £54.

9 (i) £2, (ii) 30, (iii) £16.25, (iv) £60, (v) £18.75.

10 (i) £7, (ii) £15, (iii) £80, (iv) £110, (v) 140.67.

11 (i) 160, (ii) 80, (iii) 330, (iv) 182, (v) 640.

12 (i) £150, (ii) £150.

13 (i) £154, (ii) 3657.42, (iii) 459.36, (iv) 1600.72.

14 (i) 407.55, (ii) £6.9m, (iii) 249.75, (iv) 259.81.

15 £49.

16 £164.16.

17 £357.14.

18 £41.60.

19 £68.

20 £533.33.

APPENDIX B Using Graphs and Charts

The use of charts and diagrams can simplify the presentation of data, and make them easier to understand, but there are some basic rules that should always be observed.

(i) Each diagram should be suitably titled, labelled and—unless it is obvious from the context—the source should always be stated. A key should always be given where appropriate.

(ii) The total actual amounts concerned should always be given, particularly when percentages are plotted.

(iii) If bar charts or pie charts are used (i.e. two-dimensional diagrams), then the area of the diagram has to be proportional to the amount it represents.

(iv) Attempts to represent data in three dimensions, for example by the use of a block chart or pictogram, need to ensure that the *volume* is proportional to the amount represented.

(v) Explanations or additional details can be given in the form of footnotes.

A number of computer software packages readily convert tabular data into various forms of diagrams. Before using a package, check that it is one that obeys the above rules.

Example 1

The balance sheet of British Aerospace at 31 December 1988 can be summarised as follows:

	£m	%		£m	%
Fixed assets	2506	38.6	Capital	2114	32.6
Current assets	3988	63.4	Liabilities:		
			long-term	1435	22.1
			current	2945	45.3
	6494	100.0		6494	100.0

This information can be presented in a number of ways.

BAR CHART

A comparison of total assets with total liabilities of British Aerospace for year ended 31 December 1988. (Source: *Annual Report and Accounts*, British Aerospace, 1988.)

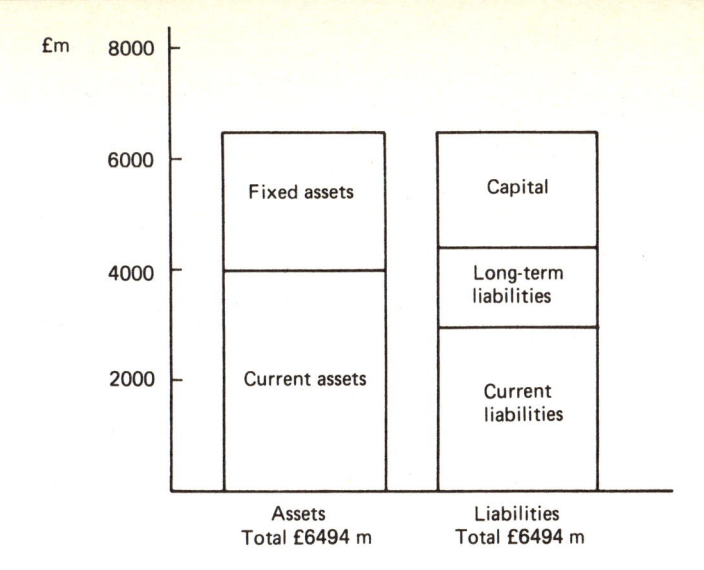

Using graphs and charts

[Bar chart showing Assets and Liabilities, both totalling £6494 m. Assets bar divided into Current assets and Fixed assets; Liabilities bar divided into Current liabilities, Long-term liabilities, and Capital. Y-axis £m scale from 0 to 8000.]

Note: Capital represents the total sum due to shareholders. Although not a liability in the ordinary sense, it nevertheless represents a source of funds similar to those obtained from creditors.

PIE CHART

A comparison of total assets with total liabilities of British Aerospace for year ended 31 December 1988. (Source: *Annual Report and Accounts*, British Aerospace, 1988.)

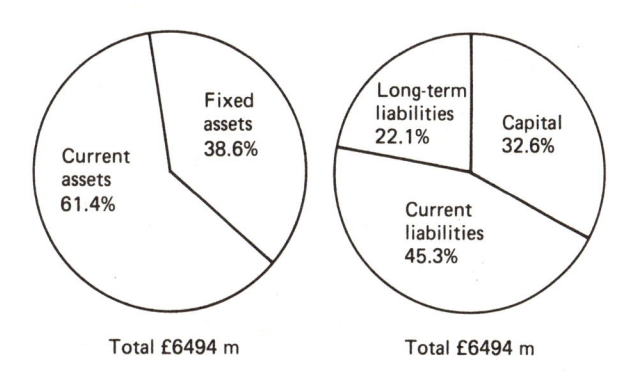

[Two pie charts. Left: Assets — Current assets 61.4%, Fixed assets 38.6%, Total £6494 m. Right: Liabilities — Long-term liabilities 22.1%, Capital 32.6%, Current liabilities 45.3%, Total £6494 m.]

Note: Although this diagram shows the percentage figures, it could equally well be used to represent the actual figures.

Example 2

Additional information can often be used to provide comparisons between years. The balance sheet of British Aerospace at 31 December 1987 can be summarised as follows:

	£m	%		£m	%
Fixed assets	996	23.0	Capital	1019	23.5
Current assets	3333	77.0	Liabilities:		
			long-term	978	22.6
			current	2332	53.9
	4329	100.0		4329	100.0

317

Appendix B

PERCENTAGE BAR CHART

A comparison of the liabilities of British Aerospace at 31 December 1988 and 1987. (Source: *Annual Report and Accounts*, British Aerospace, 1988.)

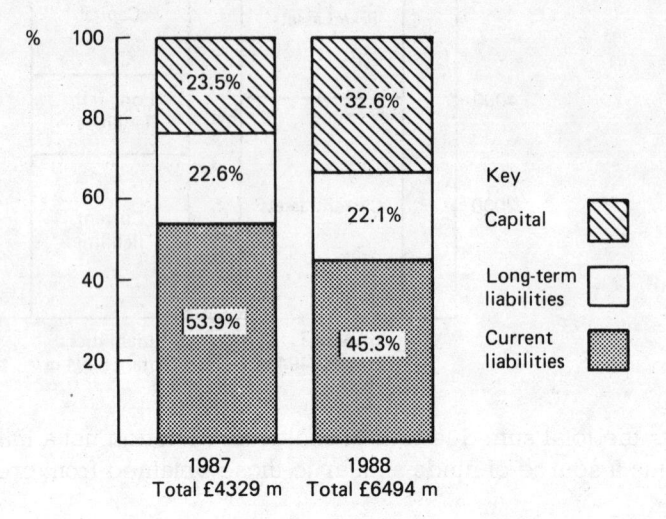

	1987	1988
Capital	23.5%	32.6%
Long-term liabilities	22.6%	22.1%
Current liabilities	53.9%	45.3%
Total	£4329 m	£6494 m

PIE CHART COMPARING ACTUAL AMOUNTS

A comparison of total assets of British Aerospace at 31 December 1988 and 1987. (Source: *Annual Report and Accounts*, British Aerospace, 1988.)

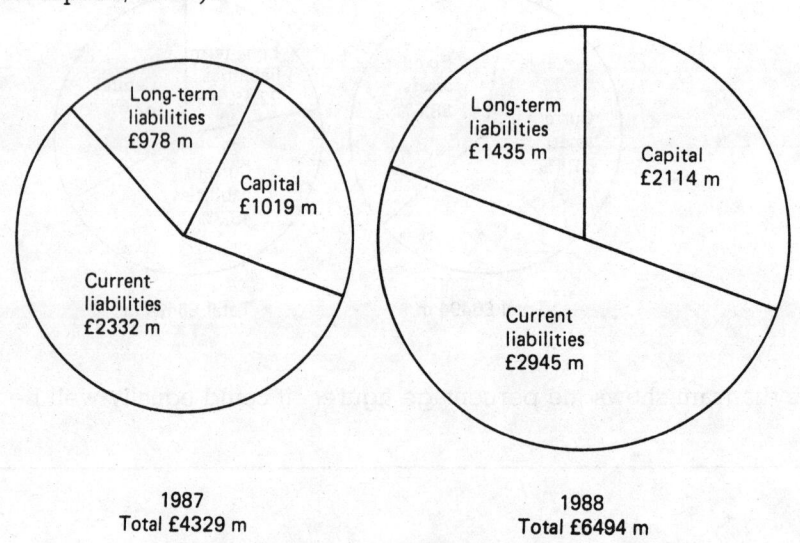

1987 — Total £4329 m
- Long-term liabilities £978 m
- Capital £1019 m
- Current liabilities £2332 m

1988 — Total £6494 m
- Long-term liabilities £1435 m
- Capital £2114 m
- Current liabilities £2945 m

Note: The radii of the circles are in the same ratio as the square roots of the actual amounts.

APPENDIX C Balancing Accounts—The Rules

When accounts are prepared in the 'T' format—which is the usual practice where manually kept accounts are concerned—definite and clearcut rules exist regarding how they should be balanced. These rules *must* be followed if confusion and mistakes are to be avoided. This balancing is carried out at the end of each page; it can also be undertaken at any other time when the balance is required.

The way in which an account is balanced depends upon the number of entries in the account, and the main rules are as follows:

Where There is Only One Entry in the Account

The figure in the account can be left as it stands, since it is already clear what the balance is.

Example

```
                         Capital account
                              May  1   Balance               b/f   500 000
```

One Entry on Each Side Coming to Same Total

Since there is no balance to carry down, and it is obvious the two sides come to the same total, it is only necessary to put a 'double underline' (the 'full stop' of book-keeping') under each figure. The double underline means that the figures above the line are not added to any figures that may subsequently be entered in the account.

Example

```
                              A. & C. Ltd
May  4  Sales                 24 000     May 30  Bank                24 000
```

Two or More Entries on Either or Both Sides

The account must be totalled. If they 'balance' (i.e. come to the same total), there will be no balance to carry down. If one side is greater than the other, then the balance must be inserted on the lightest side, and the two sides totalled (this 'proves' the balance). The balance is then *carried down* to the new period on the other side of the account where

Appendix C

it is said to have been *brought down*. If the balance is taken over the page, the terms *carried forward* and *brought forward* are used instead.

Note that the balance, after it has been carried down, sums up the true meaning of the account at the date the balancing was undertaken.

It is important that the totals of the two sides should be entered at the same level, even if this means leaving a gap on one side.

Examples

Delta Ltd

May	4	Bank	60 000	May		Purchases	90 000
	21	Bank	30 000				
			90 000				90 000

Prestwick Containers Ltd

May	31	Balance	c/d	36 000	May	5	Purchases		19 000
						16	Purchases		17 000
				36 000					36 000
					Jun	1	Balance	b/d	36 000

Omega Ltd

May	2	Sales		5 000	May	15	Bank		8 000
May	9	Sales		3 000		20	Bank		2 000
May	11	Sales		2 000		31	Balance	c/d	10 000
May	20	Sales		6 000					
May	25	Sales		4 000					
				20 000					20 000
Jun	1	Balance	b/d	10 000					

Notes

1. It is usually convenient to date balances that have been 'brought down' for the first day of the new period.
2. Balances are carried down so that further transactions can be posted to the *same* account. Students sometimes obtain the false impression from class examples that accounts are finished with once the balances have been carried down.

Index

Accounting conventions
 business entity 16
 consistency 73
 continuity 73
 matching 107-108
 materiality 163
 money measurement 12
 objectivity 131
 prudence 74
Accounting cycle 34-35, 74, 92-93
Accounting and machines 6
Accounting ratios
 profit/sales 128
 quick 42-43, 44
 return on capital employed 127
 return on capital invested 125-127
 return on total assets 128-129
Accounting requirements 3-4
Accounting structure 4-5
Accounting systems
 information provided by 4
 structure of 5
Accounts
 control 279-285
 interpretation of ledger balances 57-60
 suspense 272-274, 276
Accrued charges 103-105, 107, 169
Accumulated fund 13, 14, 224
Acid test (quick ratio) 42-43, 44
Acts of Parliament
 companies 239
 financial services 243
 partnership 230
Appropriation of partnership profit 232
Articles of association 240

Ascertained cost 118-119
Assets
 circulating 40
 current 39-40
 defined 13
 fixed 39-40
 liquidity of 14
 sale of 144-145
Audit trail 89
Authorised capital 240
Authorised value (shares) 241
AVCO (average cost of stock) 120

Bad debts
 accounting for 111-170, 209-210
 provision for 150-155, 170
 recovery of 112
Balance sheets
 alternative presentations 13-16
 clubs and societies 224-226
 company 248-252
 interpretation of 39-45, 166
 partnership 230-235
 purpose of 11-12, 166
Balancing ledger accounts, rules for 319-320
Bank accounts 22-23
Bank loans 23
Bank overdraft 23
Bank reconciliation statements 191-194
Bankruptcy 113
Bar charts 316-318
Bonus issue 241

Capital
 authorised 240
 called up 240
 circulating 40
 defined 13, 241

 fixed 39-40
 working 41, 248
Capital and company accounts 240-241, 248-249, 252
Capital employed 127, 241
Capital gains and losses 161-162
Capital income and expenditure 158-161
Capital invested 125-127, 241
Capital and partnership accounts 230-231
Capital and profit 125-128
Capital reserves 249-250
Capital and revenue 158-163, 167
Capital transactions 167-168
Carriage in and out 80-81, 168
Cash accounting 179-186
Cash analysis columns 182-183
Cash book, two and three column 179-181
Cash book and bank statements 190
Cash discount 82-84, 209
Cash drawings 114
Cash flow 44
Cash flow projections 184-185
Cash ratio 43-44
Cash security 23-24
Cash transactions, ledger postings 28-30
Cheques, dishonoured 112
Circulating capital 40
Club accounts 219-226
Coin analysis 202-203
Commission, errors of 272-273
Companies

 accounts of 244-252
 legal background of 239-242
 when not to form 241-242
Compensating errors 273
Conservatism (prudence) convention 74
Consistency, convention of 73
Consolidated fund 224
Consumption taxes 206
Continuity convention 73
Control accounts 279-285
Conventions in accounting 5-6, 73-74
Corporation tax 205-206
Correction of errors 33-34, 271-276
Cost of sales 69, 129, 168, 256, 258
Credit transactions, ledger postings 30-32
Current accounts, partners' 232
Current assets 39-40
Current liabilities 40
Current ratio 41-42

Day books 87-93
Debentures 241, 245
Delayed stocktaking 121-122
Depreciation 141-145, 169-170, 292
Diminishing balance depreciation 144
Discount allowed and received 81-84, 169, 181, 209
Dishonour of cheques 112
Dividends 240, 245
Double entry 29
 conversion to 292
Drawings by partners 230-231, 233

Index

Drawings of cash 114, 171
Drawings of goods 114–115, 171

Entity convention 16
Equity shares 240–241
Errors
 correction of 33–34, 271–276
 types of 272–273
Exempt firms (VAT) 209
Exempt goods (VAT) 208
Expenditure and income 56–60, 103–108
Expense/sales ratios 128–129

Factory cost of goods produced 258, 260
Factory overheads 257
FIFO (first-in, first-out) 119
Fixed assets 39–40
Fixed instalment (straight line) depreciation 143–144
Floating (circulating) capital 39–40
Folio columns 89
Fund
 accumulated 13, 224
 consolidated 224

Goods
 accounting for 65–72
 drawings of 114–115
Goodwill 234–235, 298
Graphs and charts 316–318
Gross profit 65

Historical costs 107–108, 131

Imprest system 185–186
Income and expenditure, nature of 56–60, 103–108
Income and expenditure accounts 221–223
Incomplete records 288–293
Inflation 131–132
Insolvency 113
Inter-firm comparisons 131
Interest 241, 245

Journal 90–93

Ledger
 balancing rules 319–320
 general procedures 19–24, 28, 166–171
 interpretation of balances 59–60
 self-balancing 279
 types of account 20–22
Liabilities
 current 40, 248–250
 defined 13
 long-term 40, 248–250
Liability
 contingent 250
 limited 239–242
LIFO (last-in, last-out) 119–120
Liquidity of assets 14
Loan account, partner 230–231
Loan capital 241

Manufacturing accounts 256–261
Materiality 162–163
Materiality convention 163
Mechanised accounting 6
Memorandum of association 240

Net profit 55
Net realisable value 121
NIC (National insurance contributions) 200
Nominal accounts 59
Note and coin analysis 202–203

Objectivity convention 131
Ordinary shares 240–241
Original documents 5
Overheads, factory 257
Overtrading 41

Par value, share 241
Partnership accounts 230–235
 goodwill in 234–235
Partnership Act 230–231
Partnership agreement 230–231
Percentage calculations 311–314
Personal accounts 59
Petty cash 185–186
Pie charts 316–318

Preference shares 240–241
Premium, share 241
Prepayments 106–107, 169
Principle, errors of 273
Profit
 calculation of 56–58
 and capital 125–128
 defined 55–103
 gross 65
 interpretation of 125–129
 net 55
 partners' appropriation 232
Profit and loss, accounting for 56–58, 166
Profit and loss account 56, 166
 company 247–250
 complications 81–84
Profit/sales (turnover) ratio 128
Provisions
 bad debts 150–155
 depreciation 142–143, 170
Prudence convention 74
Purchases 65
Purchases day book 88–89
Purchases, accounting procedure 66

Quick ratio (acid test) 42–44
Quoted companies 240

Rate of turnover of debtors and creditors 130–131
Rate of turnover of stock 129–130
Ratios
 cash 43, 44
 current 41–42, 43
 expense/sales 128–129
 profit/sales (turnover) 128
 quick (acid test) 42–43, 44
 return on capital employed 127
 return on capital invested 125–127
 return on total assets 128–129
Real accounts 59
Receipts and payments accounts 219–221

Reconciliation accounting 191–194
Retained earnings 247, 250
Return on capital employed 127
Return on capital invested 125–127
Return on total assets 127–128
Returns and allowances 77–80, 168–169
Returns day books 90
Revenue, defined 168
Revenue and capital 158–163, 167
Revenue reserves 250
Rights issues 241
Running balance accounts 21

Salaries and wages 85, 198–203
Sale of asset 144–145
Sale of firm 296–297
Sales
 accounting procedures 66–68
 nature of 65
Sales day books 90
Schedule D tax 205
Self-balancing ledgers 279–282
Share issue 240, 244
Share premium 241
Shares, company 240–241, 244–245
Single entry 288
Solvency 41–42, 43–44
Statements, reconciliation 191–194
Statements of affairs 12, 288–289
Statements of assets and liabilities 5
Statutory deductions (wages) 199–200
Stock
 consumed 168
 rate of turnover 129–130
 trading 68–73
 valuation 71–72, 118–122
Stock and issued capital 240
Stocktaking, delayed 121–122
Straight line depreciation 143–144
Subscriptions, clubs and societies 222, 223

Index

Suspense accounts 273-274, 276

Tax 200, 205-210 241-242, 247
Trade discount 81-82, 209
Trading account
  clubs and societies 223-224
  general principles 65-71, 77-80, 166
Transactions 29, 159-161, 167-171
Transport costs 80-81, 168
Trend analysis 131
Trial balances 32-34
Turnover
  rate of
    debtors and creditors 130-131
    stock 129-130

Turnover and profit 128-129

Unquoted companies 240

Valuation, stock 118-122
Value added tax 206-210
Voluntary deductions (wages) 200

Wage payment procedures 201-202
Wages and salaries 85, 198-203
Winding up 296-299
Work-in-progress 257-258
Working capital 41, 248

Zero-rated goods (VAT) 208-209